KV-512-360

McGraw-Hill's ATLAS of WORLD EVENTS

THE KEY POLITICAL, ECONOMIC, DEMOGRAPHIC, AND ENVIRONMENTAL ISSUES THAT ARE SHAPING THE WORLD TODAY

JOHN L. ALLEN, PH.D.

McGraw-Hill
New York Chicago San Francisco Lisbon London Madrid Mexico City
Milan New

A L I S
1732784

Sydney Toronto

We would like to thank Digital Wisdom Incorporated for allowing us to use their Mountain High Maps cartography software. The software was used to create maps 73, 74, 82, 83, 85–90, 92–95, 97–101, 103–106, 108–114, 116–120.

The source section for this book begins on page 191, which is to be considered an extension of this copyright page.

1 2 3 4 5 6 7 8 9 0 MID/MID 0 9 8 7 6 5

ISBN 0-07-145555-8
ISSN 1531-0221

McGraw-Hill books are available at special quantity discounts to use as premiums and sales promotions, or for use in corporate training programs. For more information, please write to the Director of Special Sales, Professional Publishing, McGraw-Hill, Two Penn Plaza, New York, NY 10121-2298. Or contact your local bookstore.

About the Author

John L. Allen is professor and chair of Geography at the University of Wyoming and emeritus professor of Geography at the University of Connecticut, where he taught from 1967 to 2000. He is a native of Wyoming. He received his bachelor's degree in 1963 and his M.A. in 1964 from the University of Wyoming, and in 1969 his Ph.D. from Clark University. His special areas of interest are perceptions of the environment and the impact of human societies on environmental systems. Dr. Allen is the author and editor of many books and articles.

Acknowledgments

Nozar Alaolmolki
Hiram College

Barbara Batterson-Rossi
Palomar College

A. Steele Becker
University of Nebraska at Kearney

Koop Berry
Walsh University

Daniel A. Bunye
South Plains College

Winifred F. Caponigri
Holy Cross College

Femi Ferreira
Hutchinson Community College

Eric J. Fournier
Samford University

William J. Frazier
Columbus State College

Hari P. Garbharran
Middle Tennessee State University

Baher Gosheh
Edinboro University of Pennsylvania

Donald Hagan
Northwest Missouri State University

Robert Janiskee
University of South Carolina

David C. Johnson
University of Louisiana

Effie Jones
Crichton College

Cub Kahn
Marylhurst University

Artimus Keiffer
Franklin College

Leonard E. Lancette
Mercer University

Donald W. Lovejoy
Palm Beach Atlantic College

Mark Maschhoff
Harris-Stowe State College

Richard Matthews
University of South Carolina

Madolia Mills
University of Colorado–Colorado Springs

Robert Mulcahy
Providence College

Otto H. Muller
Alfred University

J. Henry Owusu
University of Northern Iowa

Steven Parkansky
Morehead State University

William Preston
California Polytechnic State University, San Luis Obispo

Neil Reid
The University of Toledo

A. L. Rydant
Keene State College

Deborah Berman Santana
Mills College

Steven Slakey
University of La Verne

Rolf Sternberg
Montclair State University

Richard Ulack
University of Kentucky

David Woo
California State University, Haywood

Donald J. Zeigler
Old Dominion University

Table of Contents

Part IV Global Economic Patterns 50

Part V Global Patterns of Environmental Disturbance 68

Part VI Global Political Patterns 86

Part VII World Regions 106

Part VIII Tables

Part IX Geographic Index 179

Introduction: How to Read an Atlas

An atlas is a book containing maps which are "models" of the real world. By the term "model" we mean exactly what you think of when you think of a model: a representation of reality that is generalized, usually considerably smaller than the original, and with certain features emphasized, depending on the purpose of the model. A model of a car does not contain all of the parts of the original but it may contain enough parts that it is recognizable as a car and can be used to study principles of automotive design or maintenance. A car model designed for racing, on the other hand, may contain fewer parts but would have the mobility of a real automobile. Car models come in a wide variety of types containing almost anything you can think of relative to automobiles that doesn't require the presence of a full-size car. Since geographers deal with the real world, virtually all of the printed or published studies of that world require models. Unlike a mechanic in an automotive shop, we can't roll our study subject into the shop, take it apart, put it back together. We must use models. In other words, we must generalize our subject, and the way we do that is by using maps. Some maps are designed to show specific geographic phenomena, such as the climates of the world or the relative rates of population growth for the world's countries. We call these maps "thematic maps" and Parts I through VI of this atlas contain maps of this type. Other maps are designed to show the geographic location of towns and cities and rivers and lakes and mountain ranges and so on. These are called "reference maps" and they make up many of the maps in Part VII. All of these maps, whether thematic or reference, are models of the real world that selectively emphasize the features that we want to show on the map.

In order to read maps effectively–in other words, in order to understand the models of the world presented in the following pages–it is important for you to know certain things about maps: how they are made using what are called *projections;* how the level of mathematical proportion of the map or what geographers call *scale* affects what you see; and how geographers use *generalization* techniques such as simplification and symbols where it would be impossible to draw a small version of the real world feature. In this brief introduction, then, we'll explain to you three of the most important elements of map interpretation: projection, scale, and generalization.

MAP PROJECTIONS

Perhaps the most basic problem in *cartography,* or the art and science of map-making, is the fact that the subject of maps–the earth's surface–is what is called by mathematicians "a non-developable surface." Since the world is a sphere (or nearly so–it's actually slightly flattened at the poles and bulges a tiny bit at the equator), it is impossible to flatten out the world or any part of its curved surface without producing some kind of distortion. This "near sphere" is represented by a geographic grid or coordinate system of lines of latitude or *parallels* that run east and west and are used to measure distance north and south on the globe, and lines of longitude or *meridians* that run north and south and are used to measure distance east and west. All the lines of longitude are half circles of equal length and they all converge at the poles. These meridians are numbered from 0 degrees (Prime or Greenwich Meridian) east and west to 180 degrees. The meridian of 0 degrees and the meridian of 180 degrees are halves of the same "great circle" or line representing a plane that bisects the globe into two equal hemispheres. All lines of longitude are halves of great circles. All the lines of latitude are complete circles that are parallel to one another and are spaced equidistant on the meridians. The circumference of these circles lessens as you move north or south from the equator. Parallels of latitude are numbered from 0 degrees at the equator north and south to 90 degrees at the North and South poles. The only line of latitude that is a great circle is the equator, which equally divides the world into a northern and southern hemisphere. In the real world, all these grid lines of latitude and longitude intersect at right angles. The problem for cartographers is to convert this spherical or curved grid into a geometrical shape that is "developable"; that is, it can be flattened (such as a cylinder or cone) or is already flat (a plane). The reason the results of the conversion process are called "projections" is that we imagine a world globe (or some part of it) that is made up of wires running north-south and east-west to represent the grid lines of latitude and longitude and other wires or even solid curved plates to represent the coastlines of continents or the continents themselves. We then imagine a light source at some location inside or outside the wire globe that can "project" or cast shadows of the wires representing grid lines onto a developable surface. Sometimes the basic geometric principles of projection may be modified by other mathematical principles to yield projections that are not truly geometric but have certain desirable features. We call these types of projections "arbitrary." The three most basic types of projections are named according to the type of developable surface: cylindrical, conic, or azimuthal (plane). Each type has certain characteristic features: they may be *equal area* projections in which the size of each area on the map is a direct proportional representation of that same area in the real world but shapes are distorted; they may be *conformal* projections in which area may be distorted but shapes are shown correctly; or they may be *compromise* projections in which both shape and area are distorted but the overall picture presented is fairly close to reality. It is important to remember that all maps distort the geographic grid and continental outlines in characteristic ways. The only

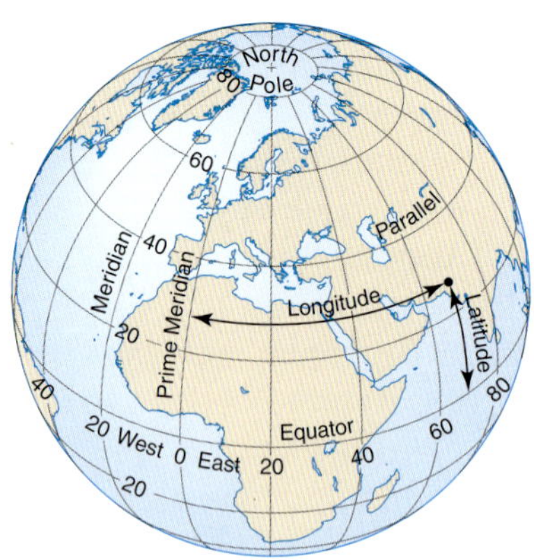
North
Pole
80
60
Parallel
Meridian
40
Prime Meridian
Longitude
Latitude
20
40
20 West
0 East
20
Equator
40
60
80
20
The Coordinate System

representation of the world that does not distort either shape or area is a globe. You can see why we must use projections–can you imagine an atlas that you would have to carry back and forth across campus that would be made up entirely of globes?

CYLINDRICAL PROJECTIONS

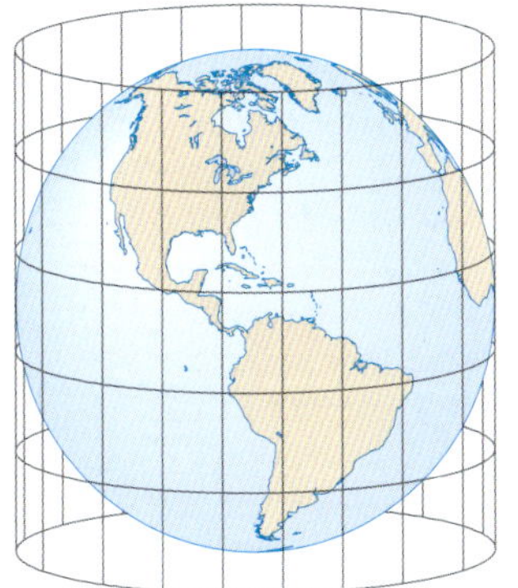

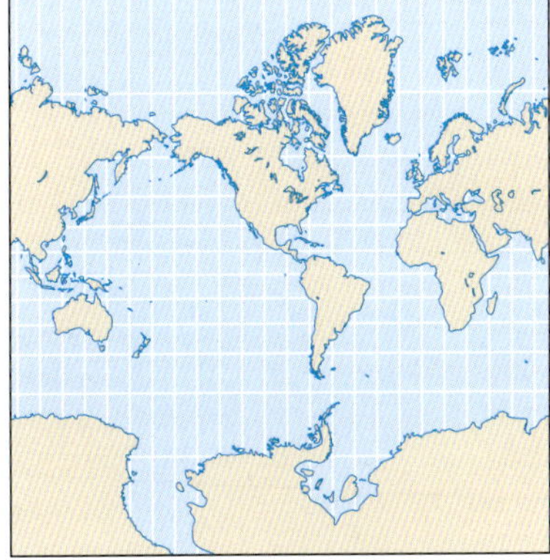

The Mercator Projection

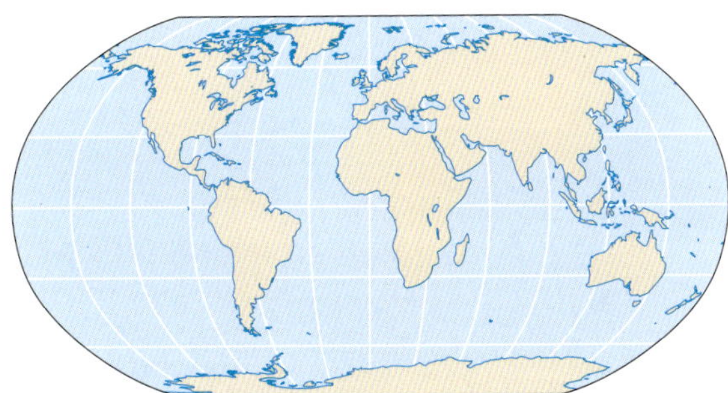

The Robinson Projection

Cylindrical projections are drawn as if the geographic grid were projected onto a cylinder. Cylindrical projections have the advantage of having all lines of latitude as true parallels or straight lines. This makes these projections quite useful for showing geographic relationships in which latitude or distance north-south is important (many physical features, such as climate, are influenced by latitude). Unfortunately, most cylindrical-type projections distort area significantly. One of the most famous is the Mercator projection shown above. This projection makes areas disproportionately large as you move toward the pole, making Greenland, which is actually about one-seventh the size of South America, appear to be as large as the southern continent. But the Mercator projection has the quality of conformality: landmasses on the map are true in shape and thus all coastlines on the map intersect lines of latitude and longitude at the proper angles. This makes the Mercator projection, named after its inventor, a sixteenth-century Dutch cartographer, ideal for its original purpose as a tool for navigation–but not a good projection for attempting to show some geographical feature in which areal relationship is important. Unfortunately, the Mercator projection has often been used for wall maps for schoolrooms and the consequence is that generations of American school children have been "tricked" into thinking that Greenland is actually larger than South America. Much better cylindrical-type projections are those like the Robinson projection used in this atlas that is neither equal area nor conformal but a compromise that portrays the real world much as it actually looks, enough so that we can use it for areal comparisons.

CONIC PROJECTIONS

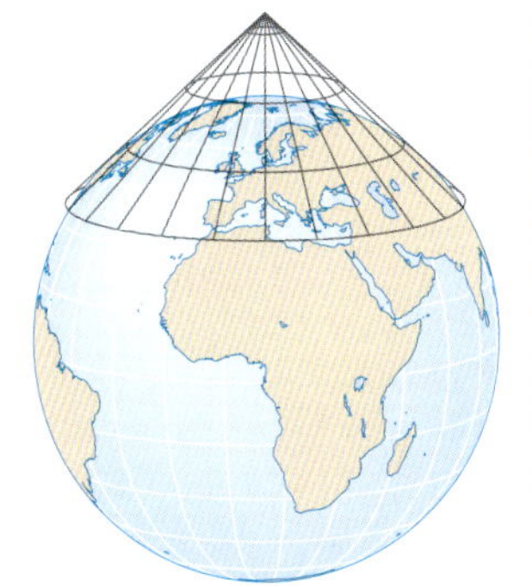

Conic Projection of Europe

Conic projections are those that are imagined as being projected onto a cone that is tangent to the globe along a standard parallel, or a series of cones tangent along several parallels or even intersecting the globe. Conic projections usually show latitude as curved lines and longitude as straight lines. They are good projections for areas with north-south extent, like the map of Europe to the right, and may be either conformal, equal area, or compromise, depending on how they are constructed. Many of the regional maps in the last map section of this atlas are conic projections.

AZIMUTHAL PROJECTIONS

Azimuthal projections are those that are imagined as being projected onto a plane or flat surface. They are named for one of their essential properties. An "azimuth" is a line of compass bearing and azimuthal projections have the property of yielding true compass directions from the center of the map. This makes azimuthal maps useful for navigation purposes, particularly air navigation. But, because they distort area and shape so greatly, they are seldom used for maps designed to show geographic relationships. When they are used as illustrative rather than navigation maps, it is often in the "polar case" projection shown below where the plane has been made tangent to the globe at the North Pole.

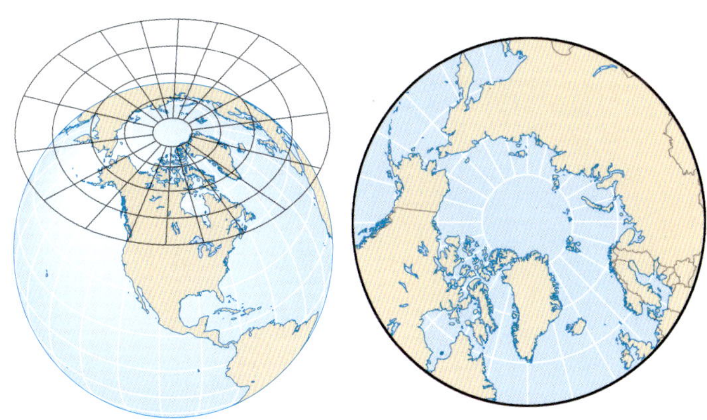

Azimuthal Projection of the North Polar Region

MAP SCALE

Since maps are models of the real world, it follows that they are not the same size as the real world or any portion of it. Every map, then, is subject to generalization, which is another way of saying that maps are drawn to certain scales. The term *scale* refers to the mathematical quality of *proportional representation,* and is expressed as a ratio between an area of the real world or the distance between places on the real world and the same area or distance on the map. We show map scale on maps in three different ways. Sometimes we simply use the proportion and write what is called a *natural scale* or representative fraction": for example, we might show on a map the mathematical proportion of 1:62,500. A map at this scale is one that is one sixty-two thousand five-hundredth the size of the same area in the real world. Other times we convert the proportion to a written description that approximates the relationship between distance on the map and distance in the real world. Since there are nearly 62,500 inches in a mile, we would refer to a map having a natural scale of 1:62,500 as having an "inch-mile" scale of "1 inch represents 1 mile." If we draw a line one inch long on this map, that line represents a distance of approximately one mile in the real world. Finally, we usually use a graphic or linear scale: a bar or line, often graduated into miles or kilometers, that shows graphically the proportional representation. A graphic scale for our 1:62,500 map might be about five inches long, divided into five equal units clearly labeled as "1 mile," "2 miles," and so on. Our examples below show all three kinds of scales.

The most important thing to keep in mind about scale, and the reason why knowing map scale is important to being able to read a map correctly, is the relationship between proportional representation and generalization. A map that fills a page but shows the whole world is much more highly generalized than a map that fills a page but shows a single city. On the world map, the city may appear as a dot. On the city map, streets and other features may be clearly seen. We call the first map, the world map, a *small-scale* map because the proportional representation is a small number. A page-size map showing the whole world may be drawn at a scale of 1:150,000,000. That is a very small number indeed–hence the term *small-scale* map even though the area shown is large. Conversely, the second map, a city map, may be drawn at a scale of 1:250,000. That is still a very small number but it is a great deal larger than 1:150,000,000! And so we'd refer to the city map as a *large scale* map, even though it shows only a small area. On our world map, geographical features are generalized greatly and many features can't even be shown at all. On the city map, much less generalization occurs–we can show specific features that we couldn't on the world map–but generalization still takes place. The general rule is that the smaller the map scale, the greater the degree of generalization;

Map 1 Small Scale Map of the United States

CANADA
Seattle
Portland
Minneapolis/ St. Paul
Milwaukee
Detroit
Buffalo
Boston
New York
Cleveland
Chicago
Pittsburgh
Philadelphia
Baltimore
Washington, D.C.
UNITED STATES
San Francisco
San Jose
Denver
Indianapolis
St. Louis
Cincinnati
Los Angeles
San Diego
Atlanta
ATLANTIC OCEAN
Dallas/ Ft. Worth
Houston
New Orleans
PACIFIC OCEAN
MEXICO
Miami
Gulf of Mexico
Scale: 1 to 76,000,000
1 inch = 1200 miles
500 Miles
500 Kilometers

Map 2 Map of the Northeast

Scale: 1 to 17,500,000
1 inch = 277 miles
100 200 Miles
100 200 Kilometers
CANADA
MAINE
VERMONT
NEW HAMPSHIRE
NEW YORK
Manchester
Lowell
Boston
MASS.
Lake Ontario
Syracuse
Rochester
Buffalo
Springfield
Worcester
Providence
RHODE ISLAND
Hartford
Waterbury
New Haven
CONNECTICUT
Bridgeport
Stamford
Lake Erie
Erie
PENNSYLVANIA
Newark
Jersey City
New York
Allentown
Altoona
NEW JERSEY
ATLANTIC OCEAN
Pittsburgh
Philadelphia
Baltimore

Map 3 Map of Southeastern New England

NEW HAMPSHIRE
Manchester
Nashua
Lawrence
Fitchburg
Lowell
Leominster
Gloucester
ATLANTIC OCEAN
Worcester
Framingham
Waltham
Brookline
Cambridge
Boston
Quincy
MASSACHUSETTS
Brockton
Woonsocket
Providence
Cape Cod Bay
Taunton
Fall River
New Bedford
Newport
RHODE ISLAND
Westerly
New London
Nantucket
Montauk
Scale: 1 to 7,000,000
1 inch = 108 miles
10 20 30 Miles
10 20 30 Kilometers

Map 4 Large Scale Map of Boston, MA

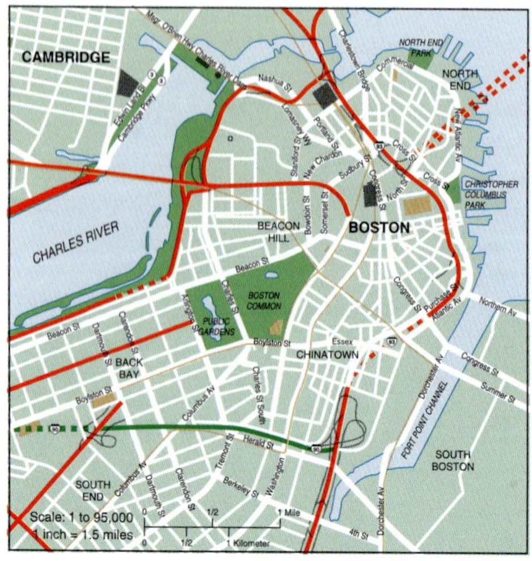
CAMBRIDGE
NORTH END
CHARLES RIVER
BEACON HILL
BOSTON
BOSTON COMMON
PUBLIC GARDENS
CHINATOWN
BACK BAY
CHRISTOPHER COLUMBUS PARK
FORT POINT CHANNEL
SOUTH END
SOUTH BOSTON
Scale: 1 to 95,000
1 inch = 1.5 miles
1/2 1 Mile
1/2 1 Kilometer

the larger the map scale, the less the degree of generalization. The only map that would not generalize would be a map at a scale of 1:1. and that map wouldn't be very handy to use. Examine the relationship between scale and generalization in the four maps on the previous page.

GENERALIZATION ON MAPS

A review of the four maps on the previous page should give you some indication of how cartographers generalize on maps. One thing that you should have noticed is that the first map, that of the United States, is much simpler than the other three and that the level of *simplification* decreases with each map. When a cartographer simplifies map data, information that is not important for the purposes of the map is just left off. For example, on the first map the objective may have been to show cities over 1 million in population. To do that clearly and effectively, it is not necessary to show and label rivers and lakes. The map has been simplified by leaving those items out. The final map, on the other hand, is more complex and shows and labels geographic features that are important to the character of the city of Boston; therefore, the Charles River is clearly indicated on the map.

Another type of generalization is *classification*. Map 1 on the previous page shows cities over 1 million in population. Map 2 shows cities of several different sizes and a different symbol is used for each size classification or category. Many of the thematic maps used in this atlas rely on classification to show data. A thematic map showing population growth rates (see Map 24 on page 37) will use different colors to show growth rates in different classification levels or what are sometimes called *class intervals*. Thus, there will be one color applied to all countries with population growth rates between 1.0 percent and 1.4 percent, another color applied to all countries with population growth rates between 1.5 percent and 2.1 percent, and so on. Classification is necessary because it is impossible to find enough symbols or colors to represent precise values. Classification may also be used for qualitative data, such as the national or regional origin of migrating populations. Cartographers show both quantitative and qualitative classification levels or class intervals in important sections of maps called *legends*. These legends, as in the samples shown below, make it possible for the reader of the map to interpret the patterns shown.

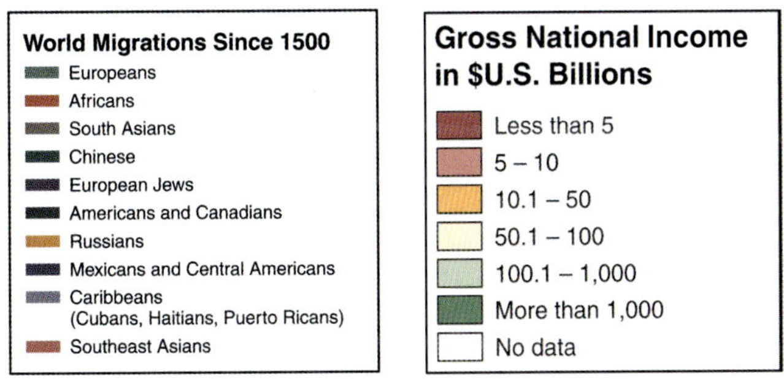
World Migrations Since 1500
Europeans
Africans
South Asians
Chinese
European Jews
Americans and Canadians
Russians
Mexicans and Central Americans
Caribbeans
(Cubans, Haitians, Puerto Ricans)
Southeast Asians
Gross National Income in $U.S. Billions
Less than 5
5 – 10
10.1 – 50
50.1 – 100
100.1 – 1,000
More than 1,000
No data

Map Legends from Maps 23 and 37

A third technique of generalization is *symbolization* and we've already noted several different kinds of symbols: those used to represent cities on the preceding maps, or the colors used to indicate population growth levels on Map 24. One general category of map symbols is quantitative in nature and this category can further be divided into a number of different types. For example, the symbols showing city size on Maps 1 and 2 on the preceding page can be categorized as *ordinal* in that they show relative differences in quantities (the size of cities). A cartographer might also use lines of different widths to express the quantities of movement of people or goods between two or more points as on Map 23 (see page 35).

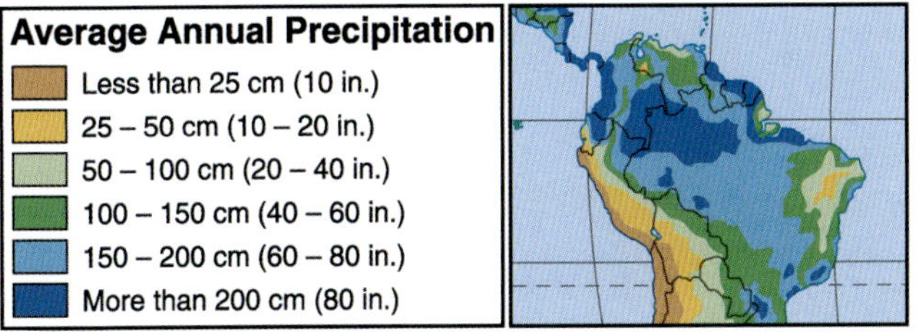
Average Annual Precipitation
Less than 25 cm (10 in.)
25 – 50 cm (10 – 20 in.)
50 – 100 cm (20 – 40 in.)
100 – 150 cm (40 – 60 in.)
150 – 200 cm (60 – 80 in.)
More than 200 cm (80 in.)

Interval Symbols

The color symbols used to show rates of population growth can be categorized as *interval* in that they express certain levels of a mathematical quantity (the percentage of population growth). Interval symbols are often used to show physical geographic characteristics such as inches of precipitation, degrees of temperature, or elevation above sea level. The sample above, for example, shows precipitation (from Map 3a, page 6).

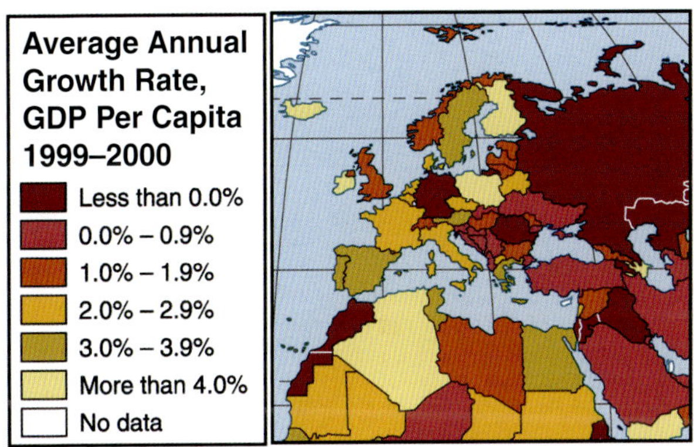
Average Annual Growth Rate, GDP Per Capita 1999–2000
Less than 0.0%
0.0% – 0.9%
1.0% – 1.9%
2.0% – 2.9%
3.0% – 3.9%
More than 4.0%
No data

Ratio Symbols

Still another type of mathematical symbolization is the *ratio* in which sets of mathematical quantities are compared: the number of persons per square mile (population density) or the growth in gross national product per capita (per person). The map above shows GDP change per capita (from Map 39, page 53).

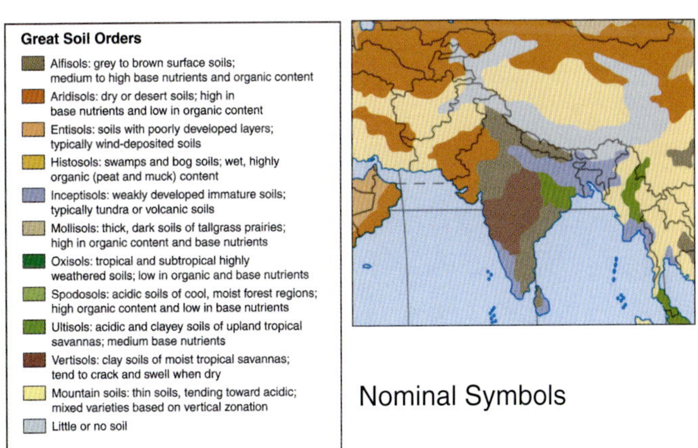
Great Soil Orders
Alfisols: grey to brown surface soils; medium to high base nutrients and organic content
Aridisols: dry or desert soils; high in base nutrients and low in organic content
Entisols: soils with poorly developed layers; typically wind-deposited soils
Histosols: swamps and bog soils; wet, highly organic (peat and muck) content
Inceptisols: weakly developed immature soils; typically tundra or volcanic soils
Mollisols: thick, dark soils of tallgrass prairies; high in organic content and base nutrients
Oxisols: tropical and subtropical highly weathered soils; low in organic and base nutrients
Spodosols: acidic soils of cool, moist forest regions; high organic content and low in base nutrients
Ultisols: acidic and clayey soils of upland tropical savannas; medium base nutrients
Vertisols: clay soils of moist tropical savannas; tend to crack and swell when dry
Mountain soils: thin soils, tending toward acidic; mixed varieties based on vertical zonation
Little or no soil

Nominal Symbols

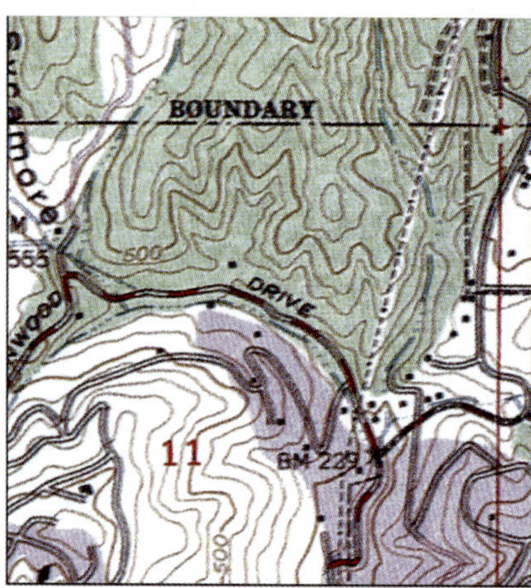
BOUNDARY
DRIVE
500
555
11
BM 229
500

Interpolation

Finally, there are a vast number of cartographic symbols that are not mathematical but show differences in the kind of information being portrayed. These symbols are called *nominal* and they range from the simplest differences such as land and water to more complex differences such as those between different types of vegetation. Shapes or patterns or colors or iconographic drawings may all be used as nominal symbols on maps. The sample map at the bottom of page xiii uses color to show the distribution of soil types.

The final technique of generalization is what cartographers refer to as *interpolation*. Here, the maker of a map may actually show more information on the map than is actually supplied by the original data. In understanding the process of interpolation is it necessary for you to visualize the quantitative data shown on maps as being three dimensional: *x* values provide geographic location along a north-south axis of the map; *y* values provide geographic location along the east-west axis of the map; and *z* values are those values of whatever data (for example, temperature) are being shown on the map at specific points. We all can imagine a real three-dimensional surface in which the *x* and y values are directions and the *z* values are the heights of mountains and the depths of valleys. On a topographic map showing a real three-dimensional surface, contour lines are used to connect points of equal elevation above sea level. These contour lines are not measured directly; they are estimated by interpolation on the basis of the elevation points that are provided.

It is harder to imagine the statistical surface of a temperature map in which the *x* and *y* values are directions and the *z* values represent degrees of temperature at precise points. But that is just what cartographers do. And to obtain the values between two or more specific points where *z* values exist, they interpolate based on a class interval they have decided is appropriate and use *isolines* (which are statistical equivalents of a contour line) to show increases or decreases in value. The diagram below shows an example of an interpolation process. Occasionally interpolation is referred to as *induction.* By whatever name, it is one of the most difficult parts of the cartographic process.

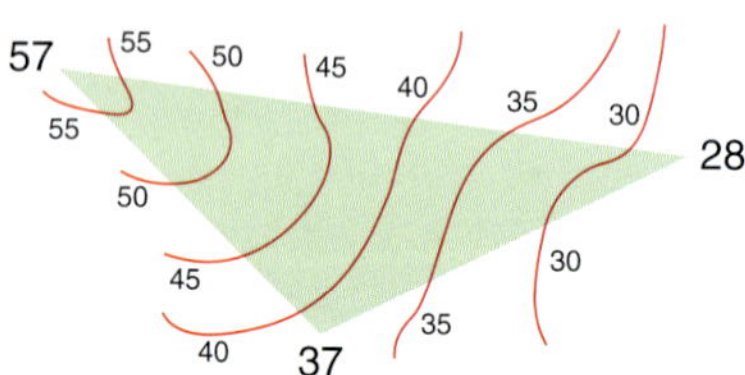
57
55
50
45
40
35
30
28
55
50
45
40
37
35
30

Degrees of Temperature (Celsius)
Interval = 5 degrees

And you thought all you had to do to read an atlas was look at the maps! You've now learned that it is a bit more involved than that. As you read and study this atlas, keep in mind the principles of projection and scale and generalization (including simplification, classification, symbolization, and interpolation) and you'll do just fine. Good luck and enjoy your study of the world of maps as well as maps of the world!

Part I

Global Physical Patterns

Map 1 World Political Divisions

The international system includes the political units called "states" or countries as the most important component. The boundaries of countries are the primary source of political division in the world and for most people nationalism is the strongest source of political identity. State boundaries are an important indicator of cultural, linguistic, economic, and other geographic divisions as well, and the states themselves normally serve as the base level for which most global statistics are available. The subfield of geography known as "political geography" has as its primary concern the geographic or spatial character of this international system and its components.

U.S.
CANADA
UNITED STATES
NORTH PACIFIC OCEAN
NORTH ATLANTIC OCEAN
MEXICO
Tropic of Cancer
Equator
GUYANA
SURINAME
FRENCH GUIANA (FR)
COLOMBIA
VENEZUELA
ECUADOR
PERU
BRAZIL
BOLIVIA
PARAGUAY
CHILE
ARGENTINA
URUGUAY
WESTERN SAMOA
TONGA
Tropic of Capricorn
SOUTH PACIFIC OCEAN
SOUTH ATLANTIC OCEAN
Antarctic Circle
THE BAHAMAS
0 300 Miles
0 300 Kilometers
CUBA
DOMINICAN REPUBLIC
JAMAICA
HAITI
PUERTO RICO
BELIZE
GUATEMALA
HONDURAS
CARIBBEAN SEA
ST. KITTS AND NEVIS
ANTIGUA AND BARBUDA
DOMINICA
MARTINIQUE
ST. LUCIA
ST. VINCENT AND THE GRENADINES
BARBADOS
GRENADA
EL SALVADOR
NICARAGUA
COSTA RICA
PANAMA
TRINIDAD AND TOBAGO
Scale: 1 to 111,922,000
0 1000 2000 Miles
0 1000 2000 3000 Kilometers

Note: All world maps are Robinson projection.

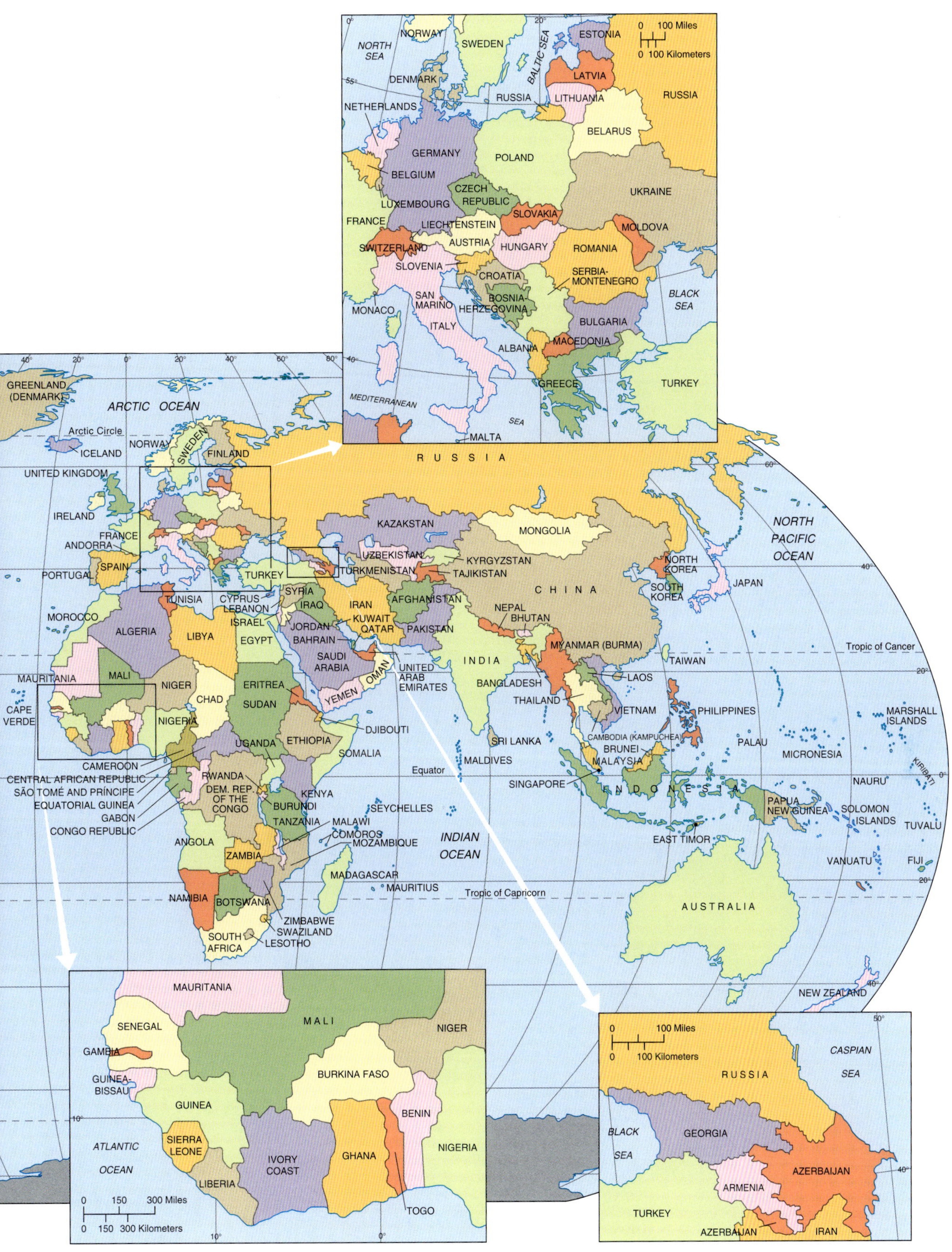
NORWAY
SWEDEN
NORTH SEA
BALTIC SEA
ESTONIA
0 100 Miles
0 100 Kilometers
LATVIA
DENMARK
RUSSIA
LITHUANIA
NETHERLANDS
BELARUS
GERMANY
POLAND
BELGIUM
CZECH REPUBLIC
UKRAINE
LUXEMBOURG
SLOVAKIA
FRANCE
LIECHTENSTEIN
MOLDOVA
AUSTRIA
SWITZERLAND
HUNGARY
ROMANIA
SLOVENIA
CROATIA
SERBIA-MONTENEGRO
BLACK SEA
SAN MARINO
BOSNIA-HERZEGOVINA
MONACO
BULGARIA
ITALY
MACEDONIA
ALBANIA
TURKEY
GREECE
MEDITERRANEAN SEA
MALTA
GREENLAND (DENMARK)
ARCTIC OCEAN
Arctic Circle
ICELAND
FINLAND
UNITED KINGDOM
R U S S I A
IRELAND
KAZAKSTAN
MONGOLIA
NORTH PACIFIC OCEAN
ANDORRA
UZBEKISTAN
KYRGYZSTAN
SPAIN
PORTUGAL
TURKMENISTAN
TAJIKISTAN
NORTH KOREA
C H I N A
JAPAN
SOUTH KOREA
TUNISIA
CYPRUS
LEBANON
SYRIA
IRAQ
IRAN
AFGHANISTAN
MOROCCO
ISRAEL
JORDAN
KUWAIT
NEPAL
BHUTAN
ALGERIA
LIBYA
EGYPT
BAHRAIN
QATAR
PAKISTAN
MYANMAR (BURMA)
Tropic of Cancer
SAUDI ARABIA
INDIA
TAIWAN
MAURITANIA
MALI
UNITED ARAB EMIRATES
LAOS
NIGER
ERITREA
OMAN
BANGLADESH
CHAD
YEMEN
THAILAND
CAPE VERDE
SUDAN
VIETNAM
PHILIPPINES
NIGERIA
DJIBOUTI
MARSHALL ISLANDS
CAMBODIA (KAMPUCHEA)
UGANDA
ETHIOPIA
SRI LANKA
PALAU
BRUNEI
SOMALIA
MALDIVES
MICRONESIA
CAMEROON
MALAYSIA
KIRIBATI
Equator
CENTRAL AFRICAN REPUBLIC
RWANDA
SINGAPORE
NAURU
SÃO TOMÉ AND PRÍNCIPE
DEM. REP. OF THE CONGO
KENYA
I N D O N E S I A
EQUATORIAL GUINEA
BURUNDI
SEYCHELLES
PAPUA NEW GUINEA
SOLOMON ISLANDS
GABON
TANZANIA
MALAWI
CONGO REPUBLIC
COMOROS
TUVALU
INDIAN OCEAN
EAST TIMOR
ANGOLA
MOZAMBIQUE
ZAMBIA
VANUATU
FIJI
MADAGASCAR
MAURITIUS
Tropic of Capricorn
NAMIBIA
BOTSWANA
AUSTRALIA
ZIMBABWE
SWAZILAND
SOUTH AFRICA
LESOTHO
MAURITANIA
NEW ZEALAND
MALI
NIGER
SENEGAL
GAMBIA
0 100 Miles
0 100 Kilometers
CASPIAN SEA
RUSSIA
GUINEA-BISSAU
BURKINA FASO
GUINEA
BENIN
BLACK SEA
GEORGIA
SIERRA LEONE
ATLANTIC OCEAN
NIGERIA
GHANA
IVORY COAST
AZERBAIJAN
ARMENIA
LIBERIA
0 150 300 Miles
0 150 300 Kilometers
TOGO
TURKEY
AZERBAIJAN
IRAN

Map 2 World Physical Features

ARCTIC OCEAN
GREENLAND
NORTH AMERICA
SOUTH AMERICA
NORTH PACIFIC OCEAN
NORTH ATLANTIC OCEAN
SOUTH PACIFIC OCEAN
SOUTH ATLANTIC OCEAN
CANADA BASIN
BEAUFORT SEA
CHUKCHI SEA
BERING SEA
Bering Strait
BROOKS RANGE
Mt. McKinley 20,320 ft.
Mt. Logan 19,551 ft.
Gulf of Alaska
Mt. Fairweather 15,300 ft.
Mt. Waddington 13,163 ft.
Mt. Rainier 14,410 ft.
Mt. Robson 12,972 ft.
Mt. Columbia 12,294 ft.
ALEUTIAN ISLANDS
ALEUTIAN TRENCH
QUEEN ELIZABETH ISLANDS
VICTORIA ISLAND
BANKS I.
BAFFIN ISLAND
Baffin Bay
Davis Strait
Hudson Bay
Great Bear Lake
Great Slave Lake
L. Winnipeg
The Great Lakes
LABRADOR SEA
LAURENTIAN PLATEAU
NEWFOUNDLAND
Strait of Belle Isle
APPALACHIAN MTS.
GREAT PLAINS
CENTRAL LOWLAND
ROCKY MTS.
SIERRA MADRE
Gulf of Mexico
Cape Hatteras
Cape Sable
Cape Cod
BERMUDA
NORTH AMERICAN BASIN
Pico de Orizaba 18,406 ft.
WEST INDIES
CARIBBEAN SEA
Tropic of Cancer
Cabo San Lucas
HAWAIIAN ISLANDS
Mauna Kea 13,796 ft.
HAWAIIAN RIDGE
MIDWAY IS.
Equator
GALAPAGOS ISLANDS
COCOS RIDGE
Pico Bolívar 16,427 ft.
Chimborazo 20,702 ft.
GUIANA HIGHLANDS
LLANOS
AMAZON BASIN
SELVAS
CAMPOS
BRAZILIAN HIGHLANDS
PLATEAU OF MATO GROSSO
ANDES MOUNTAINS
GREAT CENTRAL LOWLAND
Nevado Huascarán 22,133 ft.
NAZCA RIDGE
ATACAMA TRENCH
Nevado Ojos del Salado 22,615 ft.
Cerro Aconcagua 22,831 ft.
PAMPAS
Río de la Plata
Tropic of Capricorn
EAST PACIFIC RISE
SOUTHWEST PACIFIC BASIN
PHOENIX ISLANDS
WESTERN SAMOA
TONGA IS.
TONGA
SOCIETY IS.
TUAMOTU ARCHIPELAGO
KERMADEC IS.
KERMADEC TRENCH
CHATHAM ISLANDS
CHONOS ARCH.
Strait of Magellan
FALKLAND ISLANDS
Cape Horn
Drake Passage
SOUTH GEORGIA
SOUTH SANDWICH TRENCH
PACIFIC-ANTARCTIC RIDGE
BELLINGSHAUSEN PLAIN
Antarctic Circle
ANTARCTIC PENINSULA
WEDDELL SEA
ROSS SEA
Vinson Massif 16,066 ft.
MID-ATLANTIC RIDGE
REYKJANES RIDGE
RIO GRANDE RISE
AZORES
MADEIRA
CANARY ISLANDS
Pico de Teide 12,188 ft.
CAPE VERDE PLAIN
CAPE VERDE ISLANDS
Gunnbjørn Fjeld 12,139 ft.

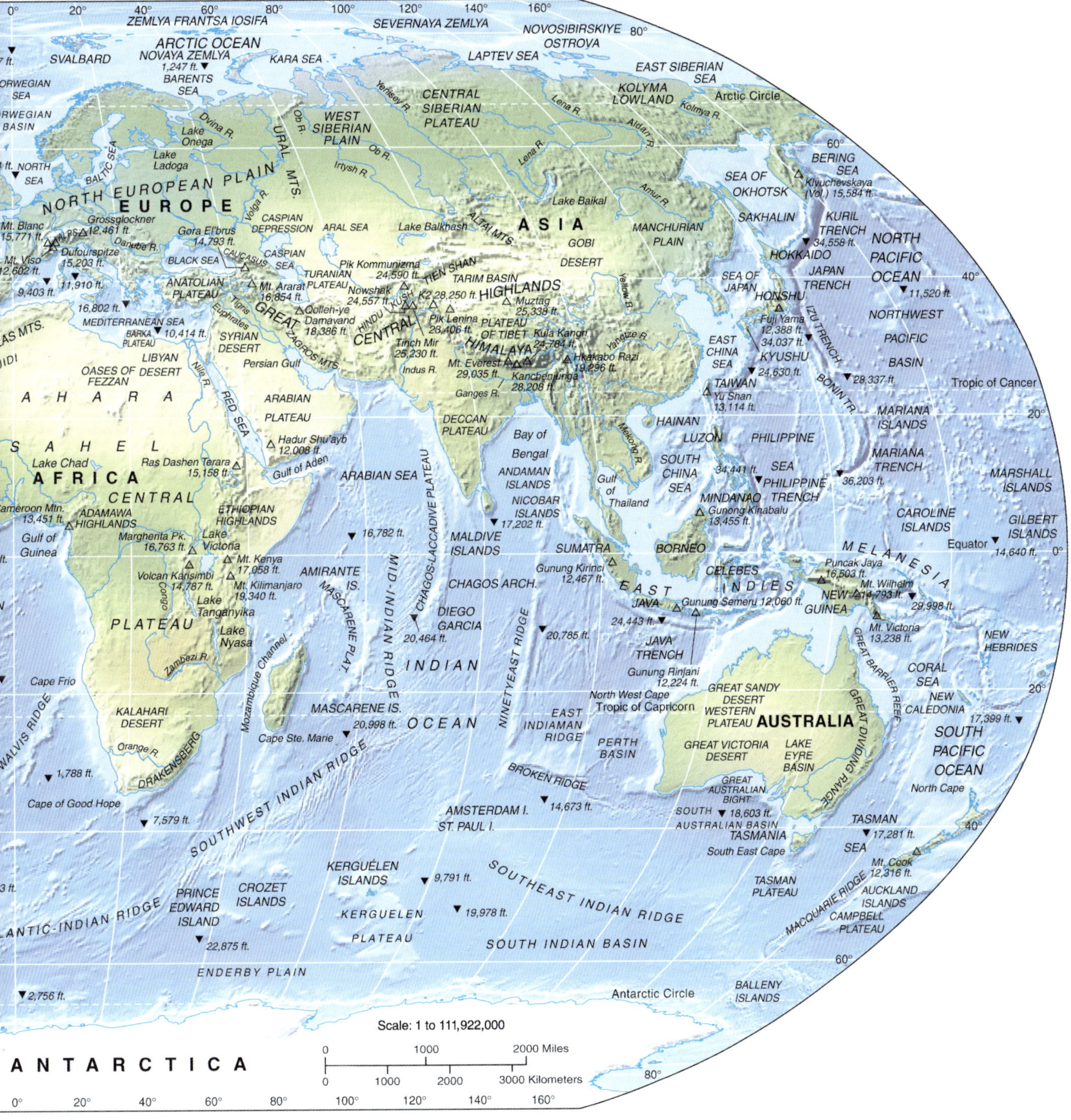
ZEMLYA FRANTSA IOSIFA
SEVERNAYA ZEMLYA
NOVOSIBIRSKIYE OSTROVA
ARCTIC OCEAN
SVALBARD
NOVAYA ZEMLYA
1,247 ft.
KARA SEA
LAPTEV SEA
BARENTS SEA
EAST SIBERIAN SEA
KOLYMA LOWLAND
Arctic Circle
CENTRAL SIBERIAN PLATEAU
WEST SIBERIAN PLAIN
Lake Onega
Lake Ladoga
BALTIC SEA
NORTH SEA
NORTH EUROPEAN PLAIN
EUROPE
URAL MTS.
BERING SEA
Klyuchevskaya (Vol.) 15,584 ft.
SEA OF OKHOTSK
SAKHALIN
KURIL TRENCH
34,558 ft.
NORTH PACIFIC OCEAN
Lake Baikal
ASIA
GOBI DESERT
MANCHURIAN PLAIN
ALTAI MTS.
Lake Balkhash
ARAL SEA
CASPIAN DEPRESSION
CASPIAN SEA
Mt. Blanc 15,771 ft.
Grossglockner 12,461 ft.
Dufourspitze 15,203 ft.
Mt. Viso 12,602 ft.
Gora El'brus 18,481 ft.
CAUCASUS
BLACK SEA
ANATOLIAN PLATEAU
Mt. Ararat 16,854 ft.
TURANIAN PLATEAU
Pik Kommunizma 24,590 ft.
TIEN SHAN
TARIM BASIN
HIGHLANDS
K2 28,250 ft.
Nowshak 24,557 ft.
HINDU KUSH
Pik Lenina 23,406 ft.
PLATEAU OF TIBET
Muztag 25,338 ft.
Kula Kangri 24,784 ft.
HIMALAYA
Qolleh-ye Damavand 18,386 ft.
GREAT ZAGROS MTS.
MEDITERRANEAN SEA
BARKA PLATEAU
10,414 ft.
16,802 ft.
11,910 ft.
9,403 ft.
SYRIAN DESERT
Tirich Mir 25,230 ft.
Mt. Everest 29,035 ft.
Kanchenjunga 28,208 ft.
Hkakabo Razi 19,296 ft.
Persian Gulf
LIBYAN DESERT
OASES OF FEZZAN
SAHARA
ARABIAN PLATEAU
RED SEA
Hadur Shu'ayb 12,008 ft.
SAHEL
Lake Chad
AFRICA
Ras Dashen Terara 15,158 ft.
Gulf of Aden
ARABIAN SEA
CENTRAL
ETHIOPIAN HIGHLANDS
Cameroon Mtn. 13,451 ft.
ADAMAWA HIGHLANDS
Gulf of Guinea
Margherita Pk. 16,763 ft.
Lake Victoria
Mt. Kenya 17,058 ft.
Mt. Kilimanjaro 19,340 ft.
Volcan Karisimbi 14,787 ft.
Lake Tanganyika
Lake Nyasa
PLATEAU
AMIRANTE IS.
MASCARENE PLAT.
Mozambique Channel
Zambezi R.
Cape Frio
WALVIS RIDGE
KALAHARI DESERT
Orange R.
DRAKENSBERG
1,788 ft.
Cape of Good Hope
7,579 ft.
Cape Ste. Marie
MASCARENE IS.
20,998 ft.
SOUTHWEST INDIAN RIDGE
DECCAN PLATEAU
Bay of Bengal
ANDAMAN ISLANDS
NICOBAR ISLANDS
17,202 ft.
16,782 ft.
MALDIVE ISLANDS
CHAGOS-LACCADIVE PLATEAU
MID-INDIAN RIDGE
CHAGOS ARCH.
DIEGO GARCIA
20,464 ft.
NINETYEAST RIDGE
INDIAN OCEAN
20,785 ft.
EAST INDIAMAN RIDGE
PERTH BASIN
BROKEN RIDGE
14,673 ft.
AMSTERDAM I.
ST. PAUL I.
KERGUÉLEN ISLANDS
9,791 ft.
SOUTHEAST INDIAN RIDGE
19,978 ft.
KERGUELEN PLATEAU
SOUTH INDIAN BASIN
PRINCE EDWARD ISLAND
CROZET ISLANDS
ATLANTIC-INDIAN RIDGE
22,875 ft.
ENDERBY PLAIN
2,756 ft.
ANTARCTICA
Antarctic Circle
BALLENY ISLANDS
SEA OF JAPAN
HOKKAIDO
JAPAN TRENCH
HONSHU
Fuji Yama 12,388 ft.
34,037 ft.
IZU TRENCH
KYUSHU
24,630 ft.
EAST CHINA SEA
TAIWAN
Yu Shan 13,114 ft.
11,520 ft.
NORTHWEST PACIFIC BASIN
BONIN TR.
28,337 ft.
Tropic of Cancer
MARIANA ISLANDS
MARIANA TRENCH
36,203 ft.
MARSHALL ISLANDS
HAINAN
LUZON
PHILIPPINE SEA
SOUTH CHINA SEA
34,441 ft.
PHILIPPINE TRENCH
Gulf of Thailand
MINDANAO
Gunong Kinabalu 13,455 ft.
CAROLINE ISLANDS
GILBERT ISLANDS
Equator
14,640 ft.
BORNEO
SUMATRA
Gunung Kirinci 12,467 ft.
CELEBES
EAST INDIES
MELANESIA
Puncak Jaya 16,503 ft.
Mt. Wilhelm 14,793 ft.
NEW GUINEA
29,998 ft.
JAVA
Gunung Semeru 12,060 ft.
24,443 ft.
JAVA TRENCH
Gunung Rinjani 12,224 ft.
Mt. Victoria 13,238 ft.
GREAT BARRIER REEF
NEW HEBRIDES
CORAL SEA
North West Cape
Tropic of Capricorn
GREAT SANDY DESERT
WESTERN PLATEAU
AUSTRALIA
NEW CALEDONIA
17,399 ft.
SOUTH PACIFIC OCEAN
GREAT VICTORIA DESERT
LAKE EYRE BASIN
GREAT DIVIDING RANGE
GREAT AUSTRALIAN BIGHT
North Cape
SOUTH AUSTRALIAN BASIN
18,603 ft.
TASMANIA
South East Cape
TASMAN SEA
17,281 ft.
Mt. Cook 12,316 ft.
TASMAN PLATEAU
MACQUARIE RIDGE
AUCKLAND ISLANDS
CAMPBELL PLATEAU
Scale: 1 to 111,922,000
0 1000 2000 Miles
0 1000 2000 3000 Kilometers

Map 3a Average Annual Precipitation

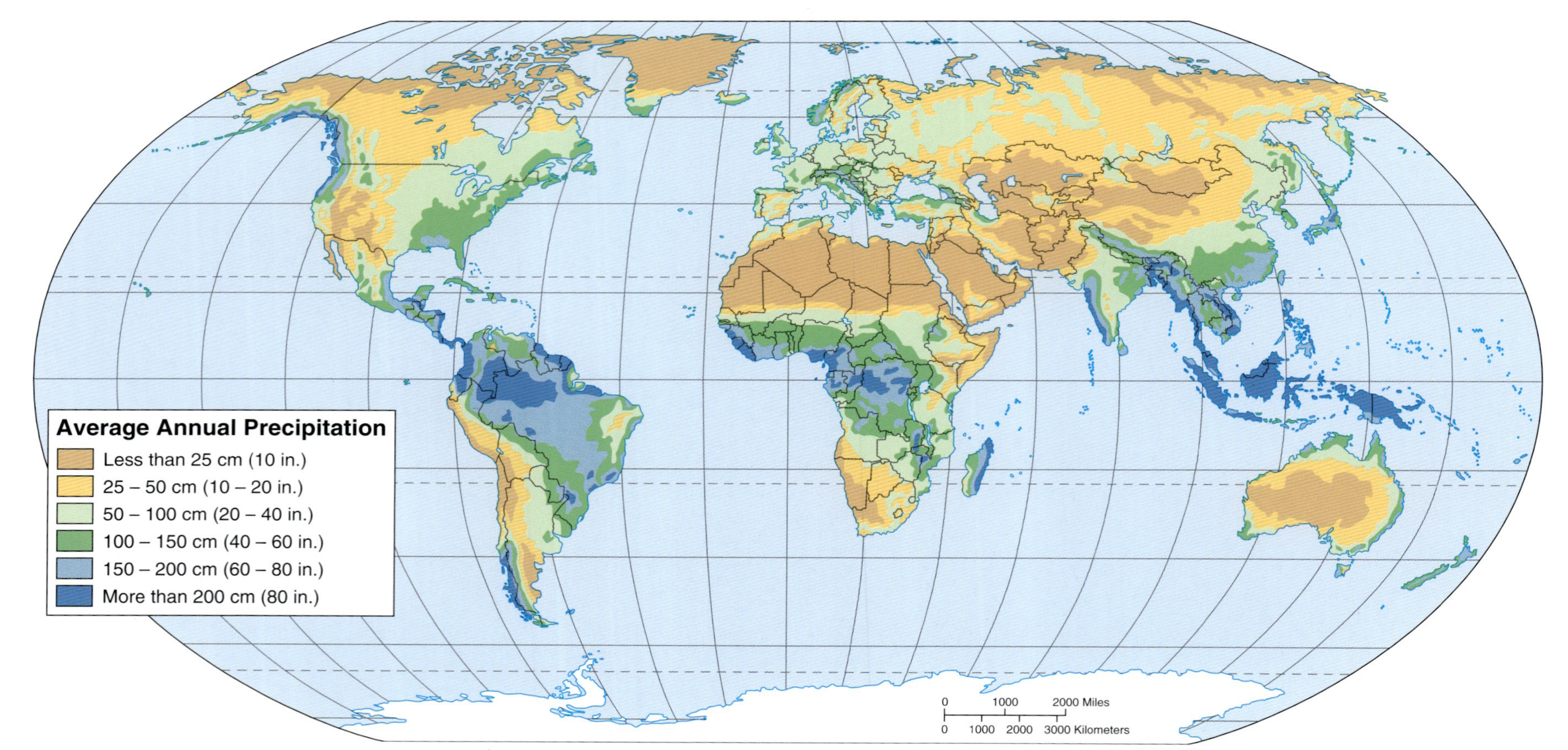
Average Annual Precipitation
Less than 25 cm (10 in.)
25 – 50 cm (10 – 20 in.)
50 – 100 cm (20 – 40 in.)
100 – 150 cm (40 – 60 in.)
150 – 200 cm (60 – 80 in.)
More than 200 cm (80 in.)
0 1000 2000 Miles
0 1000 2000 3000 Kilometers

The two most important physical geographic variables are precipitation and temperature, the essential elements of weather and climate. Precipitation is a conditioner of both soil type and vegetation. More than any other single environmental element, it influences where people do or do not live. Water is the most precious resource available to humans, and water availability is largely a function of precipitation. Water availability is also a function of several precipitation variables that do not appear on this map: the seasonal distribution of precipitation (is precipitation or drought concentrated in a particular season?), the ratio between precipitation and temperature (how much of the water that comes to the earth in the form of precipitation is lost through mechanisms such as evaporation and transpiration that are a function of temperature?), and the annual variability of precipitation (how much do annual precipitation totals for a place or region tend to vary from the "normal" or average precipitation?). In order to obtain a complete understanding of precipitation, these variables should be examined along with the more general data presented on this map. The study of precipitation and other climatic elements is the concern of the branch of physical geography called "climatology."

Map 3b Seasonal Average Precipitation, November Through April

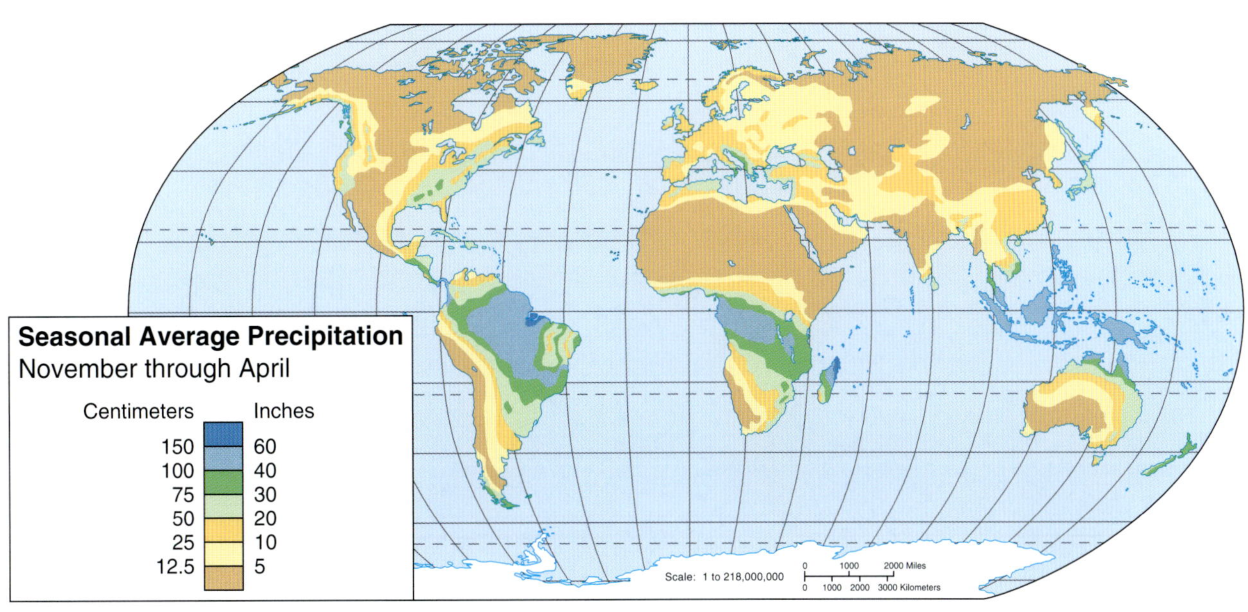
Seasonal Average Precipitation
November through April
Centimeters
Inches
150
60
100
40
75
30
50
20
25
10
12.5
5
Scale: 1 to 218,000,000
0 1000 2000 Miles
0 1000 2000 3000 Kilometers

Map 3c Seasonal Average Precipitation, May Through October

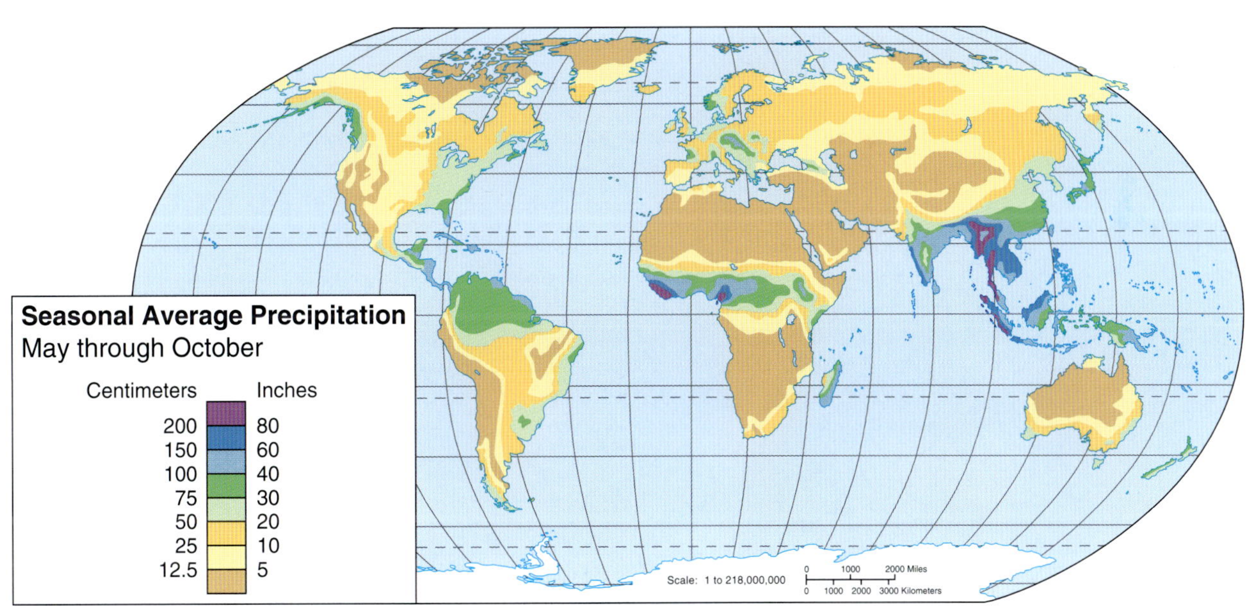
Seasonal Average Precipitation
May through October
Centimeters
Inches
200
80
150
60
100
40
75
30
50
20
25
10
12.5
5
Scale: 1 to 218,000,000
0 1000 2000 Miles
0 1000 2000 3000 Kilometers

Seasonal average precipitation is nearly as important as annual precipitation totals in determining the habitability of an area. Critical factors are such things as whether precipitation coincides with the growing season and thus facilitates agriculture or during the winter when it is less effective in aiding plant growth, and whether precipitation occurs during summer with its higher water loss through evaporation and transpiration or during the winter when more of it can go into storage. Several of the world's great climate zones have pronounced seasonal precipitation rhythms. The tropical and subtropical savanna grasslands have a long winter dry season and abundant precipitation in the summer. The Mediterranean climate is the only major climate with a marked dry season during the summer, making agriculture possible only through irrigation or other adjustments to cope with drought during the period of plant growth. And the great monsoon climates of south and southeast Asia have their winter dry season and summer rain that have conditioned the development of Asian agriculture and the rhythms of Asian life.

Map 3d Variation in Average Annual Precipitation

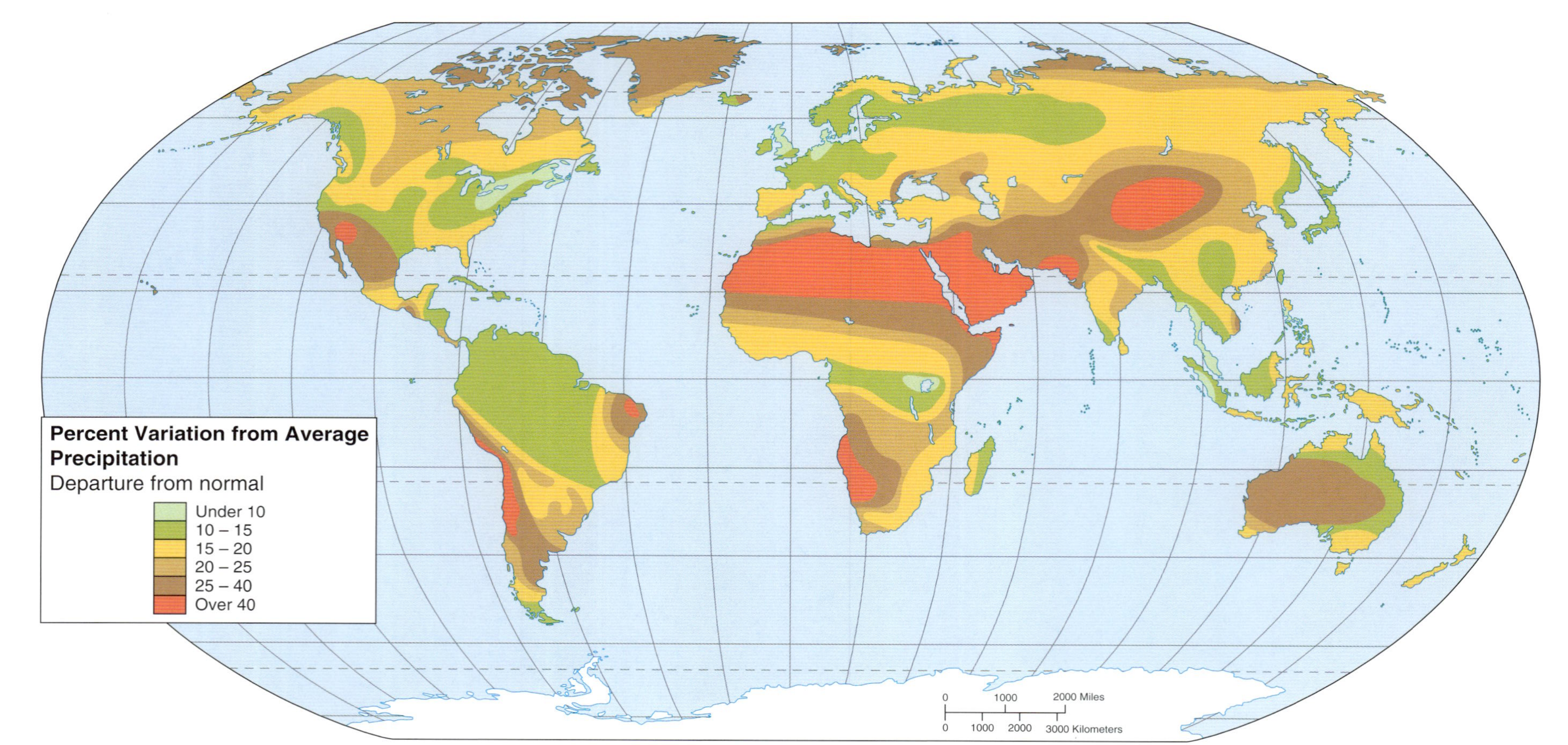

Percent Variation from Average Precipitation
Departure from normal
Under 10
10 – 15
15 – 20
20 – 25
25 – 40
Over 40
0 1000 2000 Miles
0 1000 2000 3000 Kilometers

While annual precipitation totals and seasonal distribution of precipitation are important variables, the variability of precipitation from one year to the next may be even more critical. You will note from the map that there is a general spatial correlation between the world's drylands and the amount of annual variation in precipitation. Generally, the drier the climate, the more likely it is that there will be considerable differences in rainfall and/or snowfall from one year to the next. We might determine that the average precipitation of the mid-Sahara is 2 inches per year. What this really means is that a particular location in the Sahara during one year might receive .5″, during the next year 3.5″, and during a third year 2″. If you add these together and divide by the number of years, the "average" precipitation is 2″ per year. The significance of this is that much of the world's crucial agricultural output of cereals (grains) comes from dryland climates (the Great Plains of the United States, the Pampas of Argentina, the steppes of Ukraine and Russia, for example), and variations in annual rainfall totals can have significant impacts on levels of grain production and, therefore, important consequences for both economic and political processes.

Map 4a Temperature Regions and Ocean Currents

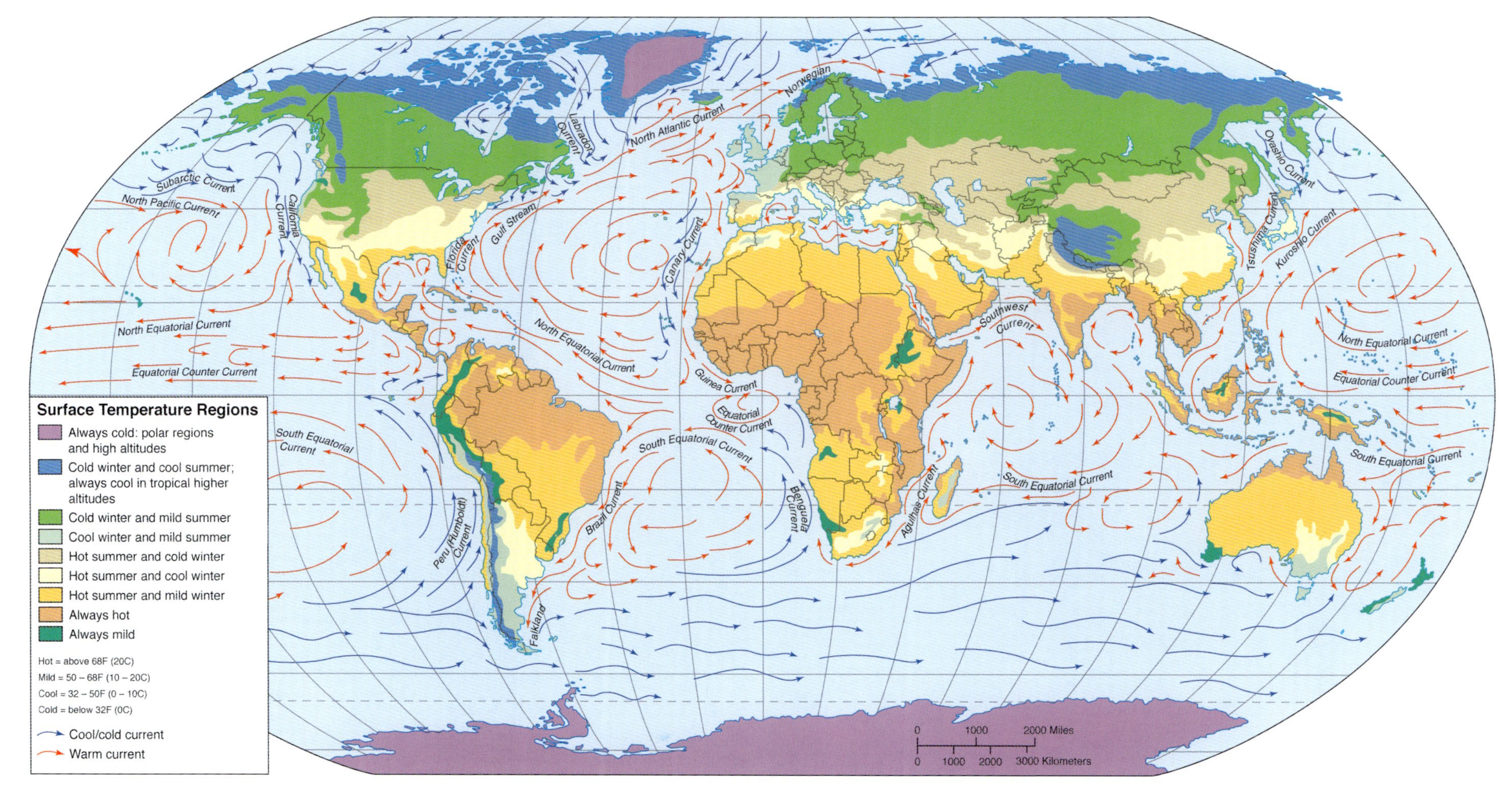

Surface Temperature Regions
Always cold: polar regions and high altitudes
Cold winter and cool summer; always cool in tropical higher altitudes
Cold winter and mild summer
Cool winter and mild summer
Hot summer and cold winter
Hot summer and cool winter
Hot summer and mild winter
Always hot
Always mild
Hot = above 68F (20C)
Mild = 50 – 68F (10 – 20C)
Cool = 32 – 50F (0 – 10C)
Cold = below 32F (0C)
Cool/cold current
Warm current
Subarctic Current
North Pacific Current
California Current
North Equatorial Current
Equatorial Counter Current
South Equatorial Current
Labrador Current
North Atlantic Current
Norwegian
Gulf Stream
Florida Current
Canary Current
North Equatorial Current
Guinea Current
Equatorial Counter Current
South Equatorial Current
Peru (Humboldt) Current
Brazil Current
Falkland
Benguela Current
Agulhas Current
Southwest Current
South Equatorial Current
Oyashio Current
Tsushima Current
Kuroshio Current
North Equatorial Current
Equatorial Counter Current
South Equatorial Current
0 1000 2000 Miles
0 1000 2000 3000 Kilometers

Along with precipitation, temperature is one of the two most important environmental variables, defining the climate conditions so essential for the distribution of such human activities as agriculture and the distribution of the human population. The seasonal rhythm of temperature, including such measures as the average annual temperature range (difference between the average temperature of the warmest month and that of the coldest month), is an additional variable not shown on the map but, like the seasonality of precipitation, should be a part of any comprehensive study of climate. The ocean currents illustrated exert a significant influence over the climate of adjacent regions and are the most important mechanism for redistributing surplus heat from the equatorial region into middle and high latitudes. Physical geographers known as "climatologists" study the phenomenon of temperature and related climatic characteristics.

Map 4b Average January Temperature

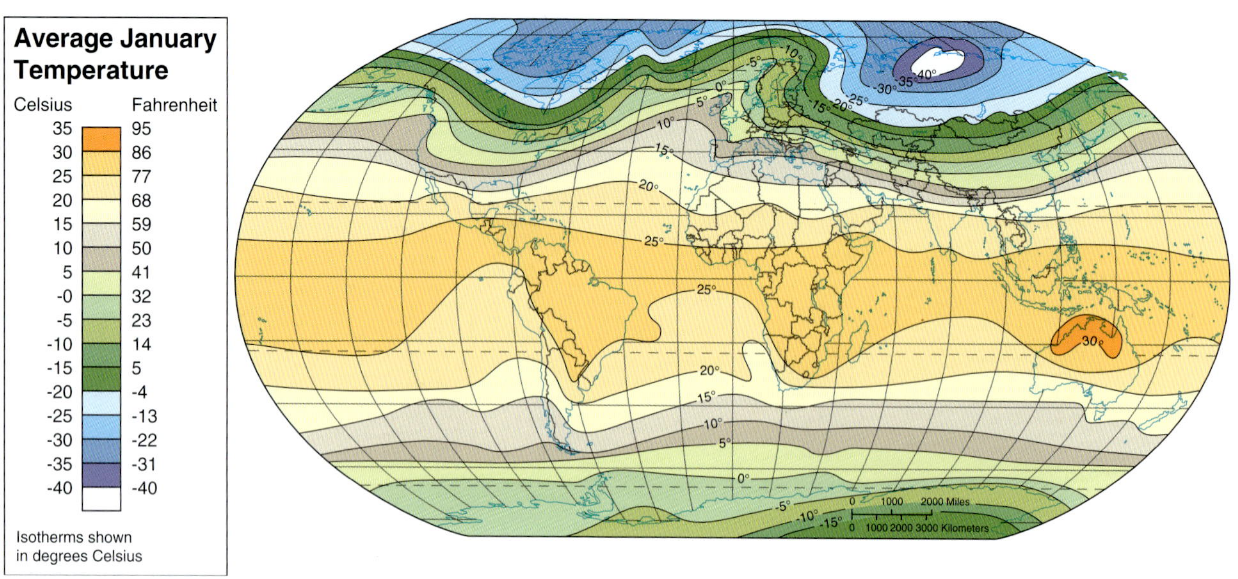
Average January Temperature
Celsius Fahrenheit
35 95
30 86
25 77
20 68
15 59
10 50
5 41
-0 32
-5 23
-10 14
-15 5
-20 -4
-25 -13
-30 -22
-35 -31
-40 -40
Isotherms shown in degrees Celsius
0 1000 2000 Miles
0 1000 2000 3000 Kilometers

Map 4c Average July Temperature

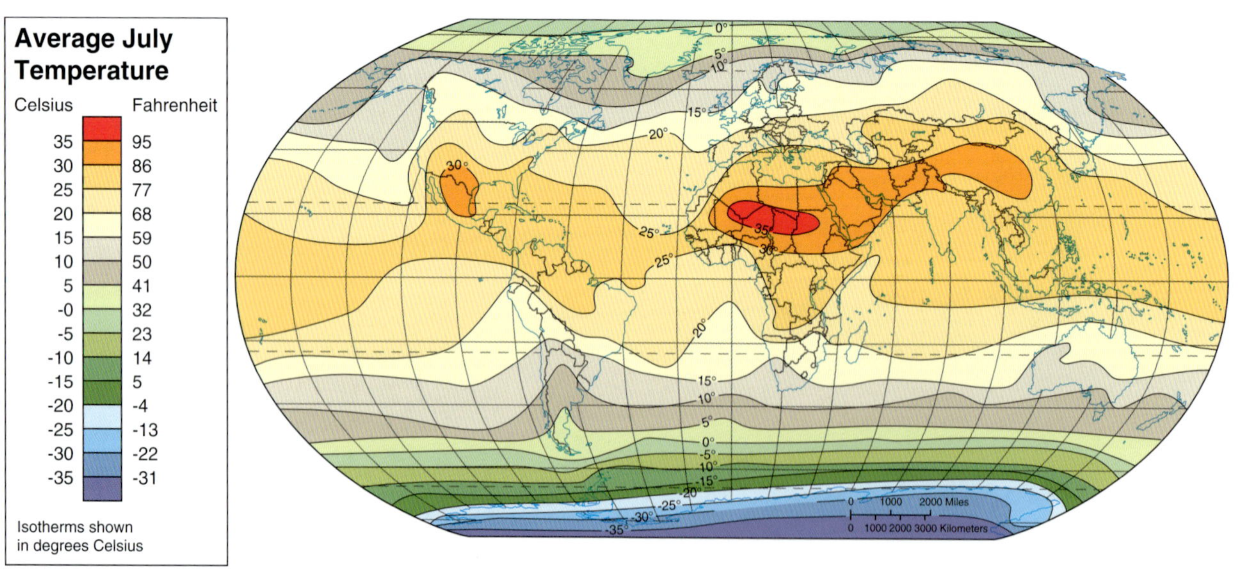
Average July Temperature
Celsius Fahrenheit
35 95
30 86
25 77
20 68
15 59
10 50
5 41
-0 32
-5 23
-10 14
-15 5
-20 -4
-25 -13
-30 -22
-35 -31
Isotherms shown in degrees Celsius
0 1000 2000 Miles
0 1000 2000 3000 Kilometers

Where moisture availability tends to mark the seasons in the tropics and subtropics, in the mid-latitudes, seasons are marked by temperature. Temperature is determined by latitudinal transition, by altitude or elevation above sea level, and by location of a place relative to the world's landmasses and oceans. The most important of these controls is latitude, and temperatures generally become lower with increasing latitude. Proximity to water, however, tends to moderate temperature extremes, and "maritime" climates influenced by the oceans will be warmer in the winter and cooler in the summer than continental climates in the same general latitude. Maritime climates will also show smaller temperature ranges, the difference between January and July temperatures, while climates of the continental interiors, far from the moderating influences of the oceans, will tend to have greater temperature ranges. In the Northern Hemisphere, where there are both large landmasses and oceans, the range is great. But in the Southern Hemisphere, dominated by water and, hence, by the more moderate maritime air masses, the temperature range is comparatively small. Significant temperature departures from the "normal" produced by latitude may also be the result of elevation. With exceptions, lower temperatures produced by topography are difficult to see on maps of this scale.

Map 5a Atmospheric Pressure and Predominant Surface Winds, January

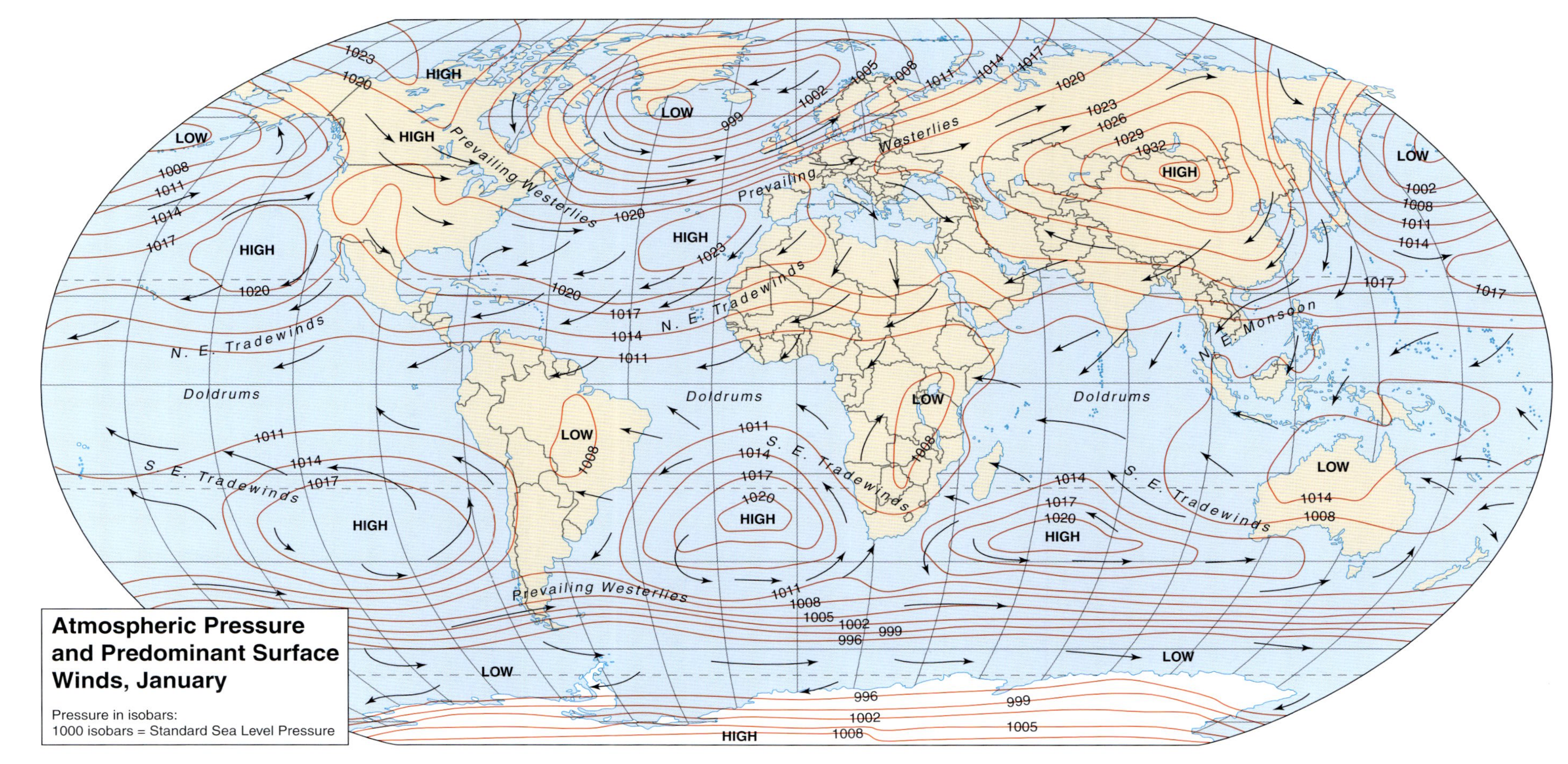
Atmospheric Pressure and Predominant Surface Winds, January
Pressure in isobars:
1000 isobars = Standard Sea Level Pressure
HIGH
LOW
Prevailing Westerlies
Prevailing
Westerlies
N. E. Tradewinds
S. E. Tradewinds
Doldrums
N. E. Monsoon
1002
1005
1008
1011
1014
1017
1020
1023
1026
1029
1032
996
999

Map 5b Atmospheric Pressure and Predominant Surface Winds, July

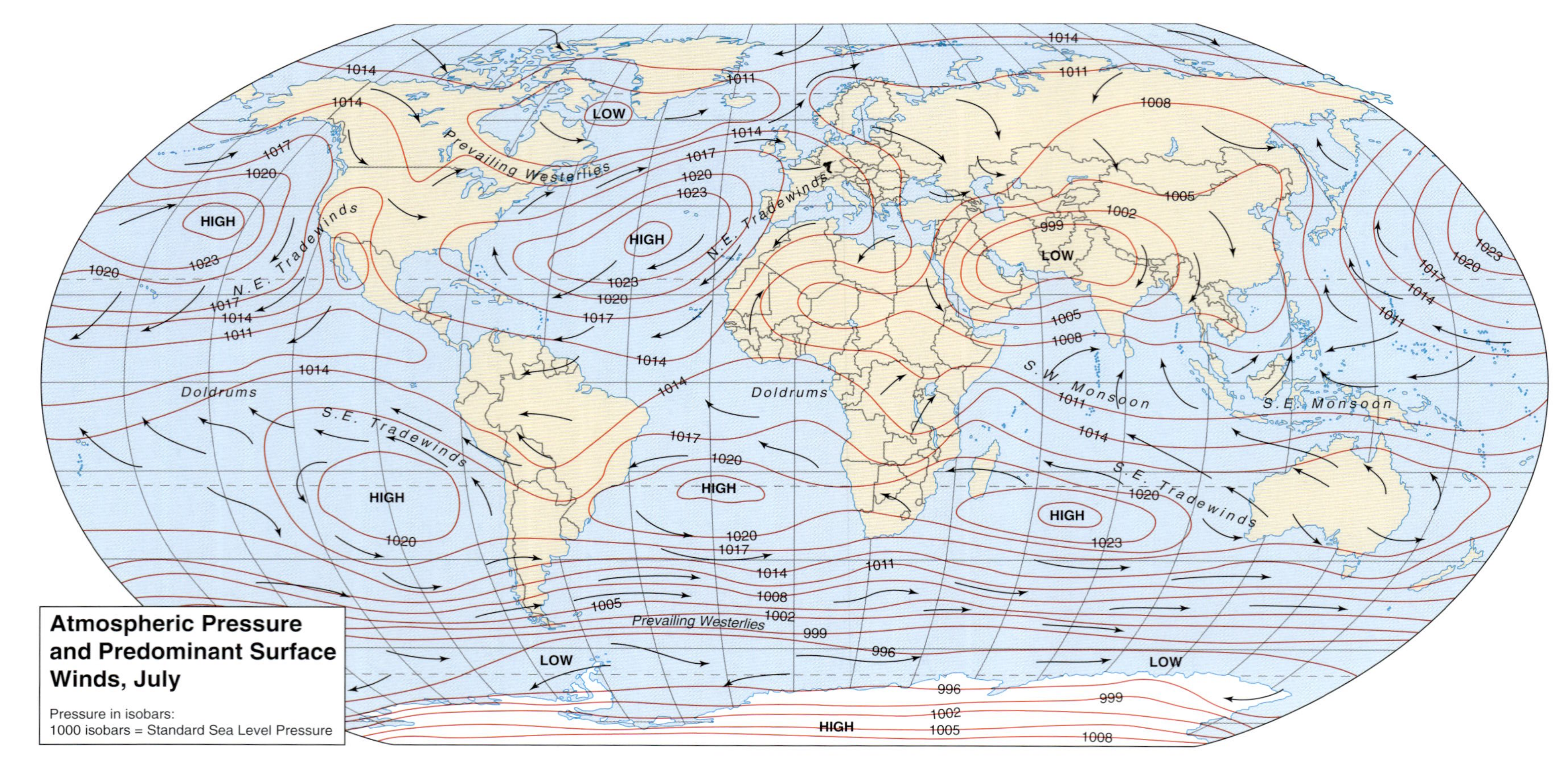

Atmospheric Pressure and Predominant Surface Winds, July
Pressure in isobars:
1000 isobars = Standard Sea Level Pressure
HIGH
LOW
Prevailing Westerlies
N. E. Tradewinds
S. E. Tradewinds
Doldrums
S. W. Monsoon
S. E. Monsoon
1014
1011
1008
1005
1002
999
996
1017
1020
1023

Atmospheric pressure, or the density of air, is a function largely of air temperature: the colder the air, the denser and heavier it is, hence the higher its pressure; the warmer the air, the lighter and less stable it is, hence the lower its pressure. Global pressure systems are the alternating low and high pressure systems that, from the equator north and south, include: the equatorial low (sometimes called the intertropical convergence) centered on the equator for much of the year; the subtropical highs with their centers near the 30th degrees of north and south latitude; the subpolar lows or polar front centered near the 60th parallel of north and south latitude; and the polar highs near the north and south poles. Air flows from high pressure to low pressure regions, and this air flow constitutes the earth's major surface winds such as the tropical tradewinds and the prevailing westerlies. This flow of air is one of the chief mechanisms by which surplus heat energy from the equatorial region is redistributed to higher latitudes. It is also the primary conditioner of the world's major precipitation belts, with rainfall and snowfall associated primarily with lower atmospheric pressure conditions.

Map 6 Climate Regions

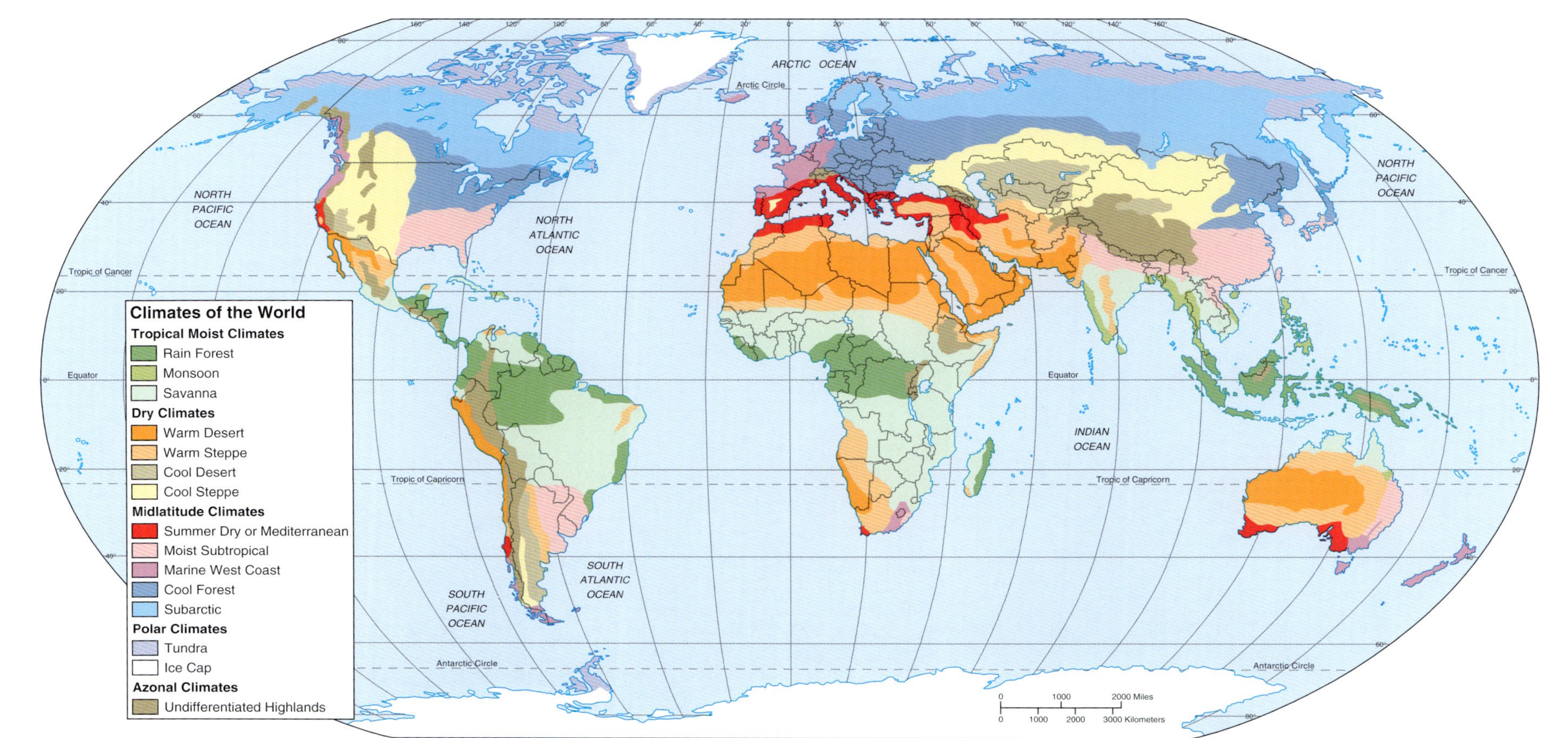

ARCTIC OCEAN
Arctic Circle
NORTH PACIFIC OCEAN
NORTH ATLANTIC OCEAN
Tropic of Cancer
Equator
Tropic of Capricorn
SOUTH PACIFIC OCEAN
SOUTH ATLANTIC OCEAN
INDIAN OCEAN
Antarctic Circle
Climates of the World
Tropical Moist Climates
Rain Forest
Monsoon
Savanna
Dry Climates
Warm Desert
Warm Steppe
Cool Desert
Cool Steppe
Midlatitude Climates
Summer Dry or Mediterranean
Moist Subtropical
Marine West Coast
Cool Forest
Subarctic
Polar Climates
Tundra
Ice Cap
Azonal Climates
Undifferentiated Highlands
0 1000 2000 Miles
0 1000 2000 3000 Kilometers

Of the world's many patterns of physical geography, climate or the long-term average of weather conditions such as temperature and precipitation is the most important. It is climate that conditions the distribution of natural vegetation and the types of soils that will exist in an area. Climate also influences the availability of our most crucial resource: water. From an economic standpoint, the world's most important activity is agriculture; no other element of physical geography is more important for agriculture than climate. Ultimately, it is agricultural production that determines where the bulk of human beings live, and therefore, climate is a basic determinant of the distribution of human populations as well. The study of climates or "climatology" is one of the most important branches of physical geography.

The climate classification system shown on this map is based on that developed by Wladimir Köppen. To establish his climate regions, Köppen used the climatic parameters of *precipitation, temperature*, and *evapotranspiration* as they impacted certain kinds of major vegetative associations. Hence the names for many of the climate regions are also the names of vegetative regions.

Map 7 Vegetation Types

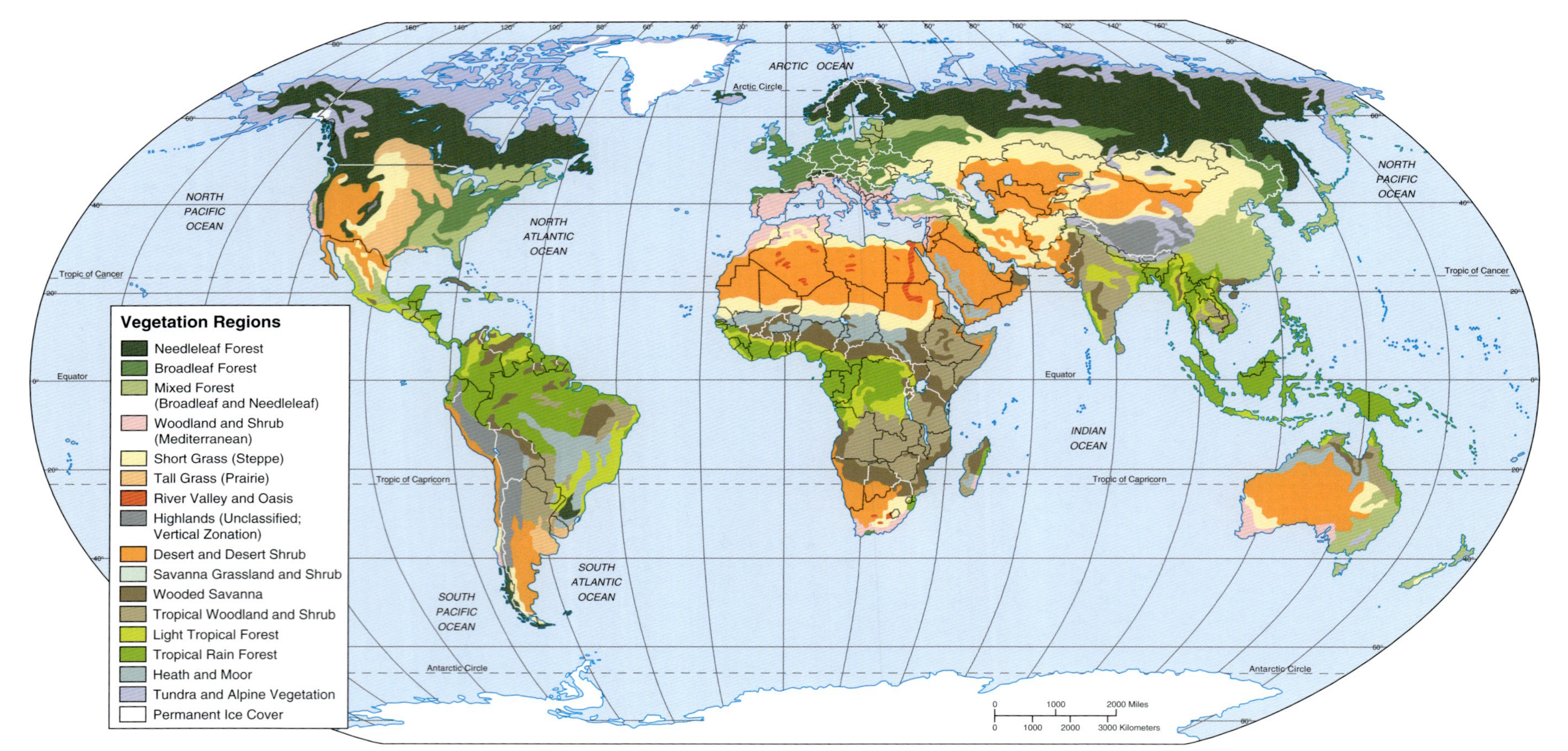
Vegetation Regions
Needleleaf Forest
Broadleaf Forest
Mixed Forest (Broadleaf and Needleleaf)
Woodland and Shrub (Mediterranean)
Short Grass (Steppe)
Tall Grass (Prairie)
River Valley and Oasis
Highlands (Unclassified; Vertical Zonation)
Desert and Desert Shrub
Savanna Grassland and Shrub
Wooded Savanna
Tropical Woodland and Shrub
Light Tropical Forest
Tropical Rain Forest
Heath and Moor
Tundra and Alpine Vegetation
Permanent Ice Cover
ARCTIC OCEAN
Arctic Circle
NORTH PACIFIC OCEAN
NORTH ATLANTIC OCEAN
SOUTH PACIFIC OCEAN
SOUTH ATLANTIC OCEAN
INDIAN OCEAN
Tropic of Cancer
Equator
Tropic of Capricorn
Antarctic Circle
0 1000 2000 Miles
0 1000 2000 3000 Kilometers

Vegetation is the most visible consequence of the distribution of temperature and precipitation. The global pattern of vegetative types or "habitat classes" and the global pattern of climate are closely related and make up one of the great global spatial correlations. But not all vegetation types are the consequence of temperature and precipitation or other climatic variables. Many types of vegetation in many areas of the world are the consequence of human activities, particularly the grazing of domesticated livestock, burning, and forest clearance. This map shows the pattern of natural or "potential" vegetation, or vegetation as it might be expected to exist without significant human influences, rather than the actual vegetation that results from a combination of environmental and human factors. Physical geographers who are interested in the distribution and geographic patterns of vegetation are "biogeographers."

Map 8 Soil Orders

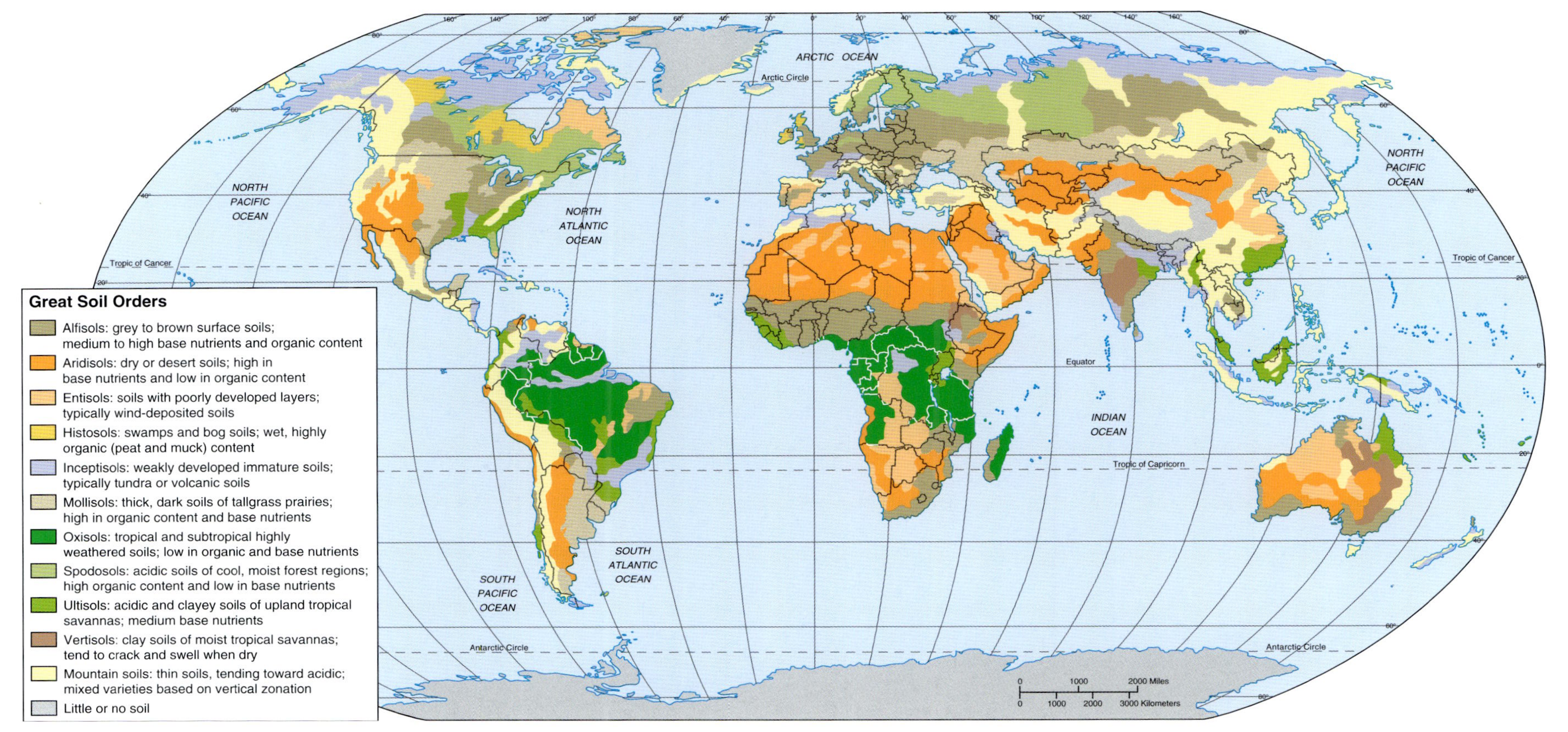

ARCTIC OCEAN
Arctic Circle
NORTH PACIFIC OCEAN
NORTH ATLANTIC OCEAN
Tropic of Cancer
Equator
INDIAN OCEAN
Tropic of Capricorn
SOUTH ATLANTIC OCEAN
SOUTH PACIFIC OCEAN
Antarctic Circle
0 1000 2000 Miles
0 1000 2000 3000 Kilometers
Great Soil Orders
Alfisols: grey to brown surface soils; medium to high base nutrients and organic content
Aridisols: dry or desert soils; high in base nutrients and low in organic content
Entisols: soils with poorly developed layers; typically wind-deposited soils
Histosols: swamps and bog soils; wet, highly organic (peat and muck) content
Inceptisols: weakly developed immature soils; typically tundra or volcanic soils
Mollisols: thick, dark soils of tallgrass prairies; high in organic content and base nutrients
Oxisols: tropical and subtropical highly weathered soils; low in organic and base nutrients
Spodosols: acidic soils of cool, moist forest regions; high organic content and low in base nutrients
Ultisols: acidic and clayey soils of upland tropical savannas; medium base nutrients
Vertisols: clay soils of moist tropical savannas; tend to crack and swell when dry
Mountain soils: thin soils, tending toward acidic; mixed varieties based on vertical zonation
Little or no soil

The characteristics of soil are one of the three primary physical geographic factors, along with climate and vegetation, that determine the habitability of regions for humans. In particular, soils influence the kinds of agricultural uses to which land is put. Since soils support the plants that are the primary producers of all food in the terrestrial food chain, their characteristics are crucial to the health and stability of ecosystems. Two types of soil are shown on this map: zonal soils, the characteristics of which are based on climatic patterns; and azonal soils, such as alluvial (water-deposited) or aeolian (wind-deposited) soils, the characteristics of which are derived from forces other than climate. However, many of the azonal soils, particularly those dependent upon drainage conditions, appear over areas too small to be readily shown on a map of this scale. Thus, almost none of the world's swamp or bog soils appear on this map. People who study the geographic characteristics of soils are most often "soil scientists," a discipline closely related to that branch of physical geography called "geomorphology."

Map 9 Ecological Regions

Ecological regions are distinctive areas within which unique sets of organisms and environments are found. We call the study of the relationships between organisms and their environmental surroundings "ecology." Within each of the ecological regions portrayed on the map, a particular combination of vegetation, wildlife, soil, water, climate, and terrain defines that region's habitability, or ability to support life, including human life. Like climate and landforms, ecological relationships are crucial to the existence of agriculture, the most basic of our economic activities, and important for many other kinds of economic activity as well. Biogeographers are especially concerned with the concept of ecological regions since such regions so clearly depend upon the geographic distribution of plants and animals in their environmental settings.

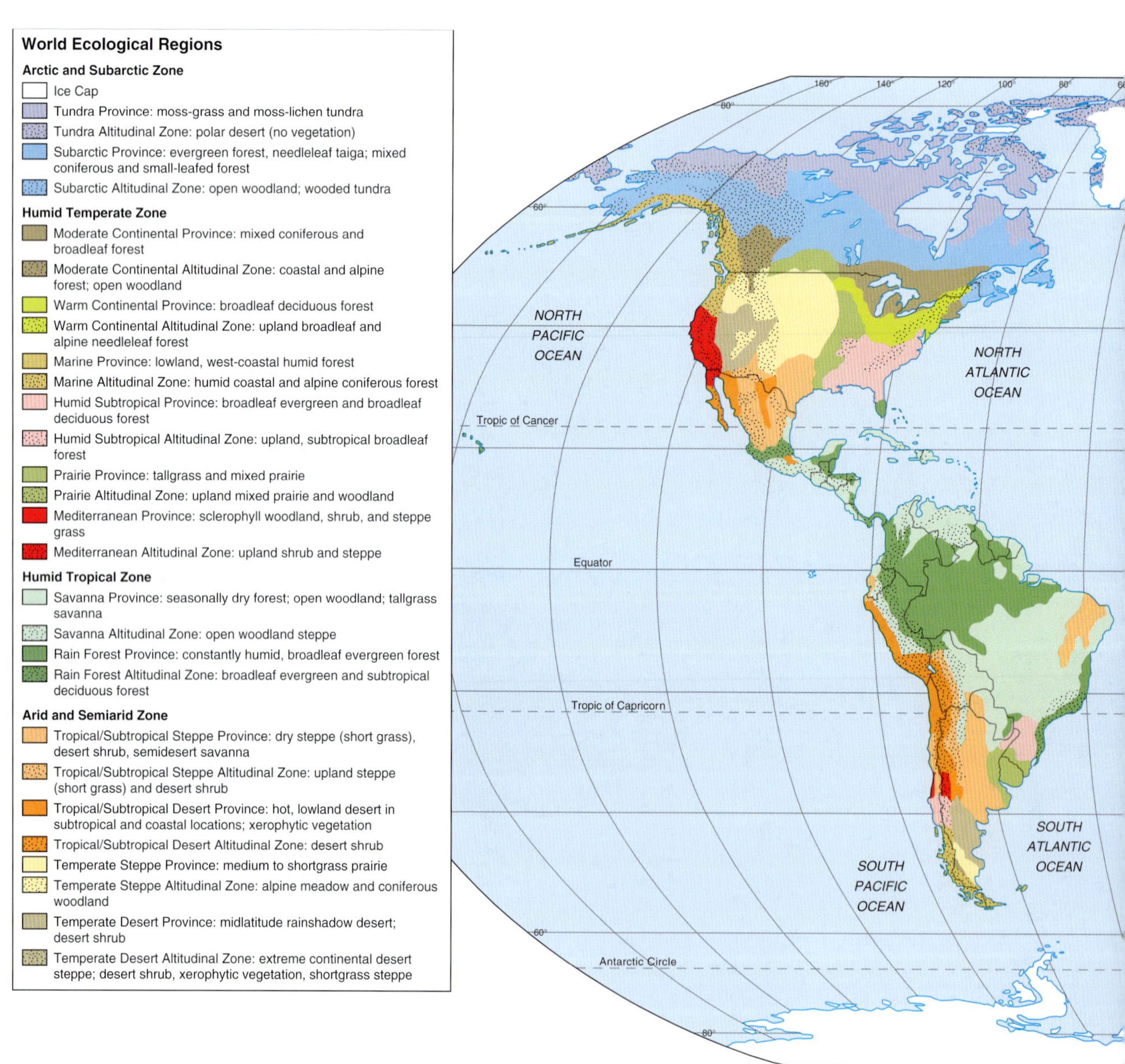

World Ecological Regions
Arctic and Subarctic Zone
Ice Cap
Tundra Province: moss-grass and moss-lichen tundra
Tundra Altitudinal Zone: polar desert (no vegetation)
Subarctic Province: evergreen forest, needleleaf taiga; mixed coniferous and small-leafed forest
Subarctic Altitudinal Zone: open woodland; wooded tundra
Humid Temperate Zone
Moderate Continental Province: mixed coniferous and broadleaf forest
Moderate Continental Altitudinal Zone: coastal and alpine forest; open woodland
Warm Continental Province: broadleaf deciduous forest
Warm Continental Altitudinal Zone: upland broadleaf and alpine needleleaf forest
Marine Province: lowland, west-coastal humid forest
Marine Altitudinal Zone: humid coastal and alpine coniferous forest
Humid Subtropical Province: broadleaf evergreen and broadleaf deciduous forest
Humid Subtropical Altitudinal Zone: upland, subtropical broadleaf forest
Prairie Province: tallgrass and mixed prairie
Prairie Altitudinal Zone: upland mixed prairie and woodland
Mediterranean Province: sclerophyll woodland, shrub, and steppe grass
Mediterranean Altitudinal Zone: upland shrub and steppe
Humid Tropical Zone
Savanna Province: seasonally dry forest; open woodland; tallgrass savanna
Savanna Altitudinal Zone: open woodland steppe
Rain Forest Province: constantly humid, broadleaf evergreen forest
Rain Forest Altitudinal Zone: broadleaf evergreen and subtropical deciduous forest
Arid and Semiarid Zone
Tropical/Subtropical Steppe Province: dry steppe (short grass), desert shrub, semidesert savanna
Tropical/Subtropical Steppe Altitudinal Zone: upland steppe (short grass) and desert shrub
Tropical/Subtropical Desert Province: hot, lowland desert in subtropical and coastal locations; xerophytic vegetation
Tropical/Subtropical Desert Altitudinal Zone: desert shrub
Temperate Steppe Province: medium to shortgrass prairie
Temperate Steppe Altitudinal Zone: alpine meadow and coniferous woodland
Temperate Desert Province: midlatitude rainshadow desert; desert shrub
Temperate Desert Altitudinal Zone: extreme continental desert steppe; desert shrub, xerophytic vegetation, shortgrass steppe
160°
140°
120°
100°
80°
60°
NORTH
PACIFIC
OCEAN
NORTH
ATLANTIC
OCEAN
Tropic of Cancer
Equator
Tropic of Capricorn
SOUTH
PACIFIC
OCEAN
SOUTH
ATLANTIC
OCEAN
Antarctic Circle

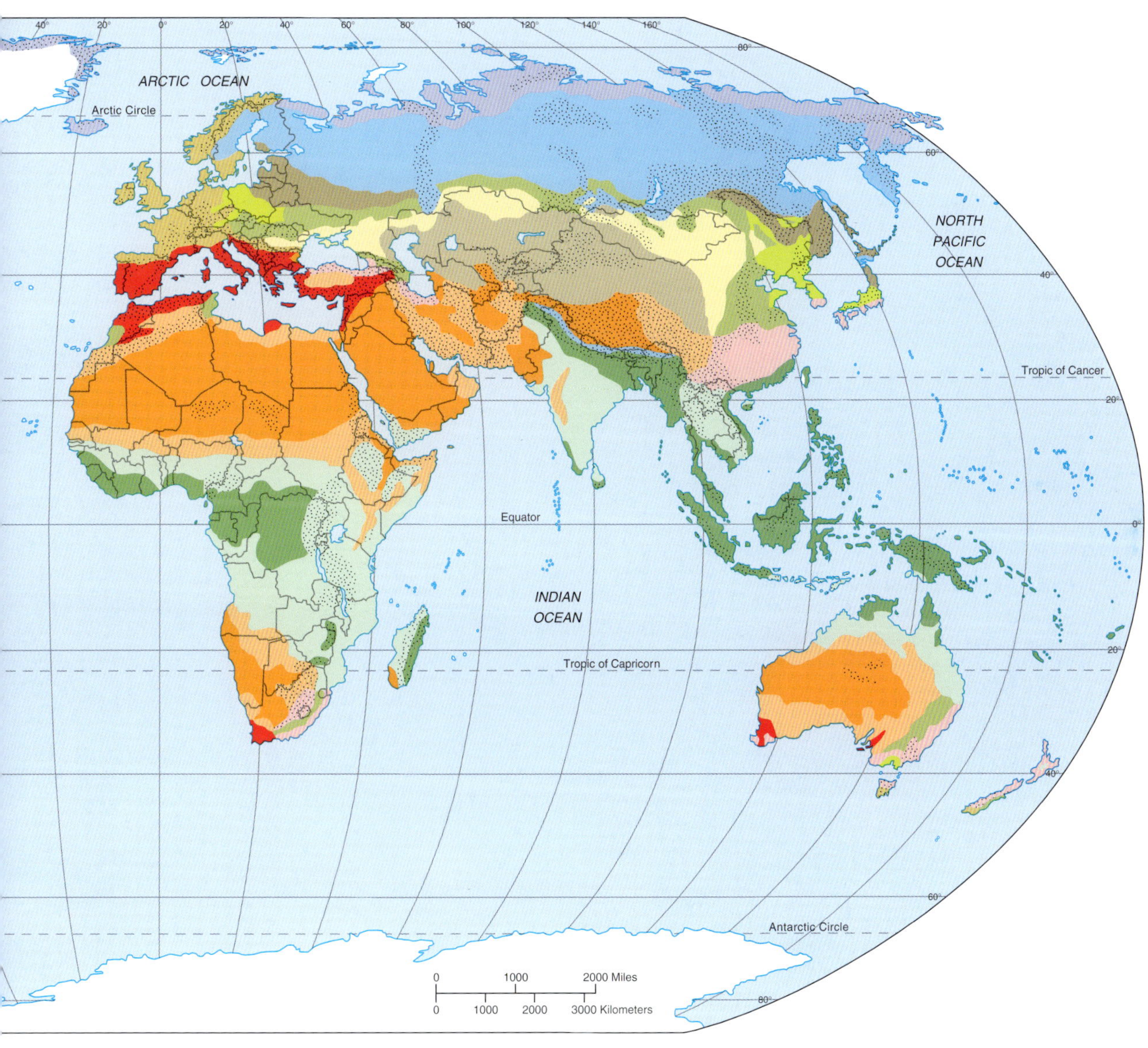

ARCTIC OCEAN
Arctic Circle
NORTH PACIFIC OCEAN
Tropic of Cancer
Equator
INDIAN OCEAN
Tropic of Capricorn
Antarctic Circle
0 1000 2000 Miles
0 1000 2000 3000 Kilometers

Map 10 Plate Tectonics

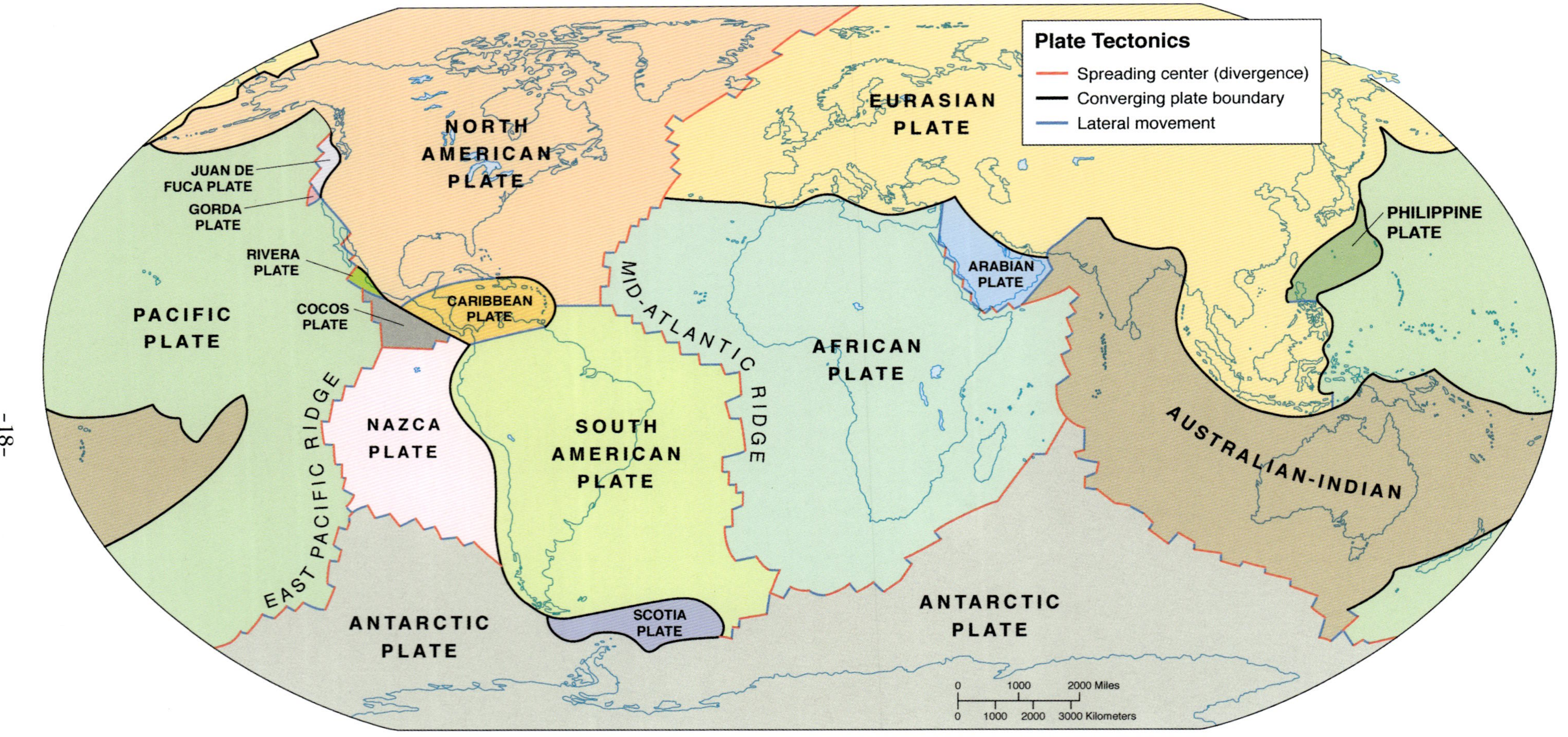
Plate Tectonics
Spreading center (divergence)
Converging plate boundary
Lateral movement
EURASIAN PLATE
NORTH AMERICAN PLATE
JUAN DE FUCA PLATE
GORDA PLATE
RIVERA PLATE
COCOS PLATE
CARIBBEAN PLATE
PACIFIC PLATE
PHILIPPINE PLATE
ARABIAN PLATE
AFRICAN PLATE
MID-ATLANTIC RIDGE
NAZCA PLATE
SOUTH AMERICAN PLATE
EAST PACIFIC RIDGE
AUSTRALIAN-INDIAN
ANTARCTIC PLATE
SCOTIA PLATE
ANTARCTIC PLATE
0 1000 2000 Miles
0 1000 2000 3000 Kilometers

An understanding of the forces that shape the primary features of the earth's surface—the continents and ocean basins—requires a view of the earth's crust as fragments or "lithospheric plates" that shift position relative to one another. There are three dominant types of plate movement: *convergence,* in which plates move together, compressing former ocean floor or continental rocks together to produce mountain ranges, or producing mountain ranges through volcanic activity if one plate slides beneath another; *divergence,* in which the plates move away from one another, producing rifts in the earth's crust through which molten material wells up to produce new sea floors and mid-oceanic ridges; and *lateral shift,* in which plates move horizontally relative to one another, causing significant earthquake activity. All the major forms of these types of shifts are extremely slow and take place over long periods of geologic time. The movement of crustal plates, or what is known as "plate tectonics," is responsible for the present shape and location of the continents but is also the driving force behind some much shorter-term earth phenomena like earthquakes and volcanoes. A comparison of the map of plates with maps of hazards and terrain will reveal some interesting relationships.

Map 11 Topography

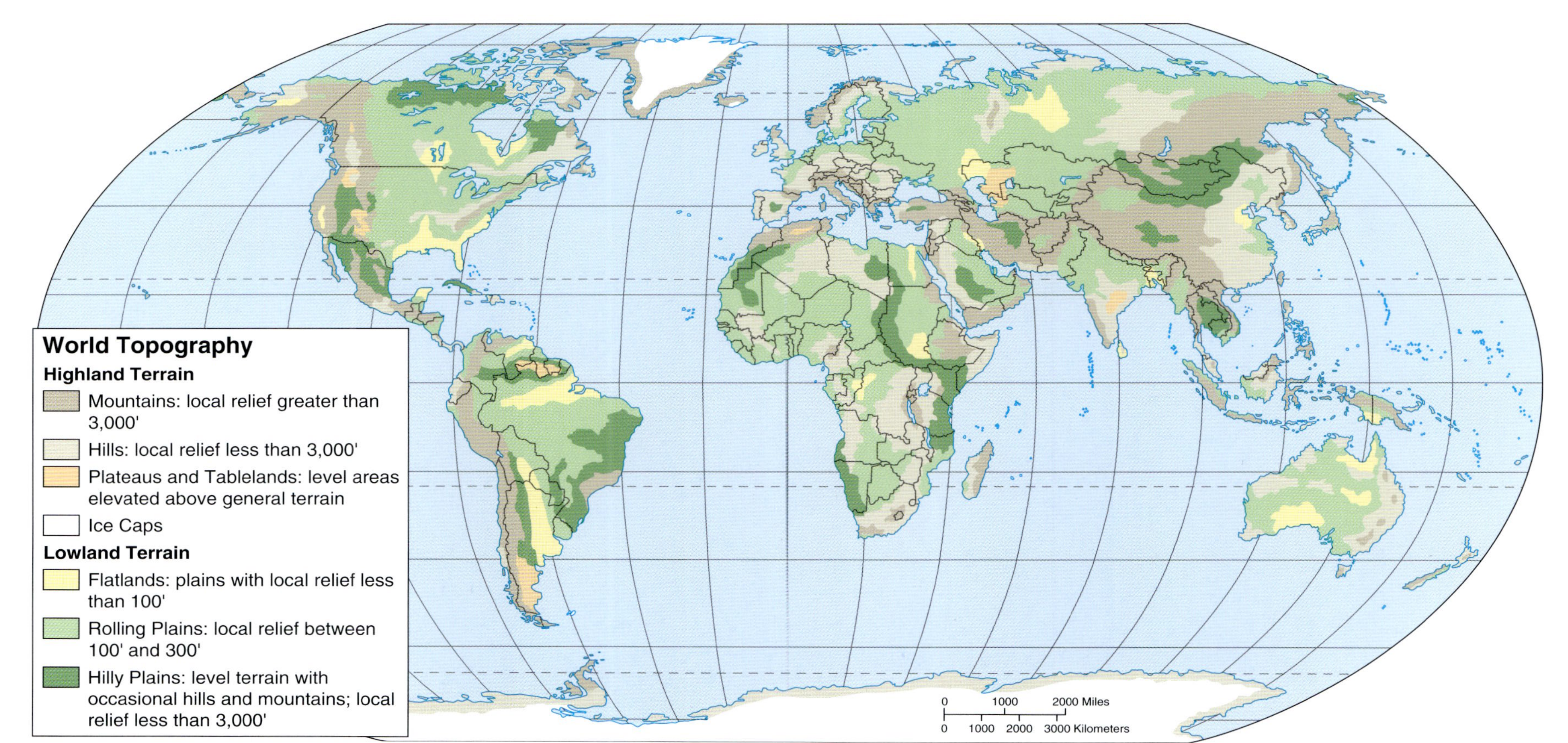
World Topography
Highland Terrain
Mountains: local relief greater than 3,000'
Hills: local relief less than 3,000'
Plateaus and Tablelands: level areas elevated above general terrain
Ice Caps
Lowland Terrain
Flatlands: plains with local relief less than 100'
Rolling Plains: local relief between 100' and 300'
Hilly Plains: level terrain with occasional hills and mountains; local relief less than 3,000'
0 1000 2000 Miles
0 1000 2000 3000 Kilometers

Topography or terrain, also called "landforms," is second only to climate as a conditioner of human activity, particularly agriculture but also the location of cities and industry. A comparison of this map of mountains, valleys, plains, plateaus, and other features of the earth's surface with a map of land use (Map 15) shows that most of the world's productive agricultural zones are located in lowland and relatively level regions. Where large regions of agricultural productivity are found, we also tend to find urban concentrations and, with cities, we find industry. There is also a good spatial correlation between the map of topography and the map showing the distribution and density of the human population (Map 14). Normally the world's major landforms are the result of extremely gradual primary geologic activity such as the long-term movement of crustal plates. This activity occurs over hundreds of millions of years. Also important is the more rapid (but still slow by human standards) geomorphological or erosional activity of water, wind, glacial ice, and waves, tides, and currents. Some landforms may be produced by abrupt or "cataclysmic" events such as a major volcanic eruption or a meteor strike, but such events are relatively rare and their effects are usually too minor to show up on a map of this scale. The study of the processes that shape topography is known as "geomorphology" and is an important branch of physical geography.

Map 12a Resources: Mineral Fuels

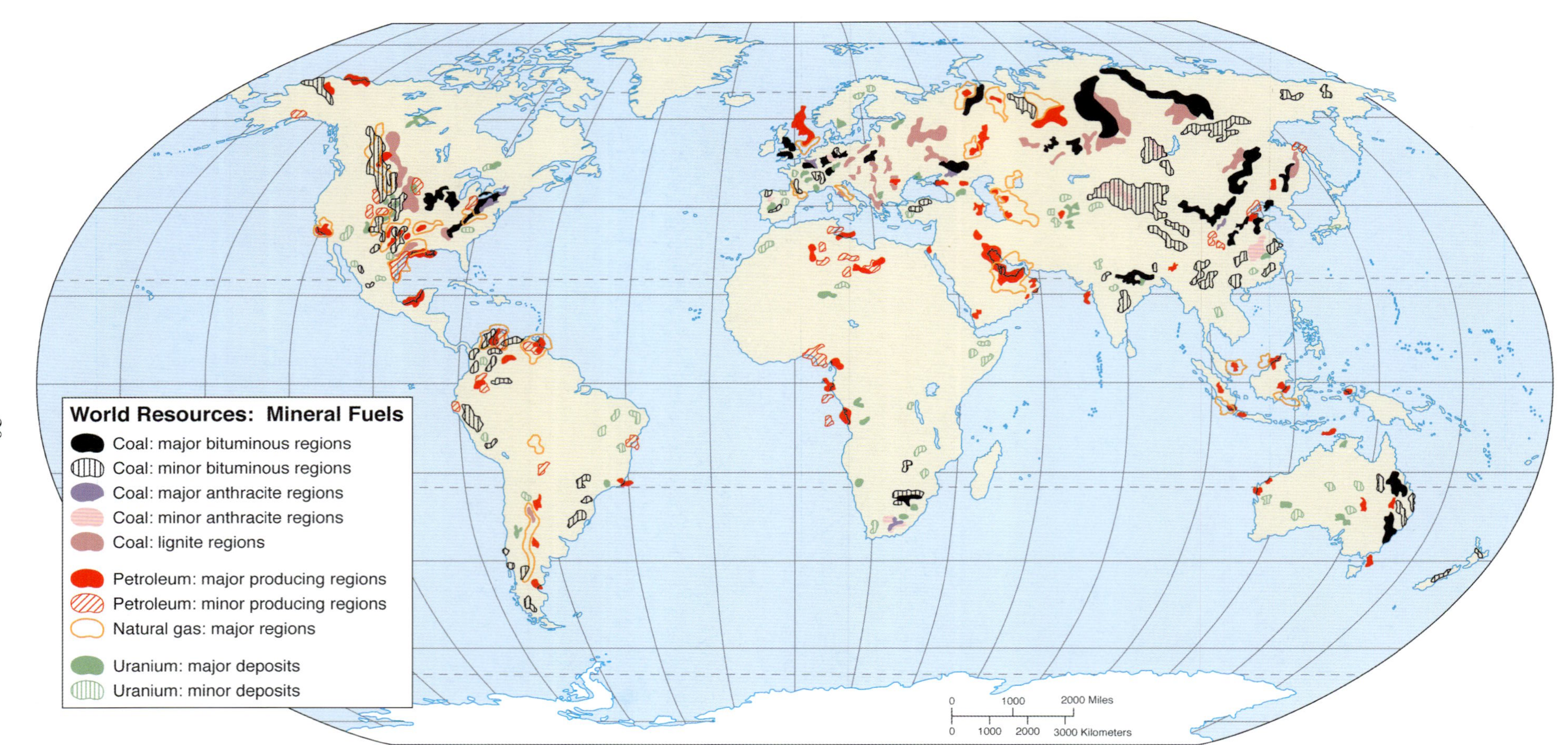
World Resources: Mineral Fuels
Coal: major bituminous regions
Coal: minor bituminous regions
Coal: major anthracite regions
Coal: minor anthracite regions
Coal: lignite regions
Petroleum: major producing regions
Petroleum: minor producing regions
Natural gas: major regions
Uranium: major deposits
Uranium: minor deposits
0 1000 2000 Miles
0 1000 2000 3000 Kilometers

The extraction and transportation of mineral fuels rank with agriculture and forestry as "primary" human activities that impact on the environment at a global scale. Nearly all of the most highly publicized environmental disasters of recent decades—the Prince William Sound oil spill or the Chernobyl nuclear accident, for example—have involved mineral fuels that were being stored, transported, or used. And the continuing extraction of mineral fuels like oil, natural gas, coal, and uranium produces high levels of atmospheric, soil, and water pollution. The location of mineral fuels tells us a great deal about where environmental degradation is likely to be occurring or to occur in the future. One need only look at the levels of atmospheric pollution and vegetative disruption in central and eastern Europe to recognize the damaging consequences of heavy reliance on coal as a domestic and industrial fuel. The location of mineral fuels also tells us something about existing or potential levels of economic development with those countries possessing abundant reserves of mineral fuels having more of a chance to maintain or attain higher levels of prosperity.

Map 12b Resources: Critical Metals

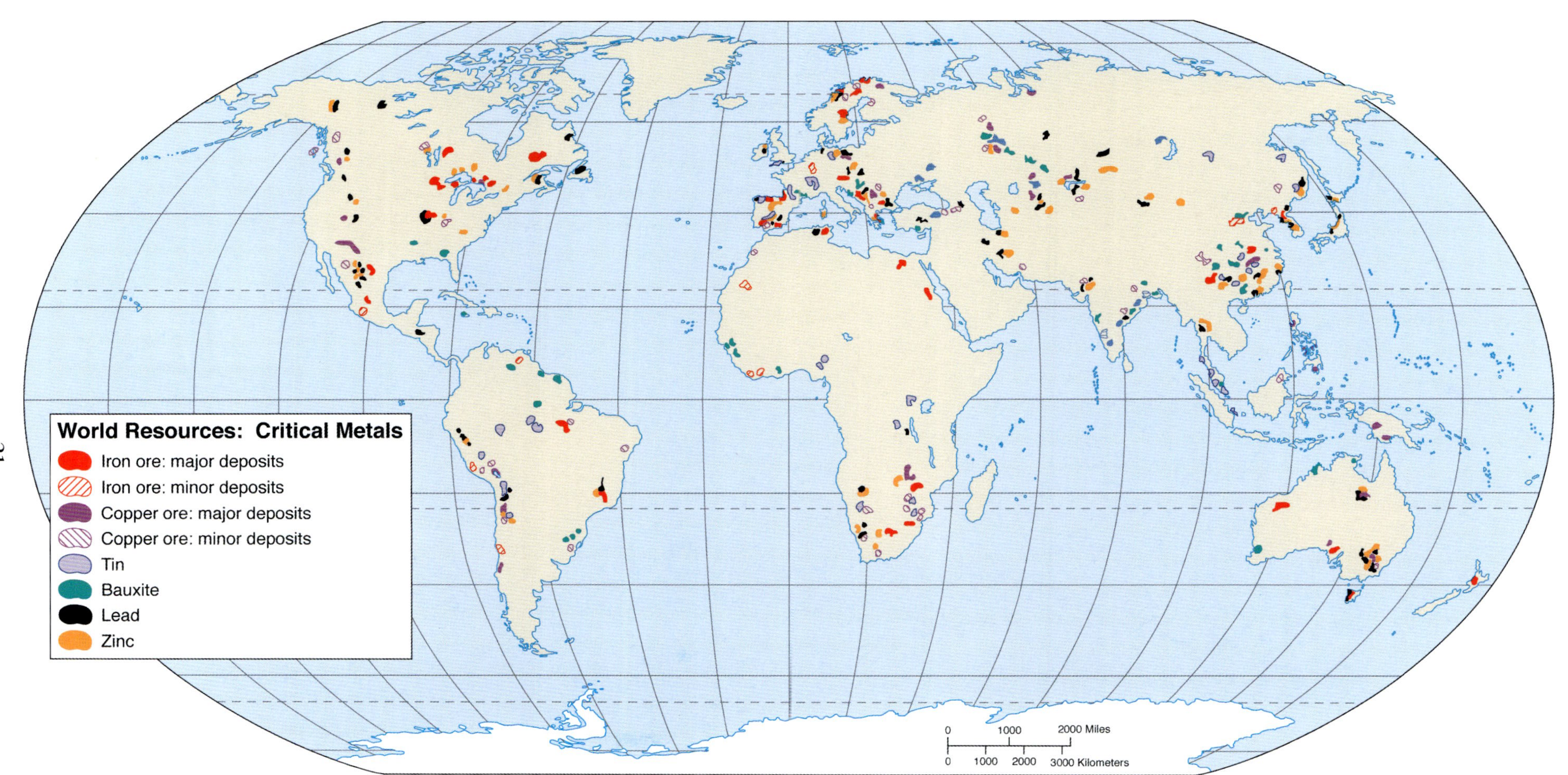
World Resources: Critical Metals
Iron ore: major deposits
Iron ore: minor deposits
Copper ore: major deposits
Copper ore: minor deposits
Tin
Bauxite
Lead
Zinc
0 1000 2000 Miles
0 1000 2000 3000 Kilometers

The location of deposits of critical metals such as iron, copper, tin, and others is an important determinant of the location of mining activities, like mineral fuel extraction, a "primary" economic activity. Also like mineral fuel extraction, mining for critical metallic ores makes significant environmental impact, particularly on vegetation, soils, and water resources. Some of the world's most dramatic examples of human modification of environments are located in areas of metallic ore extraction: the open pit copper mining areas of Arizona and Utah, for example. Environmental impact aside, those countries with significant critical metal deposits tend to stand a better chance of reaching higher levels of economic development, as long as they can extract and market the ores themselves rather than having the extraction process controlled by outside concerns. The average Bolivian, for example, does not benefit greatly from the fact that his/her country is an important producer of tin and other metals. Bolivia is a "colonial dependency" country and the wealth generated by metallic ore production there tends to flow out of the country to Europe and North America. On the other hand, another South American country, Brazil, is paying for much of its own current economic development by utilizing its reserves of iron and other metals and more of the wealth from the extraction of those resources stays within the country.

Map 13 Natural Hazards

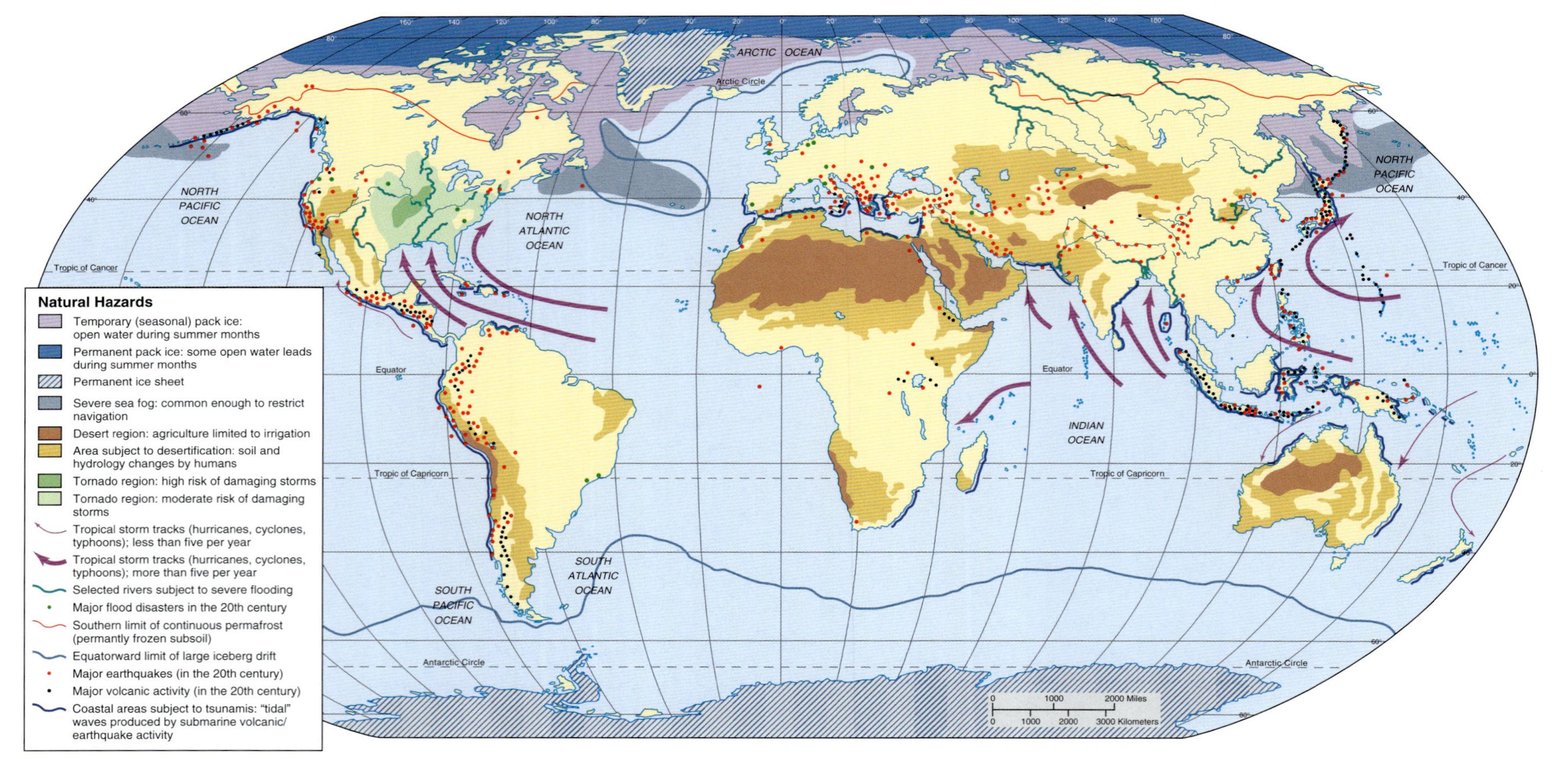

Natural Hazards
Temporary (seasonal) pack ice: open water during summer months
Permanent pack ice: some open water leads during summer months
Permanent ice sheet
Severe sea fog: common enough to restrict navigation
Desert region: agriculture limited to irrigation
Area subject to desertification: soil and hydrology changes by humans
Tornado region: high risk of damaging storms
Tornado region: moderate risk of damaging storms
Tropical storm tracks (hurricanes, cyclones, typhoons); less than five per year
Tropical storm tracks (hurricanes, cyclones, typhoons); more than five per year
Selected rivers subject to severe flooding
Major flood disasters in the 20th century
Southern limit of continuous permafrost (permantly frozen subsoil)
Equatorward limit of large iceberg drift
Major earthquakes (in the 20th century)
Major volcanic activity (in the 20th century)
Coastal areas subject to tsunamis: "tidal" waves produced by submarine volcanic/earthquake activity
ARCTIC OCEAN
Arctic Circle
NORTH PACIFIC OCEAN
NORTH ATLANTIC OCEAN
Tropic of Cancer
Equator
Tropic of Capricorn
INDIAN OCEAN
SOUTH PACIFIC OCEAN
SOUTH ATLANTIC OCEAN
Antarctic Circle
0 1000 2000 Miles
0 1000 2000 3000 Kilometers

Unlike other elements of physical geography, most natural hazards are unpredictable. However, there are certain regions where the probability of the occurrence of a particular natural hazard is high. This map shows regions affected by major natural hazards at rates that are higher than the global norm. The presence of persistent natural hazards may influence the types of modifications that people make in the environment and certainly influence the styles of housing and other elements of cultural geography. Natural hazards may also undermine the utility of an area for economic purposes and some scholars suggest that regions of environmental instability may be regions of political instability as well. The study of natural hazards has become an important activity for "resource geographers" whose areas of interest overlap both human and physical fields of geography.

Part II

Global Human Patterns

Map 14 Past Population Distributions and Densities

The map of the world at 100,000 B.P. (Before Present) shows the distributions of hominids who at that time had spread from their probable origin in Africa into parts of the Old World. At 30,000 B.P. few places in the Old World remained uninhabited. All the people then were hunters and gatherers who subsisted on wild foods. The environment probably was not at its carrying capacity for human populations until about 15, 000 B.P.

By 10,000 B.P. hunting and gathering people had spread throughout the world. Plant and animal domestication (farming and pastoralism) had begun in some parts of the Old World

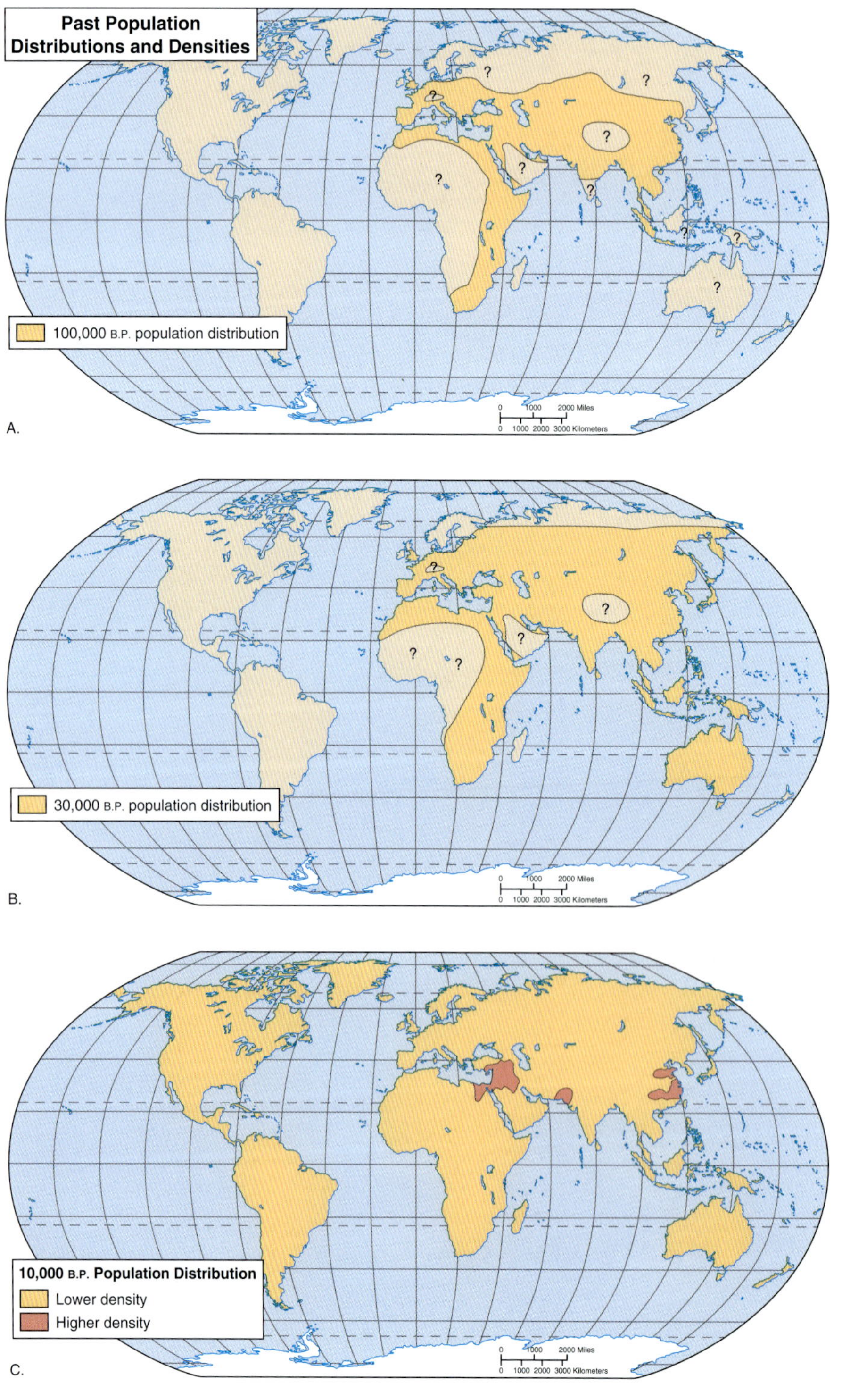

Past Population Distributions and Densities
100,000 B.P. population distribution
A.
30,000 B.P. population distribution
B.
10,000 B.P. Population Distribution
Lower density
Higher density
C.

perhaps as a response to behavioral changes necessitated by the population, which now exceeded the environmental carrying capacity. Farming supports higher population densites than hunting and gathering. Urban civilization with cities dependent on their hinterlands had developed by 5000 B.P. The maps of A.D. 1 and A.D. 1500 approximate actual population density on a scale of one dot to every million people. A chart provides total world population figures for different time periods. Compare these maps to the contemporary population density map on the following page.

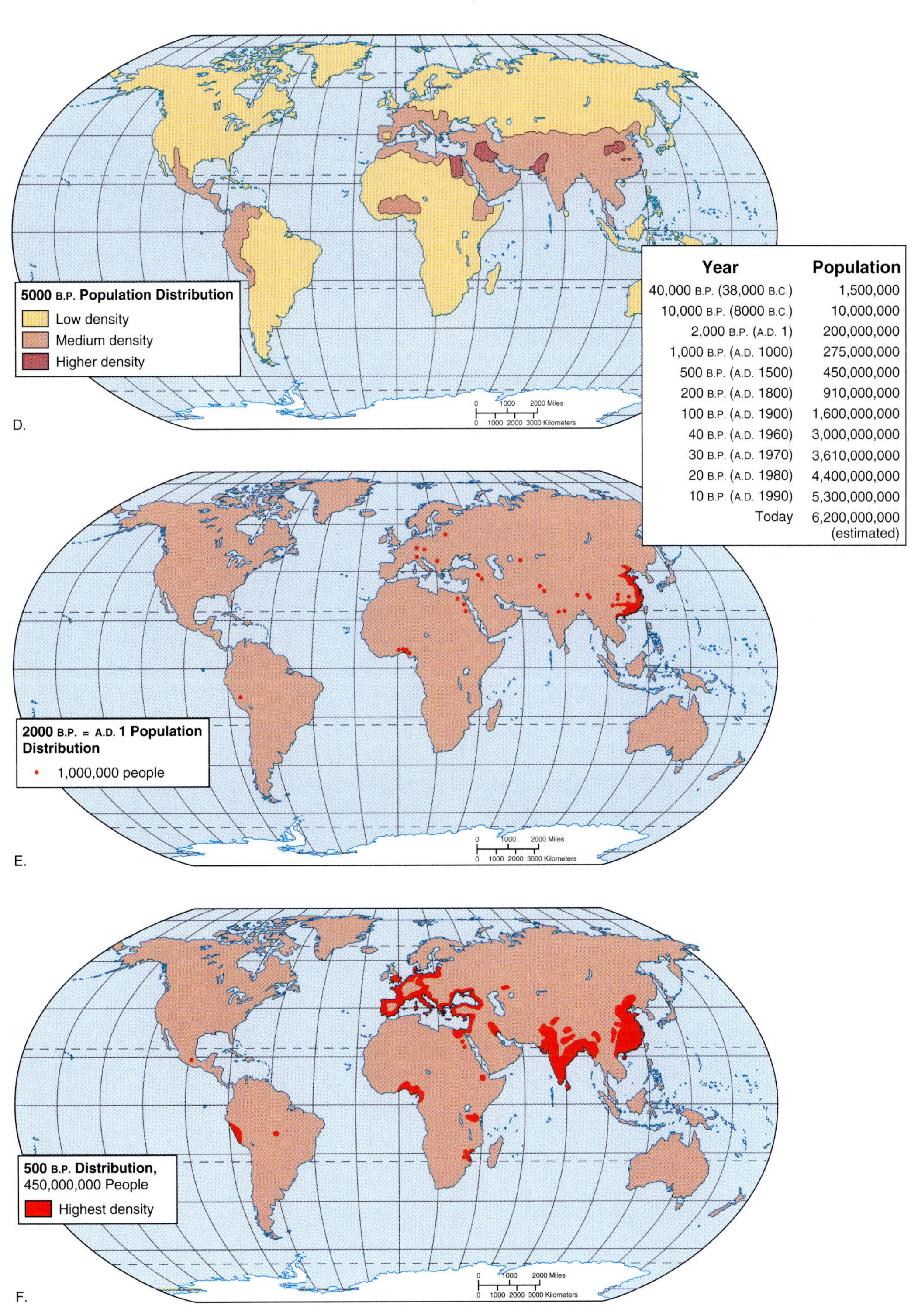

5000 B.P. Population Distribution
Low density
Medium density
Higher density
0 1000 2000 Miles
0 1000 2000 3000 Kilometers
D.
2000 B.P. = A.D. 1 Population Distribution
1,000,000 people
0 1000 2000 Miles
0 1000 2000 3000 Kilometers
E.
500 B.P. Distribution, 450,000,000 People
Highest density
0 1000 2000 Miles
0 1000 2000 3000 Kilometers
F.

Year	Population
40,000 B.P. (38,000 B.C.)	1,500,000
10,000 B.P. (8000 B.C.)	10,000,000
2,000 B.P. (A.D. 1)	200,000,000
1,000 B.P. (A.D. 1000)	275,000,000
500 B.P. (A.D. 1500)	450,000,000
200 B.P. (A.D. 1800)	910,000,000
100 B.P. (A.D. 1900)	1,600,000,000
40 B.P. (A.D. 1960)	3,000,000,000
30 B.P. (A.D. 1970)	3,610,000,000
20 B.P. (A.D. 1980)	4,400,000,000
10 B.P. (A.D. 1990)	5,300,000,000
Today	6,200,000,000 (estimated)

Map 15 Population Density

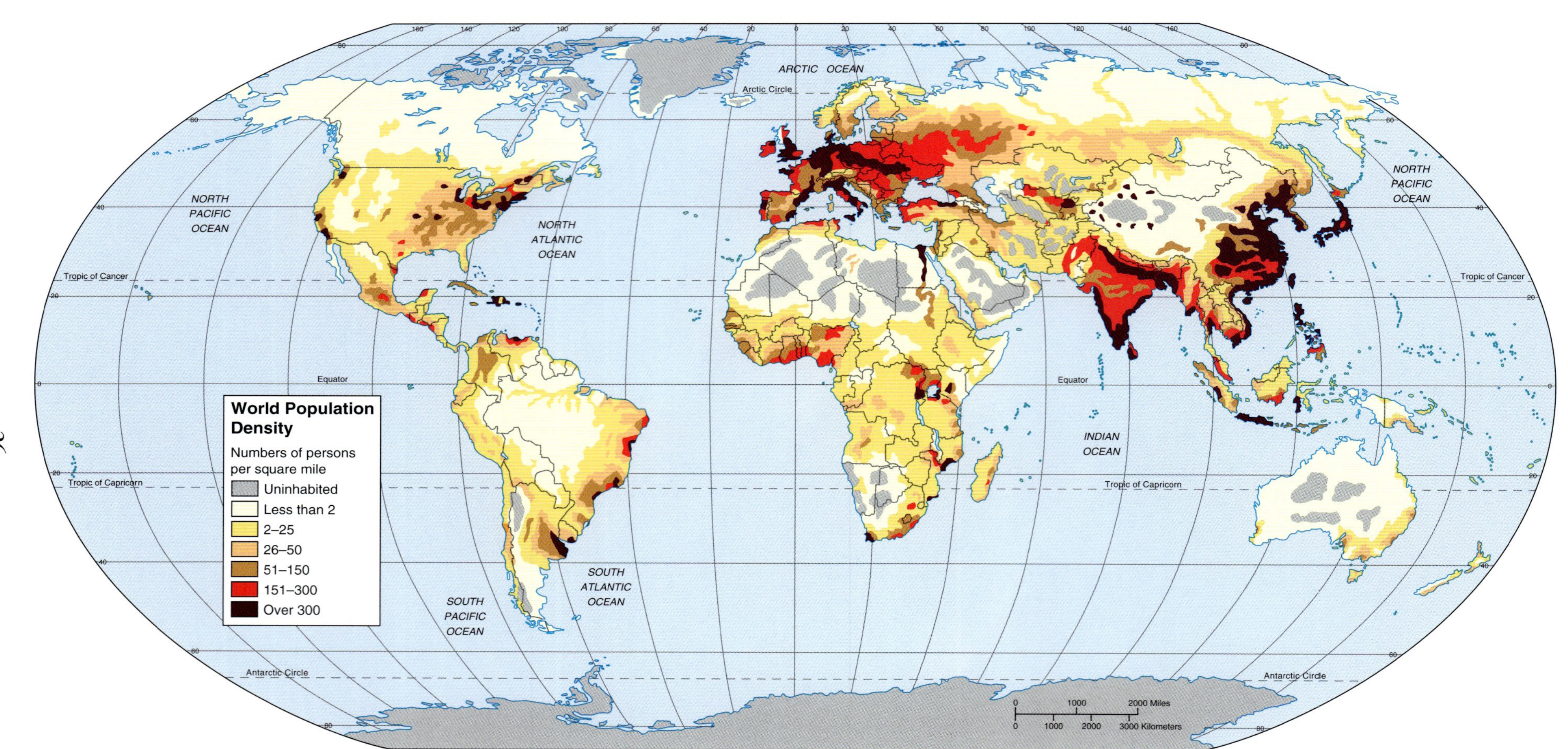

ARCTIC OCEAN
Arctic Circle
NORTH PACIFIC OCEAN
NORTH ATLANTIC OCEAN
SOUTH PACIFIC OCEAN
SOUTH ATLANTIC OCEAN
INDIAN OCEAN
NORTH PACIFIC OCEAN
Tropic of Cancer
Equator
Tropic of Capricorn
Antarctic Circle
World Population Density
Numbers of persons per square mile
Uninhabited
Less than 2
2–25
26–50
51–150
151–300
Over 300
0 1000 2000 Miles
0 1000 2000 3000 Kilometers

No feature of human activity is more reflective of geographic relationships than where people live. In the areas of densest populations, a mixture of natural and human factors has combined to allow maximum food production, maximum urbanization, and maximum centralization of economic activities. Three great concentrations of human population appear on the map—East Asia, South Asia, and Europe—with a fourth, lesser concentration in eastern North America. While population growth is relatively slow in three of these population clusters, in the fourth—South Asia—growth is still rapid and South Asia is expected to become even more densely populated in the early years of the twenty-first century, while density of the other regions is expected to remain about as it now appears. In Europe and North America, the relatively stable population growth rates are the result of economic development that has caused population growth to level off within the last century. In East Asia, the growth rates have also begun to decline. In the case of Japan, Taiwan, the Koreas, and other more highly developed nations of the Pacific Rim, the reduced growth is the result of economic development. In China, at least until recently, lowered population growth rates have resulted from strict family planning. The areas of future high density of population, in addition to those already existing, are likely to be in Middle and South America and in Central Africa, where population growth rates are well above the world average.

Map 16 Land Use, 1500

Europeans began to explore the world in the late 1400s. They encountered many independent people with self-sustaining economies at that time. Foraging people practiced hunting and gathering, utilizing the wild forms of plants and animals in their environments. Horticultural people practiced a simple form of agriculture using hoes or digging sticks as their basic tools. They sometimes cleared their land by burning and then planted crops. Pastoralists herded animals as their basic subsistence pattern. Complex state-level societies, such as the Mongols, had pastoralism as their base. Intensive agriculturalists based their societies on complicated irrigation systems and/or the plow and draft animals. Wheat and rice were two kinds of crops that supported large populations. In many of the areas of intensive agriculture—particularly in MesoAmerica, Europe, Southwest Asia, South Asia, and East Asia-complex patterns of market economies had begun to develop well before the 15th century and the beginnings of European expansion.

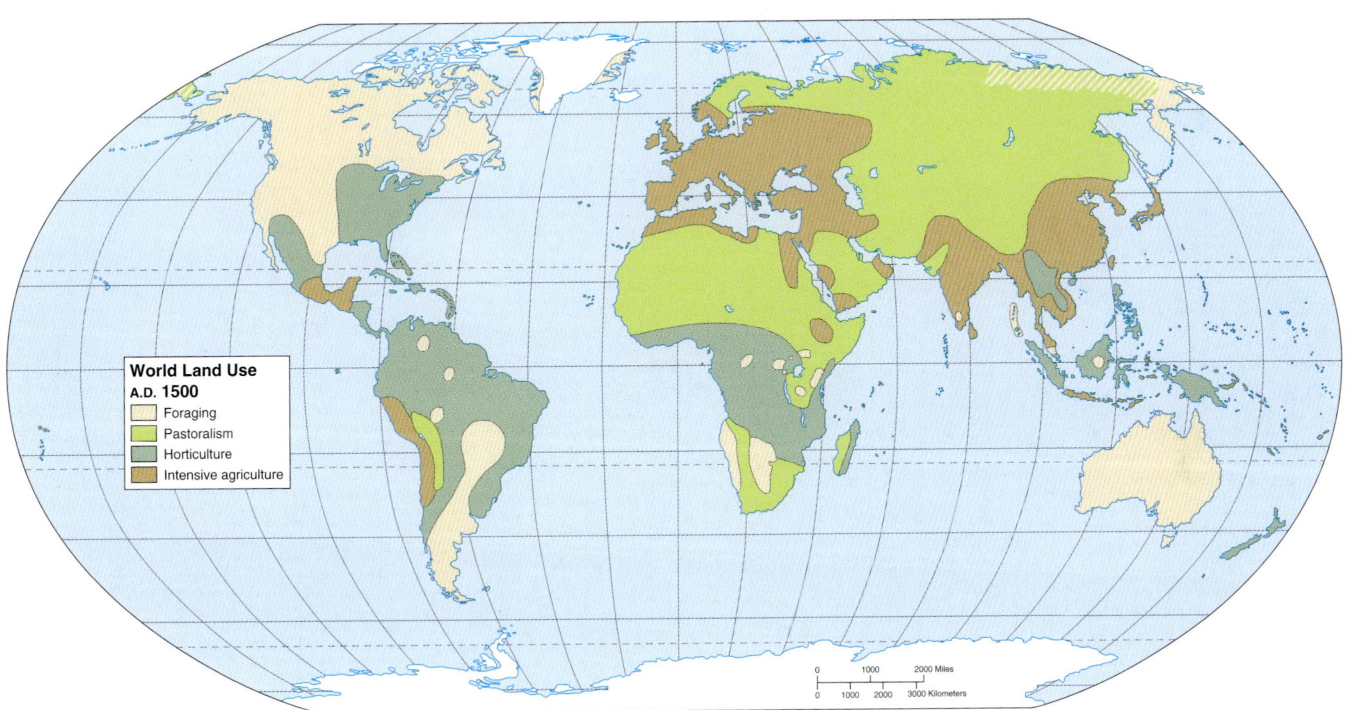
World Land Use
A.D. 1500
Foraging
Pastoralism
Horticulture
Intensive agriculture
0
1000
2000 Miles
0
1000
2000
3000 Kilometers

Map 17 Economic Activities

Land uses can be categorized as lying somewhere on a scale between extensive uses, in which human activities are dispersed over relatively large areas, and intensive uses, in which human activities are concentrated in relatively small areas. Many of the most important land use patterns of the world (such as urbanization, industry, mining, or transportation) are intensive and therefore relatively small in area and not easily seen on maps of this scale. Hence, even in the areas identified as "Manufacturing and Commerce" on the map there are many land uses that are not strictly industrial or commercial in nature, and, in fact, more extensive land uses (farming, residential, open space) may actually cover more ground than the intensive industrial or commercial activities. On the other hand, the more extensive land uses, like agriculture and forestry, tend to dominate the areas in which they are found. Thus, primary economic activities such as agriculture and forestry tend to dominate the world map of land use because of their extensive character. Much of this map is, therefore, a map that shows the global variations in agricultural patterns. Note, among other things, the differences between land use patterns in the more developed countries of the temperate zones and the less developed countries of the tropics.

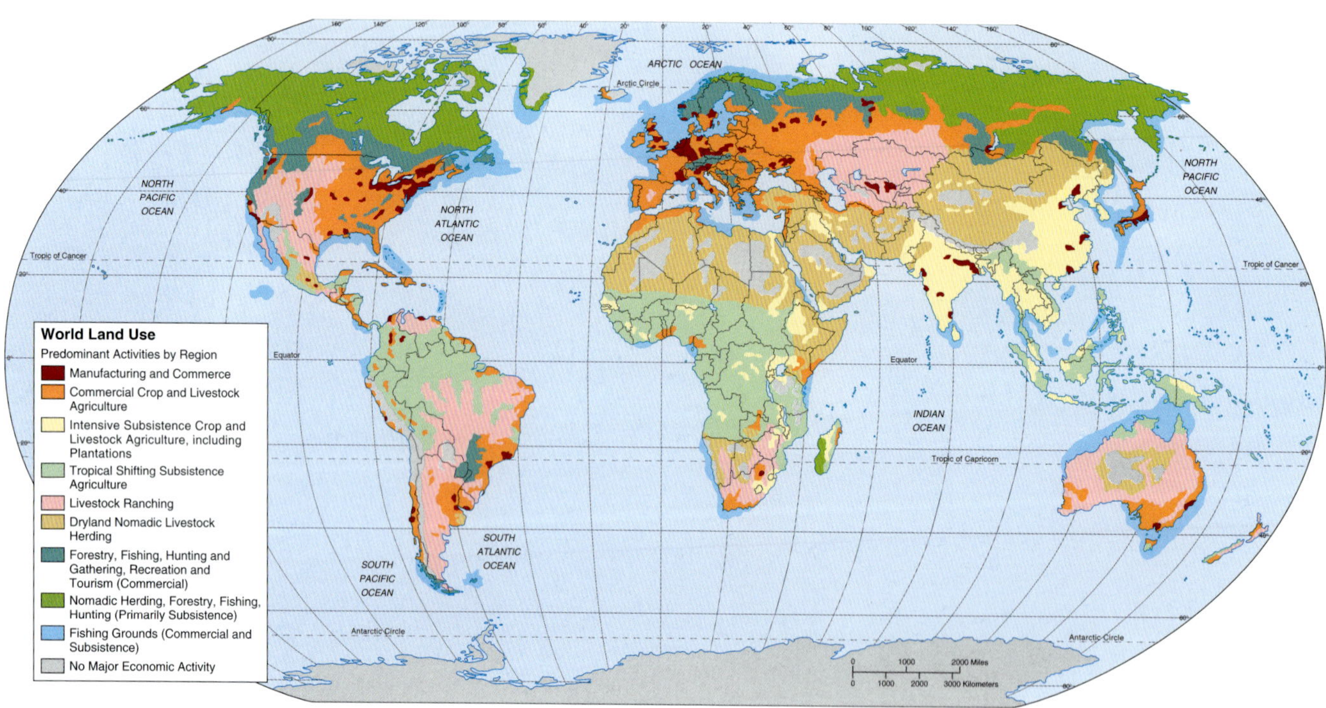
World Land Use
Predominant Activities by Region
Manufacturing and Commerce
Commercial Crop and Livestock Agriculture
Intensive Subsistence Crop and Livestock Agriculture, including Plantations
Tropical Shifting Subsistence Agriculture
Livestock Ranching
Dryland Nomadic Livestock Herding
Forestry, Fishing, Hunting and Gathering, Recreation and Tourism (Commercial)
Nomadic Herding, Forestry, Fishing, Hunting (Primarily Subsistence)
Fishing Grounds (Commercial and Subsistence)
No Major Economic Activity
ARCTIC OCEAN
Arctic Circle
NORTH PACIFIC OCEAN
NORTH ATLANTIC OCEAN
NORTH PACIFIC OCEAN
Tropic of Cancer
Tropic of Cancer
Equator
Equator
INDIAN OCEAN
Tropic of Capricorn
SOUTH PACIFIC OCEAN
SOUTH ATLANTIC OCEAN
Antarctic Circle
Antarctic Circle
0 1000 2000 Miles
0 1000 2000 3000 Kilometers

Map 18 Urbanization

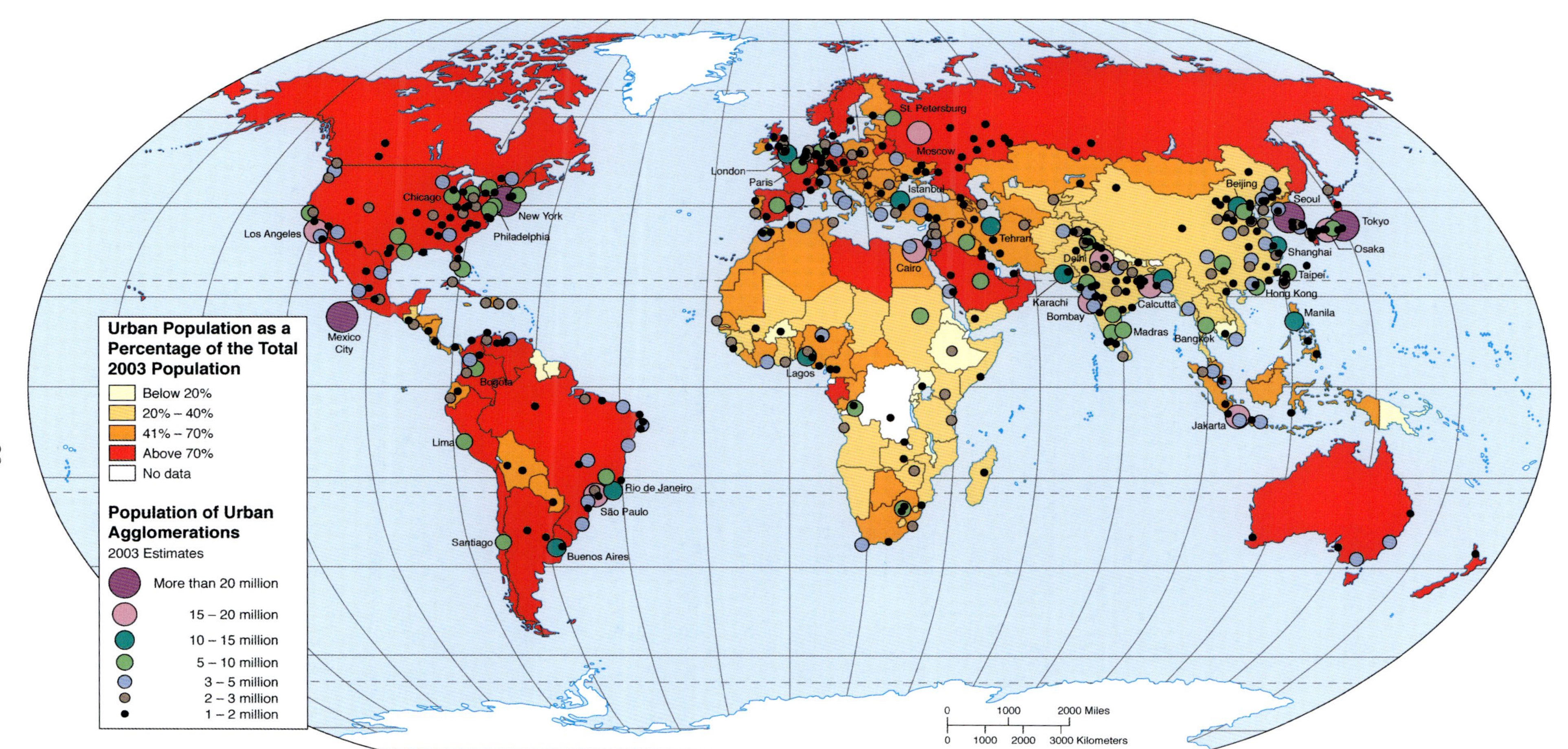

Urban Population as a Percentage of the Total 2003 Population
Below 20%
20% – 40%
41% – 70%
Above 70%
No data
Population of Urban Agglomerations
2003 Estimates
More than 20 million
15 – 20 million
10 – 15 million
5 – 10 million
3 – 5 million
2 – 3 million
1 – 2 million
Los Angeles
Mexico City
Chicago
New York
Philadelphia
Bogotá
Lima
Rio de Janeiro
São Paulo
Santiago
Buenos Aires
London
Paris
St. Petersburg
Moscow
Istanbul
Cairo
Lagos
Tehran
Karachi
Bombay
Delhi
Calcutta
Madras
Bangkok
Beijing
Seoul
Tokyo
Osaka
Shanghai
Taipei
Hong Kong
Manila
Jakarta
0 1000 2000 Miles
0 1000 2000 3000 Kilometers

The degree to which a region's population is concentrated in urban areas is a major indicator of a number of things: the potential for environmental impact, the level of economic development, and the problems associated with human concentrations. Urban dwellers are rapidly becoming the norm among the world's people and rates of urbanization are increasing worldwide, with the greatest increases in urbanization taking place in developing regions. Whether in developed or developing countries, those who live in cities exert an influence on the environment, politics, economics, and social systems that go far beyond the confines of the city itself. Acting as the focal points for the flow of goods and ideas, cities draw resources and people not just from their immediate hinterland but from the entire world. This process creates far-reaching impacts as resources are extracted, converted through industrial processes, and transported over great distances to metropolitan regions, and as ideas spread or *diffuse* along with the movements of people to cities and the flow of communication from them. The significance of urbanization can be most clearly seen, perhaps, in North America where, in spite of vast areas of relatively unpopulated land, well over 90 percent of the population lives in urban areas.

Map 19 Religions

Religious adherence is one of the fundamental defining characteristics of human culture, the style of life adopted by a people and passed from one generation to the next. Because of the importance of religion for culture, a depiction of the spatial distribution of religions is as close as we can come to a map of cultural patterns. More than just a set of behavioral patterns having to do with worship and ceremony, religion is a vital conditioner of the ways that people deal with one another, with their institutions, and with the environments

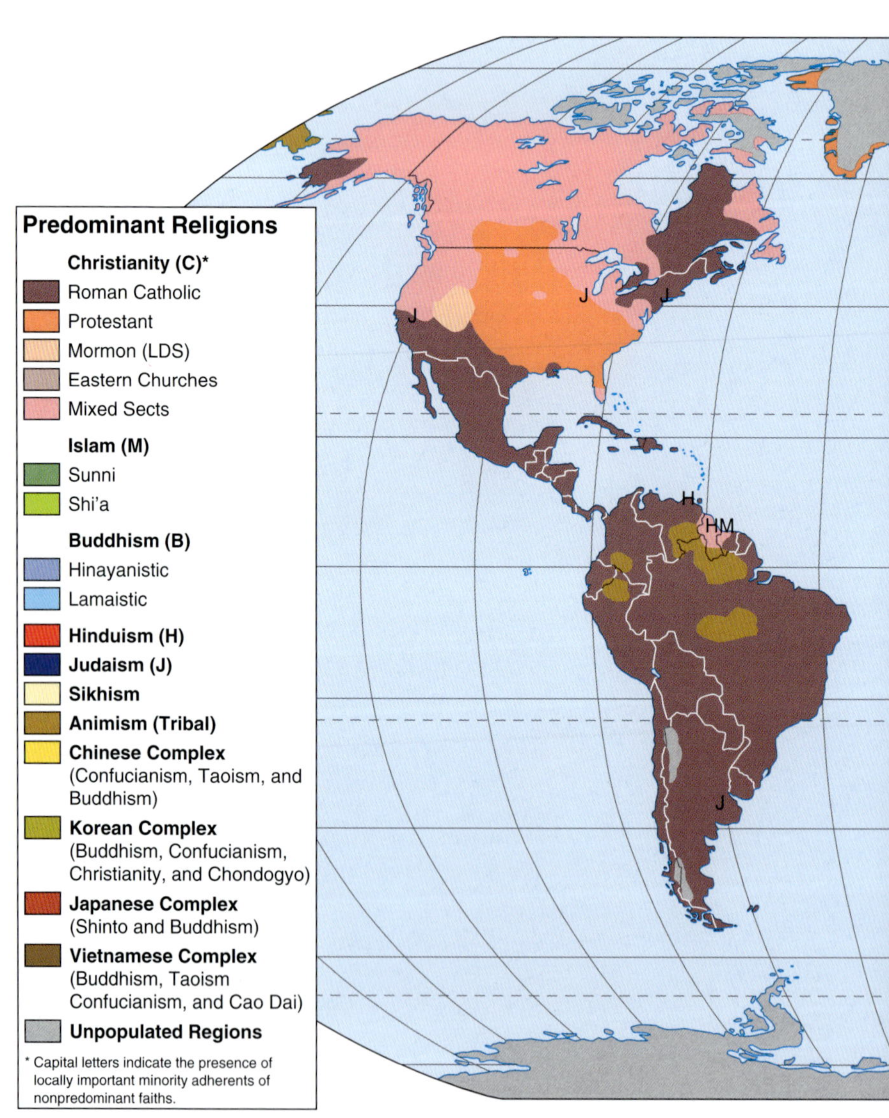

Predominant Religions
Christianity (C)*
Roman Catholic
Protestant
Mormon (LDS)
Eastern Churches
Mixed Sects
Islam (M)
Sunni
Shi'a
Buddhism (B)
Hinayanistic
Lamaistic
Hinduism (H)
Judaism (J)
Sikhism
Animism (Tribal)
Chinese Complex
(Confucianism, Taoism, and Buddhism)
Korean Complex
(Buddhism, Confucianism, Christianity, and Chondogyo)
Japanese Complex
(Shinto and Buddhism)
Vietnamese Complex
(Buddhism, Taoism Confucianism, and Cao Dai)
Unpopulated Regions
* Capital letters indicate the presence of locally important minority adherents of nonpredominant faiths.
J
J
J
J
H
HM
J

they occupy. In many areas of the world, the ways in which people make a living, the patterns of occupation that they create on the land, and the impacts that they make on ecosystems are the direct consequences of their adherence to a religious faith. An examination of the map in the context of international and intranational conflict will also show that tension between countries and the internal stability of states is also a function of the spatial distribution of religion.

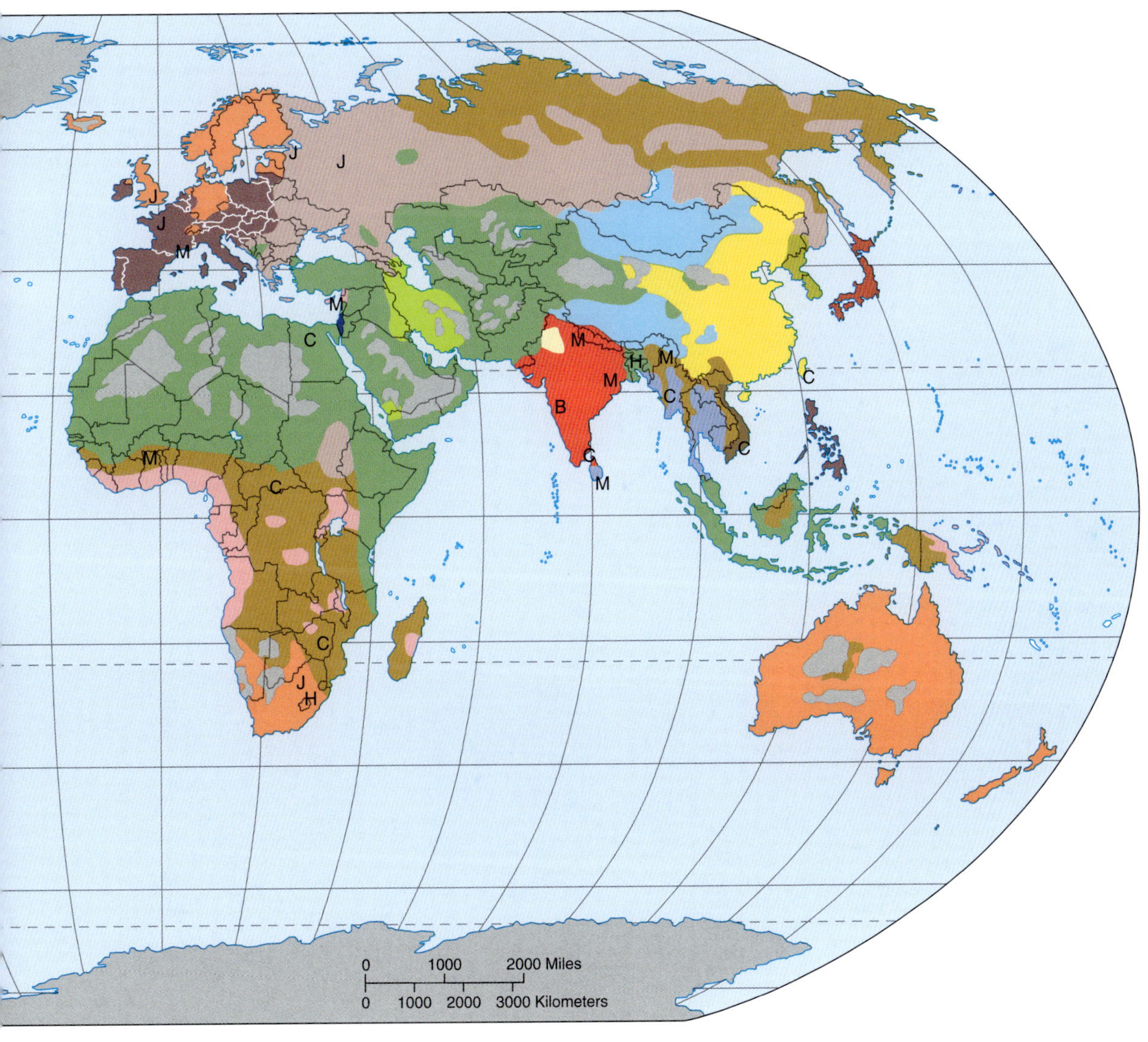
J
J
J
J
M
M
C
M
M
B
H
M
C
C
C
M
M
C
C
C
J
H
0 1000 2000 Miles
0 1000 2000 3000 Kilometers

Map 20 Languages

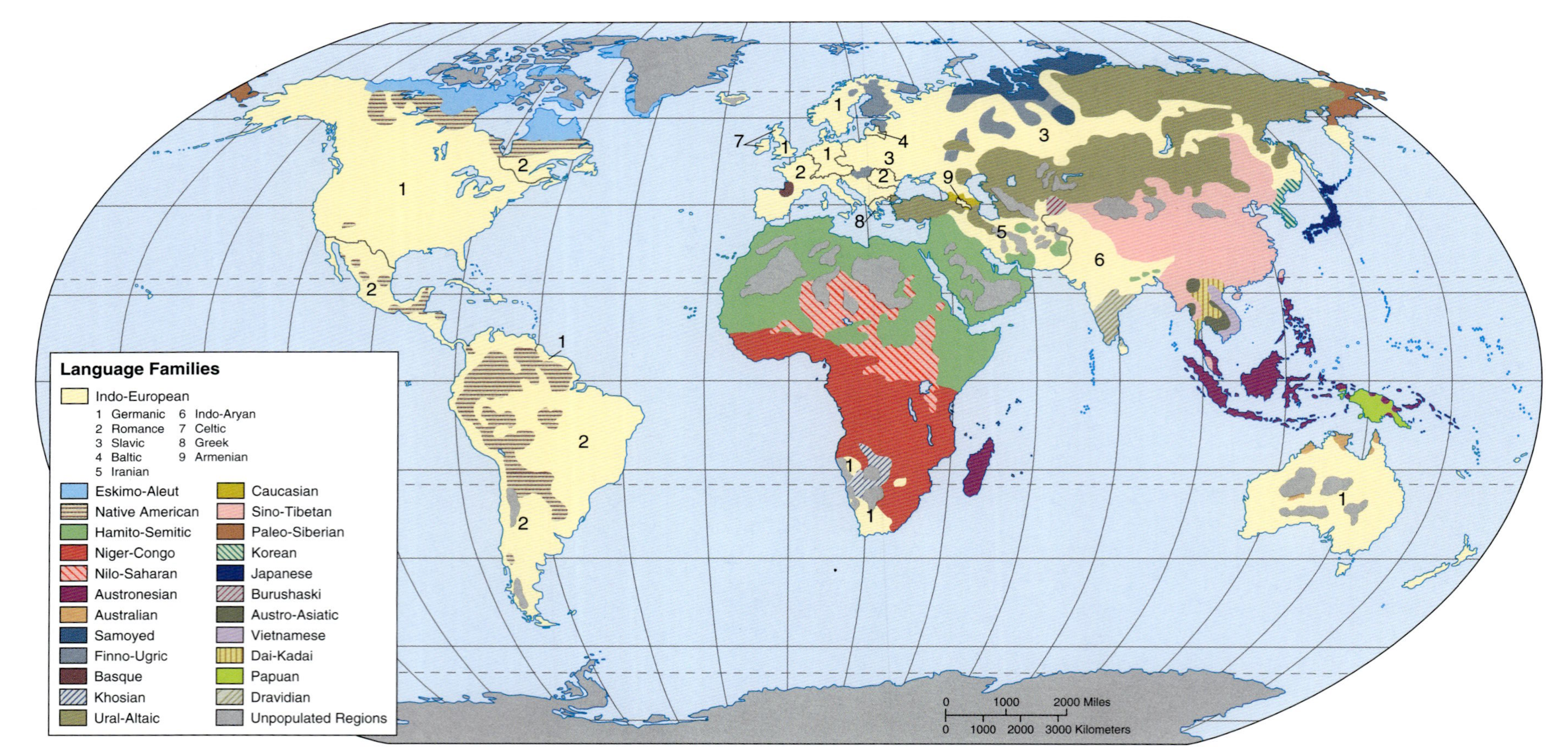
Language Families
Indo-European
1 Germanic
2 Romance
3 Slavic
4 Baltic
5 Iranian
6 Indo-Aryan
7 Celtic
8 Greek
9 Armenian
Eskimo-Aleut
Native American
Hamito-Semitic
Niger-Congo
Nilo-Saharan
Austronesian
Australian
Samoyed
Finno-Ugric
Basque
Khosian
Ural-Altaic
Caucasian
Sino-Tibetan
Paleo-Siberian
Korean
Japanese
Burushaski
Austro-Asiatic
Vietnamese
Dai-Kadai
Papuan
Dravidian
Unpopulated Regions
0 1000 2000 Miles
0 1000 2000 3000 Kilometers

Language, like religion, is an important identifying characteristic of culture. Indeed, it is perhaps the most durable of all those identifying characteristics or *cultural traits:* language, religion, institutions, material technologies, and ways of making a living. After centuries of exposure to other languages or even conquest by speakers of other languages, the speakers of a specific tongue will often retain their own linguistic identity. Language helps us to locate areas of potential conflict, particularly in regions where two or more languages overlap. Many, if not most, of the world's conflict zones are also areas of linguistic diversity. Knowing the distribution of languages helps us to understand some of the reasons behind important current events: for example, linguistic identity differences played an important part in the disintegration of the Soviet Union in the early 1990s; and in areas emerging from recent colonial rule, such as Africa, the participants in conflicts over territory and power are often defined in terms of linguistic groups. Language distributions also help us to comprehend the nature of the human past by providing clues that enable us to chart the course of human migrations, as shown in the distribution of Indo-European, Austronesian, or Hamito-Semitic languages. Finally, because languages have a great deal to do with the way people perceive and understand the world around them, linguistic patterns help to explain the global variations in the ways that people interact.

Map 21 Transportation Patterns

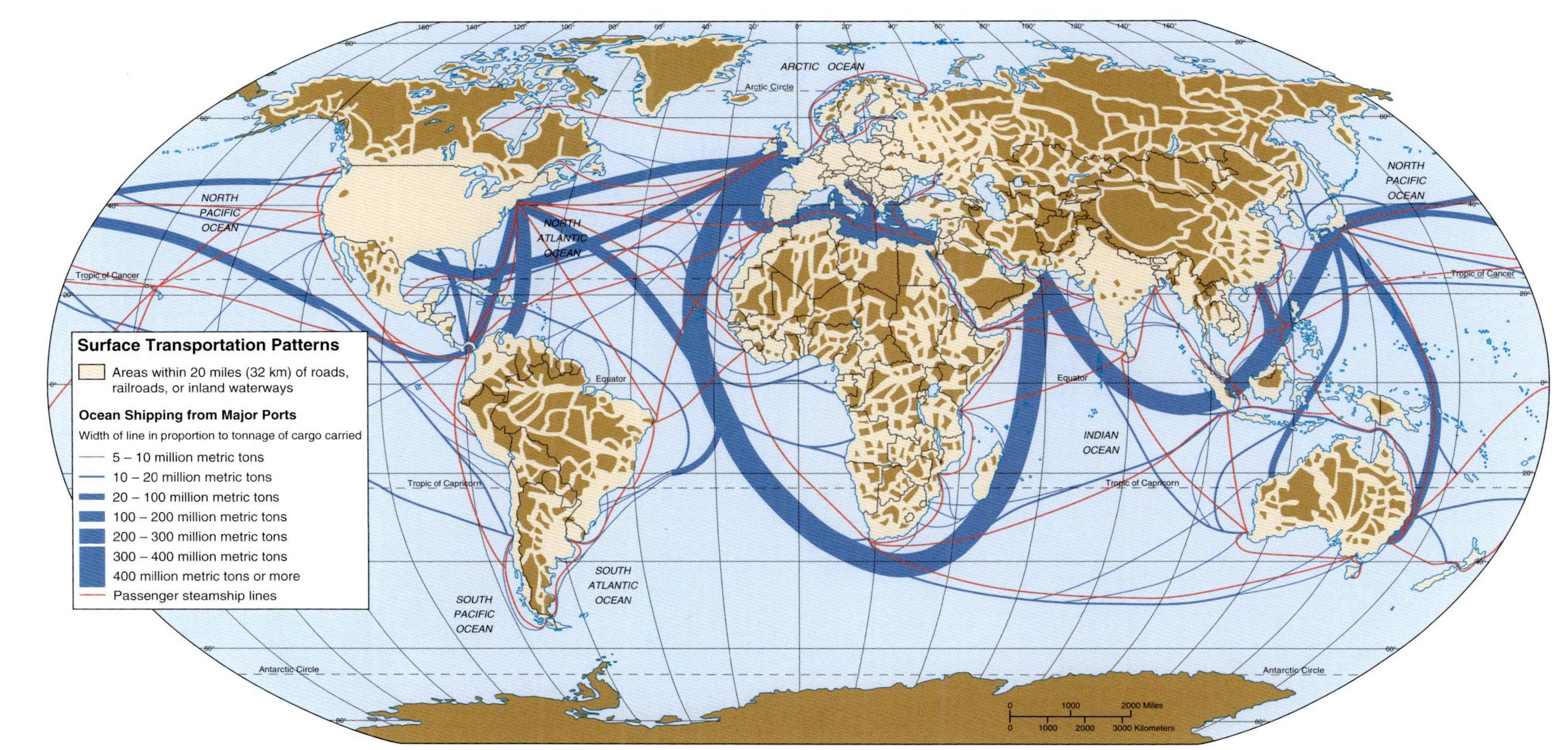
Surface Transportation Patterns
Areas within 20 miles (32 km) of roads, railroads, or inland waterways
Ocean Shipping from Major Ports
Width of line in proportion to tonnage of cargo carried
5 – 10 million metric tons
10 – 20 million metric tons
20 – 100 million metric tons
100 – 200 million metric tons
200 – 300 million metric tons
300 – 400 million metric tons
400 million metric tons or more
Passenger steamship lines
ARCTIC OCEAN
Arctic Circle
NORTH PACIFIC OCEAN
NORTH ATLANTIC OCEAN
NORTH PACIFIC OCEAN
Tropic of Cancer
Tropic of Cancer
Equator
Equator
INDIAN OCEAN
Tropic of Capricorn
Tropic of Capricorn
SOUTH PACIFIC OCEAN
SOUTH ATLANTIC OCEAN
Antarctic Circle
Antarctic Circle
0 1000 2000 Miles
0 1000 2000 3000 Kilometers

As a form of land use, transportation is second only to agriculture in its coverage of the earth's surface and is one of the clearest examples in the human world of a *network*, a linked system of lines allowing flows from one place to another. The global transportation network and its related communication web is responsible for most of the *spatial interaction,* or movement of goods, people, and ideas between places. As the chief mechanism of spatial interaction, transportation is linked firmly with the concept of a shrinking world and the development of a global community and economy. Because transportation systems require significant modification of the earth's surface, transportation is also responsible for massive alterations in the quantity and quality of water, for major soil degradations and erosion, and (indirectly) for the air pollution that emanates from vehicles utilizing the transportation system. In addition, as improved transportation technology draws together places on the earth that were formerly remote, it allows people to impact environments a great distance away from where they live.

Map 22 Linguistic Diversity

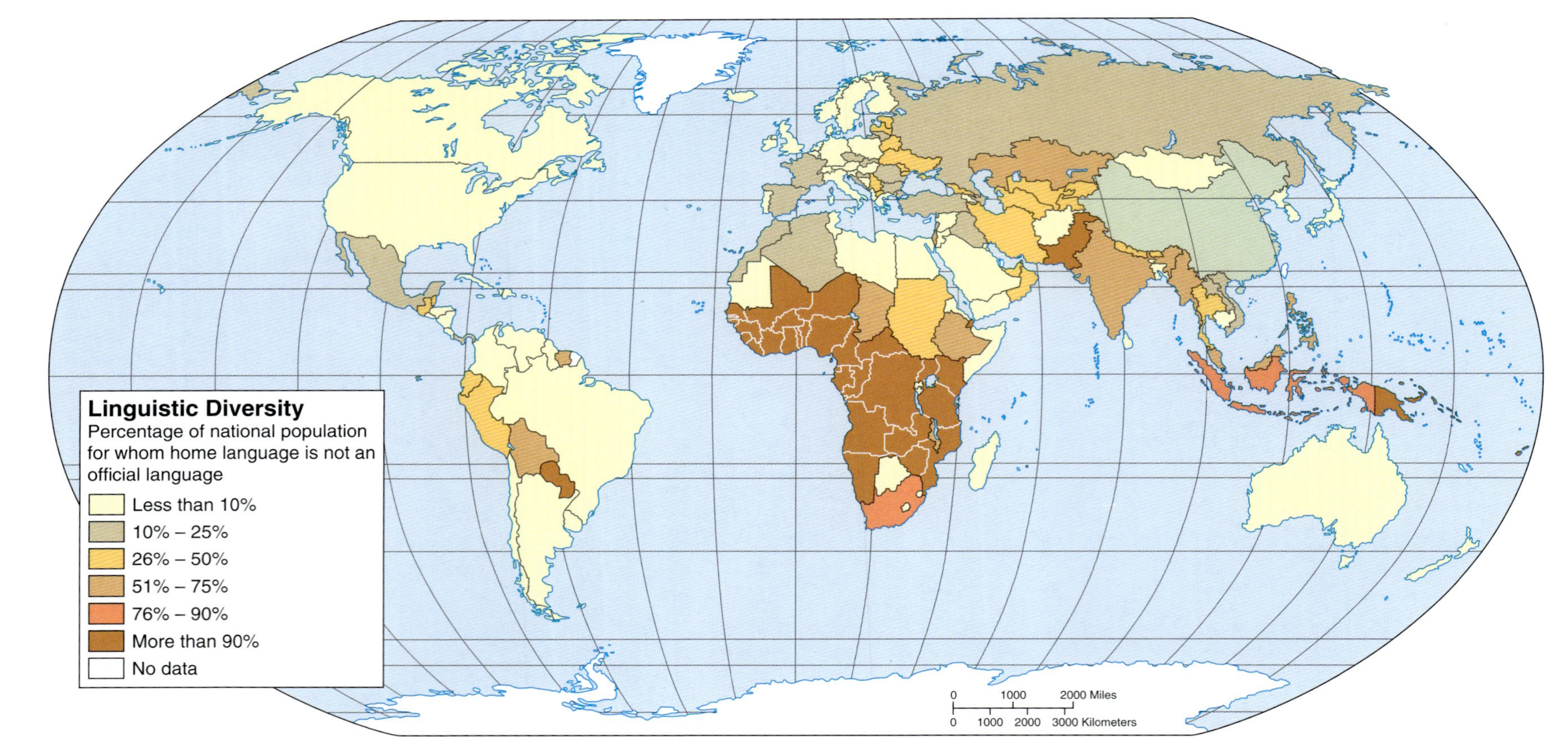
Linguistic Diversity
Percentage of national population for whom home language is not an official language
Less than 10%
10% – 25%
26% – 50%
51% – 75%
76% – 90%
More than 90%
No data
0 1000 2000 Miles
0 1000 2000 3000 Kilometers

Of the world's approximately 6,000 languages, fewer than 100 are official languages, those designated by a country as the language of government, commerce, education, and information. This means that for much of the world's population, the language that is spoken in the home is different from the official language of the country of residence. The world's former colonial areas in Middle and South America, Africa, and South and Southeast Asia stand out on the map as regions in which there is significant disparity between home languages and official languages. To complicate matters further, for most of the world's population, the primary international languages of trade and tourism (French and English) are neither home nor official languages. China is a special case as the official language is the written form of Chinese while several spoken Chinese dialects such as Mandarin and Cantonese most of them mutually unintelligible are recognized as official languages. The formal language of government and business is Mandarin."

Map 23 External Migrations in Modern Times

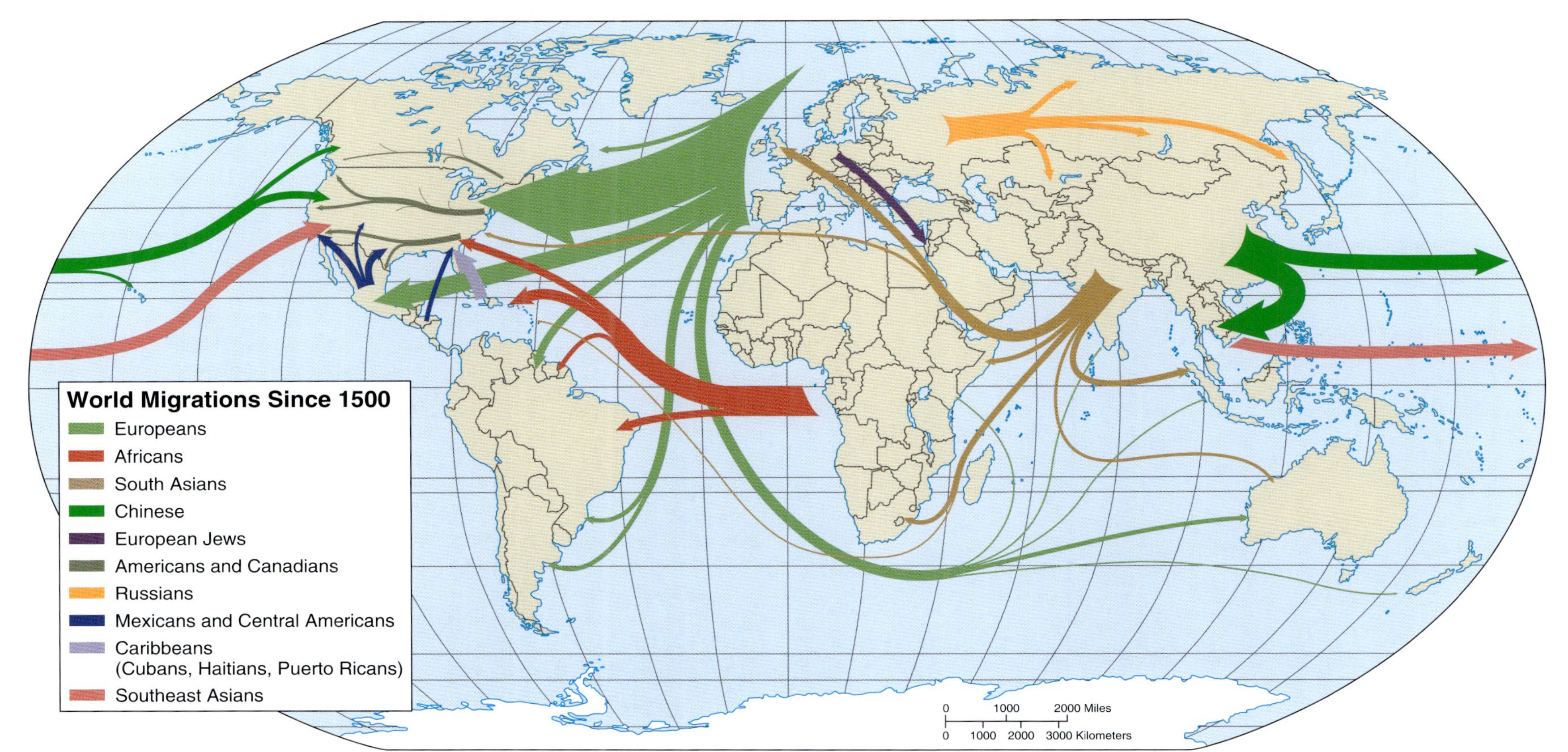

World Migrations Since 1500
Europeans
Africans
South Asians
Chinese
European Jews
Americans and Canadians
Russians
Mexicans and Central Americans
Caribbeans
(Cubans, Haitians, Puerto Ricans)
Southeast Asians
0 1000 2000 Miles
0 1000 2000 3000 Kilometers

Migration has had a significant effect on world geography, contributing to cultural change and development, to the diffusion of ideas and innovations, and to the complex mixture of people and cultures found in the world today. *Internal migration* occurs within the boundaries of a country; *external migration* is movement from one country or region to another. Over the last 50 years, the most important migrations in the world have been internal, largely the rural-to-urban migration that has been responsible for the recent rise of global urbanization. Prior to the mid-twentieth century, three types of external migrations were most important: *voluntary,* most often in search of better economic conditions and opportunities; *involuntary* or *forced,* involving people who have been driven from their homelands by war, political unrest, or environmental disasters, or who have been transported as slaves or prisoners; and *imposed,* not entirely forced but which conditions make highly advisable. Human migrations in recorded history have been responsible for major changes in the patterns of languages, religions, ethnic composition, and economies. Particularly during the last 500 years, migrations of both the voluntary and involuntary or forced type have literally reshaped the human face of the earth.

Part III

Global Demographic Patterns

Map 24 Population Growth Rates

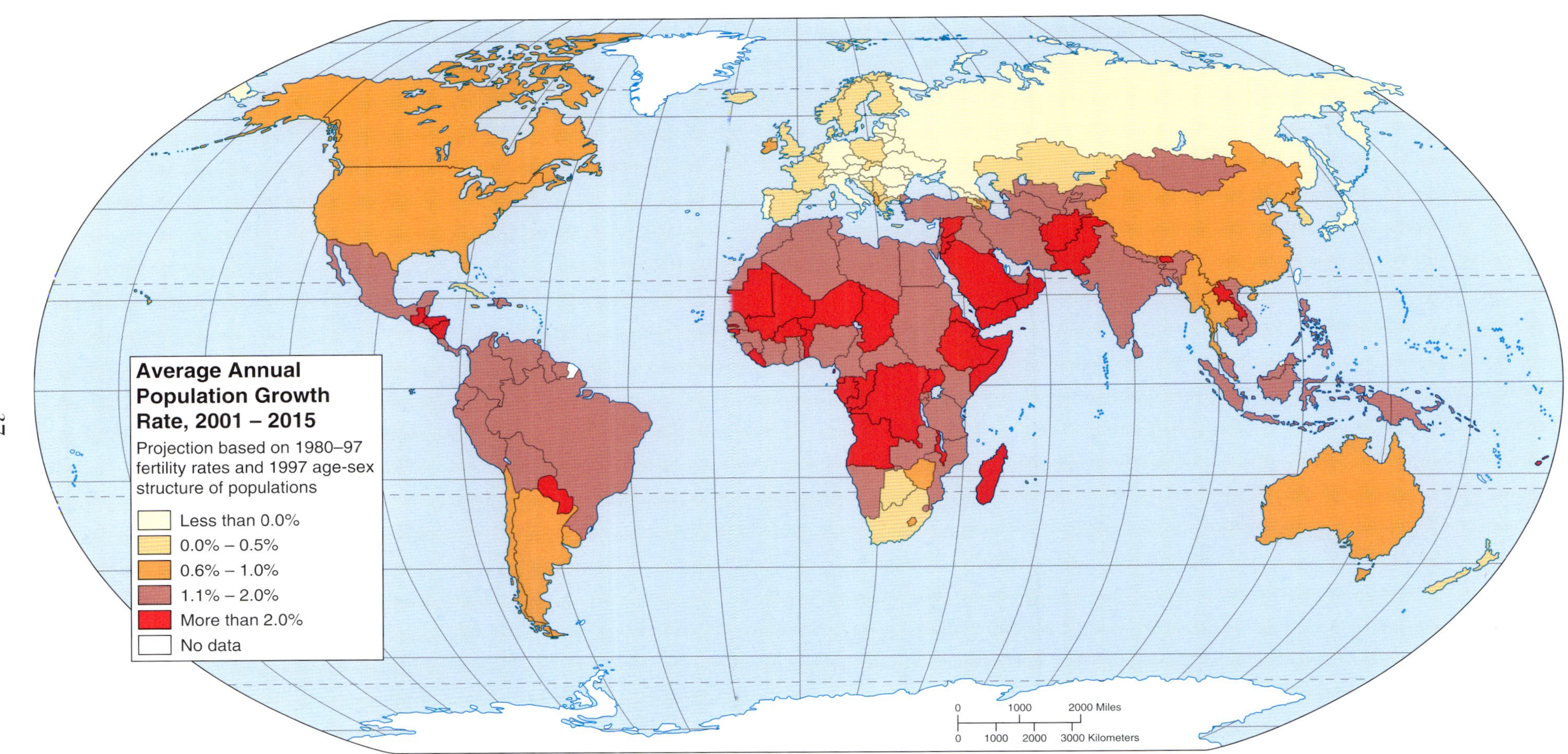
Average Annual Population Growth Rate, 2001 – 2015
Projection based on 1980–97 fertility rates and 1997 age-sex structure of populations
Less than 0.0%
0.0% – 0.5%
0.6% – 1.0%
1.1% – 2.0%
More than 2.0%
No data
0 1000 2000 Miles
0 1000 2000 3000 Kilometers

Of all the statistical measurements of human population, that of the rate of population growth is the most important. The growth rate of a population is a combination of natural change (births and deaths), in-migration, and out-migration; it is obtained by adding the number of births to the number of immigrants during a year and subtracting from that total the sum of deaths and emigrants for the same year. For a specific country, this figure will determine many things about the country's future ability to feed, house, educate, and provide medical services to its citizens. Some of the countries with the largest populations (such as India) also have high growth rates. Since these countries tend to be in developing regions, the combination of high population and high growth rates poses special problems for political stability and continuing economic development; the combination also carries heightened risks for environmental degradation. Many people believe that the rapidly expanding world population is a potential crisis that may cause environmental and human disaster by the middle of the twenty-first century.

Map 25 Total Fertility Rates

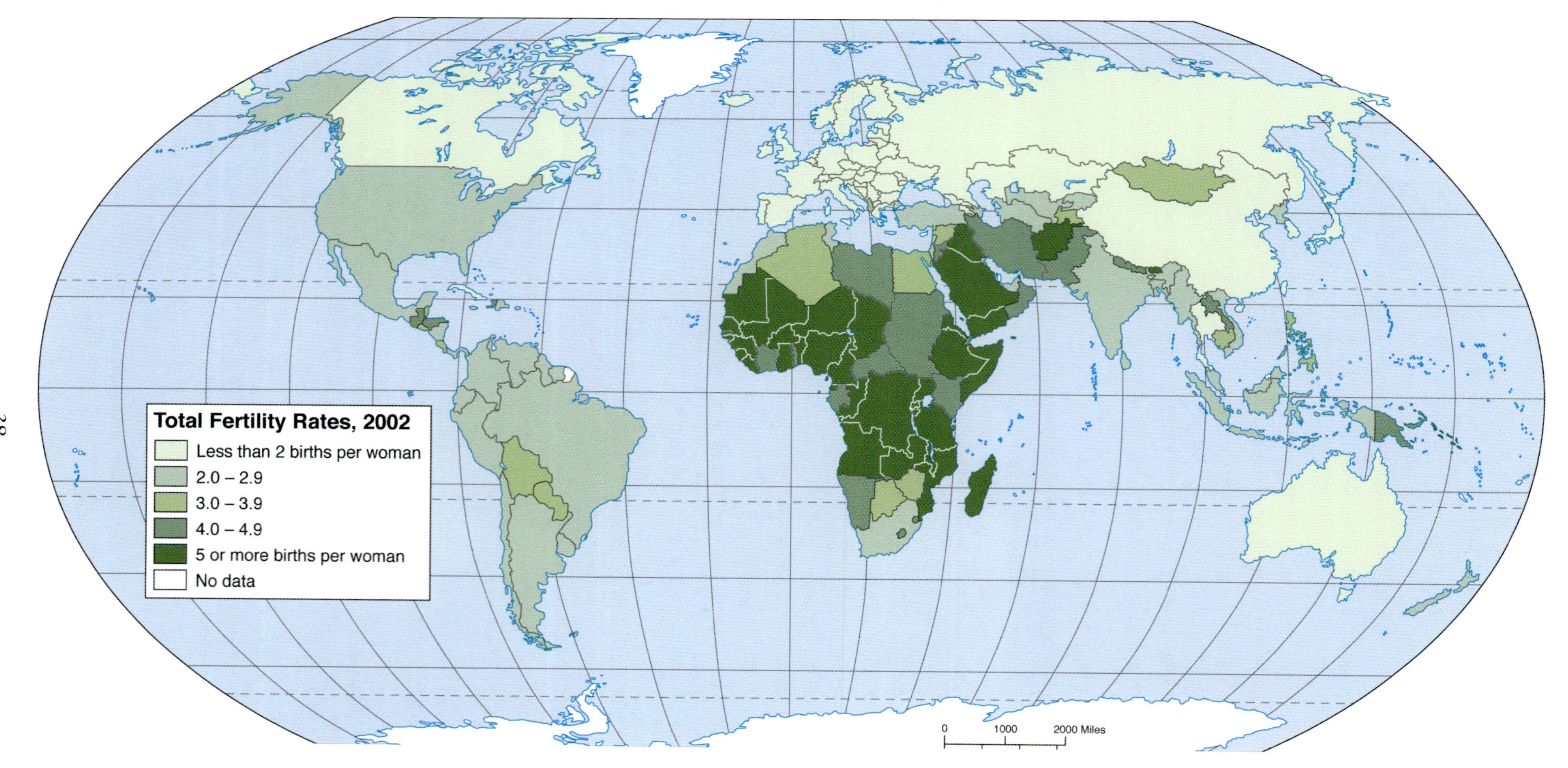
Total Fertility Rates, 2002
Less than 2 births per woman
2.0 – 2.9
3.0 – 3.9
4.0 – 4.9
5 or more births per woman
No data
0
1000
2000 Miles

The fertility rate measures the number of children that a woman is expected to bear during her lifetime, based on the age-specific fertility figures of women between 15 and 40 (the normal childbearing years). While fertility rates tell us a great deal about present population growth, with high fertility rates indicating high population growth rates, they are also indicative of potential or projected growth. A country whose women can be expected to bear many children is a country with enormous potential for population growth in the future. Given present fertility rates, for example, the number of offspring from the average German woman over the next three generations (the total number of children, grandchildren, and great-grandchildren) will be 7. During the same three generations, the average American woman will have a total of 17 children, grandchildren, and great-grandchildren. But during this time, assuming that present fertility rates are maintained, the average woman in sub-Saharan Africa will have [&em]258[&stop] children, grandchildren, and great-grandchildren. You might be interested in working out some potential population growth rates over two or three generations, using the data as presented on the map.

Map 26 Infant Mortality Rates

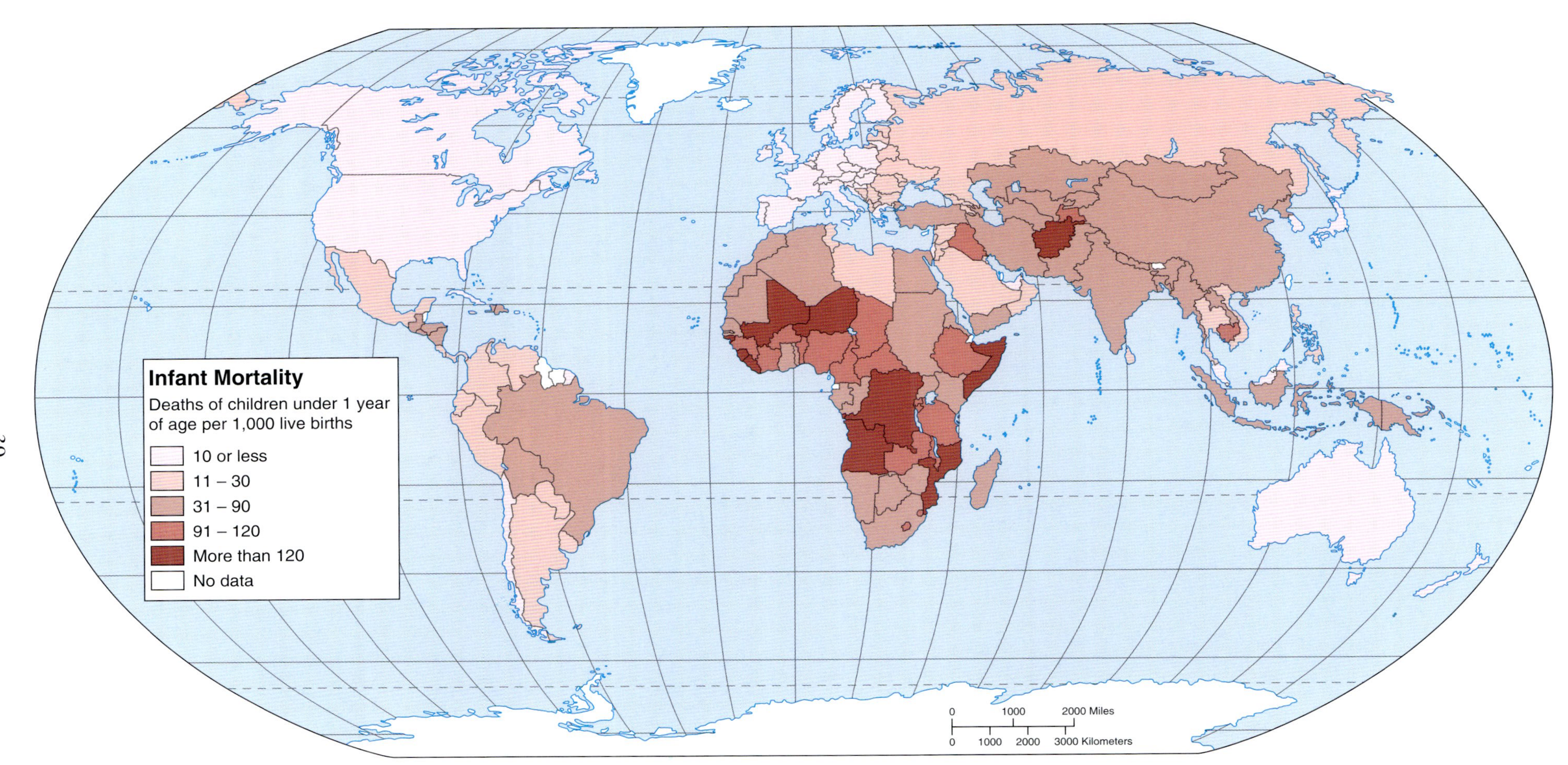

Infant Mortality
Deaths of children under 1 year of age per 1,000 live births
10 or less
11 – 30
31 – 90
91 – 120
More than 120
No data
0 1000 2000 Miles
0 1000 2000 3000 Kilometers

Infant mortality rates are calculated by dividing the number of children born in a given year who die before their first birthday by the total number of children born that year and then multiplying by 1,000; this shows how many infants have died for every 1,000 births. Infant mortality rates are prime indicators of economic development. In highly developed economies, with advanced medical technologies, sufficient diets, and adequate public sanitation, infant mortality rates tend to be quite low. By contrast, in less developed countries, with the disadvantages of poor diet, limited access to medical technology, and the other problems of poverty, infant mortality rates tend to be high.

Although worldwide infant mortality has decreased significantly during the last 2 decades, many regions of the world still experience infant mortality above the 10 percent level (100 deaths per 1,000 live births). Such infant mortality rates not only represent human tragedy at its most basic level, but also are powerful inhibiting factors for the future of human development. Comparing infant mortality rates in the midlatitudes and the tropics shows that children in most African countries are more than 10 times as likely to die within a year of birth as children in European countries.

Map 27 Child Mortality Rate

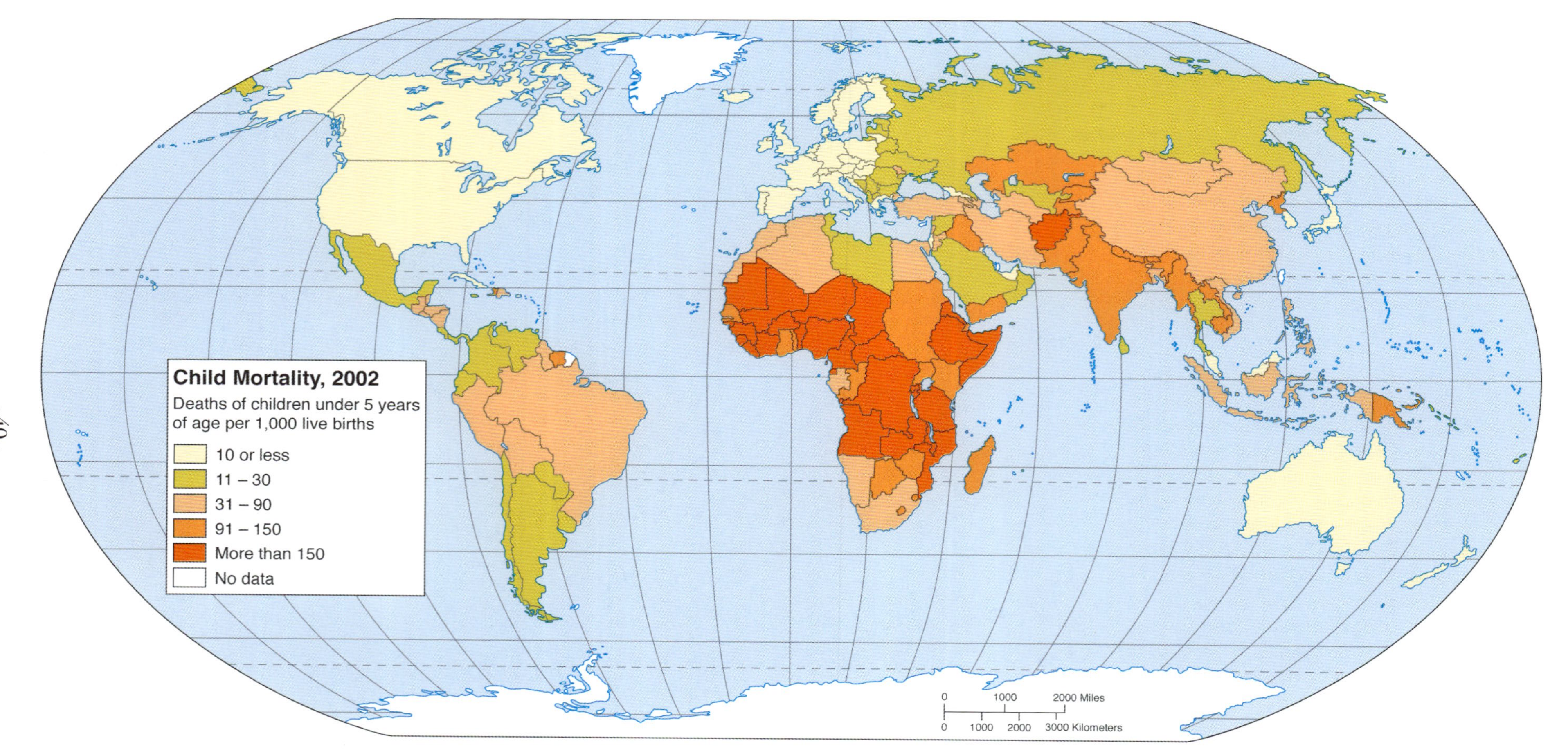

Child Mortality, 2002
Deaths of children under 5 years of age per 1,000 live births
10 or less
11 – 30
31 – 90
91 – 150
More than 150
No data
0 1000 2000 Miles
0 1000 2000 3000 Kilometers

Child mortality rates are calculated by determining the probability that a child born in a specified year will die before reaching the age 5, using current age-specific mortality rates for a population. The major sources of mortality rates are vital registration systems and estimates made from surveys and/or census reports. Along with infant mortality and average life-expectancy rates, child mortality rates, according to the World Bank, "are probably the best general indicators of a community's current health status and are often cited as overall measures of a population's welfare or quality of life." Where infant mortality often reflects health care conditions, child mortality is usually a reflection of the inadequacy of nutrition, leading to early deaths from nutritionally related diseases. In some less developed countries in Africa and Asia, child mortality is also an indicator of the widespread presence of infectious diseases such as malaria, tuberculosis, and HIV/AIDS.

Map 28 Child Malnutrition

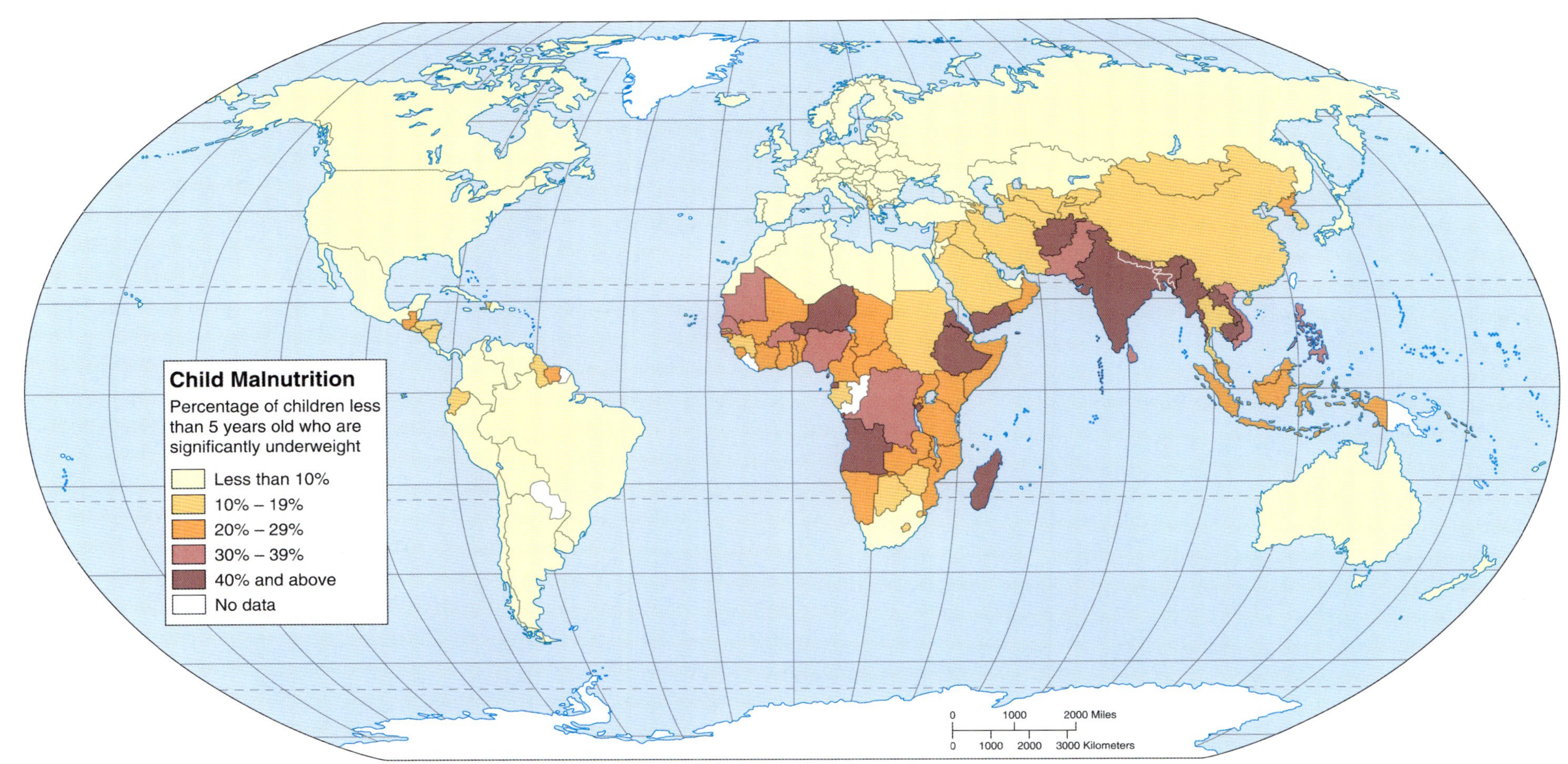

Child Malnutrition
Percentage of children less than 5 years old who are significantly underweight
Less than 10%
10% – 19%
20% – 29%
30% – 39%
40% and above
No data
0 1000 2000 Miles
0 1000 2000 3000 Kilometers

The weight of poverty is not evenly spread among the members of a population, falling disproportionately upon the weakest and most disadvantaged members of society. In most societies, these individuals are children, particularly female children. Children simply do not compete as successfully as adults for their (meager) share of the daily food supply. Where food shortages prevail, children tend to have the quality of their future lives severely compromised by poor nutrition, which, in a downward spiral, robs them of the energy necessary to compete more effectively for food. Children who are inadequately fed are less likely to do well in school, are more prone to debilitating disease, and will more often become a drain on scarce societal resources than well-fed children. Recently, health care officials in the more developed world have become concerned over the trend to "overnutrition," leading to obesity and related health problems in the world's economically developed countries. Nevertheless, child malnourishment remains one of the primary distinguishing factors between the "haves" and "have-nots."

Map 29 Primary School Enrollment

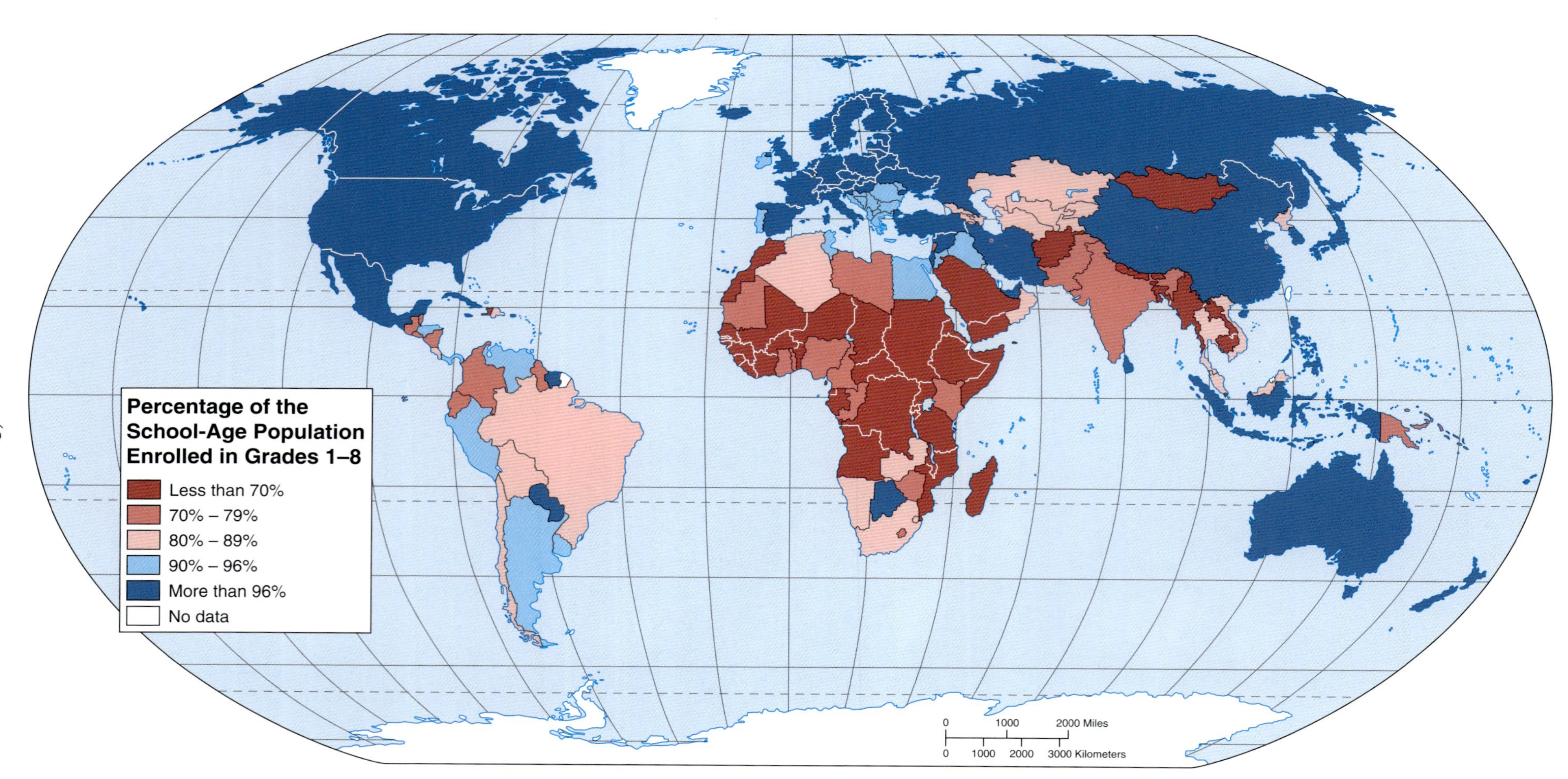

Percentage of the School-Age Population Enrolled in Grades 1–8
Less than 70%
70% – 79%
80% – 89%
90% – 96%
More than 96%
No data
0 1000 2000 Miles
0 1000 2000 3000 Kilometers

Like many of the other measures illustrated in this atlas, primary school enrollment is a clear reflection of the division of the world into "have" and "have-not" countries. It is also a measure that has changed more rapidly over the last decade than demographic and other indicators of development, as countries of even very modest means have made concerted attempts to attain relatively high percentages of primary school enrollment. That they have been able to do so is good evidence of the fact that reasonably respectable levels of human development are feasible at even modest income levels.

High primary school enrollment is also a reflection of the worldwide opinion that a major element in economic development is a well-educated, literate population. The links between human progress, as typified by higher levels of education, and economic growth are not automatic, however, and those countries without programs for maintaining the headway gained by improved education may be on the road to failure in terms of economic development.

Map 30 Average Life Expectancy at Birth

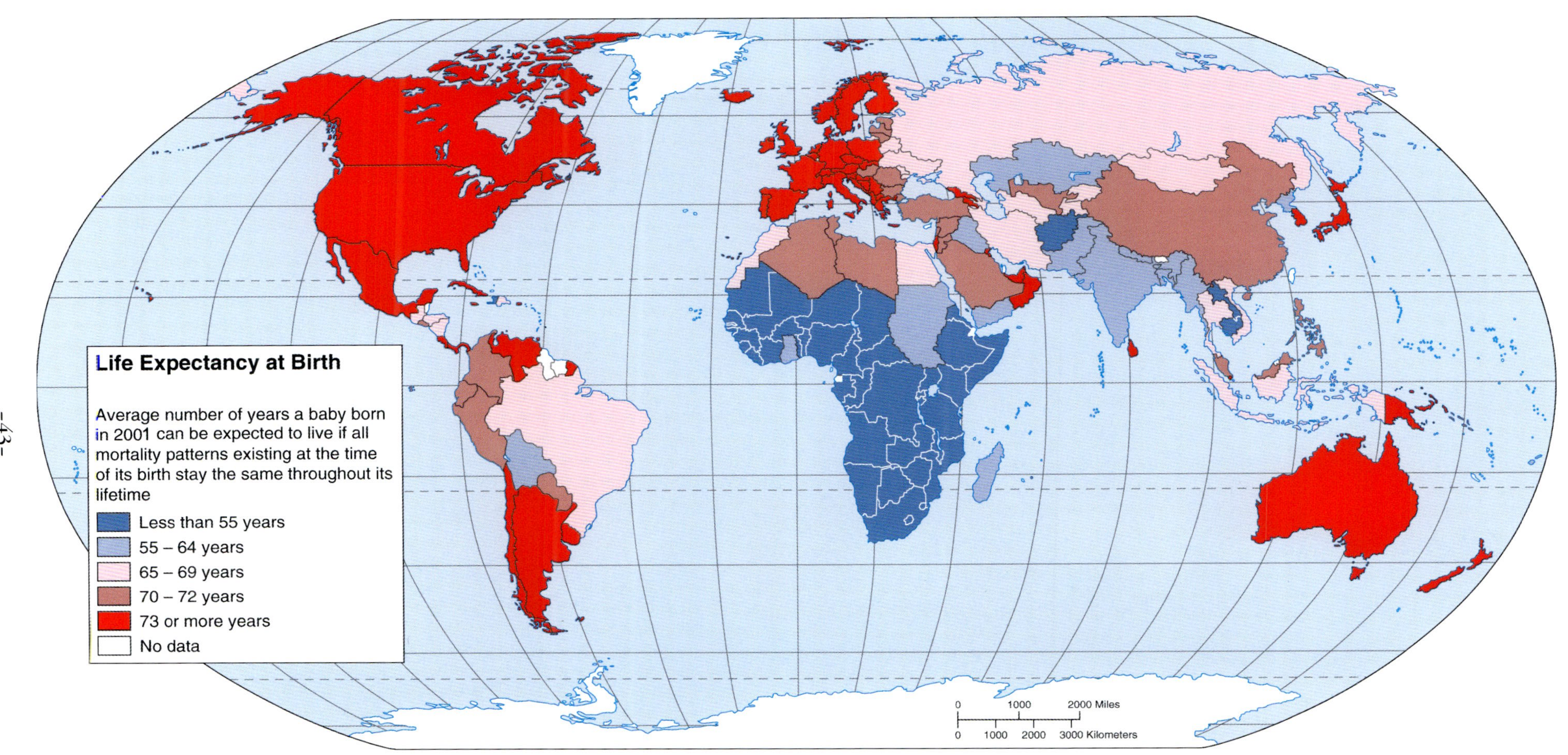
Life Expectancy at Birth
Average number of years a baby born in 2001 can be expected to live if all mortality patterns existing at the time of its birth stay the same throughout its lifetime
Less than 55 years
55 – 64 years
65 – 69 years
70 – 72 years
73 or more years
No data
0 1000 2000 Miles
0 1000 2000 3000 Kilometers

Average life expectancy at birth is a measure of the average longevity of the population of a country. Like all average measures, it is distorted by extremes. For example, a country with a high mortality rate among children will have a low average life expectancy. Thus, an average life expectancy of 45 years does not mean that everyone can be expected to die at the age of 45. More normally, what the figure means is that a substantial number of children die between birth and 5 years of age, thus reducing the average life expectancy for the entire population. In spite of the dangers inherent in misinterpreting the data, average life expectancy (along with infant mortality and several other measures) is a valid way of judging the relative health of a population. It reflects the nature of the health care system, public sanitation and disease control, nutrition, and a number of other key human need indicators. As such, it is a measure of well-being that is significant in indicating economic development and predicting political stability.

Map 31 Population by Age Group

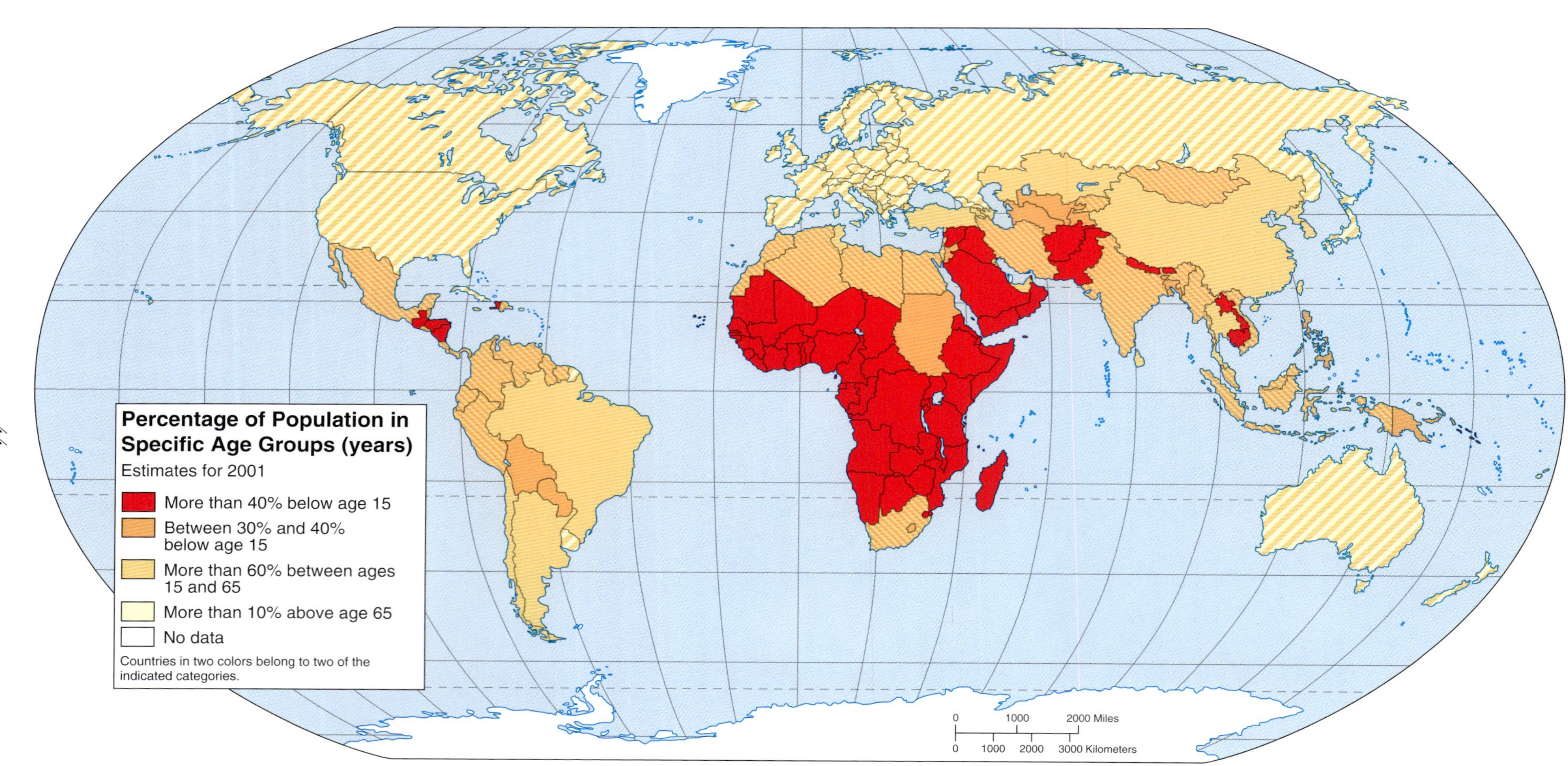

Percentage of Population in Specific Age Groups (years)
Estimates for 2001
More than 40% below age 15
Between 30% and 40% below age 15
More than 60% between ages 15 and 65
More than 10% above age 65
No data
Countries in two colors belong to two of the indicated categories.
0 1000 2000 Miles
0 1000 2000 3000 Kilometers

Of all the measurements that illustrate the dynamics of a population, age distribution may be the most significant, particularly when viewed in combination with average growth rates. The particular relevance of age distribution is that it tells us what to expect from a population in terms of growth over the next generation. If, for example, approximately 40–50 percent of a population is below the age of 15, that suggests that in the next generation about one-quarter of the total population will be women of childbearing age. When age distribution is combined with fertility rates (the average number of children born per woman in a population), an especially valid measurement of future growth potential may be derived. A simple example: Nigeria, with a 2002 population of 130 million, has 43.6 percent of its population below the age of 15 and a fertility rate of 5.5; the United States, with a 2002 population of 280 million, has 21 percent of its population below the age of 15 and a fertility rate of 2.07. During the period in which those women presently under the age of 15 are in their childbearing years, Nigeria can be expected to add a total of approximately 155 million persons to its total population. Over the same period, the United States can be expected to add only 61 million.

Map 32 Average Daily Per Capita Supply of Calories (Kilocalories)

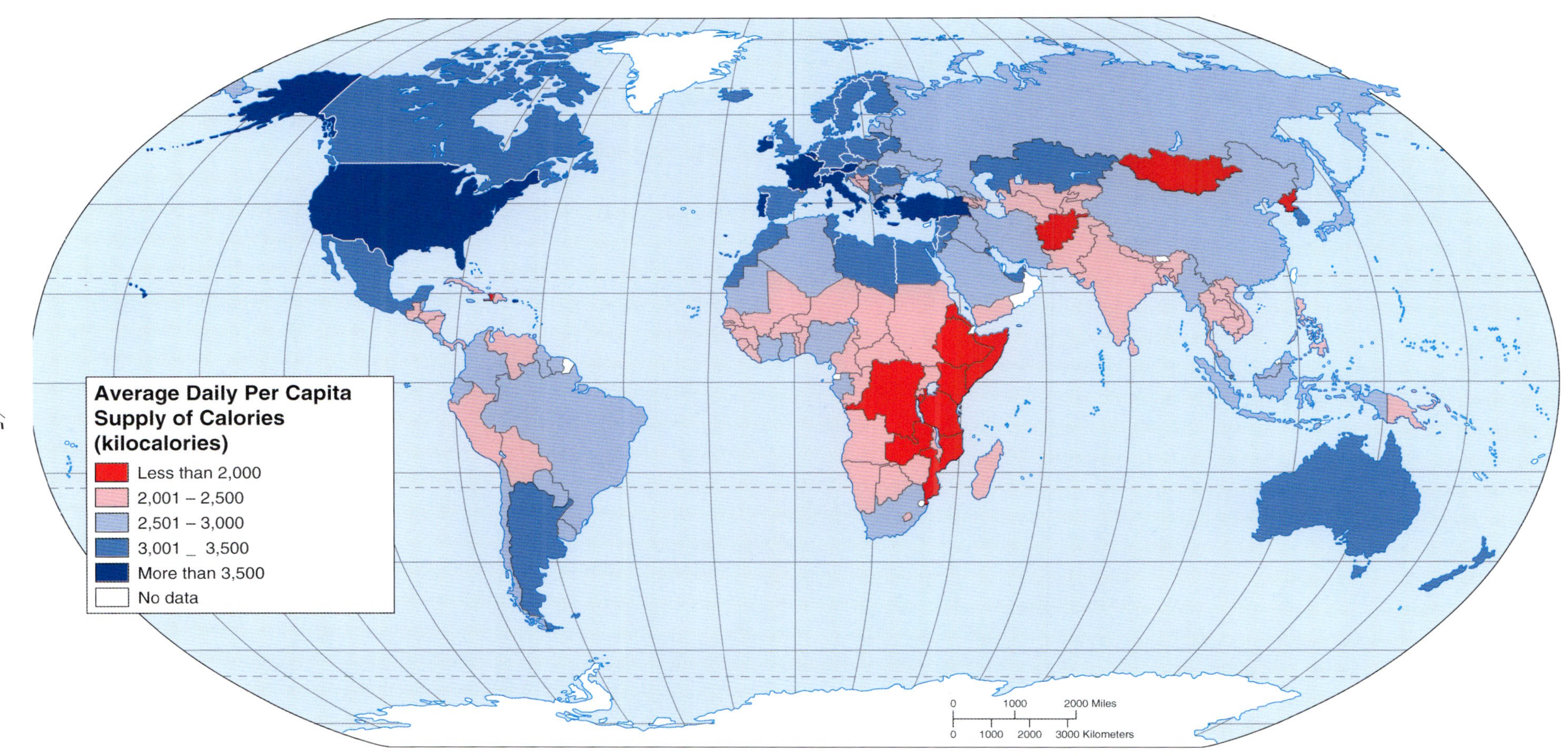

Average Daily Per Capita Supply of Calories (kilocalories)
Less than 2,000
2,001 – 2,500
2,501 – 3,000
3,001 _ 3,500
More than 3,500
No data
0 1000 2000 Miles
0 1000 2000 3000 Kilometers

The data shown on this map, which indicate the presence or absence of critical food shortages, do not necessarily indicate the presence of starvation or famine. But they certainly do indicate potential problem areas for the next decade. The measurements are in calories from *all* food sources: domestic production, international trade, drawdown on stocks or food reserves, and direct foreign contributions or aid. The quantity of calories available is that amount, estimated by the UN's Food and Agriculture Organization (FAO), that reaches consumers. The calories actually consumed may be lower than the figures shown, depending on how much is lost in a variety of ways: in home storage (to pests such as rats and mice), in preparation and cooking, through consumption by pets and domestic animals, and as discarded foods, for example. The estimate of need is not a global uniform value but is calculated for each country on the basis of the age and sex distribution of the population and the estimated level of activity of the population. Compare this map with Map 59 for a good measure of potential problem areas for food shortages within the next decade.

Map 33 Illiteracy Rates

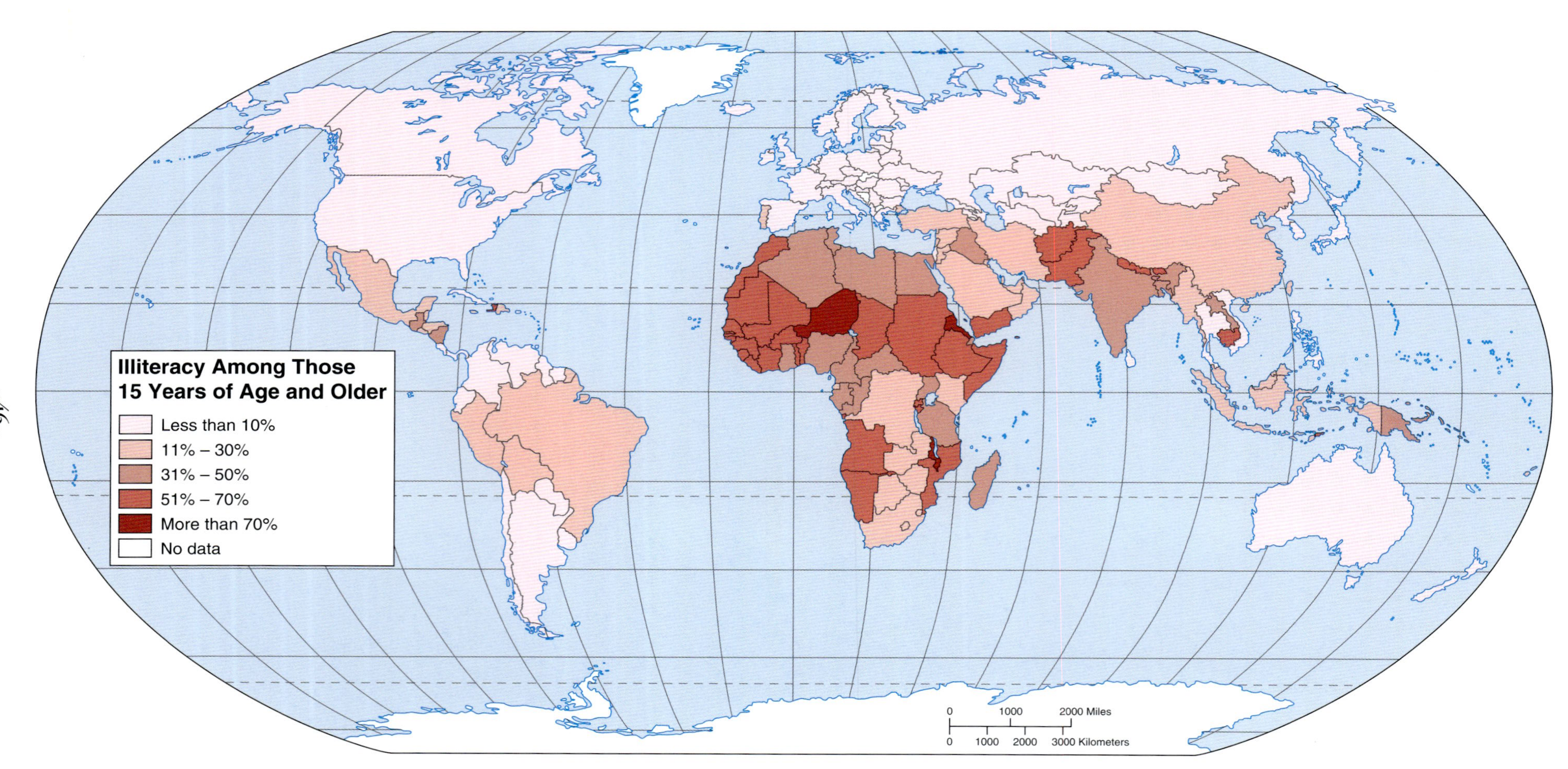
Illiteracy Among Those 15 Years of Age and Older
Less than 10%
11% – 30%
31% – 50%
51% – 70%
More than 70%
No data
0 1000 2000 Miles
0 1000 2000 3000 Kilometers

Illiteracy rates are based on the percentages of people age 15 or above (classed as adults in most countries) who are not able to write and read, with understanding, a brief, simple statement about everyday life written in their home- or official language. As might be expected, illiteracy rates tend to be higher in the less developed states, where educational systems are a low government priority. Rates of literacy or illiteracy also tend to be gender-differentiated, with women in many countries experiencing educational neglect or discrimination that makes it more likely they will be illiterate. In many developing countries, between five and ten times as many women will be illiterate as men, and the illiteracy rate for women may even exceed 90 percent. Both male and female illiteracy severely compromise economic development.

Map 34 Female/Male Inequality in Education and Employment

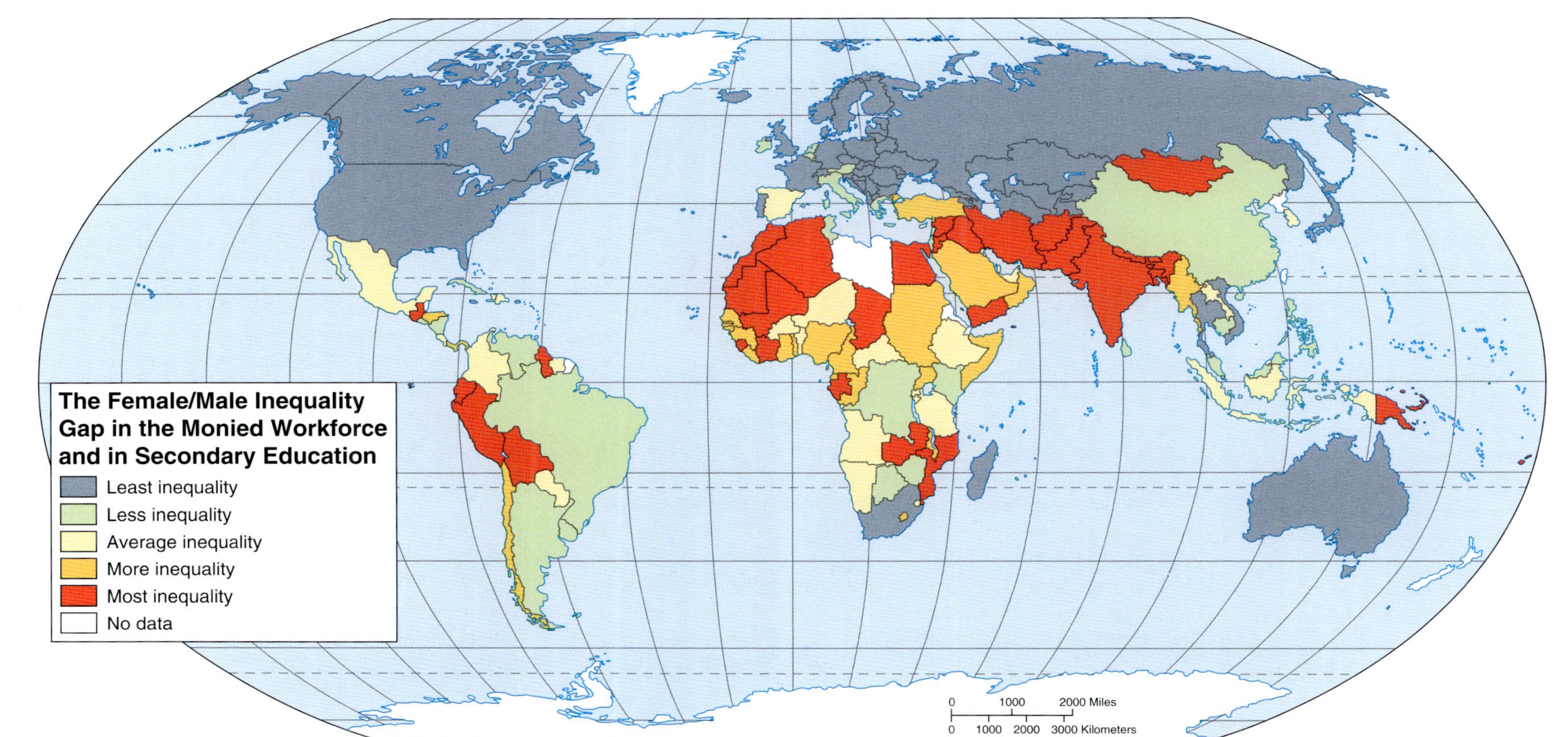
The Female/Male Inequality Gap in the Monied Workforce and in Secondary Education
Least inequality
Less inequality
Average inequality
More inequality
Most inequality
No data
0 1000 2000 Miles
0 1000 2000 3000 Kilometers

While women in developed countries, particularly in North America and Europe, have made significant advances in socioeconomic status in recent years, in most of the world they suffer from significant inequality when compared with their male counterparts. Although women have received the right to vote in most of the world's countries, in over 90 percent of these countries that right has only been granted in the last 50 years. In most regions, literacy rates for women still fall far short of those for men; In Africa and Asia, for example, only about half as many women are literate as are men. Women marry considerably younger than men and attend school for shorter periods of time. Inequalities in education and employment are perhaps the most telling indicators of the unequal status of women in most of the world. Lack of secondary education in comparison with men prevents women from entering the workforce with equally high-paying jobs. Even where women are employed in positions similar to those held by men, they still tend to receive less compensation. The gap between rich and poor involves not only a clear geographic differentiation, but a clear gender differentiation as well.

Map 35 Global Scourges: Major Infectious Diseases

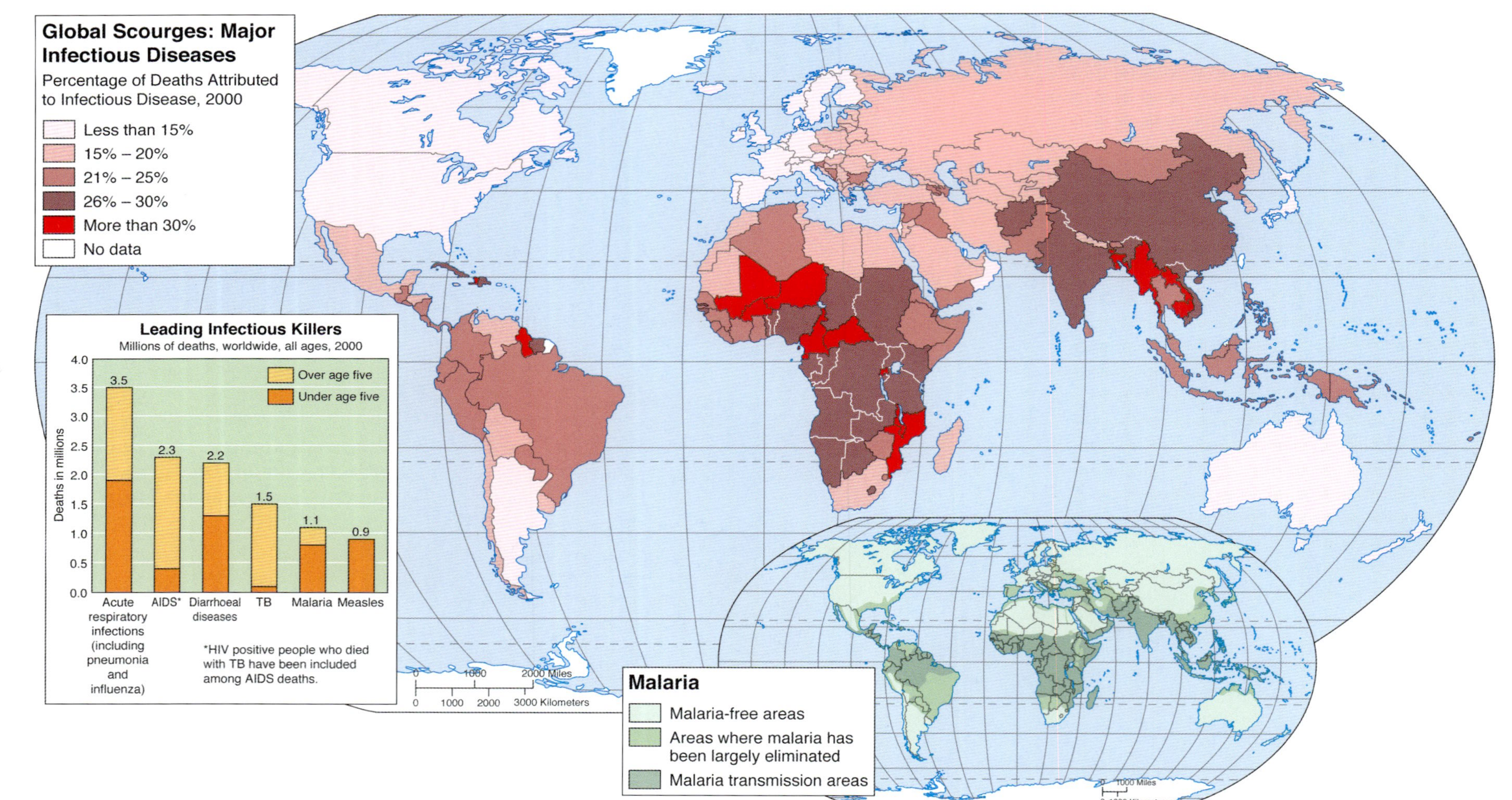

Global Scourges: Major Infectious Diseases
Percentage of Deaths Attributed to Infectious Disease, 2000
Less than 15%
15% – 20%
21% – 25%
26% – 30%
More than 30%
No data
Leading Infectious Killers
Millions of deaths, worldwide, all ages, 2000
Over age five
Under age five
Deaths in millions
4.0
3.5
3.0
2.5
2.0
1.5
1.0
0.5
0.0
3.5
2.3
2.2
1.5
1.1
0.9
Acute respiratory infections (including pneumonia and influenza)
AIDS*
Diarrhoeal diseases
TB
Malaria
Measles
*HIV positive people who died with TB have been included among AIDS deaths.
0 1000 2000 Miles
0 1000 2000 3000 Kilometers
Malaria
Malaria-free areas
Areas where malaria has been largely eliminated
Malaria transmission areas
0 1000 Miles
0 1000 Kilometers

Infectious diseases are the world's leading cause of premature death and at least half of the world's population is, at any time, at risk of contracting an infectious disease. Although we often think of infectious diseases as being restricted to the tropical world (malaria, dengue fever), many if not most of them have attained global proportions. A major case in point is HIV/AIDS, which quite probably originated in Africa but has, over the last two decades, spread throughout the entire world. Major diseases of the nineteenth century, such as cholera and tuberculosis, are making a major comeback in many parts of the world, in spite of being preventable or treatable. Part of the problem with infectious diseases is that they tend to be associated with poverty (poor nutrition, poor sanitation, substandard housing, and so on) and, therefore, are seen as a problem of undeveloped countries, with the consequent lack of funding for prevention and treatment. Infectious diseases are also tending to increase because lifesaving drugs, such as antibiotics and others used in the fight against diseases, are losing their effectiveness as bacteria develop genetic resistance to them. The problem of global warming is also associated with a spread of infectious diseases as many disease vectors (certain species of mosquito, for example) are spreading into higher latitudes with increasingly warm temperatures and are spreading disease into areas where populations have no resistance to them. Infectious diseases have become something greater than simply a health issue of poor countries. They are now major social problems with potentially enormous consequences for the entire world.

Map 36 The Index of Human Development

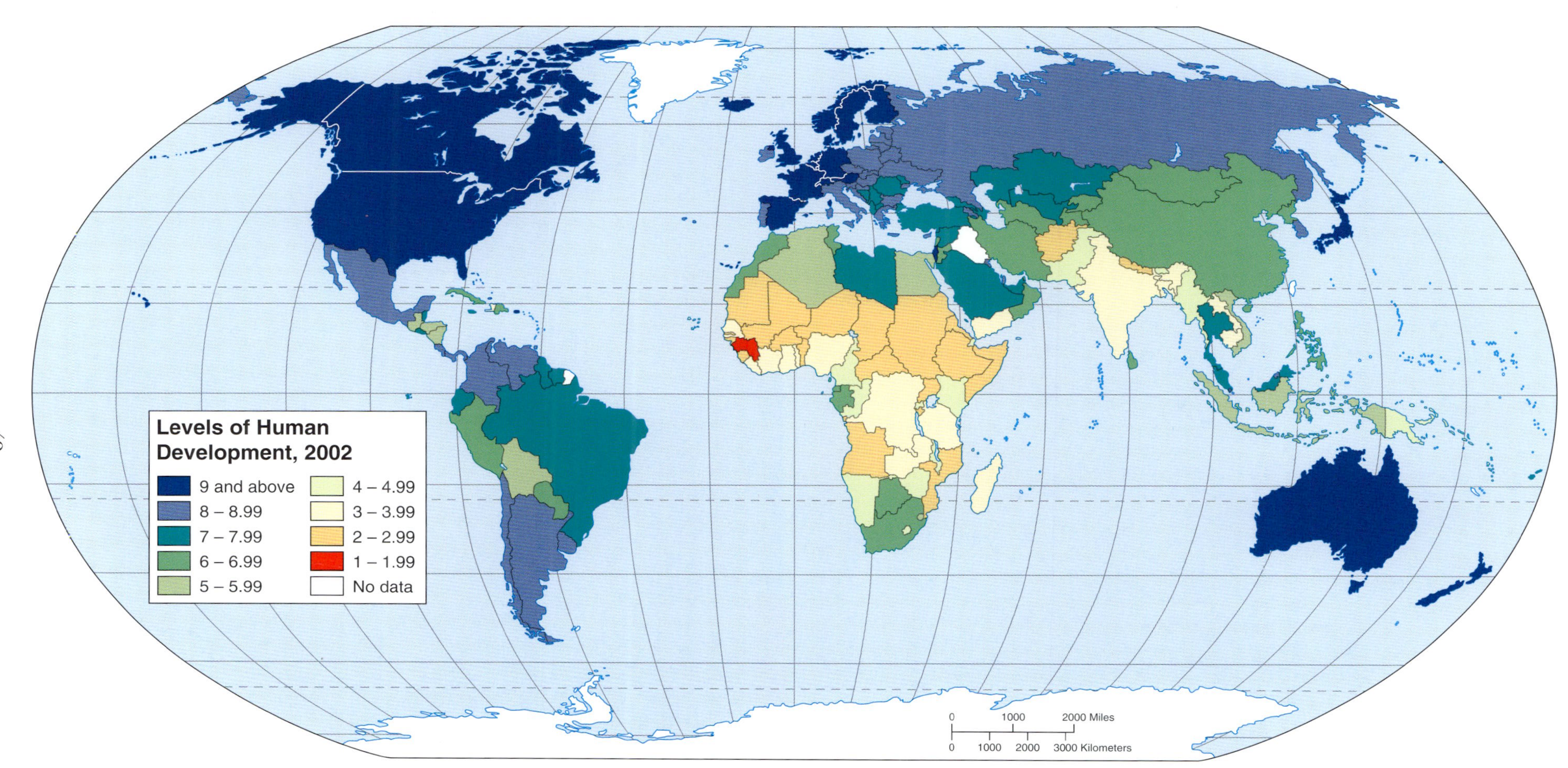

Levels of Human Development, 2002
9 and above
8 – 8.99
7 – 7.99
6 – 6.99
5 – 5.99
4 – 4.99
3 – 3.99
2 – 2.99
1 – 1.99
No data
0 1000 2000 Miles
0 1000 2000 3000 Kilometers

The development index upon which this map is based takes into account a wide variety of demographic, health, and educational data, including population growth, per capita gross domestic income, longevity, literacy, and years of schooling. The map reveals significant improvement in the quality of life in Middle and South America, although it is questionable whether the gains made in those regions can be maintained in the face of the dramatic population increases expected over the next 30 years. More clearly than anything else, the map illustrates the near-desperate situation in Africa and South Asia. In those regions, the unparalleled growth in population threatens to overwhelm all efforts to improve the quality of life. In Africa, for example, the population is increasing by 20 million persons per year. With nearly 45 percent of the continent's population aged 15 years or younger, this growth rate will accelerate as the women reach child-bearing age. Africa, along with South Asia, faces the very difficult challenge of providing basic access to health care, education, and jobs for a rapidly increasing population. The map also illustrates the striking difference in quality of life between those who inhabit the world's equatorial and tropical regions and those fortunate enough to live in the temperate zones, where the quality of life is significantly higher.

Part IV

Global Economic Patterns

Map 37 Rich and Poor Countries: Gross National Income

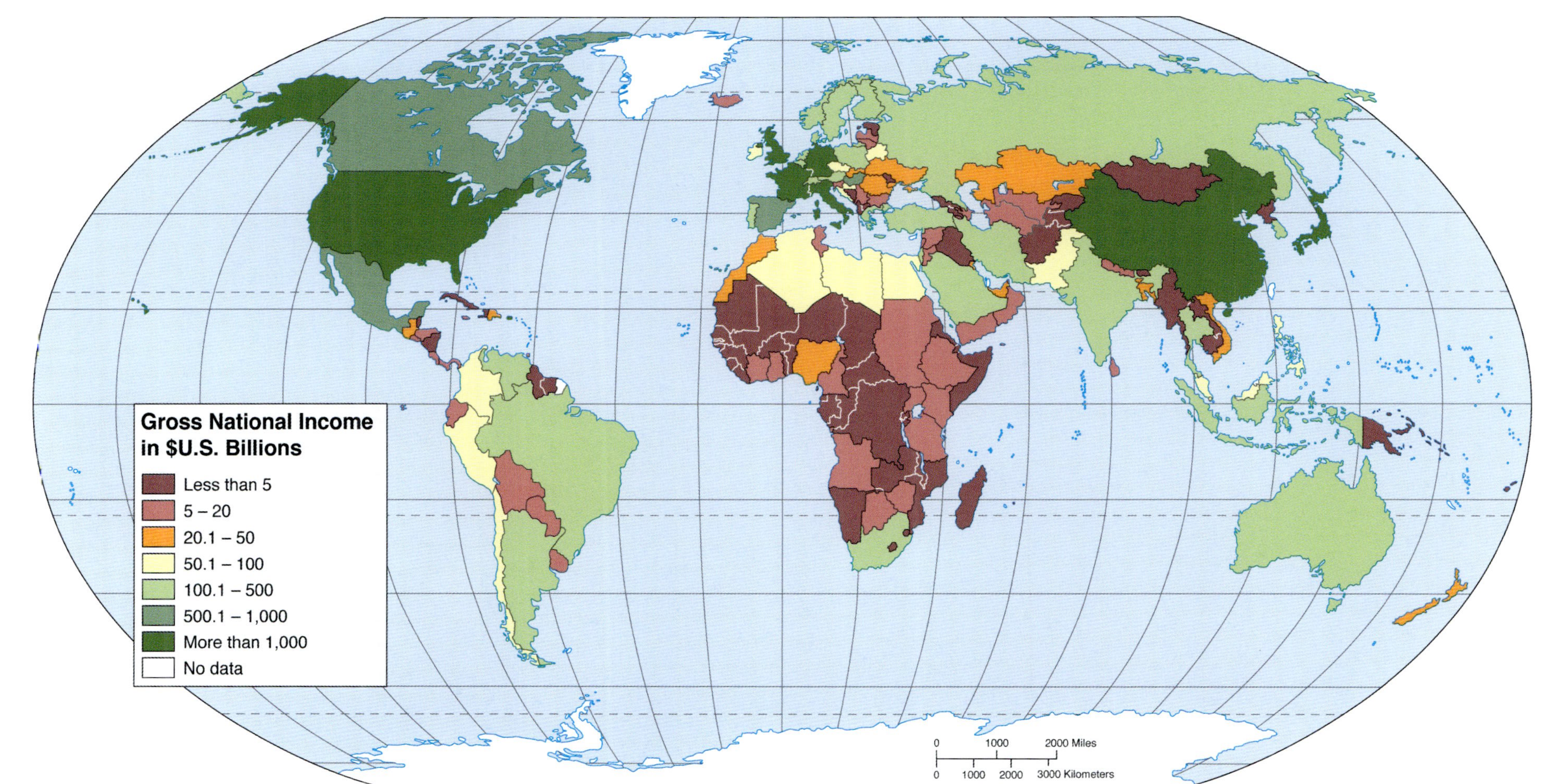
Gross National Income
in $U.S. Billions
Less than 5
5 – 20
20.1 – 50
50.1 – 100
100.1 – 500
500.1 – 1,000
More than 1,000
No data
0 1000 2000 Miles
0 1000 2000 3000 Kilometers

Gross National Income (GNI) is the broadest measure of national income and measures the total claims of a country's residents to all income from domestic and foreign products during a year. Although GNI is often misleading and commonly incomplete, it is often used by economists, geographers, political scientists, policy makers, development experts, and others not only as a measure of relative well-being but also as an instrument of assessing the effectiveness of economic and political policies. What is wrong with GNI? First of all, it does not take into account a number of real economic factors, such as, environmental deterioration, the accumulation or degradation of human and social capital, or the value of household work. Yet in spite of these deficiencies, GNI is still a reasonable way to assess the relative wealth of nations: the vast differences in wealth that separate the poorest countries from the richest. One of the more striking features of the map is the evidence it presents that such a small number of countries possess so many of the world's riches (keeping in mind that GNI provides no measure of the distribution of wealth within a country).

Map 38 Gross National Income Per Capita

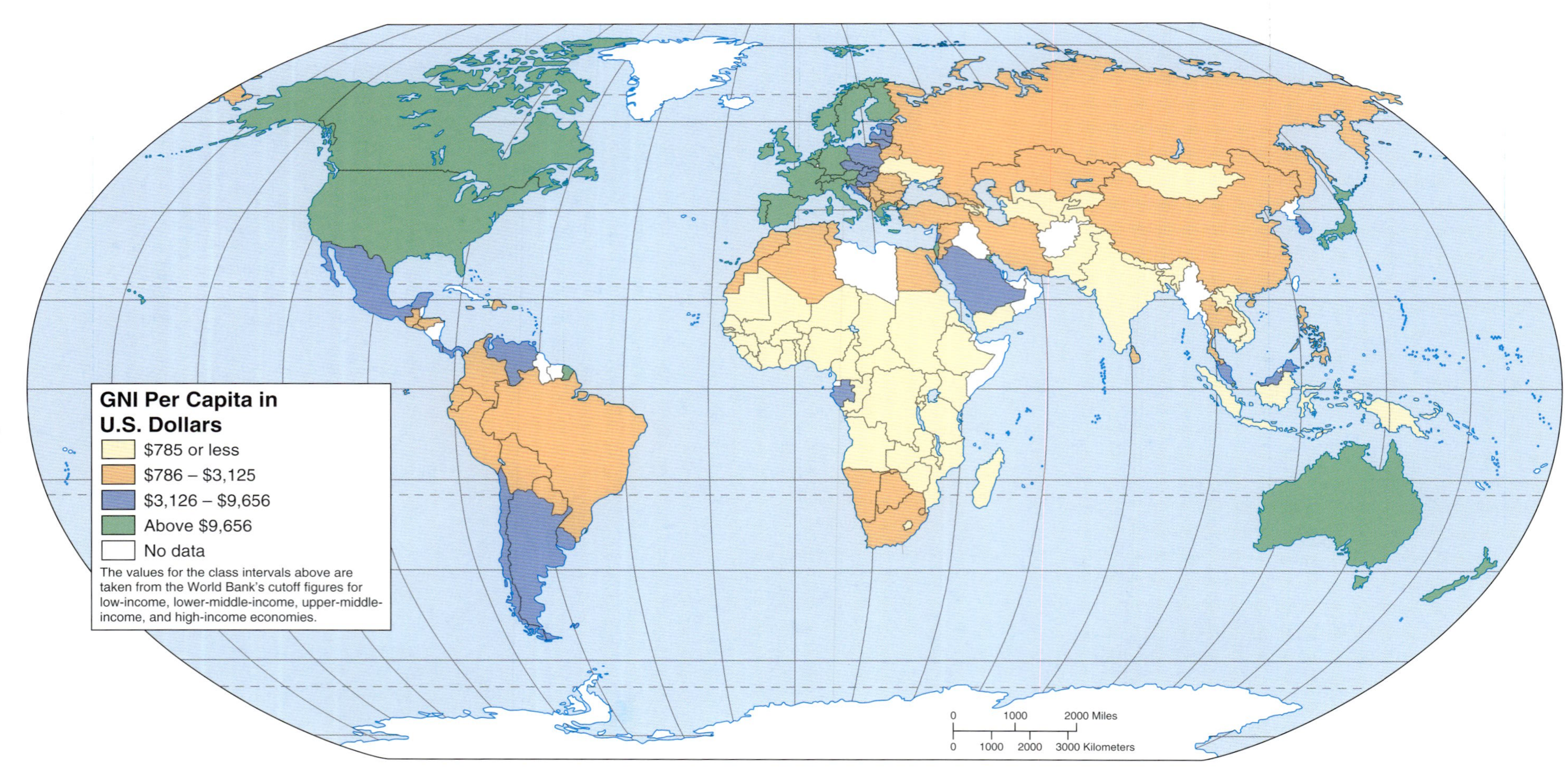
GNI Per Capita in U.S. Dollars
$785 or less
$786 – $3,125
$3,126 – $9,656
Above $9,656
No data
The values for the class intervals above are taken from the World Bank's cutoff figures for low-income, lower-middle-income, upper-middle-income, and high-income economies.
0 1000 2000 Miles
0 1000 2000 3000 Kilometers

Gross National Income (GNI) in either absolute or per capita form should be used cautiously as a yardstick of economic strength because it does not measure the distribution of wealth among a population. There are countries (most notably, the oil-rich countries of the Middle East) where per capita GNI is high but where the bulk of the wealth is concentrated in the hands of a few individuals, leaving the remainder in poverty. Even within countries in which wealth is more evenly distributed (such as those in North America or Western Europe), there is a tendency for dollars or pounds sterling or euros to concentrate in the bank accounts of a relatively small percentage of the population. Yet the mal-distribution of wealth tends to be greatest in the less developed countries, where the per capita GNI is far lower than in North America and Western Europe, and poverty is widespread. In fact, a map of GNI per capita offers a reasonably good picture of comparative economic well-being. It should be noted that a low per capita GNI does not automatically condemn a country to low levels of basic human needs and services. There are a few countries, such as Costa Rica and Sri Lanka, that have relatively low per capita GNI figures but rank comparatively high in other measures of human well-being, such as average life expectancy, access to medical care, and literacy.

Map 39 Economic Growth: GDP Change Per Capita

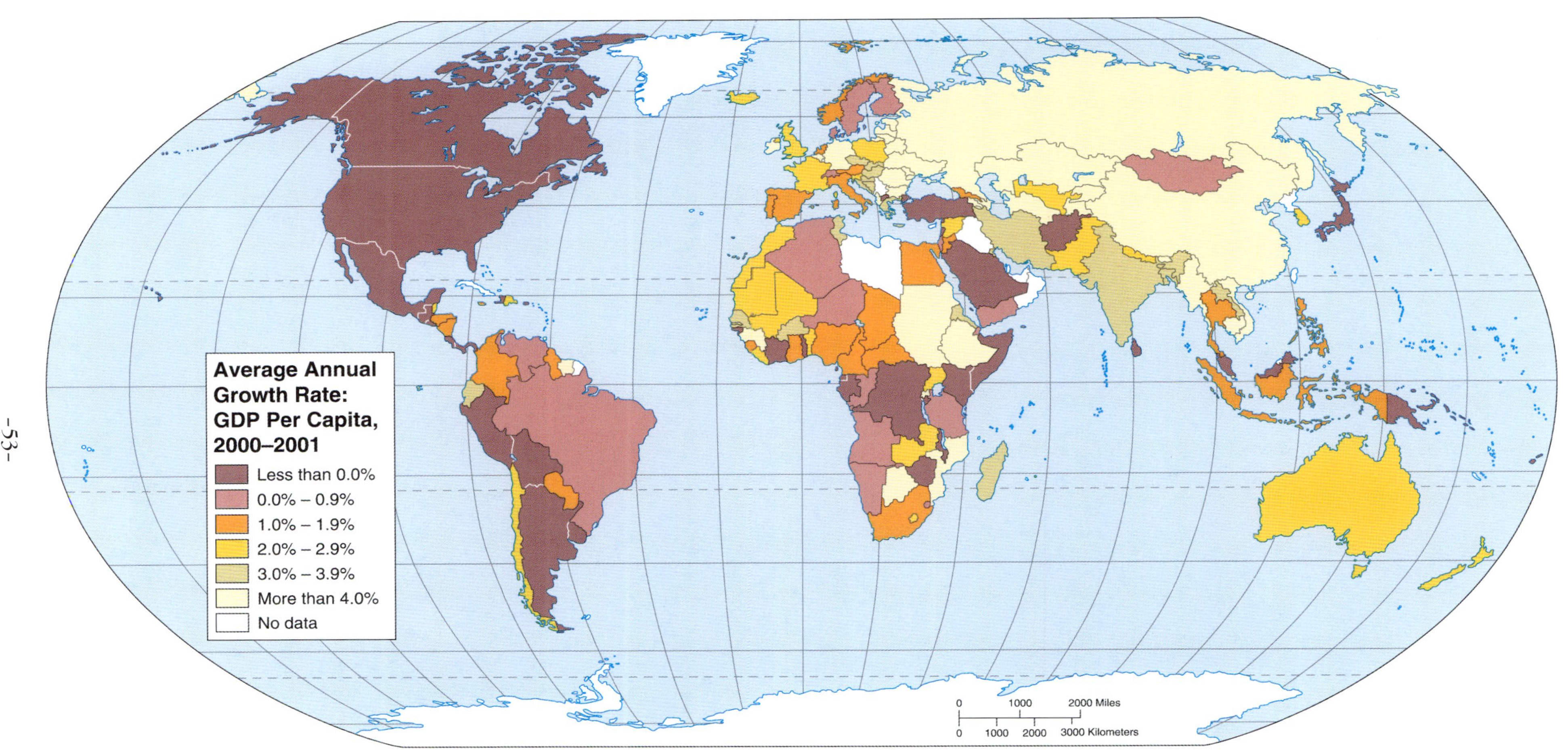
Average Annual Growth Rate: GDP Per Capita, 2000–2001
Less than 0.0%
0.0% – 0.9%
1.0% – 1.9%
2.0% – 2.9%
3.0% – 3.9%
More than 4.0%
No data
0 1000 2000 Miles
0 1000 2000 3000 Kilometers

Gross Domestic Product or GDP is Gross National Income (GNI) less receipts of primary income from foreign sources. While the calculations of GDP growth per capita are complex, the growth rate is considered by the World Bank and international economists to be a particularly good measure of economic growth. One of the worldwide tendencies measured by GDP growth per capita is for continued economic development in Africa, and in South, Southeast, and East Asia where GDP grew at rates higher than the growth rates of "richer" countries in Europe and North and South America. This should not necessarily be viewed as a case of the poor catching up with the rich; in fact, it shows the huge impact that even relatively small production increases will have in countries with small GNIs and GDPs. Nevertheless, in spite of the continuing low economic growth through most of sub-Saharan Africa, the GDP growth rate of some of the world's poorer countries is an encouraging trend.

Map 40 Total Labor Force

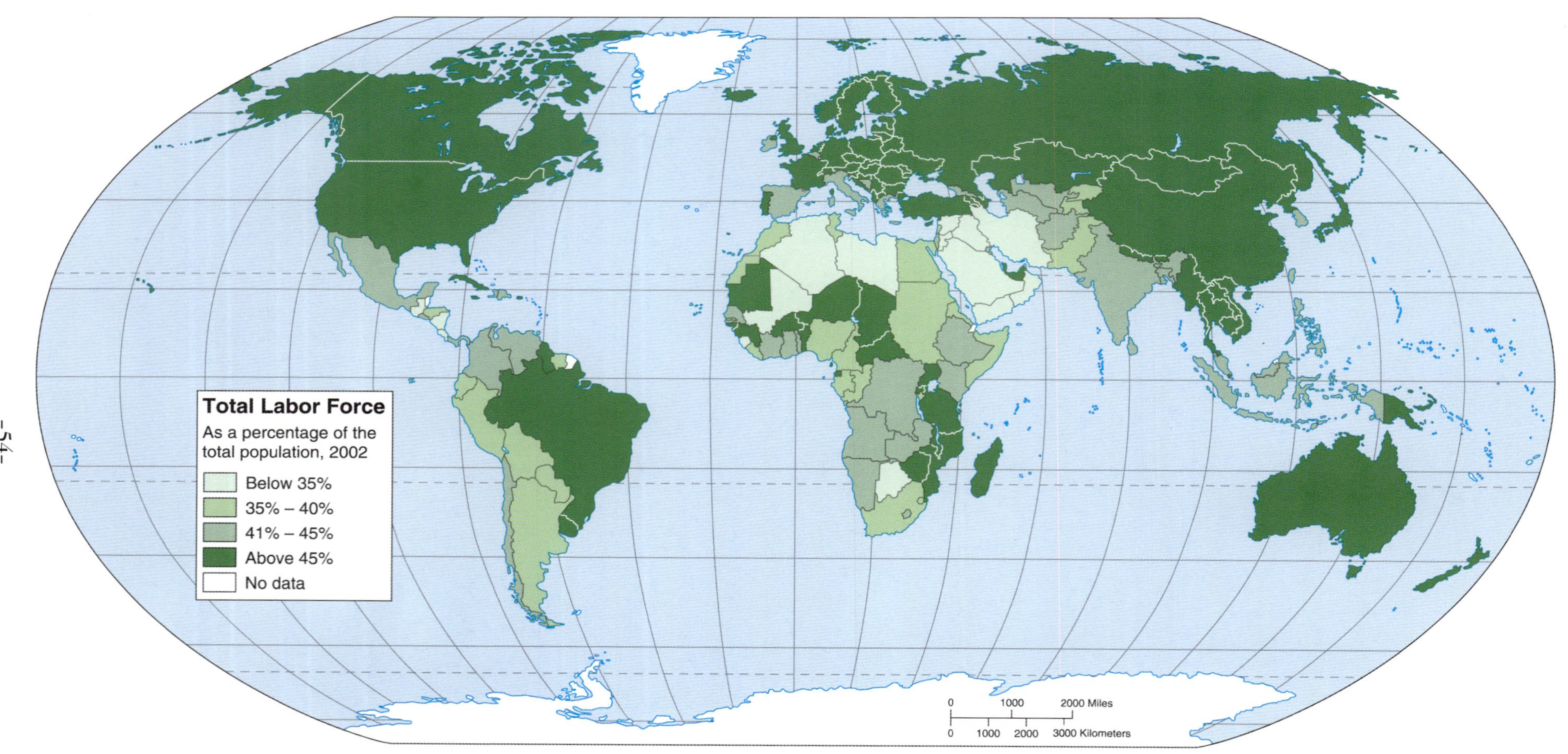
Total Labor Force
As a percentage of the total population, 2002
Below 35%
35% – 40%
41% – 45%
Above 45%
No data
0 1000 2000 Miles
0 1000 2000 3000 Kilometers

The term *labor force* refers to the economically active portion of a population, that is, all people who work or are without work but are available for and are seeking work to produce economic goods and services. The total labor force thus includes both the employed and the unemployed (as long as they are actively seeking employment). Labor force is considered a better indicator of economic potential than employment/unemployment figures, since unemployment figures will include experienced workers with considerable potential who are temporarily out of work. Unemployment figures will also incorporate persons seeking employment for the first time (many recent college graduates, for example). Generally, countries with higher percentages of total population within the labor force will be countries with higher levels of economic development. This is partly a function of levels of education and training and partly a function of the age distribution of populations. In developing countries, substantial percentages of the total population are too young to be part of the labor force. Also in developing countries a significant percentage of the population consist of women engaged in household activities or subsistence cultivation. These people seldom appear on lists of either employed or unemployed seeking employment and are the world's forgotten workers.

Map 41 Employment by Economic Activity

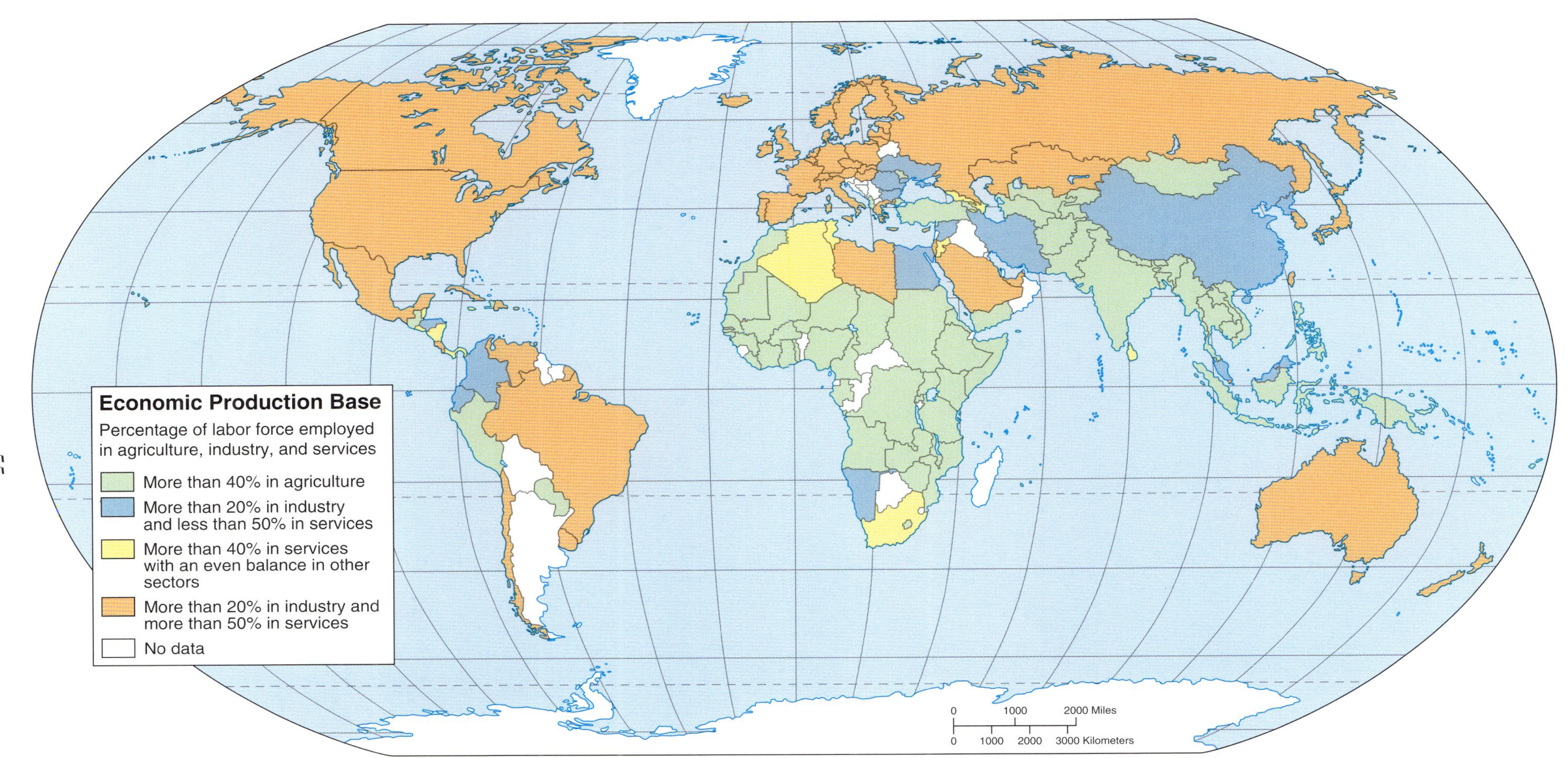
Economic Production Base
Percentage of labor force employed in agriculture, industry, and services
More than 40% in agriculture
More than 20% in industry and less than 50% in services
More than 40% in services with an even balance in other sectors
More than 20% in industry and more than 50% in services
No data
0 1000 2000 Miles
0 1000 2000 3000 Kilometers

The employment structure of a country's population is one of the best indicators of the country's position on the scale of economic development. At one end of the scale are those countries with more than 40 percent of their labor force employed in agriculture. These are almost invariably the least developed, with high population growth rates, poor human services, significant environmental problems, and so on. In the middle of the scale are two types of countries: those with more than 20 percent of their labor force employed in industry and those with a fairly even balance among agricultural, industrial, and service employment but with at least 40 percent of their labor force employed in service activities. Generally, these countries have undergone the industrial revolution fairly recently and are still developing an industrial base while building up their service activities. This category also includes countries with a disproportionate share of their economies in service activities primarily related to resource extraction. On the other end of the scale from the agricultural economies are countries with more than 20 percent of their labor force employed in industry and more than 50 percent in service activities. These countries are, for the most part, those with a highly automated industrial base and a highly mechanized agricultural system (the "postindustrial," developed countries). They also include, particularly in Middle and South America and Africa, industrializing countries that are also heavily engaged in resource extraction as a service activity.

Map 42 Economic Output per Sector

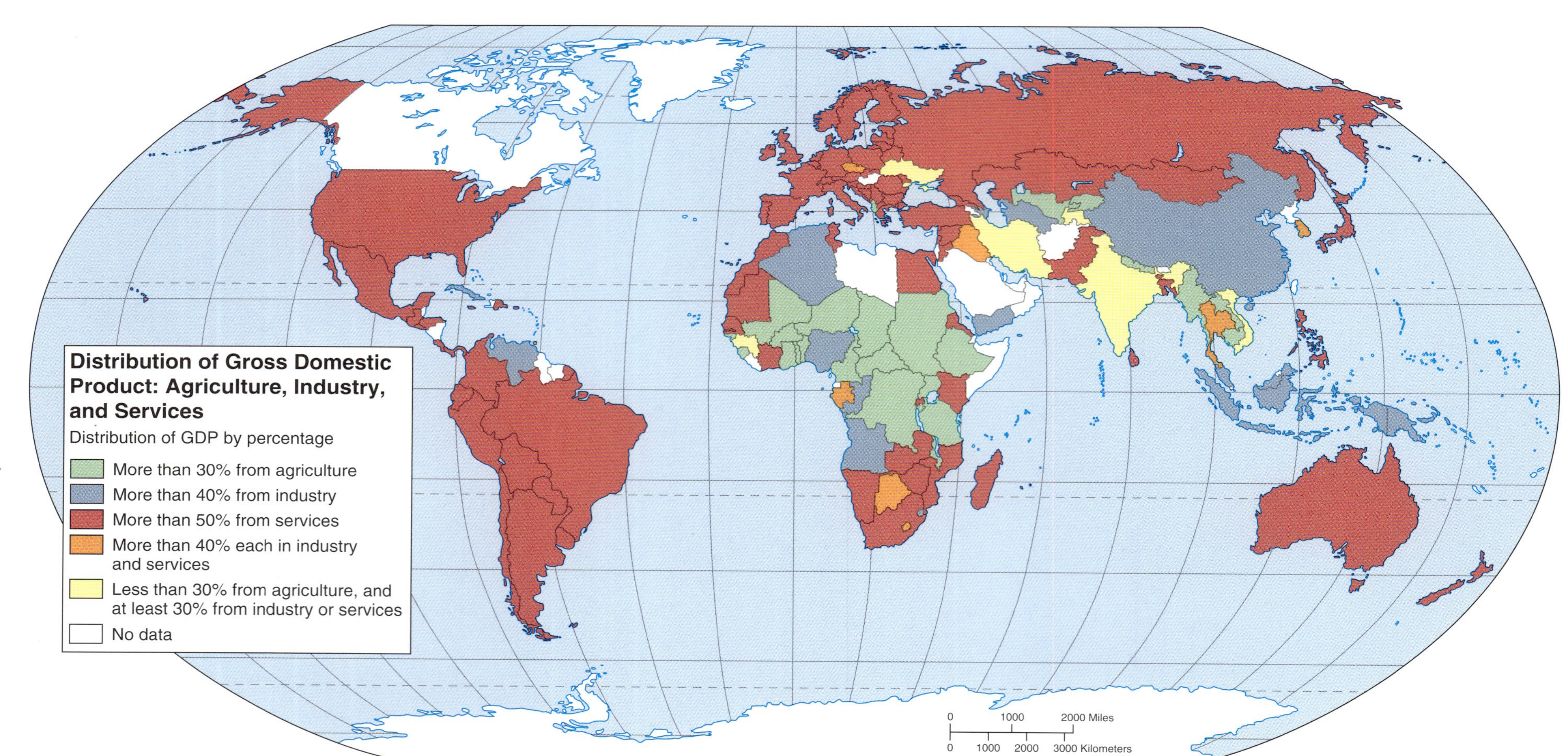
Distribution of Gross Domestic Product: Agriculture, Industry, and Services
Distribution of GDP by percentage
More than 30% from agriculture
More than 40% from industry
More than 50% from services
More than 40% each in industry and services
Less than 30% from agriculture, and at least 30% from industry or services
No data
0 1000 2000 Miles
0 1000 2000 3000 Kilometers

The percentage of the gross domestic product (the final output of goods and services produced by the domestic economy, including net exports of goods and nonfactor—nonlabor, noncapital—services) that is devoted to agricultural, industrial, and service activities is considered a good measure of the level of economic development. In general, countries with more than 40 percent of their GDP derived from agriculture are still in a *colonial dependency* economy—that is, raising agricultural goods primarily for the export market and dependent upon that market (usually the richer countries). Similarly, countries with more than 40 percent of GDP devoted to both agriculture and services often emphasize resource extractive (primarily mining and forestry) activities. These also tend to be *colonial dependency* countries, providing raw materials for foreign markets. Countries with more than 40 percent of their GDP obtained from industry are normally well along the path to economic development. Countries with more than half of their GDP based on service activities fall into two ends of the development spectrum. On the one hand are countries heavily dependent upon both extractive activities and tourism and other low-level service functions. On the other hand are countries that can properly be termed *postindustrial*: they have already passed through the industrial stage of their economic development and now rely less on the manufacture of products than on finance, research, communications, education, and other service-oriented activities.

Map 43 Agricultural Production Per Capita

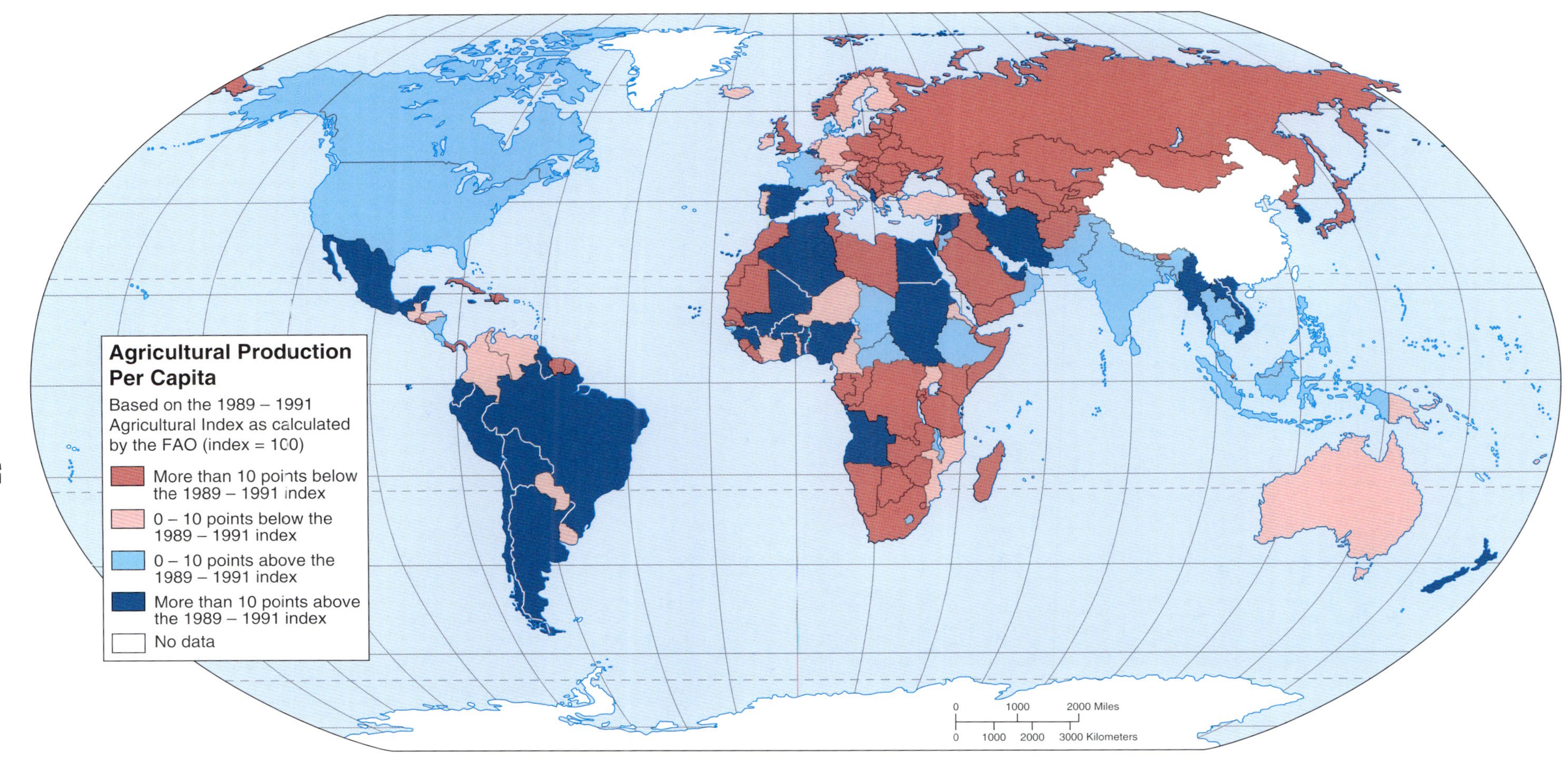

Agricultural Production Per Capita
Based on the 1989 – 1991 Agricultural Index as calculated by the FAO (index = 100)
More than 10 points below the 1989 – 1991 index
0 – 10 points below the 1989 – 1991 index
0 – 10 points above the 1989 – 1991 index
More than 10 points above the 1989 – 1991 index
No data
0 1000 2000 Miles
0 1000 2000 3000 Kilometers

Agricultural production includes the value of all crop and livestock products originating within a country for the base period of 1999–2001. The index value portrays the disposable output (after deductions for livestock feed and seed for planting) of a country's agriculture in comparison with the base period 1989–1991. Thus, the production values show not only the relative ability of countries to produce food but also show whether or not that ability has increased or decreased over a 10-year period. In general, global food production has kept up with or very slightly exceeded population growth. However, there are significant regional variations in the trend of food production keeping up with or surpassing population growth. For example, agricultural production in Africa and in Middle America has fallen, while production in South America, Asia, and Europe has risen. In the case of Africa, the drop in production reflects a population growing more rapidly than agricultural productivity. Where rapid increases in food production per capita exist (as in certain countries in South America, Asia, and Europe), most often the reason is the development of new agricultural technologies that have allowed food production to grow faster than population. In much of Asia, for example, the so-called Green Revolution of new, highly productive strains of wheat and rice made positive index values possible. Also in Asia, the cessation of major warfare allowed some countries (Cambodia, Laos, and Vietnam) to show substantial increases over the 1989–1991 index. In some cases, a drop in production per capita reflects government decisions to limit production in order to maintain higher prices for agricultural products. The United States and Japan fall into this category.

Map 44 Exports of Primary Products

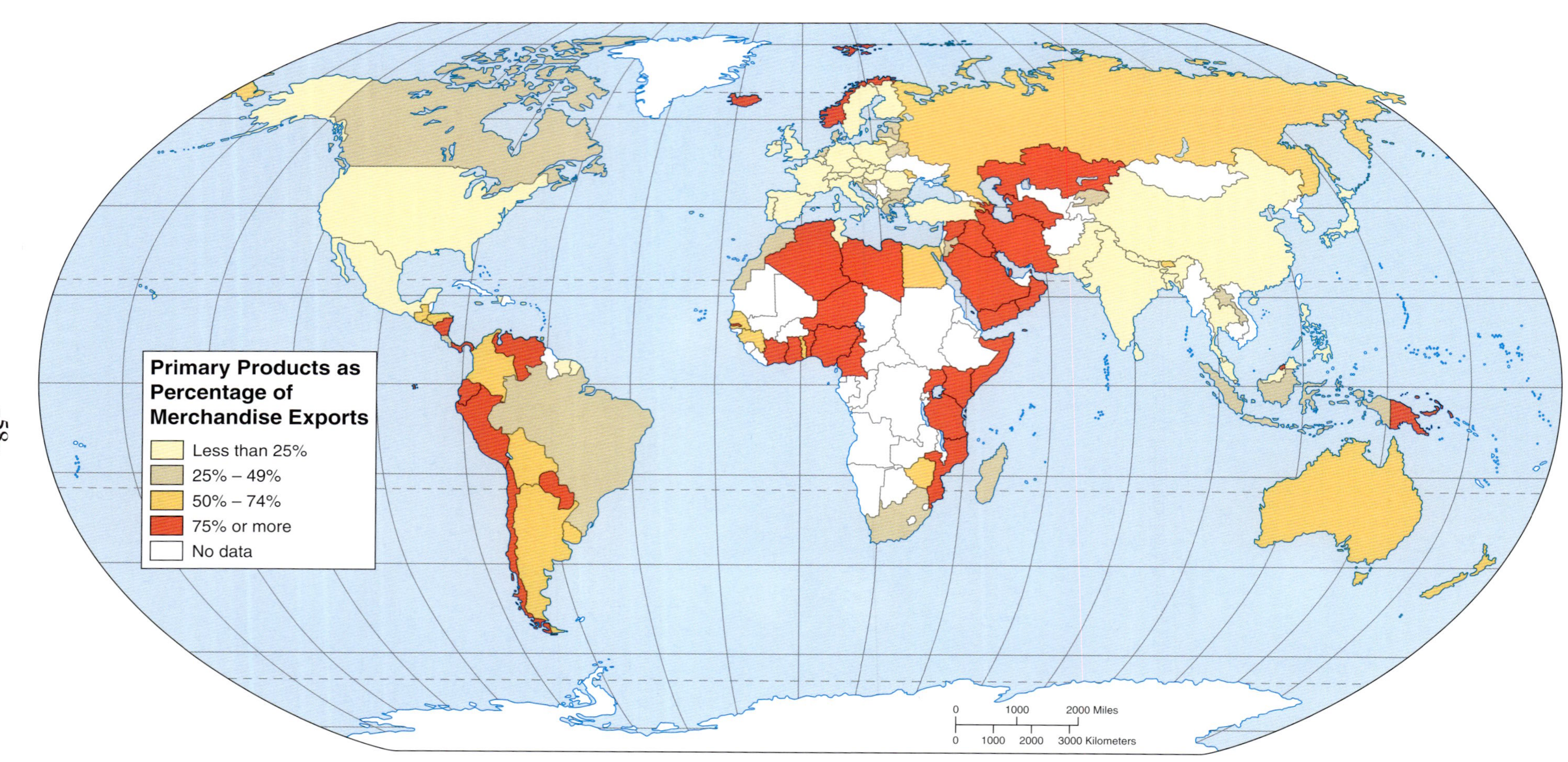
Primary Products as Percentage of Merchandise Exports
Less than 25%
25% – 49%
50% – 74%
75% or more
No data
0 1000 2000 Miles
0 1000 2000 3000 Kilometers

Primary products are those that require additional processing before they enter the consumer market: metallic ores that must be converted into metals and then into metal products such as automobiles or refrigerators; forest products such as timber that must be converted to lumber before they become suitable for construction purposes; and agricultural products that require further processing before being ready for human consumption. It is an axiom in international economics that the more a country relies on primary products for its export commodities, the more vulnerable its economy is to market fluctuations. Those countries with only primary products to export are hampered in their economic growth. A country dependent on only one or two products for export revenues is unprotected from economic shifts, particularly a changing market demand for its products. Imagine what would happen to the thriving economic status of the oil-exporting states of the Persian Gulf, for example, if an alternate source of cheap energy were found. A glance at this map, together with Map 57, shows that those countries with the lowest levels of economic development tend to be concentrated on primary products and, therefore, have economies that are especially vulnerable to economic instability.

Map 45 Dependence on Trade

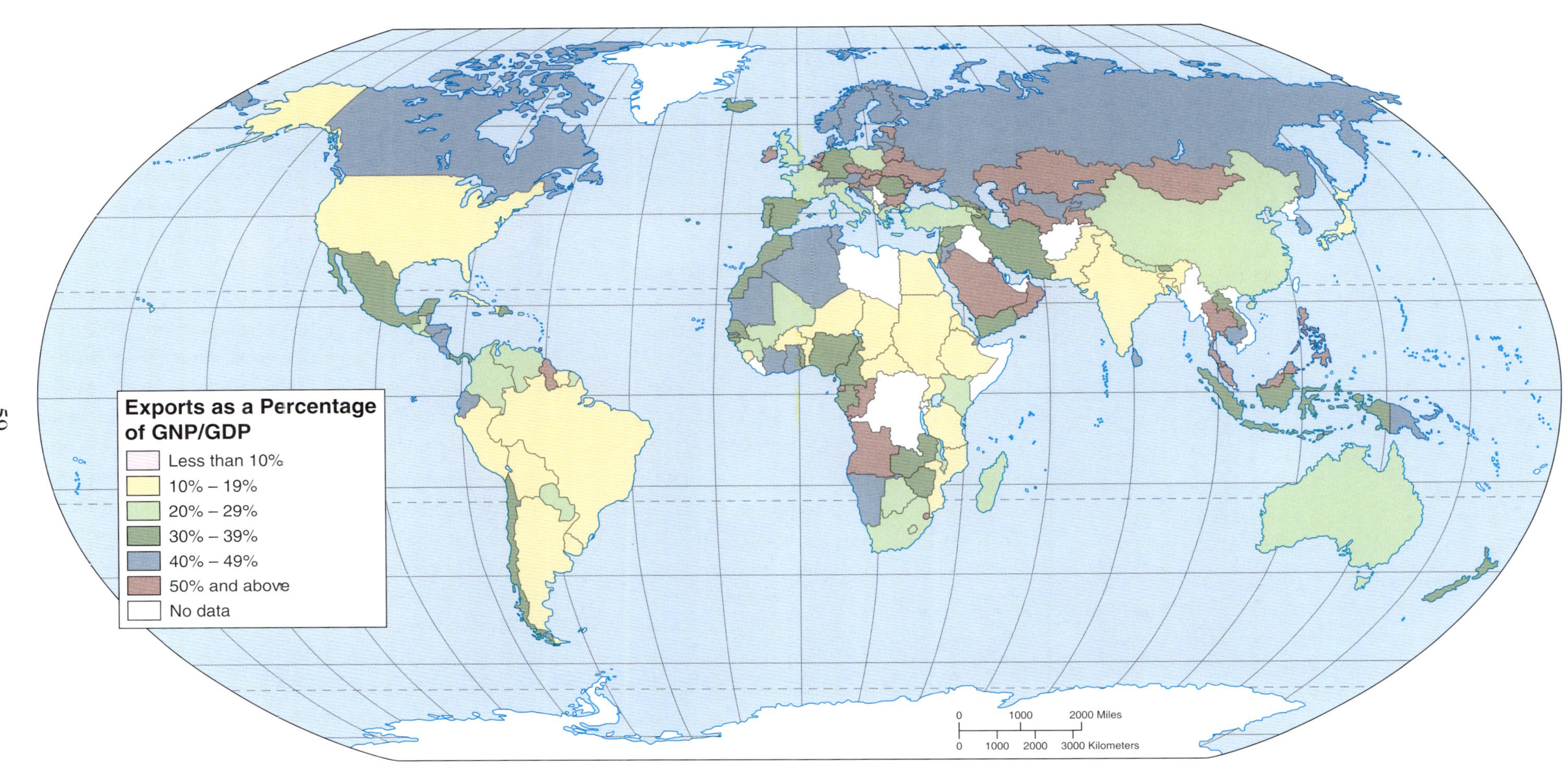

Exports as a Percentage of GNP/GDP
Less than 10%
10% – 19%
20% – 29%
30% – 39%
40% – 49%
50% and above
No data
0 1000 2000 Miles
0 1000 2000 3000 Kilometers

As the global economy becomes more and more a reality, the economic strength of virtually all countries is increasingly dependent upon trade. For many developing nations, with relatively abundant resources and limited industrial capacity, exports provide the primary base upon which their economies rest. Even countries like the United States, Japan, and Germany, with huge and diverse economies, depend on exports to generate a significant percentage of their employment and wealth. Without imports, many products that consumers want would be unavailable or more expensive; without exports, many jobs would be eliminated.

Map 46 The Indebtedness of States

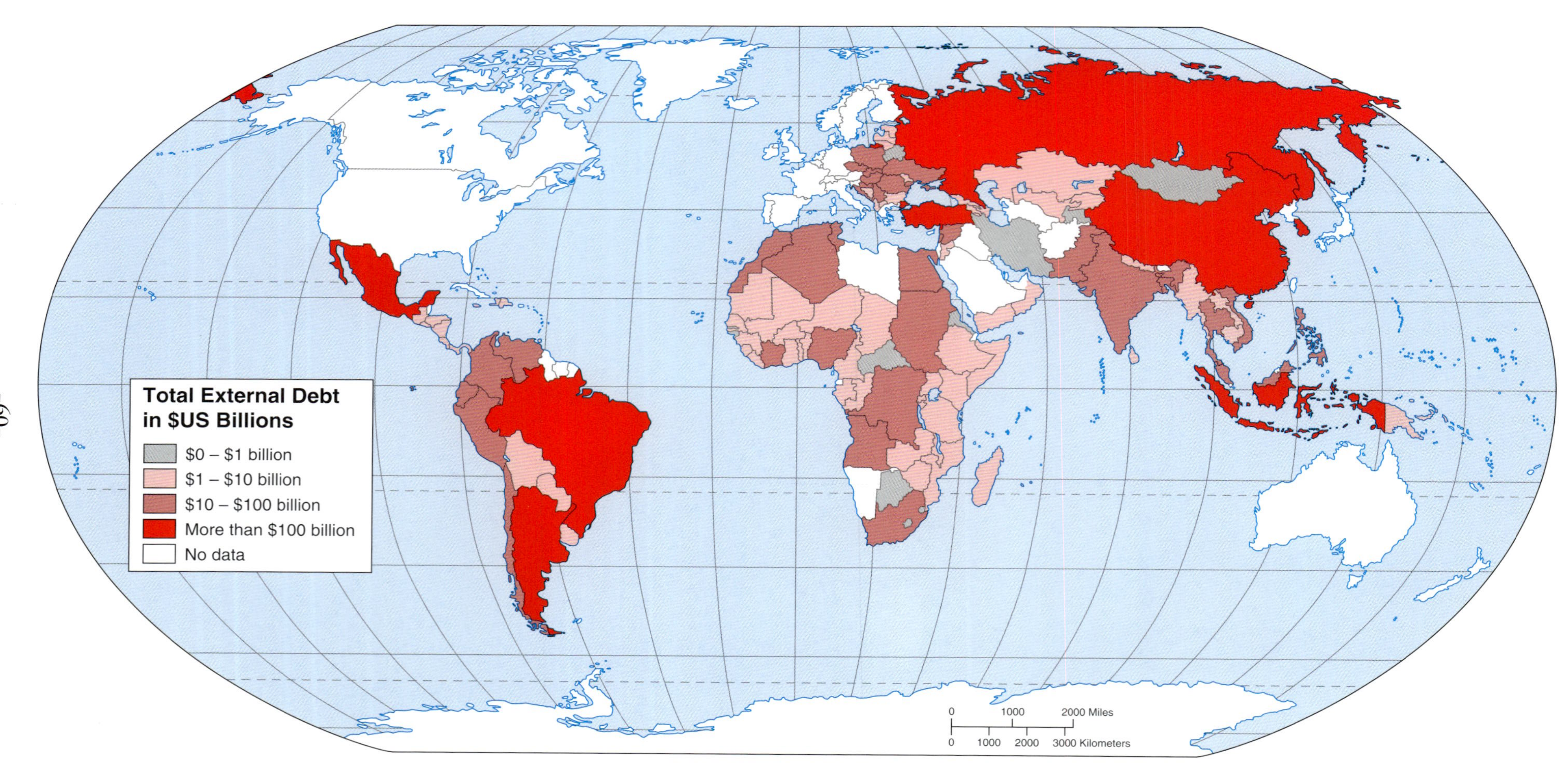

Total External Debt in $US Billions
$0 – $1 billion
$1 – $10 billion
$10 – $100 billion
More than $100 billion
No data
0 1000 2000 Miles
0 1000 2000 3000 Kilometers

Many governments spend more on a wide variety of services and activities than they collect in taxes and other revenues. In order to finance this deficit spending, governments borrow money—often from banks or other investors outside their country. Repayment of these debts, or even meeting interest payments on them, often means expending a country's export income—in other words, exchanging a country's wealth in production or, more often, resources, for debt service. Where the debt is external, as it is in most developing countries, governments become more open to outside influence in political as well as economic terms. Even internal debt service or repayment of monies owed to investors within a country gives financial establishments a measure of influence over government decisions. The amounts of debt shown on the map indicate the total external indebtedness of states.

Map 47 Global Flows of Investment Capital

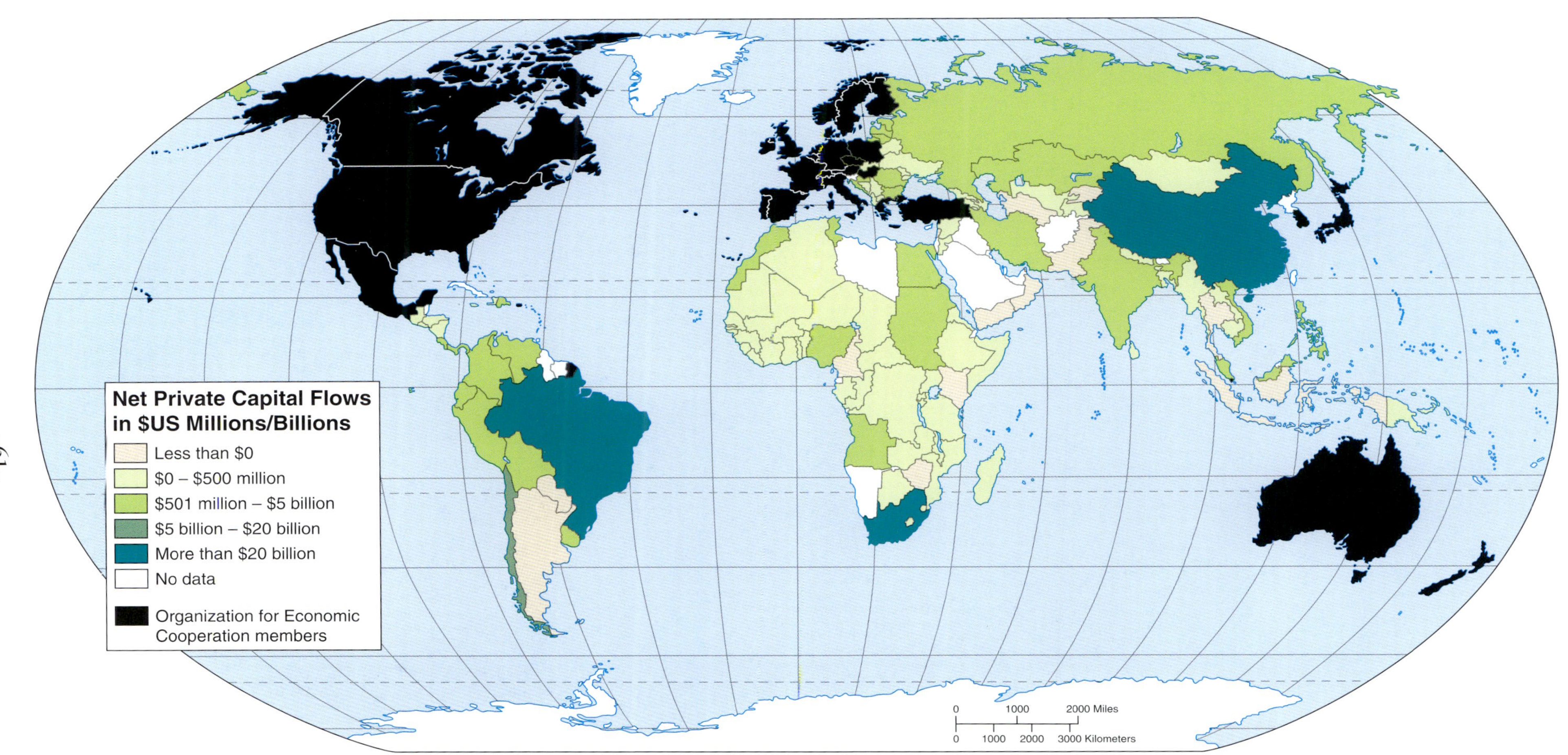
Net Private Capital Flows in $US Millions/Billions
Less than $0
$0 – $500 million
$501 million – $5 billion
$5 billion – $20 billion
More than $20 billion
No data
Organization for Economic Cooperation members
0 1000 2000 Miles
0 1000 2000 3000 Kilometers

International capital flows include private debt and nondebt flows from one country to another, shown on the map as flows into a country. Nearly all of the capital comes from those countries that are members of the Organization for Economic Cooperation and Development (OECD), shown in black on the map. Capital flows include commercial bank lending, bonds, other private credits, foreign direct investment, and portfolio investment. Most of these flows are indicators of the increasing influence developed countries exert over the developing economies. Foreign direct investment or FDI, for example, is a measure of the net inflow of investment monies used to acquire long-term management interest in businesses located somewhere other than in the economy of the investor. Usually this means the acquisition of at least 10 percent of the stock of a company by a foreign investor and is, then, a measure of what might be termed "economic colonialism": control of a region's economy by foreign investors that could, in the world of the future, be as significant as colonial political control was in the past. International capital flows have increased greatly in the last decade as the result of the increasing liberalization of developing countries, the strong economic growth exhibited by many developing countries, and the falling costs and increased efficiency of communication and transportation services.

Map 48 Central Government Expenditures Per Capita

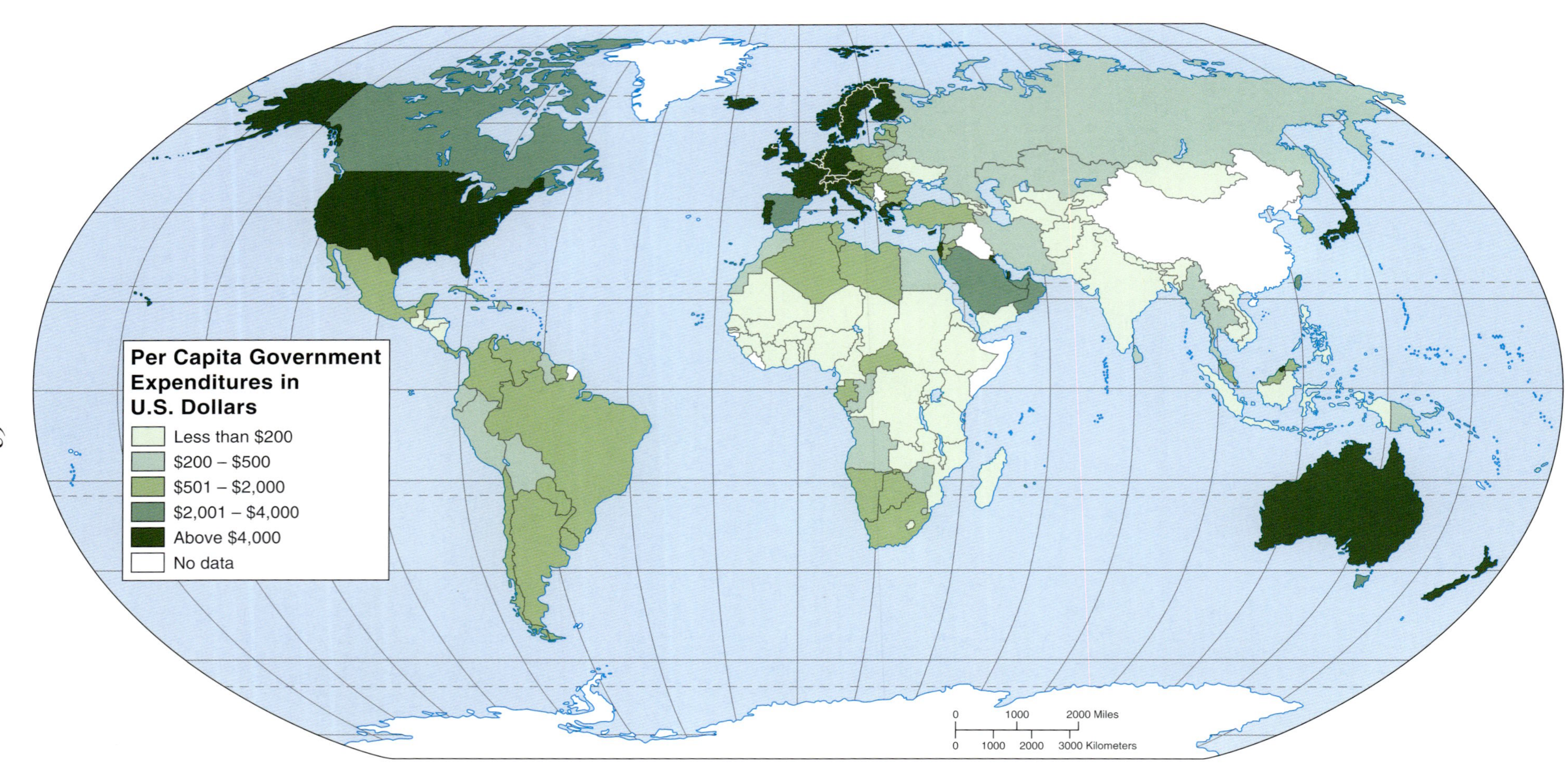

Per Capita Government Expenditures in U.S. Dollars
Less than $200
$200 – $500
$501 – $2,000
$2,001 – $4,000
Above $4,000
No data
0 1000 2000 Miles
0 1000 2000 3000 Kilometers

The amount of money that the central government of a country spends upon a variety of essential governmental functions is a measure of relative economic development, particularly when it is viewed on a per-person basis. These functions include such governmental responsibilities as agriculture, communications, culture, defense, education, fishing and hunting, health, housing, recreation, religion, social security, transportation, and welfare. Generally, the higher the level of economic development, the greater the per capita expenditures on these services. However, the data do mask some internal variations. For example, countries that spend 20 percent or more of their central government expenditures on defense will often show up in the more developed category when, in fact, all that the figures really show is that a disproportionate amount of the money available to the government is devoted to purchasing armaments and maintaining a large standing military force. Thus, the fact that Libya spends more than the average for Africa does not suggest that the average Libyan is much better off than the average Tanzanian. Nevertheless, this map—particularly when compared with Map 51, Energy Consumption Per Capita—does provide a reasonable approximation of economic development levels.

Map 49 The Relative Wealth of Nations: Purchasing Power Parity

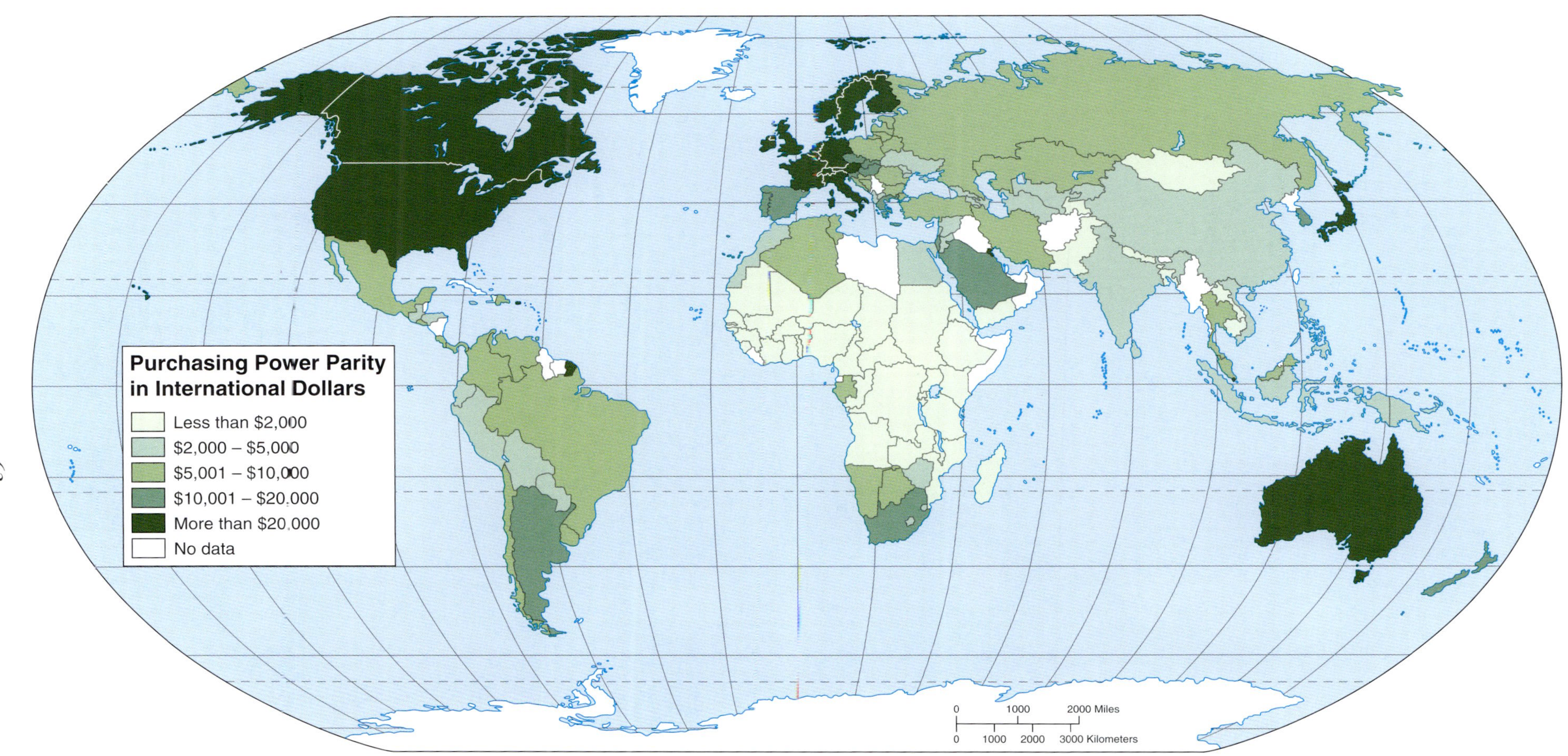

Purchasing Power Parity in International Dollars
Less than $2,000
$2,000 – $5,000
$5,001 – $10,000
$10,001 – $20,000
More than $20,000
No data
0 1000 2000 Miles
0 1000 2000 3000 Kilometers

Of all the economic measures that separate the "haves" from the "have-nots," perhaps per capita Purchasing Power Parity (PPP) is the most meaningful. While per capita figures can mask significant uneven distributions within a country, they are generally useful for demonstrating important differences between countries. Per capita GNP and GDP (Cross Domestic Product) figures, and even per capita income, have the limitation of seldom reflecting the true purchasing power of a country's currency at home. In order to get around this limitation, international economists seeking to compare national currencies developed the PPP measure, which shows the level of goods and services that holders of a country's money can acquire locally. By converting all currencies to the "international dollar," the World Bank and other organizations using PPP can now show more truly comparative values, since the new currency value shows the number of units of a country's currency required to buy the same quantity of goods and services in the local market as one U.S. dollar would buy in an average country. The use of PPP currency values can alter the perceptions about a country's true comparative position in the world economy. More than per capita income figures, PPP provides a valid measurement of the ability of a country's population to provide for itself the things that people in the developed world take for granted: adequate food, shelter, clothing, education, and access to medical care. A glance at the map shows a clear-cut demarcation between temperate and tropical zones, with most of the countries with a PPP above $5,000 in the midlatitude zones and most of those with lower PPPs in the tropical and equatorial regions. Where exceptions to this pattern occur, they usually stem from a tremendous maldistribution of wealth among a country's population.

Map 50 Energy Production Per Capita

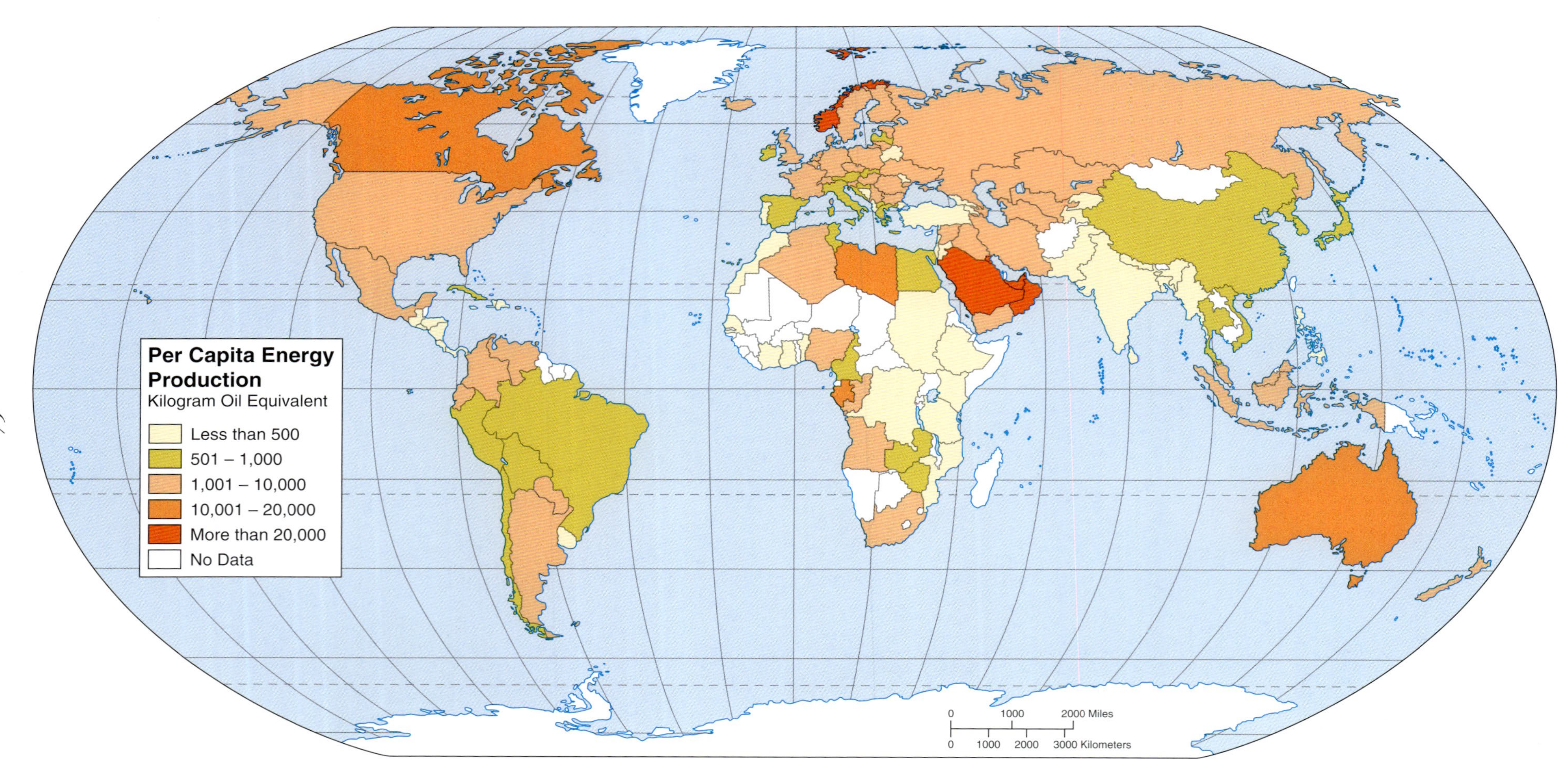
Per Capita Energy Production
Kilogram Oil Equivalent
Less than 500
501 – 1,000
1,001 – 10,000
10,001 – 20,000
More than 20,000
No Data
0 1000 2000 Miles
0 1000 2000 3000 Kilometers

Energy production per capita is a measure of the availability of mechanical energy to assist people in their work. This map shows the amount of all kinds of energy—solid fuel (primarily coal), liquid fuel (primarily petroleum), natural gas, geothermal, wind, solar, hydroelectric, nuclear, waste recycling, and indigenous heat pumps—produced per person in each country. With some exceptions, wealthier countries produce more energy per capita than poor ones. Countries such as Japan and many European states rank among the world's wealthiest, but are energy-poor and produce relatively little of their own energy. They have the ability, however, to pay for imports. On the other hand, countries such as those of the Persian Gulf or the oil-producing states of Central and South America may rank relatively low on the scale of economic development but rank high as producers of energy. In many poor countries, especially in Central and South America, Africa, South Asia, and East Asia, large proportions of energy come from traditional fuels such as firewood and animal dung. Indeed for many in the developing world, the real energy crisis is a shortage of wood for cooking and heating.

Map 51 Energy Consumption Per Capita

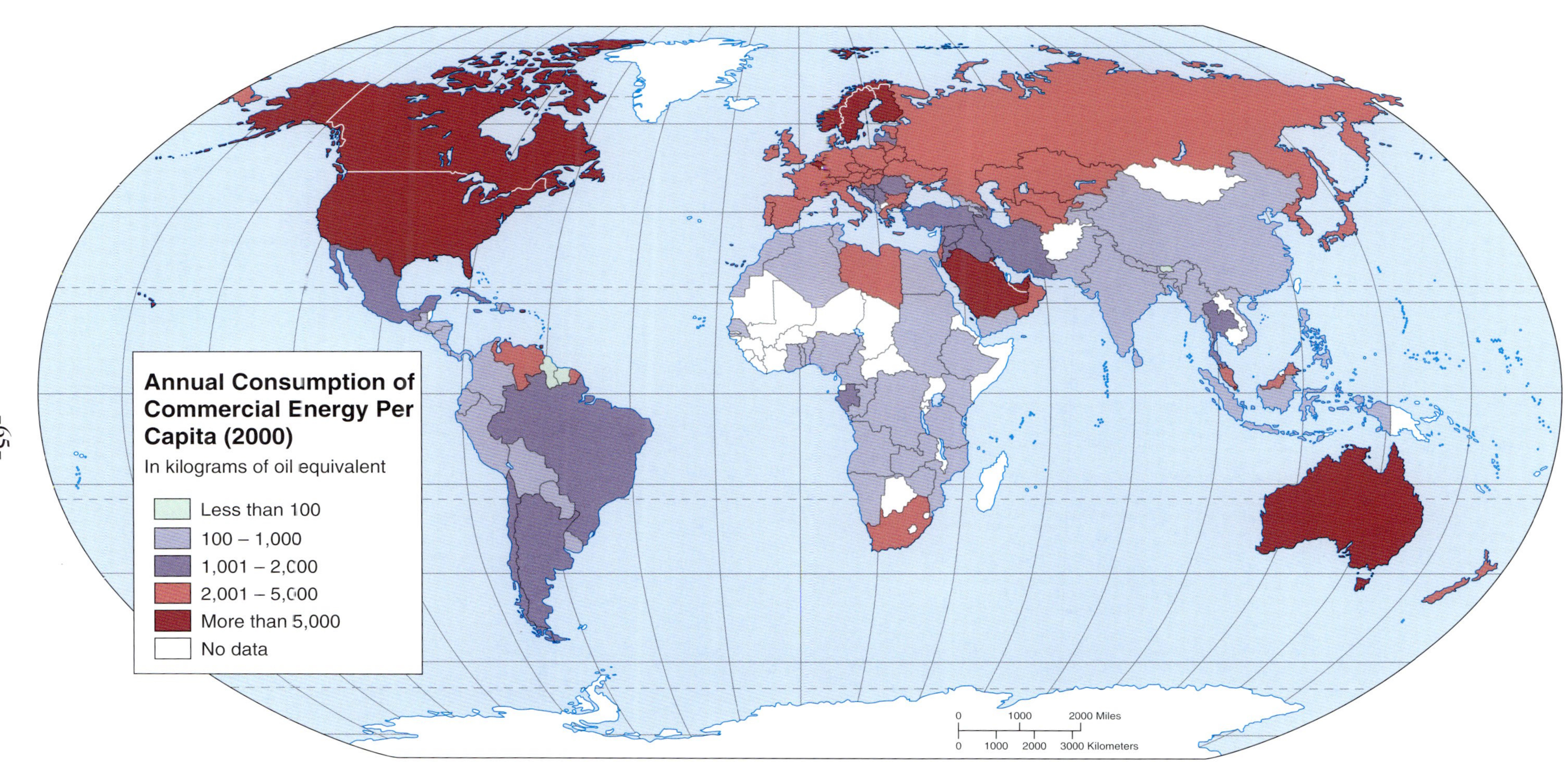
Annual Consumption of Commercial Energy Per Capita (2000)
In kilograms of oil equivalent
Less than 100
100 – 1,000
1,001 – 2,000
2,001 – 5,000
More than 5,000
No data
0 1000 2000 Miles
0 1000 2000 3000 Kilometers

Of all the quantitative measures of economic well-being, energy consumption per capita may be the most expressive. All of the countries defined by the World Bank as having high incomes consume at least 100 gigajoules of commercial energy (the equivalent of about 3.5 metric tons of coal) per person per year, with some, such as the United States and Canada, having consumption rates in the 300 gigajoule range (the equivalent of more than 10 metric tons of coal per person per year). With the exception of the oil-rich Persian Gulf states, where consumption figures include the costly "burning off" of excess energy in the form of natural gas flares at wellheads, most of the highest-consuming countries are in the Northern Hemisphere, concentrated in North America and Western Europe. At the other end of the scale are low-income countries, whose consumption rates are often less than 1 percent of those of the United States and other high consumers. These figures do not, of course, include the consumption of noncommercial energy—the traditional fuels of firewood, animal dung, and other organic matter—widely used in the less developed parts of the world.

Map 52 Energy Dependency

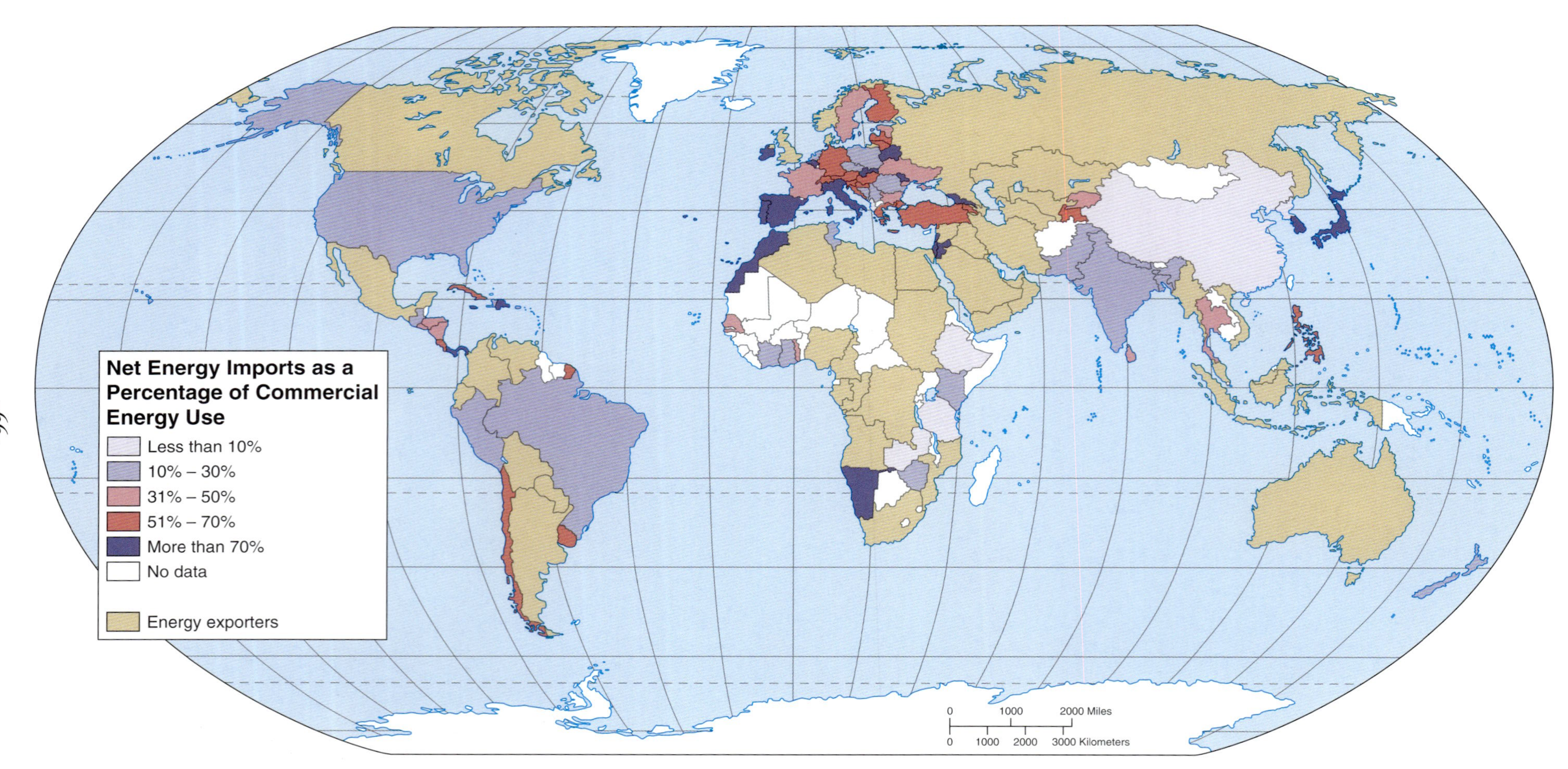
Net Energy Imports as a Percentage of Commercial Energy Use
Less than 10%
10% – 30%
31% – 50%
51% – 70%
More than 70%
No data
Energy exporters
0 1000 2000 Miles
0 1000 2000 3000 Kilometers

The patterns on the map show dependence on commercial energy before transformation to other end-use fuels such as electricity or refined petroleum products; energy from traditional sources such as fuelwood or dried animal dung is not included. Energy dependency is the difference between domestic consumption and domestic production of commercial energy and is most often expressed as a net energy import or export. A few of the world's countries are net exporters of energy; most are importers. The growth in global commercial energy use over the last decade indicates growth in the modern sectors of the economy—industry, transportation, and urbanization—particularly in the lesser developed countries. Still, the primary consumers of energy—and those having the greatest dependence on foreign sources of energy—are the more highly developed countries of Europe, North America, and Japan.

Map 53 Flows of Oil

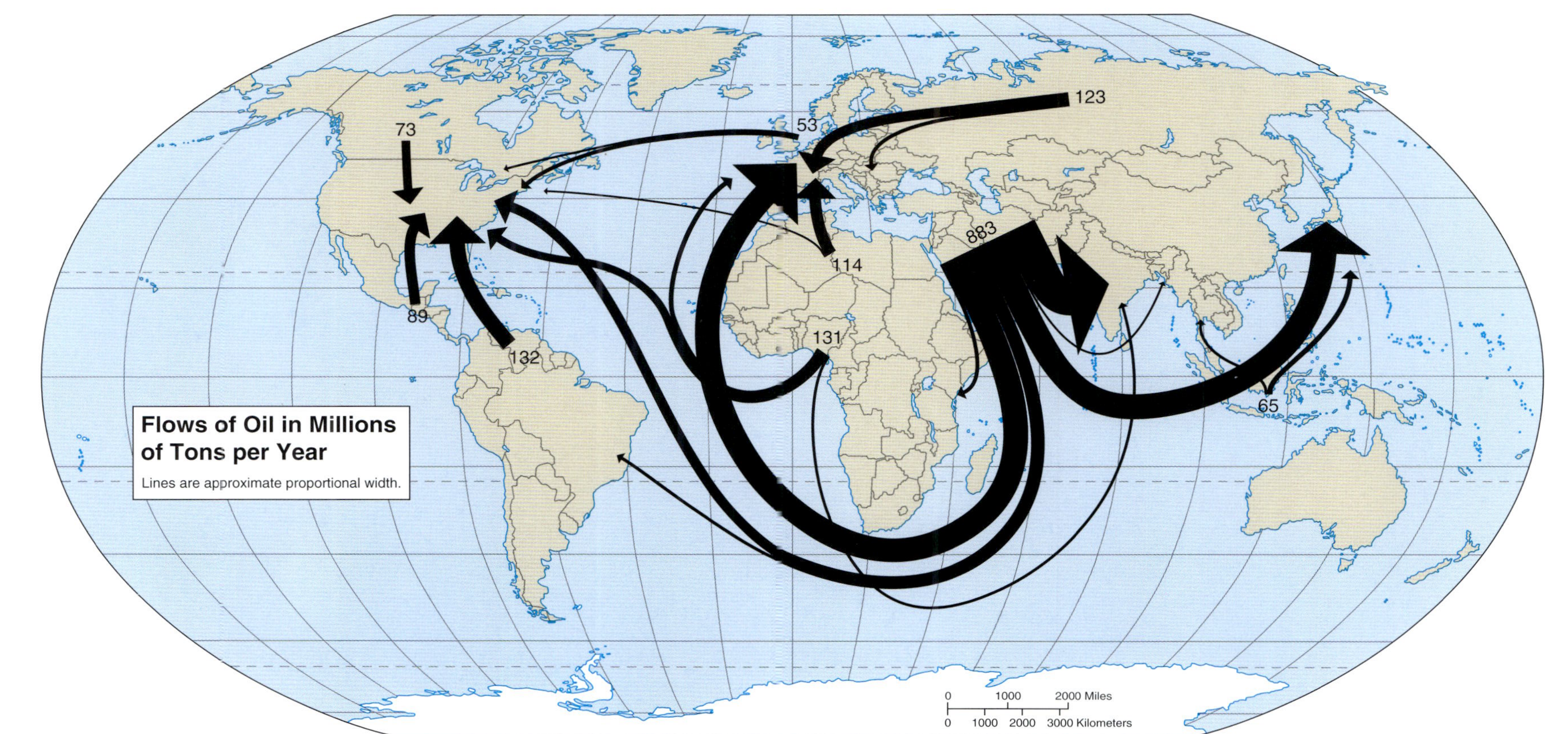
Flows of Oil in Millions of Tons per Year
Lines are approximate proportional width.
123
73
53
883
114
89
131
132
65
0 1000 2000 Miles
0 1000 2000 3000 Kilometers

The pattern of oil movements from producing region to consuming region is one of the dominant facts of contemporary international maritime trade. Supertankers carry a million tons of crude oil and charge rates in excess of $0.10 per ton per mile, making the transportation of oil not only a necessity for the world's energy-hungry countries, but also an enormously profitable proposition. One of the major negatives of these massive oil flows is the damage done to the oceanic ecosystems—not just from the well-publicized and dramatic events like the wrecking of the *Exxon Valdez* but from the incalculable amounts of oil from leakage, scrubbings, purgings, and so on, which are a part of the oil transport technology. It is clear from the map that the primary recipients of these oil flows are the world's most highly developed economies.

Part V

Global Patterns of Environmental Disturbance

Map 54 Global Air Pollution: Sources and Wind Currents

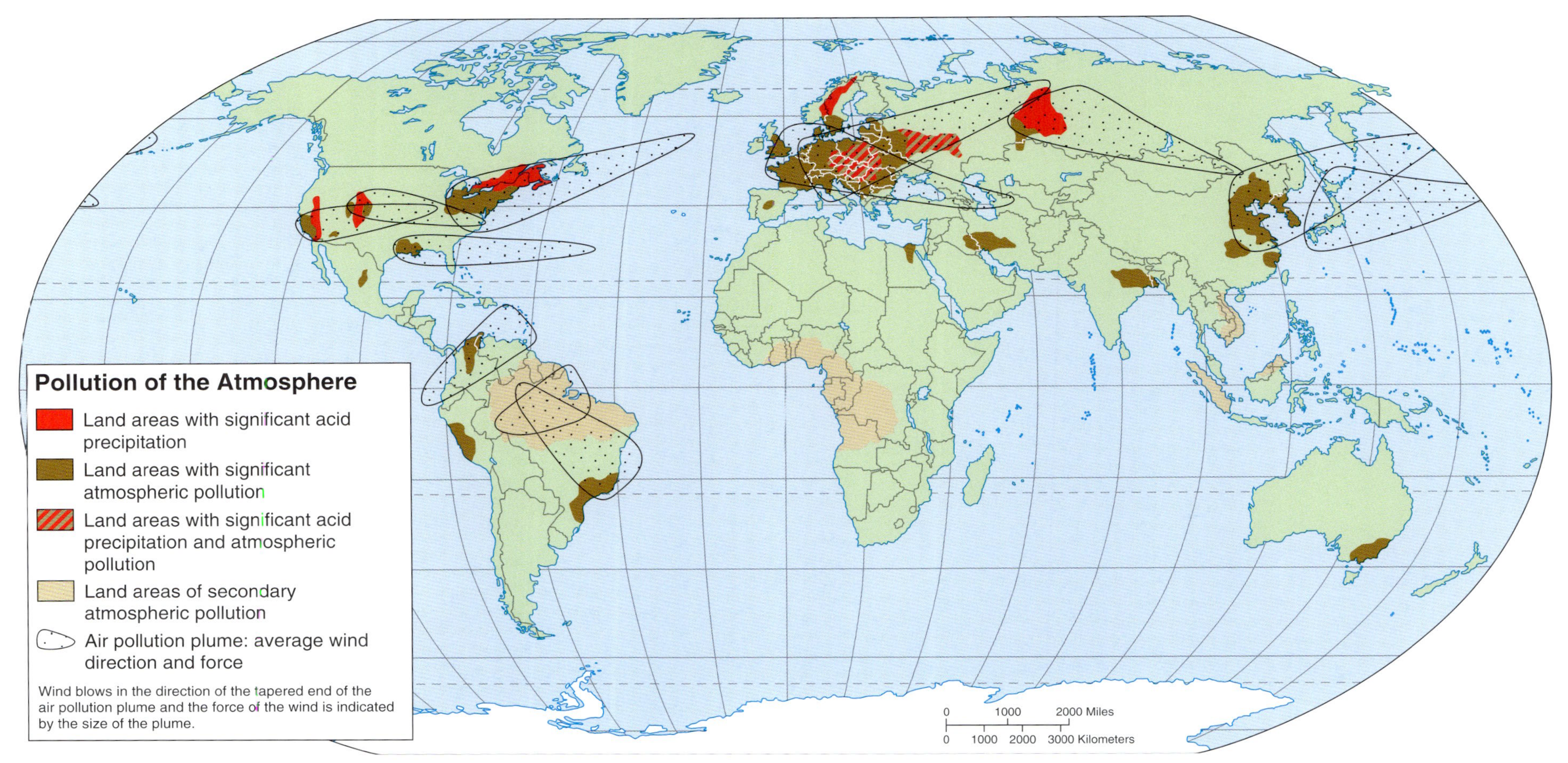

Pollution of the Atmosphere
Land areas with significant acid precipitation
Land areas with significant atmospheric pollution
Land areas with significant acid precipitation and atmospheric pollution
Land areas of secondary atmospheric pollution
Air pollution plume: average wind direction and force
Wind blows in the direction of the tapered end of the air pollution plume and the force of the wind is indicated by the size of the plume.
0 1000 2000 Miles
0 1000 2000 3000 Kilometers

Almost all processes of physical geography begin and end with the flows of energy and matter among land, sea, and air. Because of the primacy of the atmosphere in this exchange system, air pollution is potentially one of the most dangerous human modifications in environmental systems. Pollutants such as various oxides of nitrogen or sulfur cause the development of acid precipitation, which damages soil, vegetation, and wildlife and fish. Air pollution in the form of smog is often dangerous for human health. And most atmospheric scientists believe that the efficiency of the atmosphere in retaining heat—the so-called greenhouse effect—is being enhanced by increased carbon dioxide, methane, and other gases produced by agricultural and industrial activities. The result, they fear, will be a period of global warming that will dramatically alter climates in all parts of the world.

Map 55 The Acid Deposition Problem: Air, Water, Soil

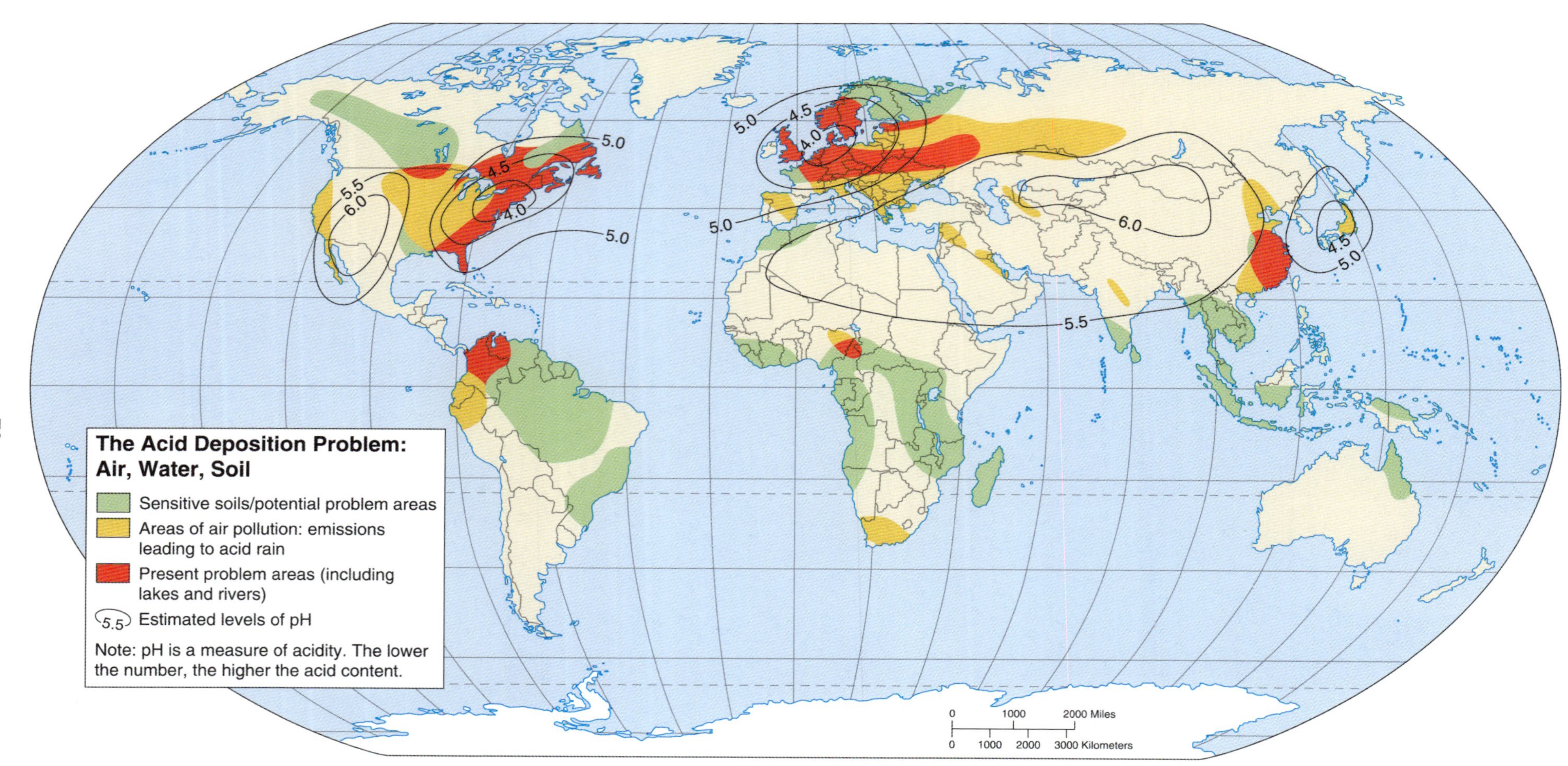

The Acid Deposition Problem: Air, Water, Soil
Sensitive soils/potential problem areas
Areas of air pollution: emissions leading to acid rain
Present problem areas (including lakes and rivers)
5.5 Estimated levels of pH
Note: pH is a measure of acidity. The lower the number, the higher the acid content.
5.0
4.5
4.0
5.5
6.0
0 1000 2000 Miles
0 1000 2000 3000 Kilometers

The term "acid precipitation" refers to increasing levels of acidity in snowfall and rainfall caused by atmospheric pollution. Oxides of nitrogen and sulfur resulting from incomplete combustion of fossil fuels (coal, oil, and natural gas) combine with water vapor in the atmosphere to produce weak acids that then "precipitate" or fall along with water or ice crystals. Some atmospheric acids formed by this process are known as "dry-acid" precipitates and they too will fall to earth, although not necessarily along with rain or snow. In some areas of the world, the increased acidity of streams and lakes stemming from high levels of acid precipitation or dry acid fallout has damaged or destroyed aquatic life. Acid precipitation and dry acid fallout also harms soil systems and vegetation, producing a characteristic burned appearance in forests that lends the same quality to landscapes that forest fires would. The region most dramatically impacted by acid precipitation is Central Europe where decades of destructive environmental practices, including the burning of high sulfur coal for commercial, industrial, and residential purposes, has produced the destruction of hundreds of thousands of acres of woodlands—a phenomenon described by the German foresters who began their study of the area following the lifting of the Iron Curtain as "Waldsterben": Forest Death.

Map 56 Major Polluters and Common Pollutants

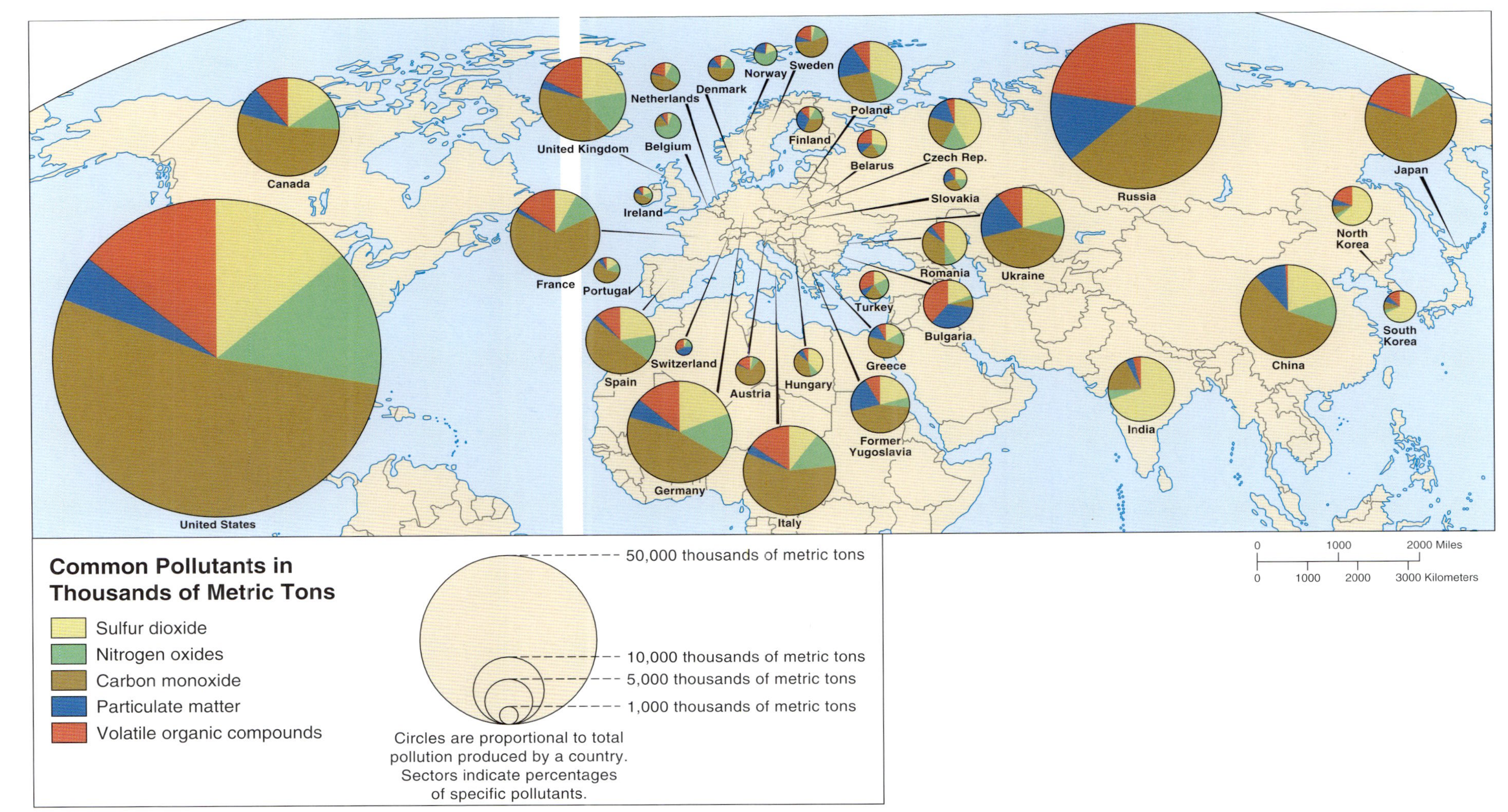
United States
Canada
United Kingdom
Netherlands
Belgium
Denmark
Norway
Sweden
Ireland
France
Portugal
Spain
Switzerland
Germany
Austria
Italy
Hungary
Poland
Finland
Belarus
Czech Rep.
Slovakia
Romania
Turkey
Bulgaria
Greece
Former Yugoslavia
Ukraine
Russia
India
China
North Korea
South Korea
Japan
Common Pollutants in Thousands of Metric Tons
Sulfur dioxide
Nitrogen oxides
Carbon monoxide
Particulate matter
Volatile organic compounds
50,000 thousands of metric tons
10,000 thousands of metric tons
5,000 thousands of metric tons
1,000 thousands of metric tons
Circles are proportional to total pollution produced by a country. Sectors indicate percentages of specific pollutants.
0 1000 2000 Miles
0 1000 2000 3000 Kilometers

More than 90 percent of the world's total of anthropogenic (human-generated) air pollutants come from the heavily populated industrial regions of North America, Europe, South Asia (primarily in India), and East Asia (mainly in China, Japan, and the two Koreas). This map shows the origins of the five most common pollutants: sulfur dioxide, nitrogen oxide, carbon monoxide, particulate matter, and volatile organic compounds. These substances are produced both by industry and by the combustion of fossil fuels that generate electricity and power trains, planes, automobiles, buses, and trucks. In addition to combining with other components of the atmosphere and with one another to produce smog, they are the chief ingredients in acid accumulations in the atmosphere, which ultimately result in acid deposition, either as acid precipitation or dry acid fallout. Like other forms of pollutants, these air pollutants do not recognize political boundaries, and regions downwind of major polluters receive large quantities of pollutants from areas over which they often have no control.

Map 57 Global Carbon Dioxide Emissions

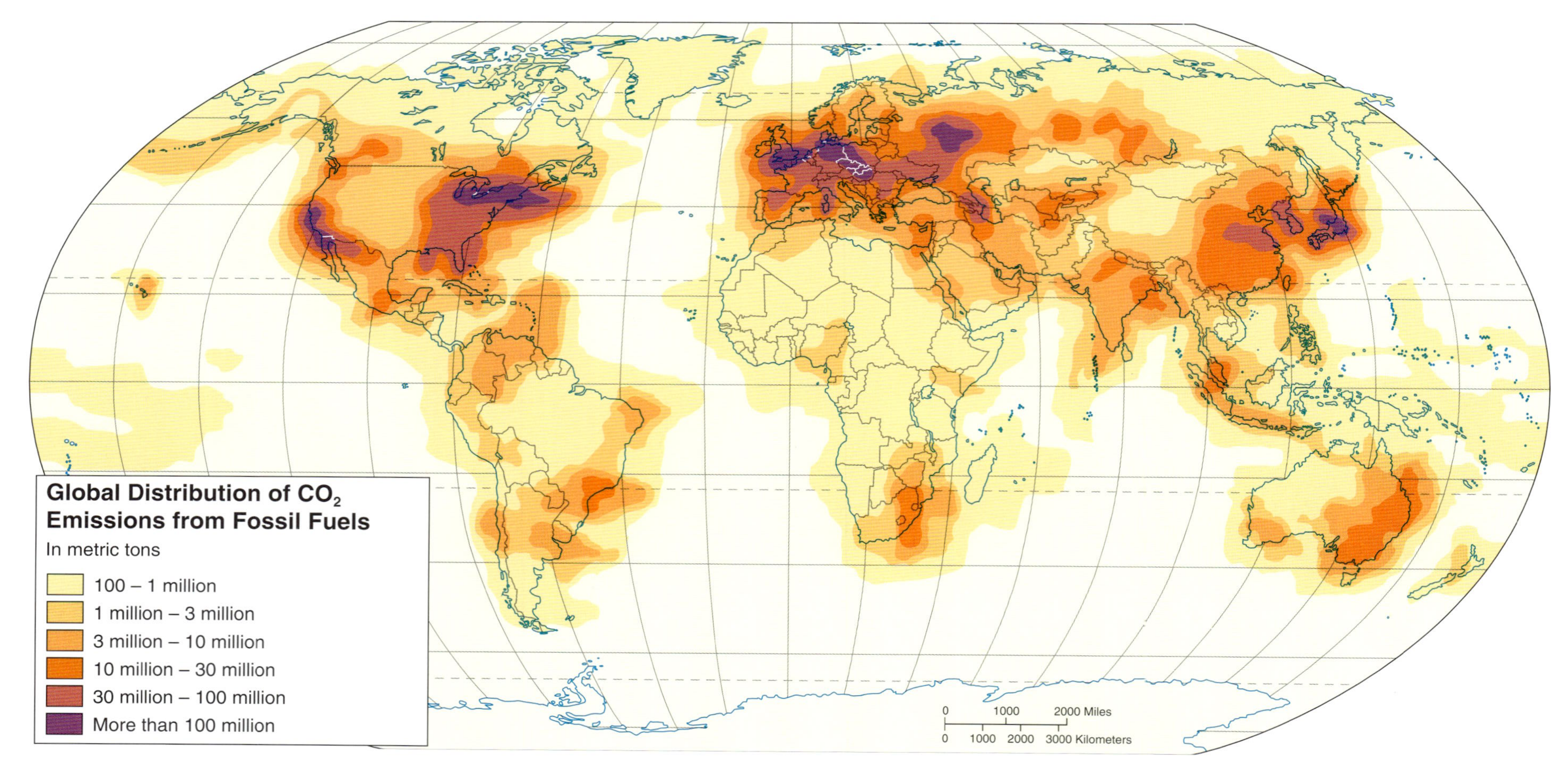

Global Distribution of CO_2 Emissions from Fossil Fuels
In metric tons
100 – 1 million
1 million – 3 million
3 million – 10 million
10 million – 30 million
30 million – 100 million
More than 100 million
0 1000 2000 Miles
0 1000 2000 3000 Kilometers

One of the most important components of the atmosphere is the gas carbon dioxide (CO^2), the byproduct of animal respiration, decomposition, and combustion. During the past 200 years, atmospheric CO^2 has risen dramatically, largely as the result of the tremendous increase in fossil fuel combustion brought on by the industrialization of the world's economy and the burning and clearing of forests by the expansion of farming. While CO^2 by itself is relatively harmless, it is an important "greenhouse gas." The gases in the atmosphere act like the panes of glass in a greenhouse roof, allowing light in but preventing heat from escaping. The greenhouse capacity of the atmosphere is crucial for organic life and is a purely natural component of the global energy cycle. But too much CO^2 and other greenhouse gases such as methane could cause the earth's atmosphere to warm up too much, producing the global warming that atmos-pheric scientists are concerned about. Researchers estimate that if greenhouse gases such as CO^2 continue to increase at their present rates, the earth's mean temperature could rise between 1.5 and 4.5 degrees Celsius by the middle of the next century. Such a rise in global temperatures would produce massive alterations in the world's climate patterns.

Map 58 Potential Global Temperature Change

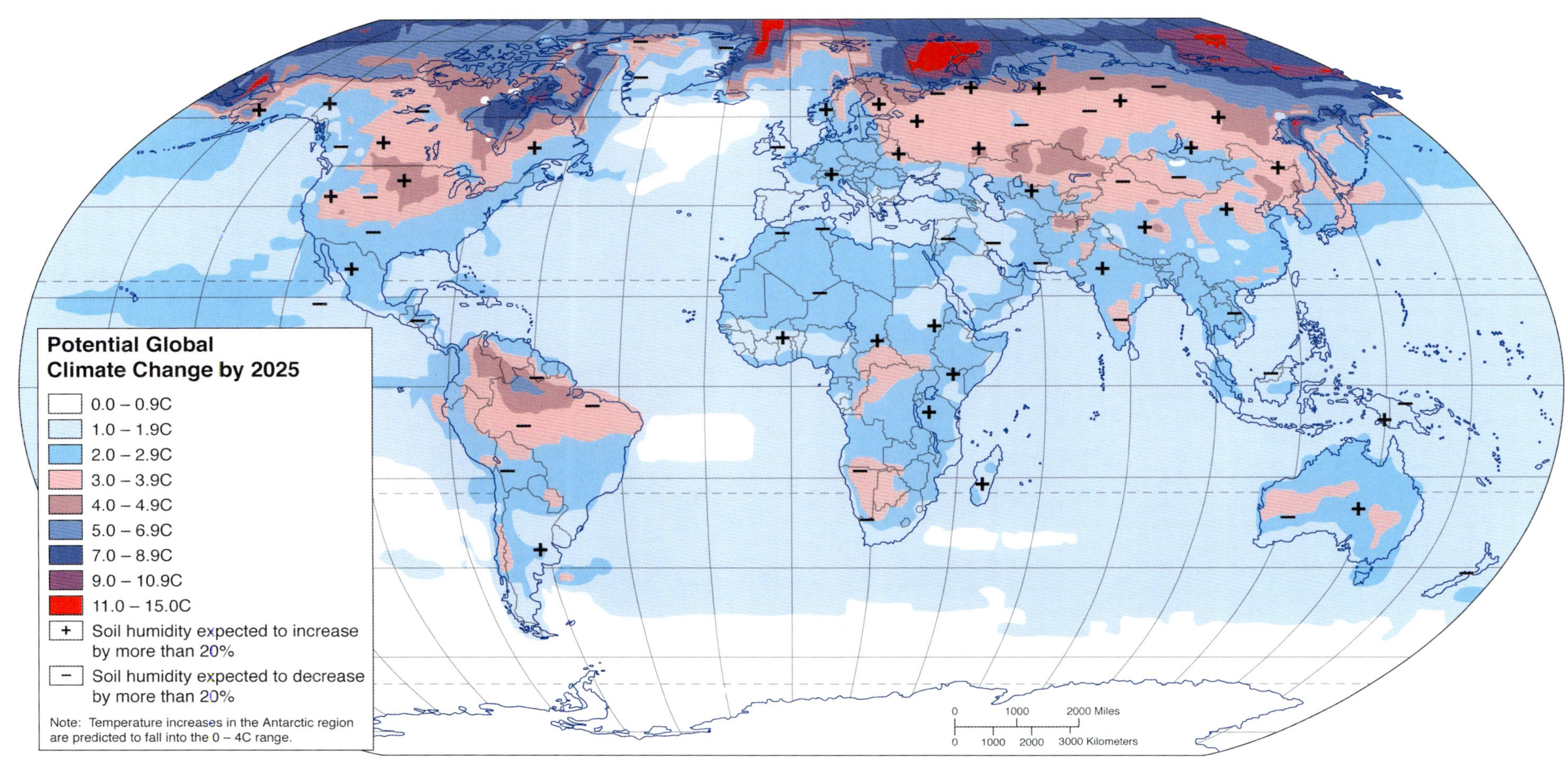

Potential Global
Climate Change by 2025
0.0 – 0.9C
1.0 – 1.9C
2.0 – 2.9C
3.0 – 3.9C
4.0 – 4.9C
5.0 – 6.9C
7.0 – 8.9C
9.0 – 10.9C
11.0 – 15.0C
+ Soil humidity expected to increase by more than 20%
− Soil humidity expected to decrease by more than 20%
Note: Temperature increases in the Antarctic region are predicted to fall into the 0 – 4C range.
0 1000 2000 Miles
0 1000 2000 3000 Kilometers

According to atmospheric scientists, one of the major problems of the twenty-first century will be "global warming," produced as the atmosphere's natural ability to trap and retain heat is enhanced by increased percentages of carbon dioxide, methane, chlorinated fluorocarbons or "CFCs," and other "greenhouse gases" in the earth's atmosphere. Computer models based on atmospheric percentages of carbon dioxide resulting from present use of fossil fuels show that warming is not just a possibility but a probability. Increased temperatures would cause precipitation patterns to alter significantly as well and would produce a number of other harmful effects, including a rise in the level of the world's oceans that could flood most coastal cities. International conferences on the topic of the enhanced greenhouse effect have resulted in several international agreements to reduce the emission of carbon dioxide or to maintain it at present levels. Unfortunately, the solution is not that simple since reduction of carbon dioxide emissions is, in the short run, expensive—particularly as long as the world's energy systems continue to be based on fossil fuels. Chief among the countries that could be hit by serious international mandates to reduce emissions are those highest on the development scale who use the highest levels of fossil fuels and, therefore, produce the highest emissions, and those on the lowest end of the development scale whose efforts to industrialize could be severely impeded by the more expensive energy systems that would replace fossil fuels.

Map 59 Water Resources: Availability of Renewable Water Per Capita

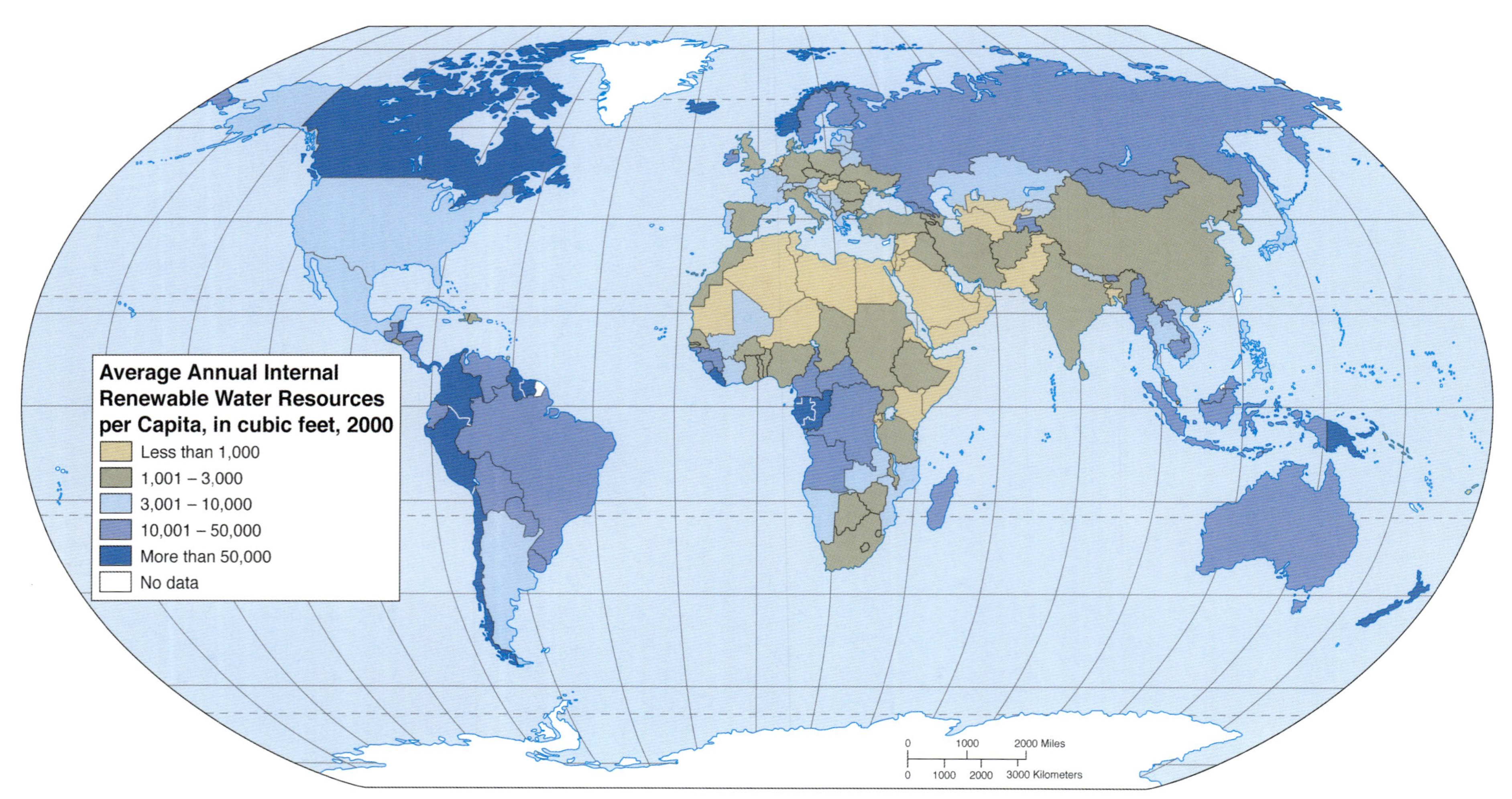
Average Annual Internal Renewable Water Resources per Capita, in cubic feet, 2000
Less than 1,000
1,001 – 3,000
3,001 – 10,000
10,001 – 50,000
More than 50,000
No data
0 1000 2000 Miles
0 1000 2000 3000 Kilometers

Renewable water resources are usually defined as the total water available from streams and rivers (including flows from other countries), ponds and lakes, and groundwater storage or aquifers. Not included in the total of renewable water would be water that comes from such nonrenewable sources as desalinization plants or melted icebergs. While the concept of renewable or flow resources is a traditional one in resource management, in fact, few resources, including water, are truly renewable when their use is excessive. The water resources shown here are indications of that principle. A country like the United States possesses truly enormous quantities of water. But the United States also uses enormous quantities of water. The result is that, largely because of excessive use, the availability of renewable water is much less than in many other parts of the world where the total supply of water is significantly less.

Map 60 Water Resources: Annual Withdrawal Per Capita

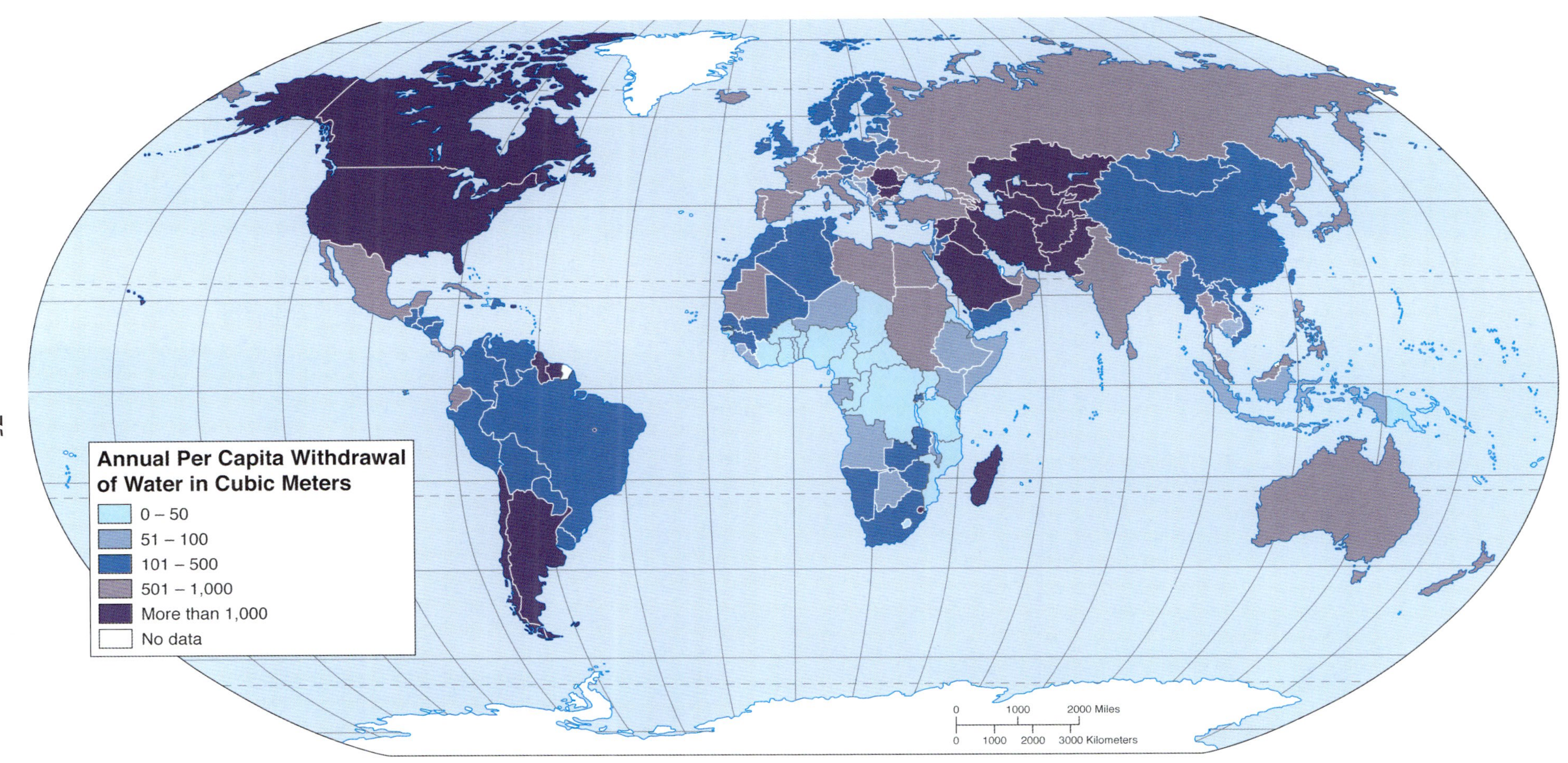

Annual Per Capita Withdrawal of Water in Cubic Meters
0 – 50
51 – 100
101 – 500
501 – 1,000
More than 1,000
No data
0 1000 2000 Miles
0 1000 2000 3000 Kilometers

Water resources must be viewed like a bank account in which deposits and withdrawals are made. As long as the deposits are greater than the withdrawals, a positive balance remains. But when the withdrawals begin to exceed the deposits, sooner or later (depending on the relative sizes of the deposits and withdrawals) the account becomes overdrawn. For many of the world's countries, annual availability of water is insufficient to cover the demand. In these countries, reserves stored in groundwater are being tapped, resulting in depletion of the water supply (think of this as shifting money from a savings account to a checking account). The water supply can maintain its status as a renewable resource only if deposits continue to be greater than withdrawals, and that seldom happens. In general, countries with high levels of economic development and countries that rely on irrigation agriculture are the most spendthrift when it comes to their water supplies.

Map 61 Pollution of the Oceans

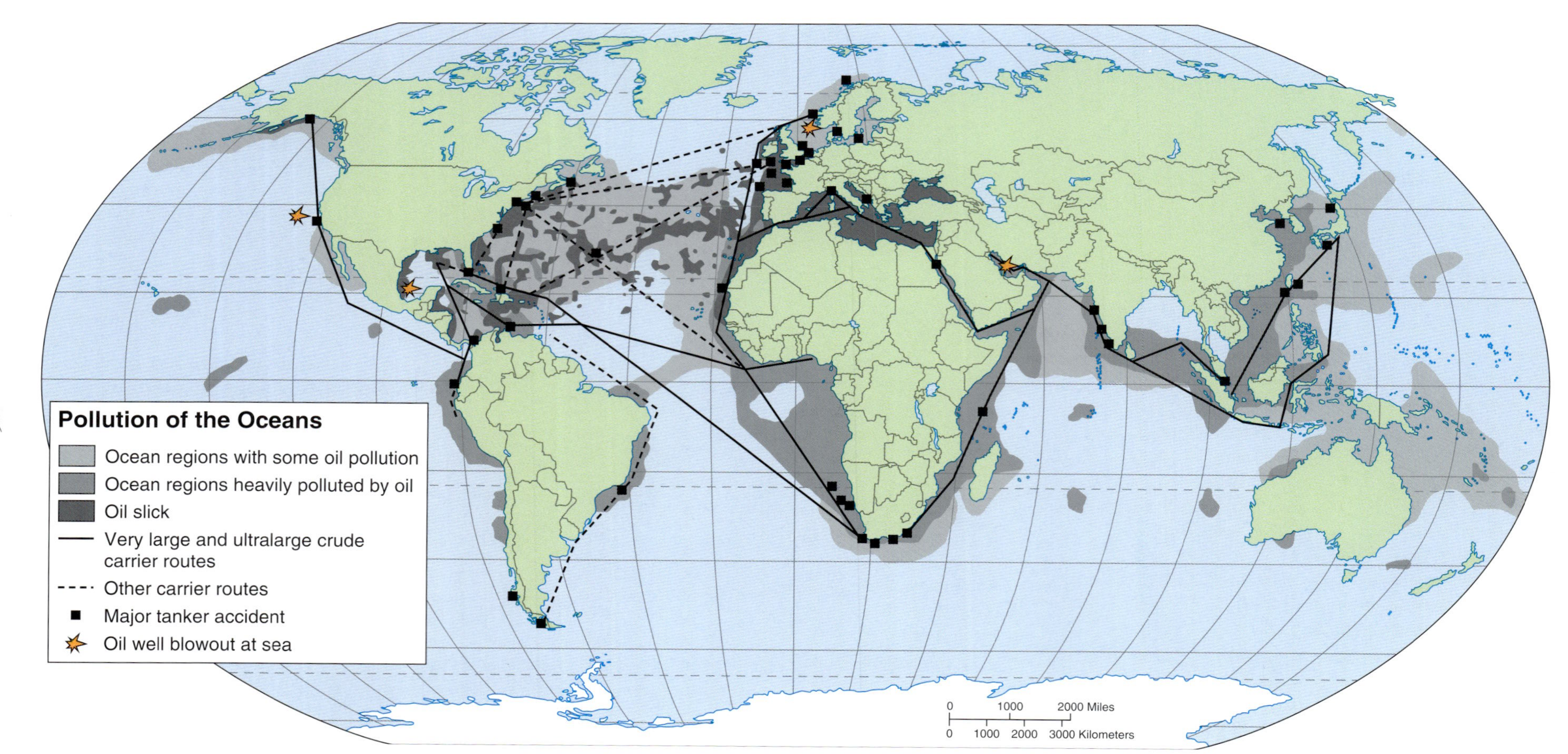
Pollution of the Oceans
Ocean regions with some oil pollution
Ocean regions heavily polluted by oil
Oil slick
Very large and ultralarge crude carrier routes
Other carrier routes
Major tanker accident
Oil well blowout at sea
0 1000 2000 Miles
0 1000 2000 3000 Kilometers

The pollution of the world's oceans has long been a matter of concern to physical geographers, oceanographers, and other environmental scientists. The great circulation systems of the ocean are one of the controlling factors of the earth's natural environment, and modifications to those systems have unknown consequences. This map is based on what we can measure: (1) areas of oceans where oil pollution has been proven to have inflicted significant damage to ocean ecosystems and life-forms (including phytoplankton, the oceans' primary food producers, equivalent to land-based vegetation) and (2) areas of oceans where unusually high concentrations of hydrocarbons from oil spills may have inflicted some damage to the oceans' biota. A glance at the map shows that there are few areas of the world's oceans where some form of pollution is not a part of the environmental system. What the map does not show in detail, because of the scale, are the dramatic consequences of large individual pollution events: the wreck of the *Exxon Valdez* and the polluting of Prince William Sound, or the environmental devastation produced by the 1991 Gulf War in the Persian Gulf.

Map 62 Food Supply From Marine and Freshwater Systems

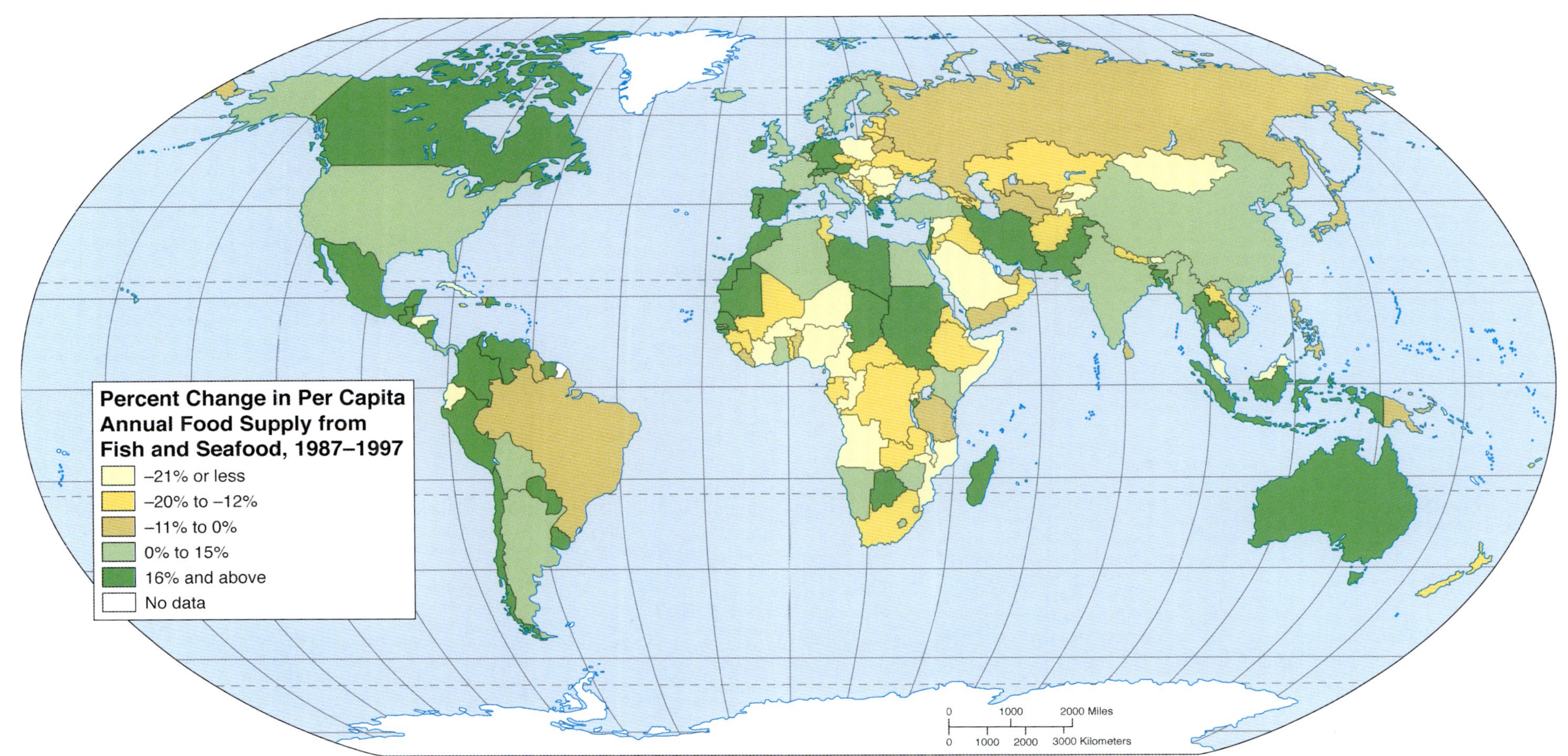
Percent Change in Per Capita Annual Food Supply from Fish and Seafood, 1987–1997
–21% or less
–20% to –12%
–11% to 0%
0% to 15%
16% and above
No data
0 1000 2000 Miles
0 1000 2000 3000 Kilometers

Not that many years ago, food supply experts were confidently predicting that the "starving millions" of the world of the future could be fed from the unending bounty of the world's oceans. While the annual catch from the sea helped to keep hunger at bay for a time, by the late 1980s it had become apparent that without serious human intervention in the form of aquaculture, the supply of fish would not be sufficient to offset the population/food imbalance that was beginning to affect so many of the world's regions. The development of factory-fishing with advanced equipment to locate fish and process them before they went to market increased the supply of food from the ocean, but in that increase was sown the seeds of future problems. The factory-fishing system, efficient in terms of economics, was costly in terms of fish populations. In some well-fished areas, the stock of fish that was viewed as near infinite just a few decades ago has dwindled nearly to the point of disappearance. This map shows both increases and decreases in the amount of individual countries' food supplies from the ocean. The increases are often the result of more technologically advanced fishing operations. The decreases are usually the result of the same thing: increased technology has brought increased harvests, which has reduced the supply of fish and shellfish and that, in turn, has increased prices. Most of the countries that have experienced sharp decreases in their supply of food from the world's oceans are simply no longer able to pay for an increasingly scarce commodity.

Map 63 Cropland Per Capita: Changes, 1987–1997

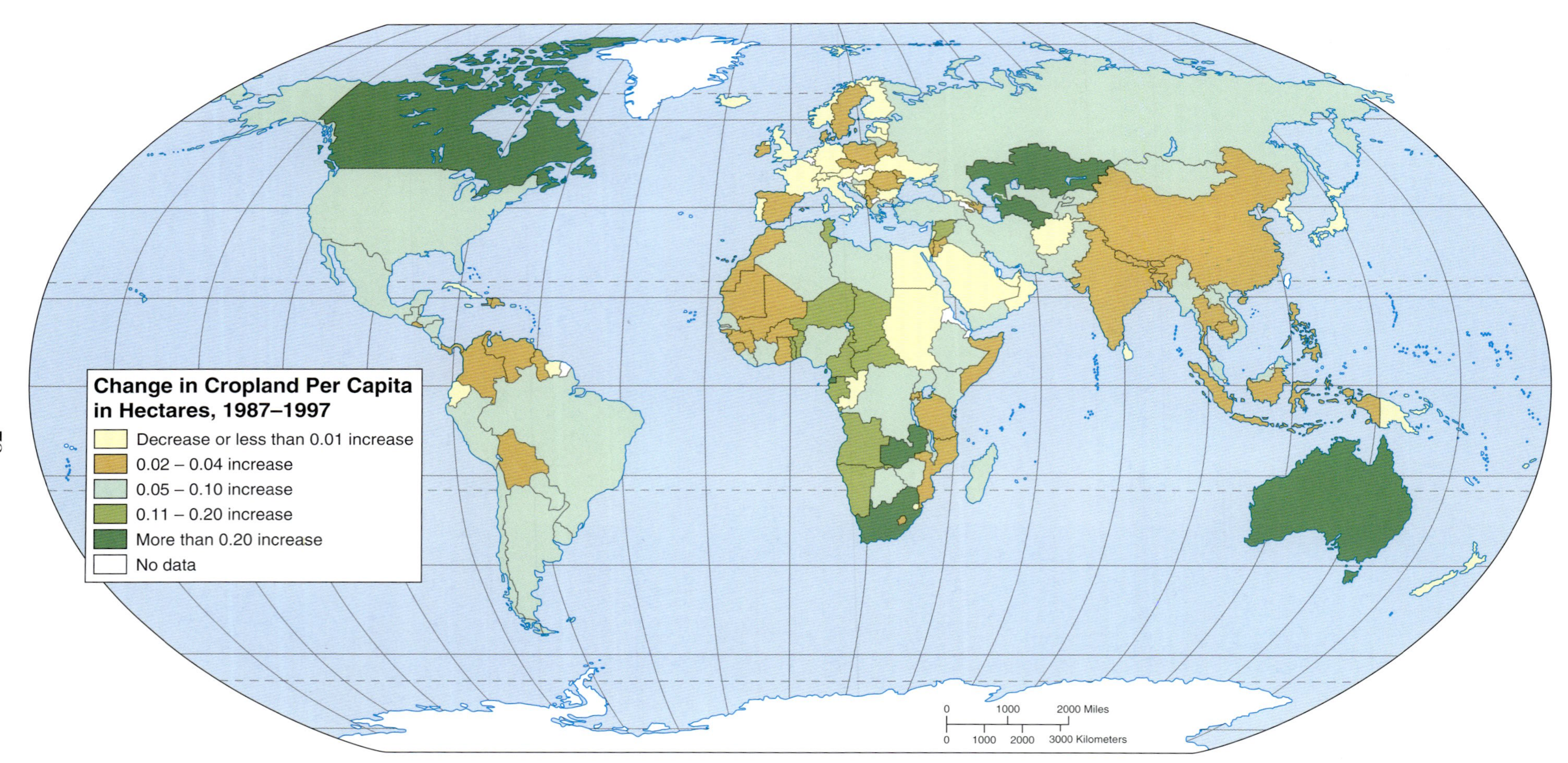

Change in Cropland Per Capita in Hectares, 1987–1997
Decrease or less than 0.01 increase
0.02 – 0.04 increase
0.05 – 0.10 increase
0.11 – 0.20 increase
More than 0.20 increase
No data
0 1000 2000 Miles
0 1000 2000 3000 Kilometers

As population has increased rapidly throughout the world, the area of cultivated land has increased at the same time; in fact, the amount of farmland per person has gone up slightly. Unfortunately, the figures that show this also tell us that since most of the best (or even good) agricultural land in 1985 was already under cultivation, most of the agricultural area added since the early 1980s involves land that would have been viewed as marginal by the fathers and grandfathers of present farmers—marginal in that it was too dry, too wet, too steep to cultivate, too far from a market, and so on. The continued expansion of agricultural area is one reason that serious famine and starvation have struck only a few regions of the globe. But land, more than any other resource we deal with, is finite, and the expansion cannot continue indefinitely. Future gains in agricultural production are most probably going to come through more intensive use of existing cropland, heavier applications of fertilizers and other agricultural chemicals, and genetically engineered crops requiring heavier applications of energy and water, than from an increase in the amount of the world's cropland.

Map 64 Annual Change in Forest Cover, 1990–1995

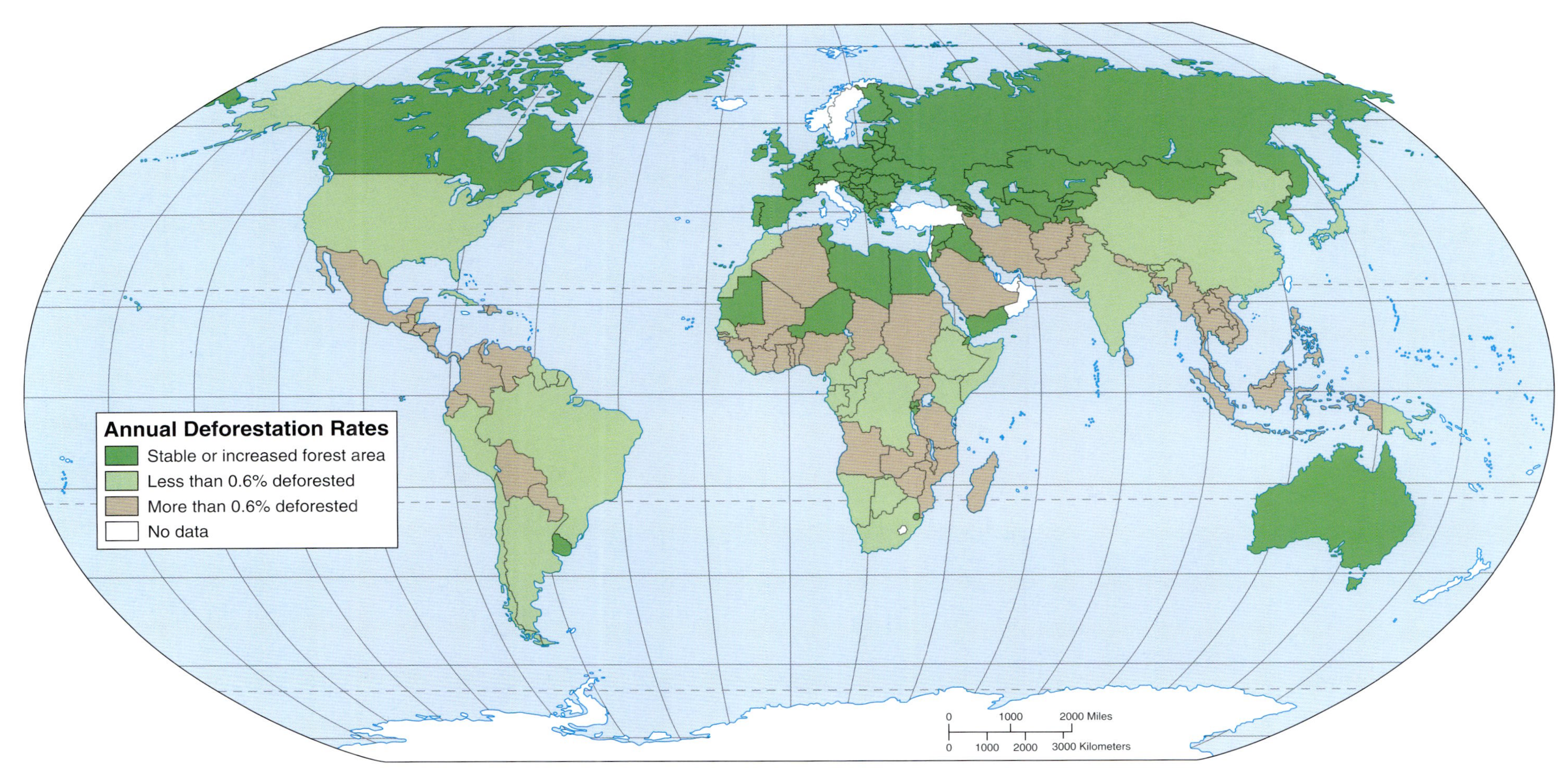

Annual Deforestation Rates
Stable or increased forest area
Less than 0.6% deforested
More than 0.6% deforested
No data
0 1000 2000 Miles
0 1000 2000 3000 Kilometers

One of the most discussed environmental problems is that of deforestation. For most people, deforestation means clearing of tropical rain forests for agricultural purposes. Yet nearly as much forest land per year—much of it in North America, Europe, and Russia—is impacted by commercial lumbering as is cleared by tropical farmers and ranchers. Even in the tropics, much of the forest clearance is undertaken by large corporations producing high-value tropical hardwoods for the global market in furniture, ornaments, and other fine wood products. Still, it is the agriculturally driven clearing of the great rain forests of the Amazon Basin, west and central Africa, Middle America, and Southeast Asia that draws public attention. Although much concern over forest clearance focuses on the relationship between forest clearance and the reduction in the capacity of the world's vegetation system to absorb carbon dioxide (and thus delay global warming), of just as great concern are issues having to do with the loss of biodiversity (large numbers of plants and animals), the near-total destruction of soil systems, and disruptions in water supply that accompany clearing.

Map 65 The Loss of Biodiversity: Globally Threatened Animal Species

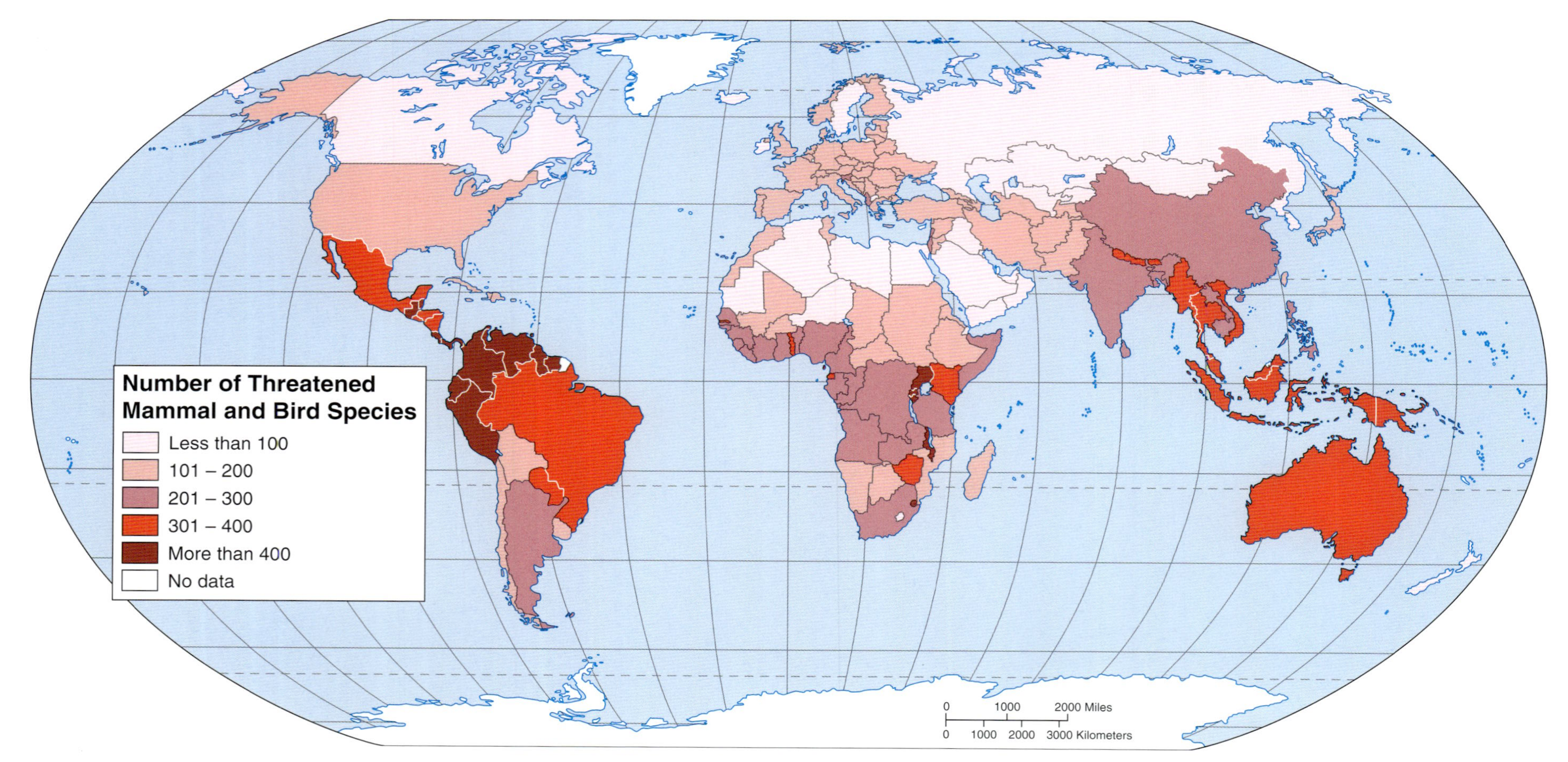
Number of Threatened
Mammal and Bird Species
Less than 100
101 – 200
201 – 300
301 – 400
More than 400
No data
0 1000 2000 Miles
0 1000 2000 3000 Kilometers

Threatened species are those in grave danger of going extinct. Their populations are becoming restricted in range, and the size of the populations required for sustained breeding is nearing a critical minimum. *Endangered species* are in immediate danger of becoming extinct. Their range is already so reduced that the animals may no longer be able to move freely within an ecozone, and their populations are at the level where the species may no longer be able to sustain breeding. Most species become threatened first and then endangered as their range and numbers continue to decrease. When people think of animal extinction, they think of large herbivorous species like the rhinoceros or fierce carnivores like lions, tigers, or grizzly bears. Certainly these animals make almost any list of endangered or threatened species. But there are literally hundreds of less conspicuous animals that are equally threatened. Extinction is normally nature's way of informing a species that it is inefficient. But conditions in the late twentieth century are controlled more by human activities than by natural evolutionary processes. Species that are endangered or threatened fall into that category because, somehow, they are competing with us or with our domesticated livestock for space and food. And in that competition the animals are always going to lose.

Map 66 The Loss of Biodiversity: Globally Threatened Plant Species

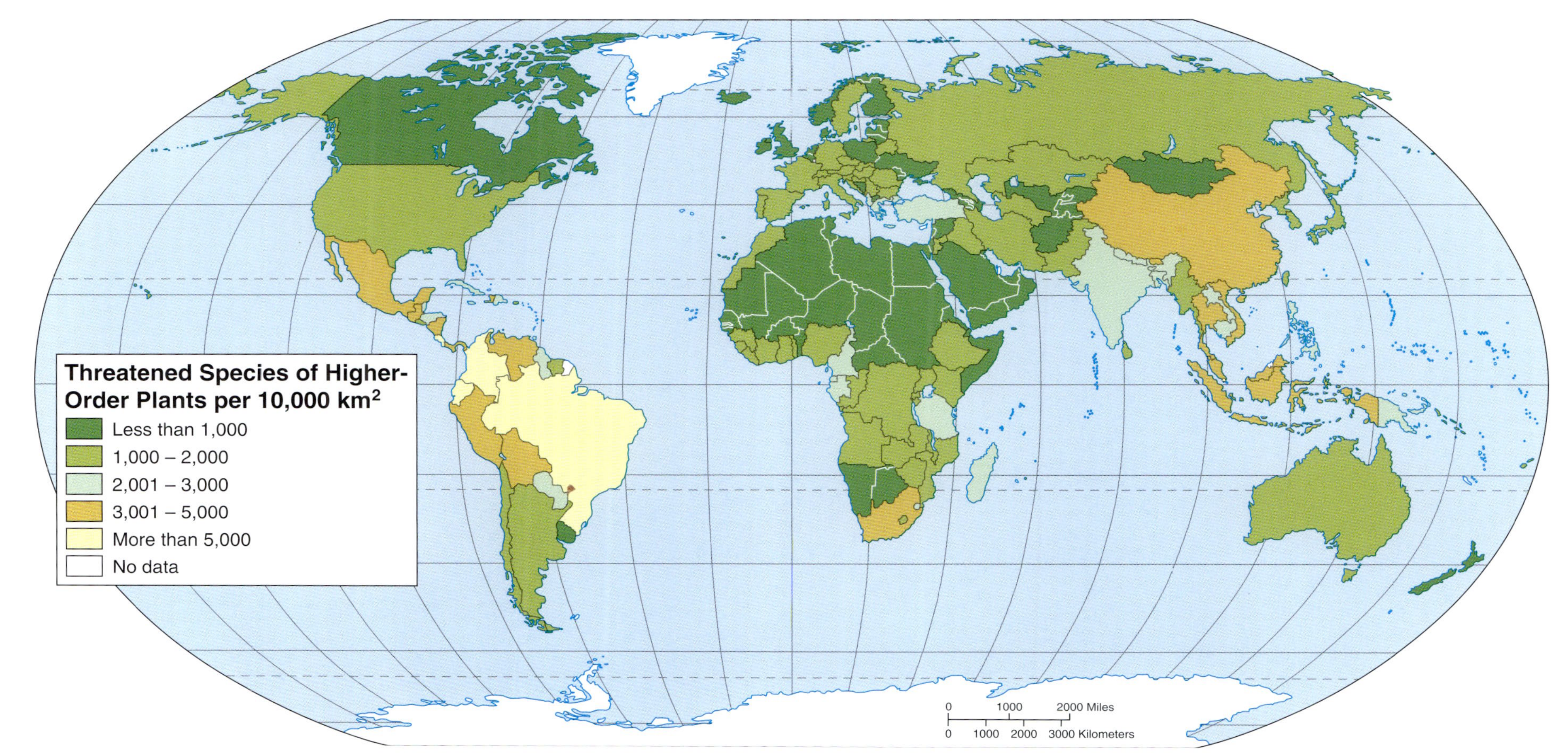
Threatened Species of Higher-Order Plants per 10,000 km²
Less than 1,000
1,000 – 2,000
2,001 – 3,000
3,001 – 5,000
More than 5,000
No data
0 1000 2000 Miles
0 1000 2000 3000 Kilometers

While most people tend to be more concerned about the animals on threatened and endangered species lists, the fact is that many more plants are in jeopardy, and the loss of plant life is, in all ecological regions, a more critical occurrence than the loss of animal populations. Plants are the primary producers in the ecosystem; that is, plants produce the food upon which all other species in the food web, including human beings, depend for sustenance. It is plants from which many of our critical medicines come, and it is plants that maintain the delicate balance between soil and water in most of the world's regions. When environmental scientists speak of a loss of biodiversity, what they are most often describing is a loss of the richness and complexity of plant life that lends stability to ecosystems. Systems with more plant life tend to be more stable than those with less. For these and other reasons, the scientific concern over extinction is greater when applied to plants than to animals. It is difficult for people to become as emotional over a teak tree as they would over an elephant. But as great a tragedy as the loss of the elephant would be, the loss of the teak would be greater.

Map 67 Hotspots of Biodiversity

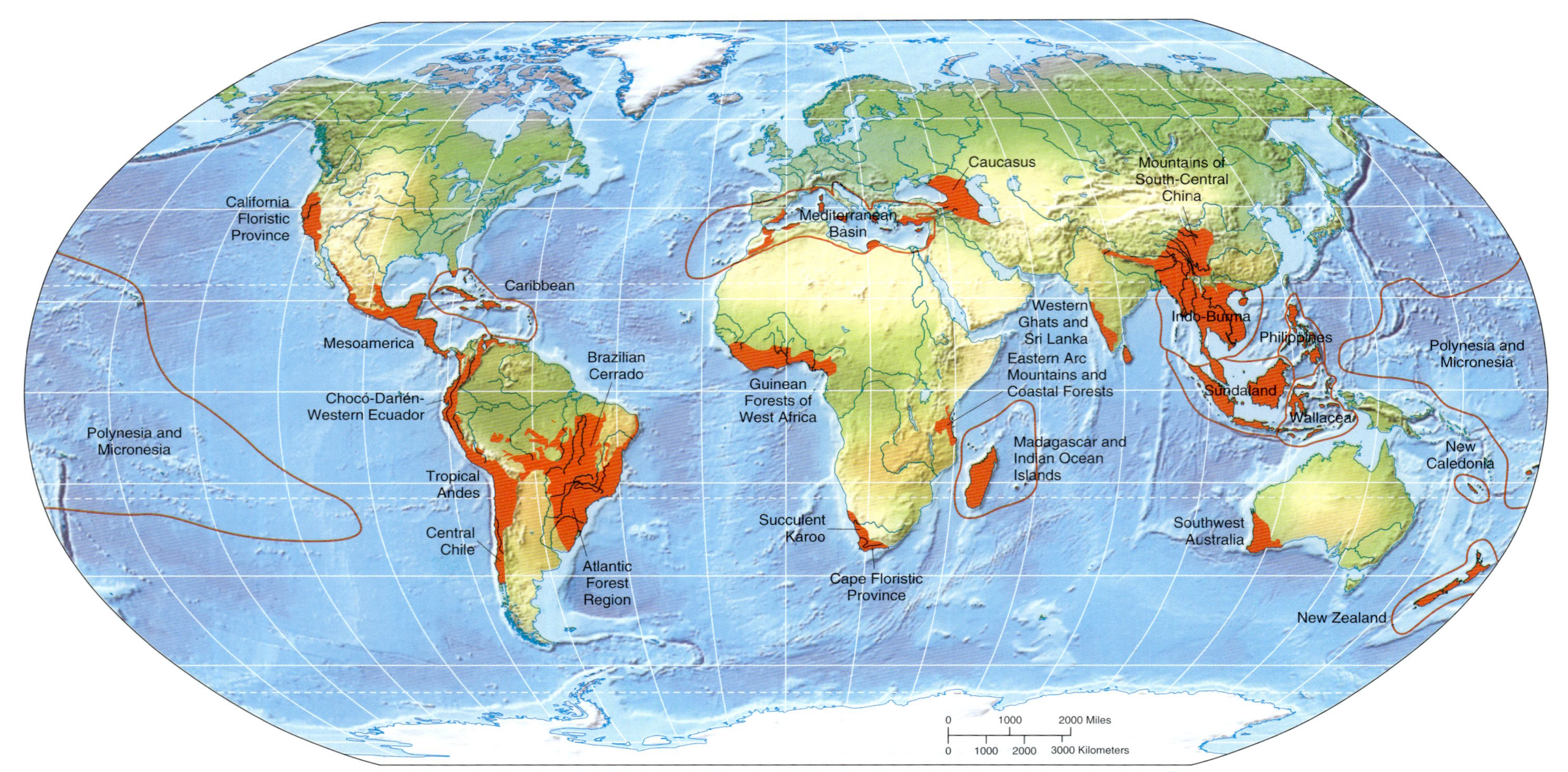
California Floristic Province
Caribbean
Mesoamerica
Chocó-Darién-Western Ecuador
Brazilian Cerrado
Polynesia and Micronesia
Tropical Andes
Central Chile
Atlantic Forest Region
Caucasus
Mediterranean Basin
Mountains of South-Central China
Western Ghats and Sri Lanka
Guinean Forests of West Africa
Eastern Arc Mountains and Coastal Forests
Indo-Burma
Philippines
Polynesia and Micronesia
Sundaland
Wallacea
Madagascar and Indian Ocean Islands
New Caledonia
Succulent Karoo
Southwest Australia
Cape Floristic Province
New Zealand
0 1000 2000 Miles
0 1000 2000 3000 Kilometers

Where we have normally thought of tropical forest basins such as Amazonia as the worlds most biologically diverse ecosystems, recent research has discovered the surprising fact that a number of hotspots of biological diversity exist outside the major tropical forest regions. These hotspot regions contain slightly less than 2 percent of the world's total land area but may contain up to 60 percent of the total world's terrestrial species of plants and animals. Geographically, the hotspot areas are characterized by vertical zonation (that is, they tend to be hilly to mountainous regions), long known to be a factor in biological complexity. They are also in coastal locations or near large bodies of water, locations that stimulate climatic variability and, hence, biological complexity. Although some of the hotspots are sparsely populated, others, such as Sundaland, are occupied by some of the world's densest populations. Protection of the rich biodiversity of these hotspots is, most biologists feel, of crucial importance to the preservation of the world's biological heritage.

Map 68 The Risks of Desertification

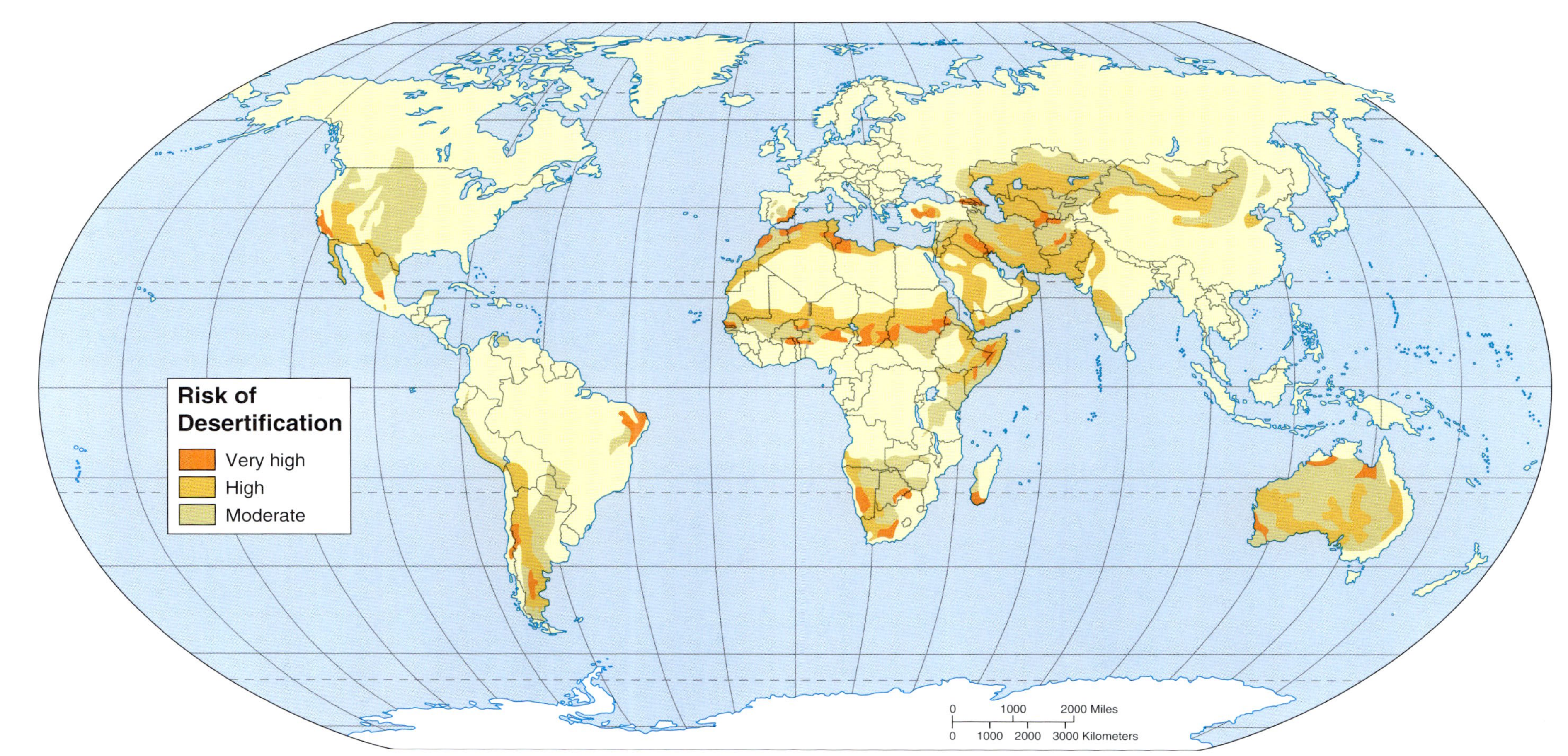
Risk of Desertification
Very high
High
Moderate
0 1000 2000 Miles
0 1000 2000 3000 Kilometers

The awkward-sounding term *desertification* refers to a reduction in the food-producing capacity of drylands through vegetation, soil, and water changes that culminate in either a drier climate or in soil and plant systems that are less efficient in their use of water. Most of the world's existing drylands—the shortgrass steppes, the tropical savannas, the bunchgrass regions of the desert fringe—are fairly intensively used for agriculture and are, therefore, subject to the kinds of pressures that culminate in desertification. Most desertification is a natural process that occurs near the margins of desert regions. It is caused by dehydration of the soil's surface layers during periods of drought and by high water loss through evaporation in an environment of high temperature and high winds. This natural process is greatly enhanced by human agricultural activities that expose topsoil to wind and water erosion. Among the most important practices that cause desertification are (1) overgrazing of rangelands, resulting from too many livestock on too small an area of land; (2) improper management of soil and water resources in irrigation agriculture, leading to accelerated erosion and to salt buildup in the soil; (3) cultivation of marginal terrain with soils and slopes that are unsuitable for farming; (4) surface disturbances of vegetation (clearing of thorn scrub, mesquite, chaparral, and similar vegetation) without soil protection efforts being made or replanting being done; and (5) soil compaction by agricultural implements, domesticated livestock, and rain falling on an exposed surface.

Map 69 Soil Degradation

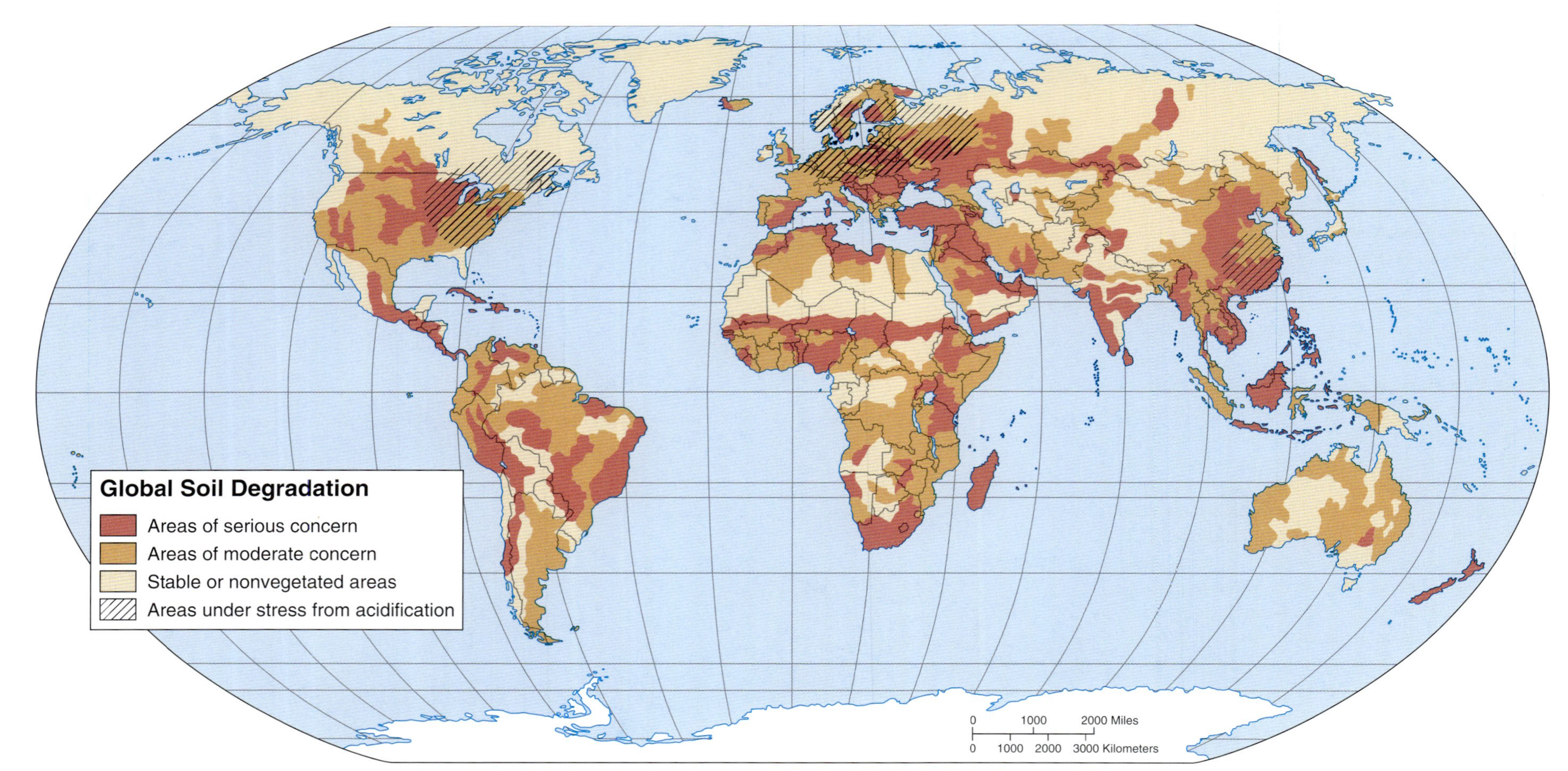
Global Soil Degradation
Areas of serious concern
Areas of moderate concern
Stable or nonvegetated areas
Areas under stress from acidification
0 1000 2000 Miles
0 1000 2000 3000 Kilometers

Recent research has shown that more than 3 billion acres of the world's surface suffer from serious soil degradation, with more than 22 million acres so severely eroded or poisoned with chemicals that they can no longer support productive crop agriculture. Most of this soil damage has been caused by poor farming practices, overgrazing of domestic livestock, and deforestation. These activities strip away the protective cover of natural vegetation forests and grasslands, allowing wind and water erosion to remove the topsoil that contains necessary nutrients and soil microbes for plant growth. But millions of acres of topsoil have been degraded by chemicals as well. In some instances these chemicals are the result of overapplication of fertilizers, herbicides, pesticides, and other agricultural chemicals. In other instances, chemical deposition from industrial and urban wastes and from acid precipitation has poisoned millions of acres of soil. As the map shows, soil erosion and pollution are not problems just in developing countries with high population densities and increasing use of marginal lands. They also afflict the more highly developed regions of mechanized, industrial agriculture. While many methods for preventing or reducing soil degradation exist, they are seldom used because of ignorance, cost, or perceived economic inefficiency.

Map 70 The Degree of Human Disturbance

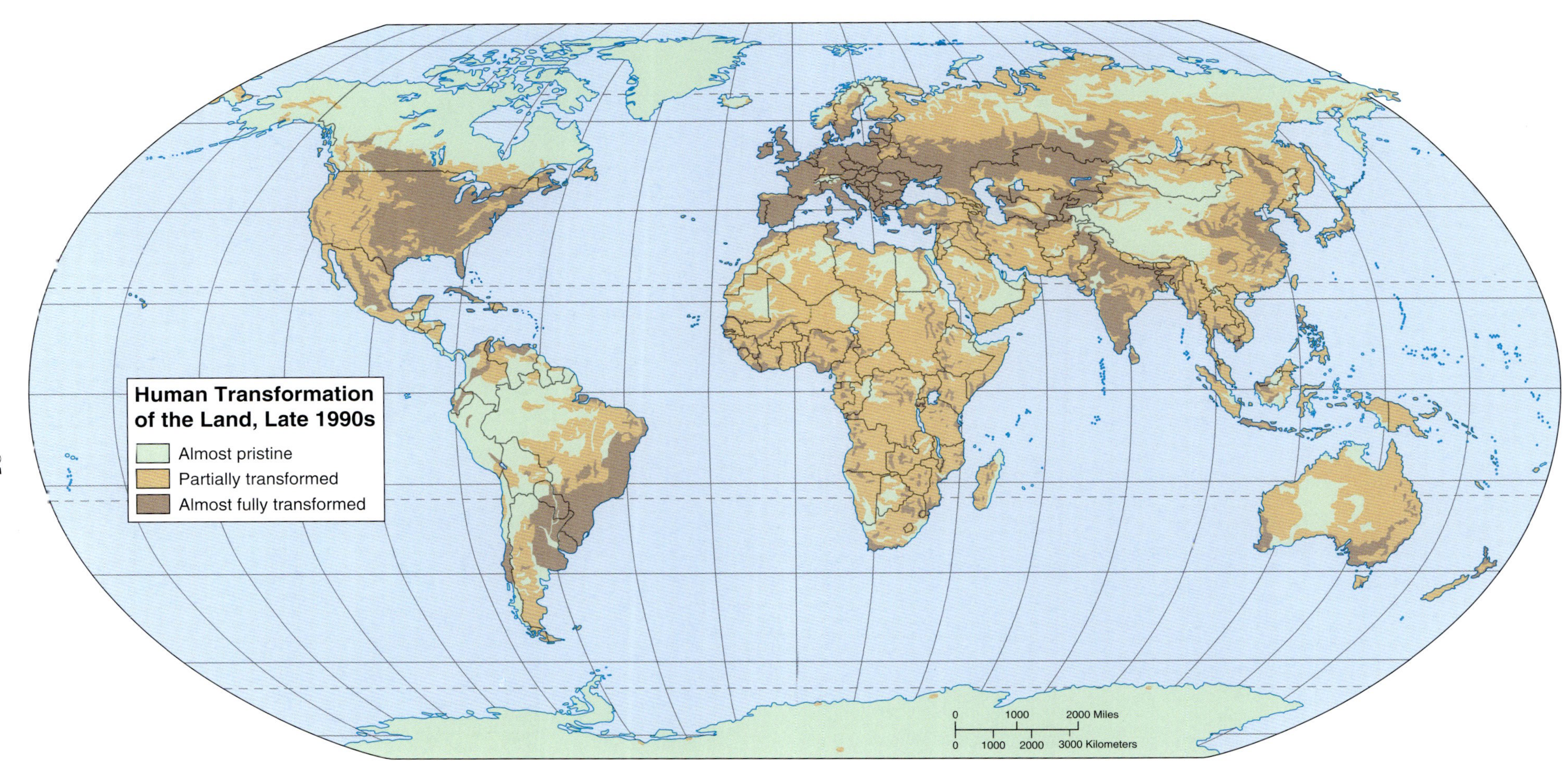

Human Transformation of the Land, Late 1990s
Almost pristine
Partially transformed
Almost fully transformed
0 1000 2000 Miles
0 1000 2000 3000 Kilometers

The data on human disturbance have been gathered from a wide variety of sources, some of them conflicting and not all of them reliable. Nevertheless, at a global scale this map fairly depicts the state of the world in terms of the degree to which humans have modified its surface. The almost pristine areas, covered with natural vegetation, generally have population densities under 10 persons per square mile. These areas are, for the most part, in the most inhospitable parts of the world: too high, too dry, too cold for permanent human habitation in large numbers. The partially transformed areas are normally agricultural areas, either subsistence (such as shifting cultivation) or extensive (such as livestock grazing). They often contain areas of secondary vegetation, regrown after removal of original vegetation by humans. They are also sometimes marked by a density of livestock in excess of carrying capacity, leading to overgrazing, which further alters the condition of the vegetation. The almost fully transformed areas are those of permanent and intensive agriculture and urban settlement. The primary vegetation of these regions has been removed, with no evidence of regrowth or with current vegetation that is quite different from natural (potential) vegetation. Soils are in a state of depletion and degradation, and, in drier lands, desertification is a factor of human occupation. The disturbed areas match closely those areas of the world with the densest human populations.

Part VI

Global Political Patterns

Map 71 Political Systems

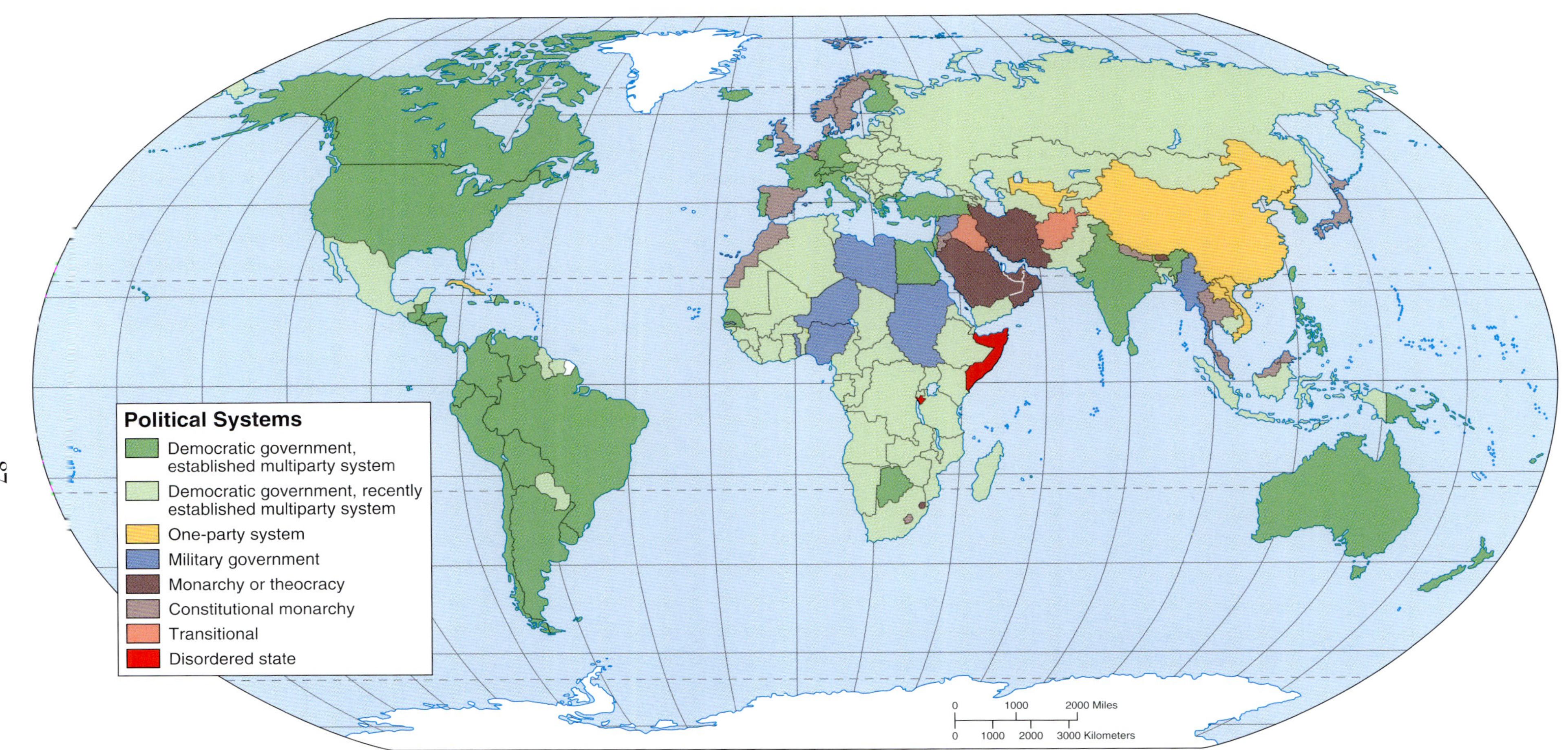

Political Systems
Democratic government, established multiparty system
Democratic government, recently established multiparty system
One-party system
Military government
Monarchy or theocracy
Constitutional monarchy
Transitional
Disordered state
0 1000 2000 Miles
0 1000 2000 3000 Kilometers

World political systems have changed dramatically during the last decade and may change even more in the future. The categories of political systems shown on the map are subject to some interpretation: established multiparty democracies are those in which elections by secret ballot with adult suffrage are and have been long-term features of the political landscape; recently established multiparty democracies are those in which the characteristic features of multiparty democracies have only recently emerged. The former Soviet satellites of eastern Europe and the republics that formerly constituted the USSR are in this category; so are states in emerging regions that are beginning to throw off the single-party rule that often followed the violent upheavals of the immediate postcolonial governmental transitions. The other categories are more or less obvious. One-party systems are states where single-party rule is constitutionally guaranteed or where a one-party regime is a fact of political life. Monarchies are countries with heads of state who are members of a royal family. In a constitutional monarchy, such as the U.K. and the Netherlands, the monarchs are titular heads of state only. Theocracies are countries in which rule is within the hands of a priestly or clerical class; today, this means primarily fundamentalist Islamic countries such as Iran. Military governments are frequently organized around a junta that has seized control of the government from civil authority; such states are often technically transitional, that is, the military claims that it will return the reins of government to civil authority when order is restored. Finally, disordered states are countries so beset by civil war or widespread ethnic conflict that no organized government can be said to exist within them.

Map 72 Sovereign States: Duration of Independence

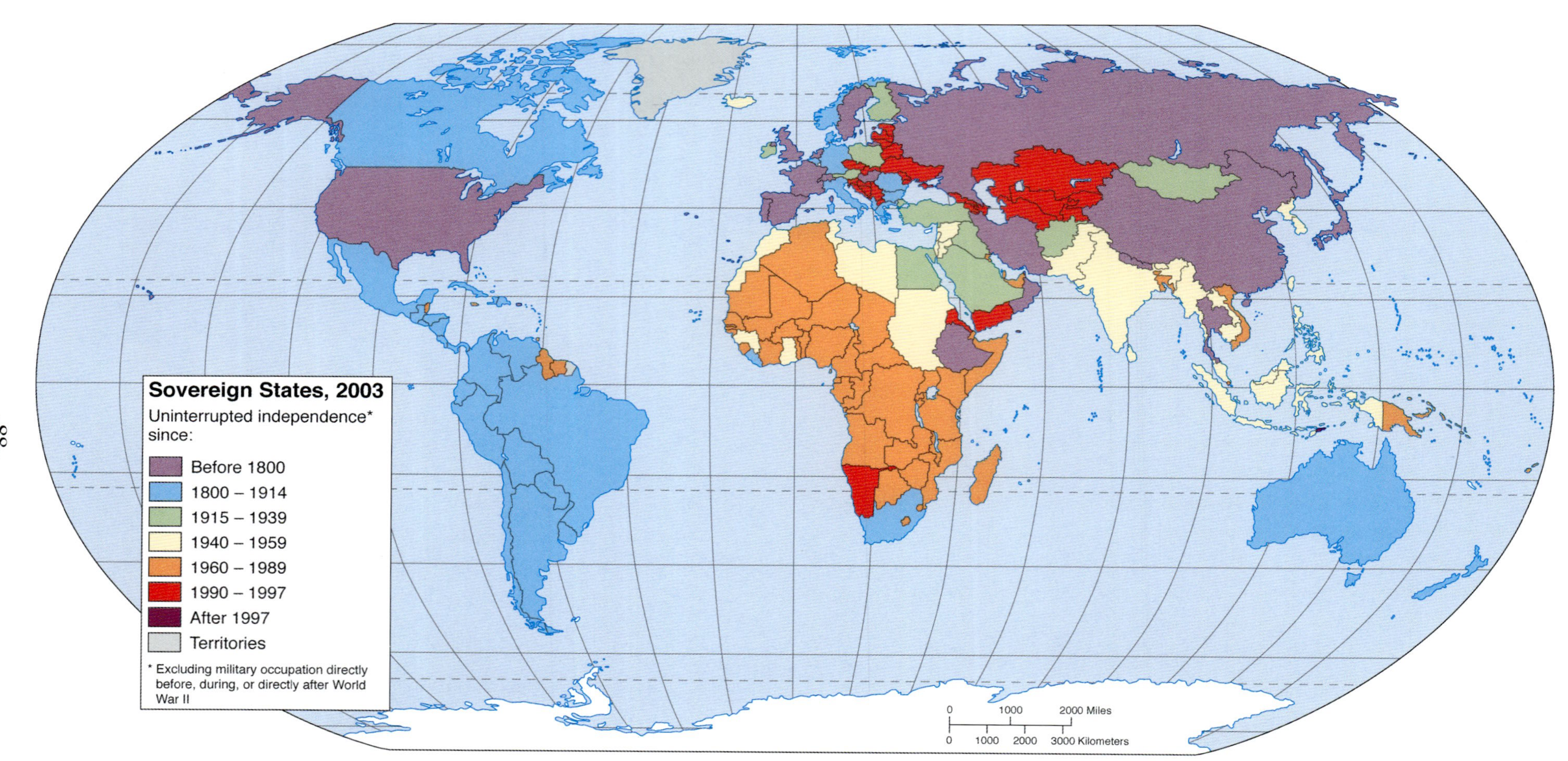

Sovereign States, 2003
Uninterrupted independence* since:
Before 1800
1800 – 1914
1915 – 1939
1940 – 1959
1960 – 1989
1990 – 1997
After 1997
Territories
* Excluding military occupation directly before, during, or directly after World War II
0 1000 2000 Miles
0 1000 2000 3000 Kilometers

Most countries of the modern world, including such major states as Germany and Italy, became independent after the beginning of the nineteenth century. Of the world's current countries, only 27 were independent in 1800. (Ten of the 27 were in Europe; the others were Afghanistan, China, Colombia, Ethiopia, Haiti, Iran, Japan, Mexico, Nepal, Oman, Paraguay, Russia, Taiwan, Thailand, Turkey, the United States, and Venezuela). Following 1800, there have been five great periods of national independence. During the first of these (1800–1914), most of the mainland countries of the Americas achieved independence.During the second period (1915–1939), the countries of Eastern Europe emerged as independent entities. The third period (1940–1959) includes World War II and the years that followed, when independence for African and Asian nations that had been under control of colonial powers first began to occur. During the fourth period (1960–1989), independence came to the remainder of the colonial African and Asian nations, as well as to former colonies in the Caribbean and the South Pacific. More than half of the world's countries came into being as independent political entities during this period. Finally, in the last few years (1990–1997), the breakup of the existing states of the Soviet Union, Yugoslavia, and Czechoslovakia created 22 countries where only 3 had existed before.

Map 73 European Colonialism 1500–2000

European nations have controlled many parts of the world during the last 500 years. The period of European expansion began when European explorers sailed the oceans in search of new trading routes and ended after World War II when many colonies in Africa and Asia gained independence. The process of colonization was very complex but normally involved the acquisition, extraction, or production of raw materials (including minerals, forest products, products from the sea, agricultural products, and animal furs/pelts) from the areas being controlled by the European colonial power in exchange for items of European manufacture. The concept of colonial dependency implied an economic structure in which the European country obtained raw materials from the colonial country in exchange for those manufactured items upon which populations in the colonial areas quickly came to depend. The colors on this map represent colonial control at its maximum extent and do not take into account shifting colonial control. In North America, for example, "New France" became British territory and "Louisiana" became Spanish territory after the Seven Years' (French and Indian) War.

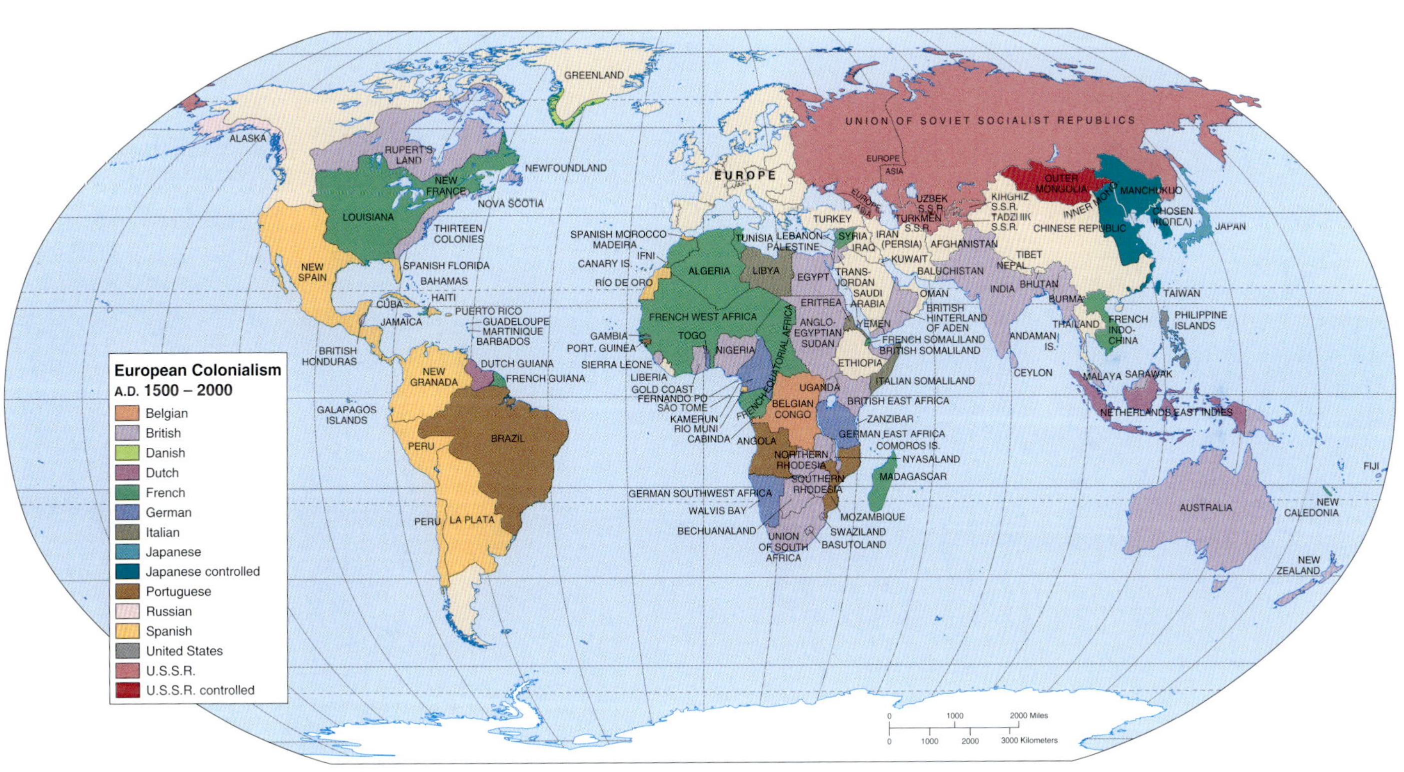

GREENLAND
ALASKA
RUPERT'S LAND
NEWFOUNDLAND
NEW FRANCE
NOVA SCOTIA
LOUISIANA
THIRTEEN COLONIES
NEW SPAIN
SPANISH FLORIDA
BAHAMAS
HAITI
CUBA
PUERTO RICO
JAMAICA
GUADELOUPE
MARTINIQUE
BARBADOS
BRITISH HONDURAS
NEW GRANADA
DUTCH GUIANA
FRENCH GUIANA
GALAPAGOS ISLANDS
PERU
BRAZIL
PERU
LA PLATA
EUROPE
UNION OF SOVIET SOCIALIST REPUBLICS
EUROPE
ASIA
EUROPE
ASIA
SPANISH MOROCCO
MADEIRA
IFNI
CANARY IS.
RÍO DE ORO
TUNISIA
ALGERIA
LIBYA
EGYPT
LEBANON
PALESTINE
SYRIA
IRAQ
IRAN (PERSIA)
TURKEY
UZBEK S.S.R.
TURKMEN S.S.R.
KIHGHIZ S.S.R.
S.S.R.
AFGHANISTAN
KUWAIT
TRANS-JORDAN
SAUDI ARABIA
BALUCHISTAN
OMAN
BRITISH HINTERLAND OF ADEN
YEMEN
ERITREA
ANGLO-EGYPTIAN SUDAN
FRENCH SOMALILAND
BRITISH SOMALILAND
ETHIOPIA
ITALIAN SOMALILAND
FRENCH WEST AFRICA
TOGO
NIGERIA
FRENCH EQUATORIAL AFRICA
GAMBIA
PORT. GUINEA
SIERRA LEONE
LIBERIA
GOLD COAST
FERNANDO PO
SÃO TOME
KAMERUN
RIO MUNI
CABINDA
UGANDA
BELGIAN CONGO
BRITISH EAST AFRICA
ZANZIBAR
GERMAN EAST AFRICA
COMOROS IS.
ANGOLA
NORTHERN RHODESIA
NYASALAND
MADAGASCAR
SOUTHERN RHODESIA
GERMAN SOUTHWEST AFRICA
WALVIS BAY
BECHUANALAND
MOZAMBIQUE
SWAZILAND
BASUTOLAND
UNION OF SOUTH AFRICA
OUTER MONGOLIA
INNER MONGOLIA
MANCHUKUO
CHOSEN
JAPAN
CHINESE REPUBLIC
TIBET
NEPAL
BHUTAN
INDIA
BURMA
TAIWAN
THAILAND
FRENCH INDO-CHINA
PHILIPPINE ISLANDS
ANDAMAN IS.
CEYLON
MALAYA
SARAWAK
NETHERLANDS EAST INDIES
FIJI
AUSTRALIA
NEW CALEDONIA
NEW ZEALAND
European Colonialism
A.D. 1500 – 2000
Belgian
British
Danish
Dutch
French
German
Italian
Japanese
Japanese controlled
Portuguese
Russian
Spanish
United States
U.S.S.R.
U.S.S.R. controlled
0 1000 2000 Miles
0 1000 2000 3000 Kilometers

Map 74 International Conflicts in the Post–World War II World

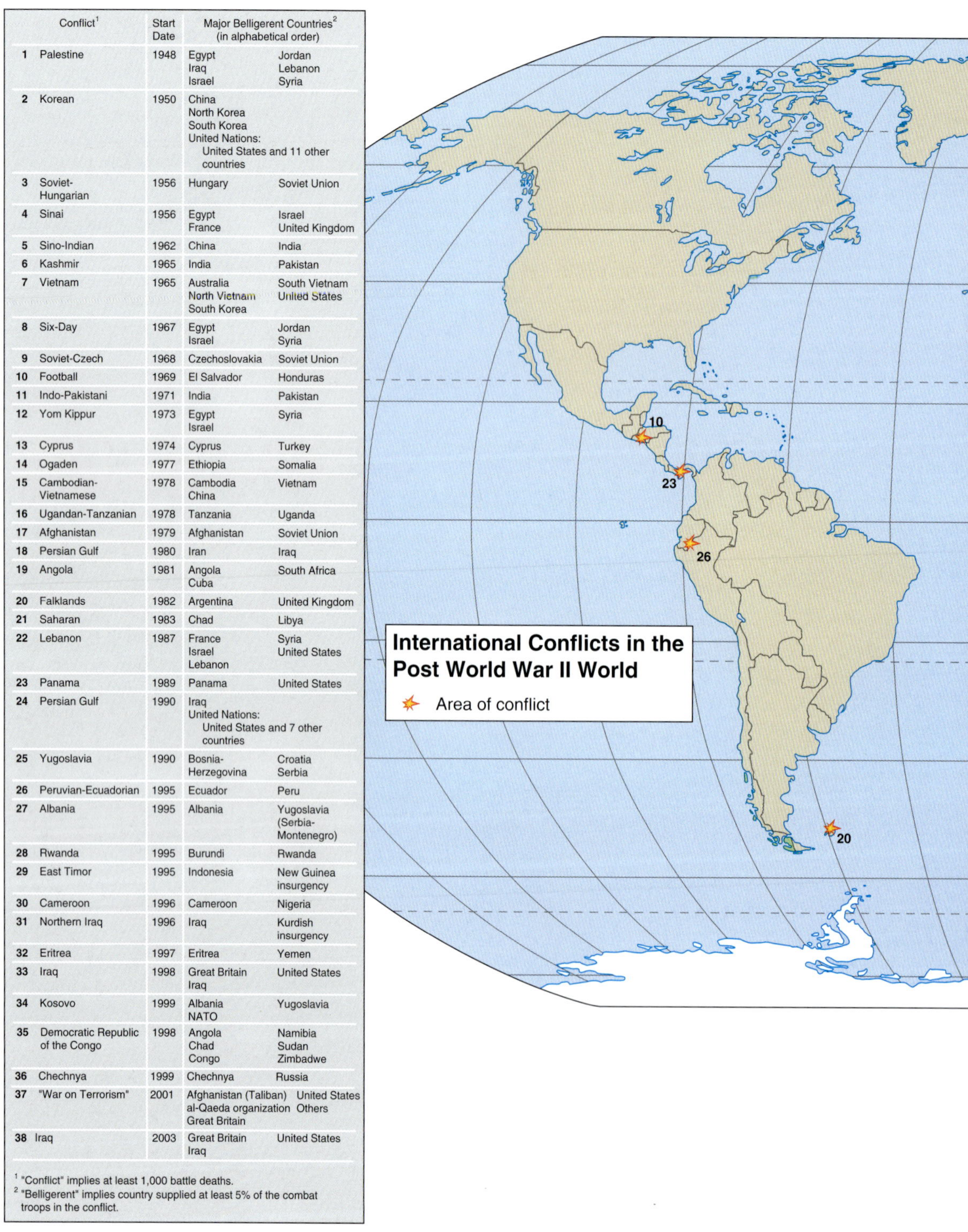

	Conflict[1]	Start Date	Major Belligerent Countries[2] (in alphabetical order)	
1	Palestine	1948	Egypt Iraq Israel	Jordan Lebanon Syria
2	Korean	1950	China North Korea South Korea United Nations: United States and 11 other countries	
3	Soviet-Hungarian	1956	Hungary	Soviet Union
4	Sinai	1956	Egypt France	Israel United Kingdom
5	Sino-Indian	1962	China	India
6	Kashmir	1965	India	Pakistan
7	Vietnam	1965	Australia North Vietnam South Korea	South Vietnam United States
8	Six-Day	1967	Egypt Israel	Jordan Syria
9	Soviet-Czech	1968	Czechoslovakia	Soviet Union
10	Football	1969	El Salvador	Honduras
11	Indo-Pakistani	1971	India	Pakistan
12	Yom Kippur	1973	Egypt Israel	Syria
13	Cyprus	1974	Cyprus	Turkey
14	Ogaden	1977	Ethiopia	Somalia
15	Cambodian-Vietnamese	1978	Cambodia China	Vietnam
16	Ugandan-Tanzanian	1978	Tanzania	Uganda
17	Afghanistan	1979	Afghanistan	Soviet Union
18	Persian Gulf	1980	Iran	Iraq
19	Angola	1981	Angola Cuba	South Africa
20	Falklands	1982	Argentina	United Kingdom
21	Saharan	1983	Chad	Libya
22	Lebanon	1987	France Israel Lebanon	Syria United States
23	Panama	1989	Panama	United States
24	Persian Gulf	1990	Iraq United Nations: United States and 7 other countries	
25	Yugoslavia	1990	Bosnia-Herzegovina	Croatia Serbia
26	Peruvian-Ecuadorian	1995	Ecuador	Peru
27	Albania	1995	Albania	Yugoslavia (Serbia-Montenegro)
28	Rwanda	1995	Burundi	Rwanda
29	East Timor	1995	Indonesia	New Guinea insurgency
30	Cameroon	1996	Cameroon	Nigeria
31	Northern Iraq	1996	Iraq	Kurdish insurgency
32	Eritrea	1997	Eritrea	Yemen
33	Iraq	1998	Great Britain Iraq	United States
34	Kosovo	1999	Albania NATO	Yugoslavia
35	Democratic Republic of the Congo	1998	Angola Chad Congo	Namibia Sudan Zimbadwe
36	Chechnya	1999	Chechnya	Russia
37	"War on Terrorism"	2001	Afghanistan (Taliban) al-Qaeda organization Great Britain	United States Others
38	Iraq	2003	Great Britain Iraq	United States

[1] "Conflict" implies at least 1,000 battle deaths.
[2] "Belligerent" implies country supplied at least 5% of the combat troops in the conflict.

International Conflicts in the Post World War II World
Area of conflict
10
23
26
20

The Korean War and the Vietnam War dominated the post–World War II period in terms of international military conflict. But numerous smaller conflicts have taken place, with fewer numbers of belligerents and with fewer battle and related casualties. These smaller international conflicts have been mostly territorial conflicts, reflecting the continual readjustment of political boundaries and loyalties brought about by the end of colonial empires, and the dissolution of the Soviet Union. Many of these conflicts were not wars in the more traditional sense, in which two or more countries formally declare war on one another, sever-

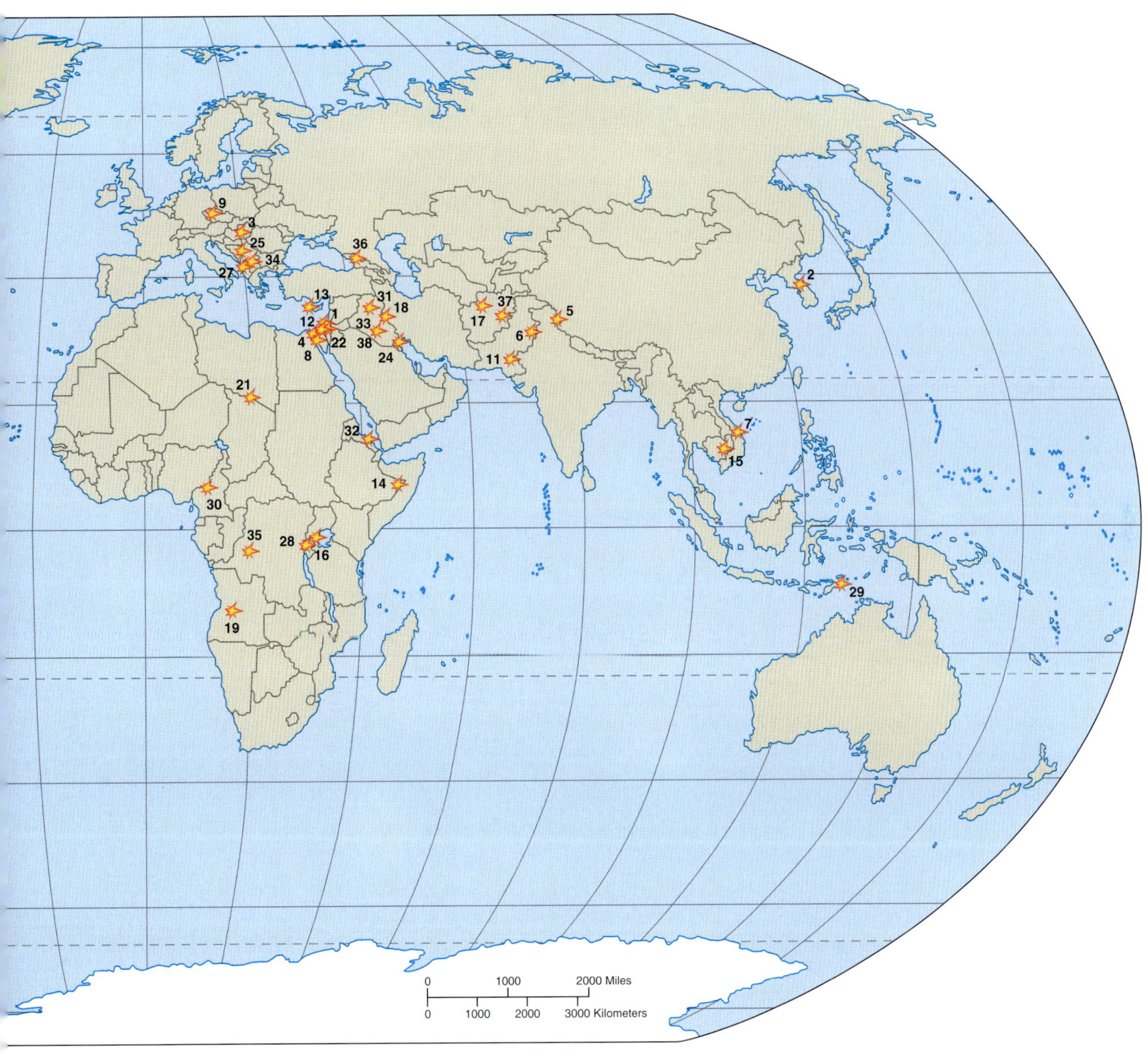
9
3
25
34
27
36
13
31
18
12
1
33
4
22
38
8
24
37
17
5
6
11
2
21
32
7
15
14
30
35
28
16
19
29
0 1000 2000 Miles
0 1000 2000 3000 Kilometers

ing diplomatic ties and devoting their entire national energies to the war effort. Rather, many of these conflicts were and are undeclared wars, sometimes fought between rival groups within the same country with outside support from other countries. The aftermath of the September 11, 2001, terrorist attacks on the United States indicate the dawn of yet another type of international conflict, namely a "war" fought between traditional nation-states and non-state actors.

Map 75 Post-Cold War International Alliances

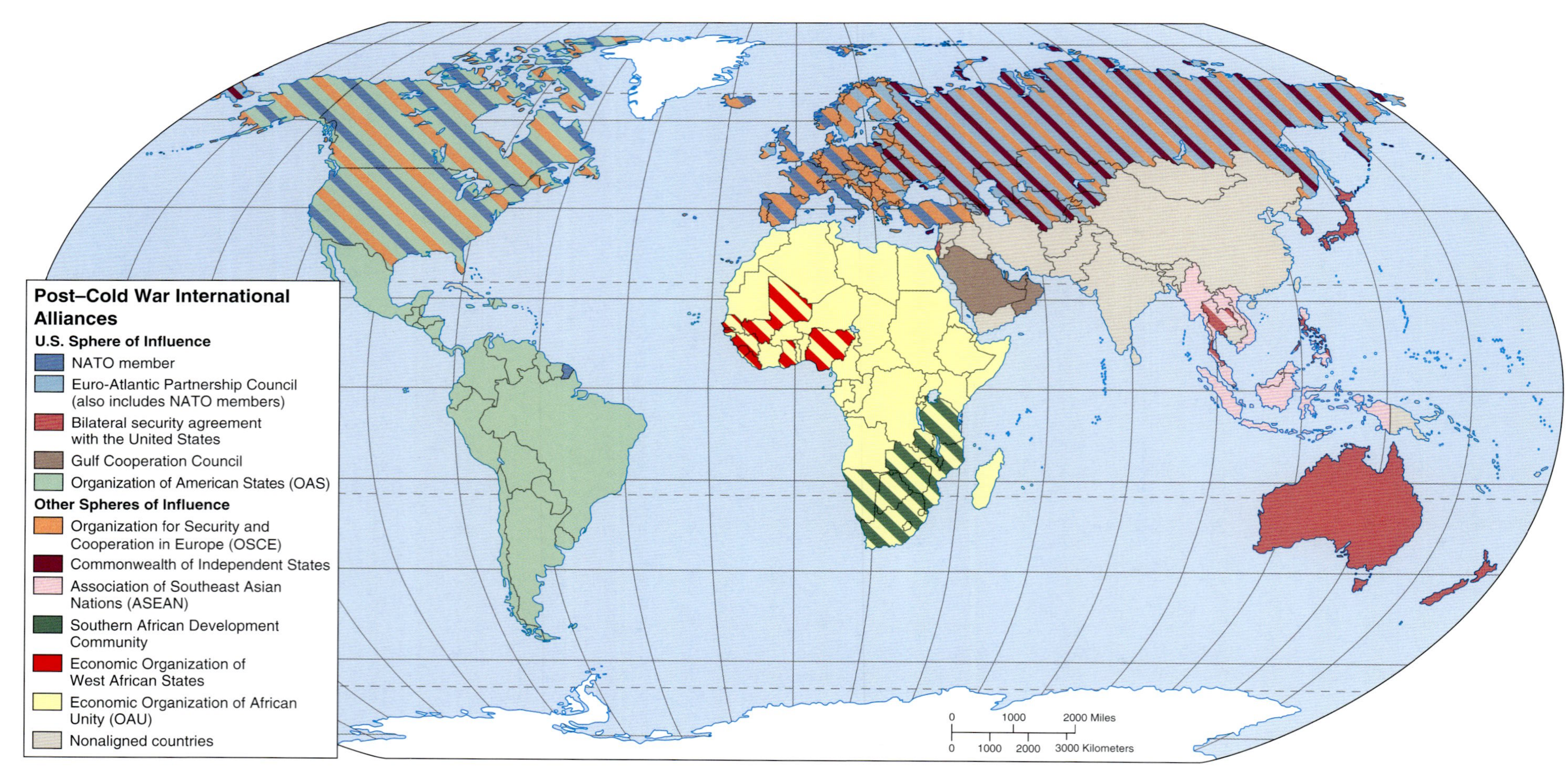

Post–Cold War International Alliances
U.S. Sphere of Influence
NATO member
Euro-Atlantic Partnership Council (also includes NATO members)
Bilateral security agreement with the United States
Gulf Cooperation Council
Organization of American States (OAS)
Other Spheres of Influence
Organization for Security and Cooperation in Europe (OSCE)
Commonwealth of Independent States
Association of Southeast Asian Nations (ASEAN)
Southern African Development Community
Economic Organization of West African States
Economic Organization of African Unity (OAU)
Nonaligned countries
0 1000 2000 Miles
0 1000 2000 3000 Kilometers

When the Warsaw Pact dissolved in 1992, the North Atlantic Treaty Organization (NATO) was left as the only major military alliance in the world. Some former Warsaw Pact members (Czech Republic, Hungary, and Poland) have joined NATO and others are petitioning for entry. The bipolar division of the world into two major military alliances is over, at least temporarily, leaving the United States alone as the world's dominant political and military power. But other international alliances, such as the Commonwealth of Independent States (including most of the former republics of the Soviet Union), will continue to be important. It may well be that during the first few decades of the twenty-first century economic alliances will begin to overshadow military ones in their relevance for the world's peoples.

Map 76 Flashpoints, 2005

Areas of conflict
SERBIA/
MONTENEGRO
Montenegro
Pec
Pristina
Kosovo
BULGARIA
Kumanovo
Tetovo
Skopje
Gostivar
Titov Velles
Stip
MACEDONIA
Varder River
Strumica
Prilep
Durres
Tirana
Lake Ohrid
Ohrid
Bitola
Lake Prespa
ALBANIA
Thesaloniki
GREECE
40

Macedonia: Since the fifteenth-century conquest of much of southeastern Europe by the Turkish Ottoman Empire, conflict in the Balkan region has been precipitated by ethnic and religious enmity between Orthodox Christians and Muslims. An area of particular concern has been the interface between predominantly Orthodox Macedonia and predominantly Muslim Albania, particularly in the border region the two share with the former Yugoslav republic of Kosovo. Tensions between the Macedonian government and its Albanian (Muslim) minority were heightened by the fallout from the conflict in Kosovo in the late 1990s between the Serbs and the Kosovar Albanians, backed by Albania. The resolution of this conflict by a NATO-led force in favor of the Kosovars led to emboldened feelings of Albanian patriotism in the region. Several sporadic incidents occurred along the Macedonian-Albanian border in late 2000, with more protracted and heavier combat between rebels and the Macedonian government forces occurring in the northern part of Macedonia (near the capital of Skopje) throughout 2001. The rebel forces assert they are only seeking to revise the Macedonian constitution and attain better rights for the Albanian minority in Macedonia. The Macedonian government is concerned that the Albanian minority centered in northern and western Macedonia wishes to secede and merge (along with Kosovo) into a Greater Albania, and suspects that Albania itself has encouraged this objective.

RUSSIA
Dagestan
Karnyshev
Kargalinskaya
Kizlyar
Mozdok
Terek
Kalinovskaya
Novy Terek
CHECHNYA
Nadterechnaya
Malgobek
Chervlennaya
Ingushetia
Terek
Sunzha
Groznyy
Gudermes
Sulak
Beslan
Nazran
Argun
Khasav"yurt
Urus-Martan
Shali
Alagir
North Ossetia
Vladikavkaz
Kirovauya
Sovetskoye
Argun River
RUSSIA
Dagestan
Botlikh
Andiyskoye Kaysu
GEORGIA
0
25 Miles
0
25 Kilometers

Chechnya: The area in southern Russia known as the Caucasus Region is home to a large variety of non-Russian ethnic groups; many are Muslim and resent centuries of Russian domination and Soviet-era totalitarianism. After the Soviet Union disintegrated in 1991, several of these ethnic groups began agitating for more autonomy from Moscow or for outright independence. One of the more vocal groups with a history of opposition to Moscow's rule were the Chechens. The Chechens declared themselves a sovereign nation in 1991 and by 1994 relations between the breakaway government in Chechnya and the Russian government had drastically deteriorated. In December of that year, Russian forces attacked Chechnya, beginning the first of two (1994–96 and 1999–present) full-scale military conflicts that have also crept into the neighboring Russian autonomous area of Dagestan, itself largely Muslim. In the mid- and late 1990s Russia experienced several terrorist attacks in cities throughout the nation, which the Russian government attributed to Islamic extremists supporting Chechen independence. As a result, a second round of the conflict began in August 1999 with a full-scale Russian military assault on Dagestan and Chechnya. This assault is ongoing and continues to face intense resistance, with heavy casualties on both sides. In 2003 and 2004 Chechen rebels increased their pressure with urban terrorist activities in Russian cities, including Moscow.

Area gained by Israel in 1949
Area occupied by Israel since 1967
City under total Palestinian control
Areas of joint control
LEBANON
SYRIA
MEDITERRANEAN
SEA
ISRAEL
Nahariyyah
Acre
Haifa
Sea of Galilee
Nazareth
Nabulus
WEST
BANK
Jordan River
Tel Aviv-Jaffa
Lod
Ramallah
Amman
Jerusalem
Jericho
Ashdod
Ashkelon
Bethlehem
GAZA
STRIP
Gaza
Hebron
DEAD
SEA
Beersheba
Dimona
NEGEV
DESERT
JORDAN
EGYPT
SINAI
PENINSULA
Elat
SAUDI
ARABIA
50 Miles
50 Kilometers

Israel and Its Neighbors: The modern state of Israel was created out of the former British Protectorate of Palestine, inhabited primarily by Muslim Arabs, after World War II. Conflict between Arabs and Israeli Jews has been a constant ever since. Much of the present tension revolves around the West Bank area, not part of the original Israeli state but taken from Jordan, an Arab country, in the Six-Day War of 1967. Many Palestinians had settled this part of Jordan after the creation of Israel and remain as a majority population in the West Bank region today. Israel has established many agricultural settlements within the region since 1967, angering Palestinian Arabs. For Israel, the West Bank is the region of ancient Judea and this region, won in battle, will not be ceded back to Palestinian Arabs without protracted or severe military action. The West Bank, inhabited by nearly 400,000 Israeli settlers and 4 million Palestinians, is also the location of most of the suicide bombings carried out by Islamic militant groups from 2001 to 2004. The U.S. government has recently agreed that Israel should retain most of its rights to the Israeli-settled areas of the West Bank.

AFGHANISTAN
CHINA
Claimed by India
Controlled by China
Gilgit
Indus River
NORTHWEST
FRONTIER
Claimed by India
Controlled by Pakistan
JAMMU
LADAKH
Pakistan-India Divided Conrol Line
AND
Kargil
AZAD KASHMIR
Jhelum
Srinagar
River
KASHMIR
Leh
Islamabad
Controlled by India
Vale
of
Kashmir
Chenab River
PAKISTAN
Jammu
INDIA
0 25 50 Miles
0 25 50 Kilometers

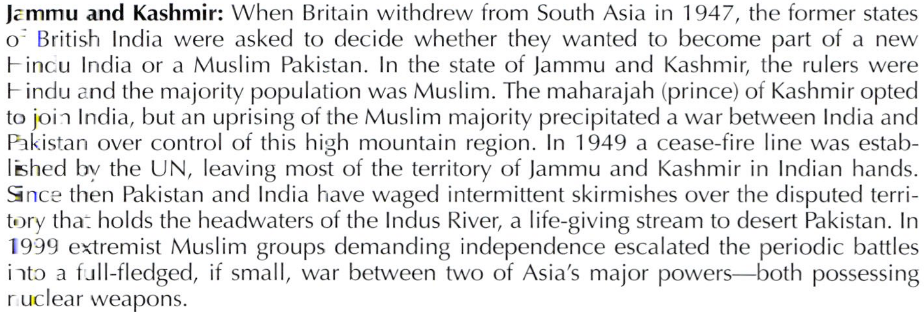

Jammu and Kashmir: When Britain withdrew from South Asia in 1947, the former states of British India were asked to decide whether they wanted to become part of a new Hindu India or a Muslim Pakistan. In the state of Jammu and Kashmir, the rulers were Hindu and the majority population was Muslim. The maharajah (prince) of Kashmir opted to join India, but an uprising of the Muslim majority precipitated a war between India and Pakistan over control of this high mountain region. In 1949 a cease-fire line was established by the UN, leaving most of the territory of Jammu and Kashmir in Indian hands. Since then Pakistan and India have waged intermittent skirmishes over the disputed territory that holds the headwaters of the Indus River, a life-giving stream to desert Pakistan. In 1999 extremist Muslim groups demanding independence escalated the periodic battles into a full-fledged, if small, war between two of Asia's major powers—both possessing nuclear weapons.

BLACK SEA
GEORGIA
ARMENIA
Yerevan
AZERBAIJAN
TURKEY
Lake Van
Tabriz
Divarbakir
KURDISTAN
Lake
Orumiyeh
Gaziantep
Kurdish
Security Zone
1991 – 2003
IRAN
Mosul
Irbil
Aleppo
Euphrates River
Dayr az Zawr
Kirkuk
SYRIA
IRAQ
Tigris River
Bakhtaran
Lake
Tharthar
0 100 200 Miles
0 100 200 Kilometers
Baghdad

Kurdistan: Where Turkey, Iran, and Iraq meet in the high mountain region of the Tauros and Zagros mountains, a nation of 25 million people exists. This nation is "Kurdistan," but the Kurds, the occupants of this area for over 3,000 years, have no state, and receive much less attention than other stateless nations like the Palestinians. Following the 1991 Gulf War between Iraq and a U.S.-led coalition of European and Arabic states, the United Nations demarcated a Kurdish "security zone" in northern Iraq. From 1991 to 2003 the Security Zone was anything but secure as Iraqi militants from the south and Turks from the north infringed on Kurdish territory, and the internal militant extremist groups, such as the Kurdish Workers' Party, staged periodic attacks on rival villages. During the 2003 U.S.-led invasion of Iraq that eliminated the Baathist regime of Saddam Hussein, the Kurds played an important role in securing the northern portions of Iraq for the U.S.-British coalition and fought alongside American troops in expelling elements of the Iraqi army from cities like Mosul and Kirkuk. Rich in oil and history, Kurdistan will probably remain as a nation without a state, shared by Iraq, Turkey, and Iran—none of which is likely to give up substantial portions of territory for the establishment of a Kurdish state.

CENTRAL AFRICAN REPUBLIC
SUDAN
CAMEROON
Congo River
UGANDA
CONGO
GABON
DEMOCRATIC REPUBLIC OF CONGO (ZAIRE)
RWANDA
Lake Victoria
Kigali
Bukavu
Bujumbura
BURUNDI
Brazzaville
Kinshasa
Kigoma
Kananga
TANZANIA
Lake Tanganyika
ATLANTIC OCEAN
Luanda
ANGOLA
Lubumbashi
MALAWI
0 200 400 Miles
0 200 400 Kilometers
ZAMBIA
Areas of renewed conflict

Congo: The war in the Democratic Republic of the Congo (formerly Zaire) has preoccupied the United Nations and African diplomats since 1999. Troops from Zimbabwe, Angola, Sudan, Chad and Namibia are now joined with the Congo's President Laurent Kabila against his former allies Rwanda, Burundi, and Uganda, who each back several separate Congolese rebel groups. The origins of the conflict lie in the overthrow of long-time dictator Mobutu Sese Seko by Kabila's army in May 1997 after a year of civil war. Kabila's failure to call elections or stabilize the country's economy led to further rounds of rebellion in the huge but fractious nation, rebellion supported by the economic and military assistance of neighboring Rwanda, Burundi, and Uganda. In October 2002, accord seemed to have been reached, and the various conflicting parties had agreed to withdraw troops. But in early 2003, new fighting flared along the country's eastern border, threatening a new and broadened war and the addition of more deaths to the 3.3 million since 1998. Diplomats have called the conflict "Africa's first world war," and fear that it may destabilize the southern half of the continent, leading to massive refugee flows and abject poverty.

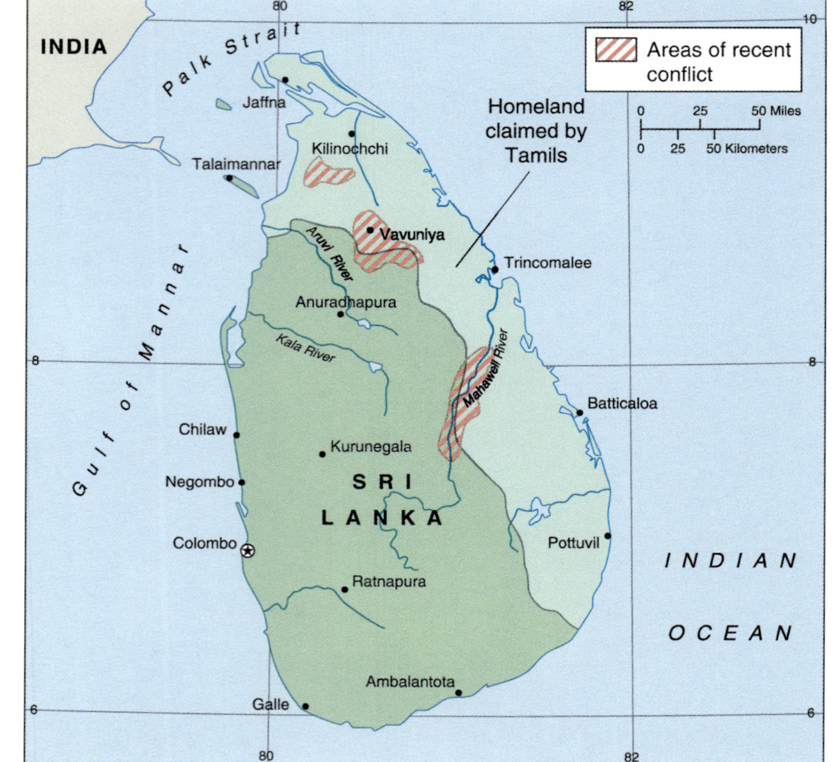
INDIA
Palk Strait
Jaffna
Areas of recent conflict
Homeland claimed by Tamils
0 25 50 Miles
0 25 50 Kilometers
Kilinochchi
Talaimannar
Vavuniya
Aruvi River
Trincomalee
Gulf of Mannar
Anuradhapura
Kala River
Mahaweli River
Batticaloa
Chilaw
Kurunegala
Negombo
SRI LANKA
Colombo
Pottuvil
INDIAN OCEAN
Ratnapura
Ambalantota
Galle
80
82
10
8
6

Sri Lanka: The island state of Sri Lanka, historically known as Ceylon, is potentially one of the most agriculturally productive regions of Asia. Unfortunately for plans related to agricultural development, two quite different peoples have occupied the island country: The Buddhist Sinhalese originally from northern India and long the dominant population in Sri Lanka, and the minority Hindu Tamil, a Dravidian people from south India. Since independence from Britain, Sri Lankan governments have sought to "resettle" the Tamil population in south India, actions that finally precipitated an armed rebellion by Tamils against the Sinhalese-dominated government. The Tamils at present are demanding a complete separation of the state into two parts, with a Tamil homeland in the north and along the east coast. At one time viewed as an island paradise, Sri Lanka is now a troubled country with an uncertain future. A cease fire between Sinhalese and Tamil fighters was brokered in 2001 by Norway but fell apart in late 2003 with the resumption of violence. In May 2004, Norwegian diplomats again made an attempt to negotiate a cease fire but with questionable results.

UZBEKISTAN
Samarkand
KYRGYZSTAN
CHINA
TAJIKISTAN
TURKMENISTAN
Dushanbe
Feyzabad
Mazar-e Sharif
Kholm
Konduz
Baghlan
Sheberghan
Meymaneh
Towraghondi
Kabul
Herat
AFGHANISTAN
Jalalabad
Peshawar
INDIA
Islamabad
Shindand
Ghazni
Farah
Indus River
Zaranj
Qandahar
Quetta
PAKISTAN
IRAN
0 100 200 Miles
0 100 200 Kilometers
Areas controlled by Northern Alliance, pre–2002
Pockets of remaining Taliban and Al-Qaeda resistance, 2004

Afghanistan: In the aftermath of the tragic September 11, 2001, terrorist attacks on the World Trade Center and the Pentagon, the United States (backed to varying degrees by its allies) has declared a massive and global "war on terrorism" and any states that may provide "safe harbor" to terrorists. To date, the most prominent target of this U.S. declaration of war has been the Taliban regime of Islamic extremists who controlled about 95 percent of the territory of the beleaguered nation of Afghanistan. International observers believe that the Taliban regime has welcomed and provided a base for the al-Qaeda terrorist network dominated by Saudi expatriate and millionaire Osama bin Laden since the late 1990s. As a result of this intelligence, the U.S. and Britain pursued a daily bombardment of key al-Qaeda and Taliban installations inside Afghanistan for several months, with key logistical support in the form of air bases and supply depots provided by the government of Pakistan (in exchange for financial considerations and political support of the non-elected Pakistani government). U.S. and allied ground troops, aided by members of the Northern Alliance of Afghan rebels opposed to the Taliban regime, and expelled the Taliban government in 2002. While now under home rule and with a duly elected government, Afghanistan still is plagued by warlords in remote areas of the country who refuse to recognize the legally constituted government. In addition, along the Afghanistan-Pakistan border, significant pockets of resistance from remnants of the former Taliban regime and from al-Qaeda forces are engaged in ongoing military conflict with American and Pakistani troops.

TURKEY
Lake Urmia
Tabriz
CASPIAN SEA
Salahaddin
Dohuk
Mahabad
Mosul
Irbil
Dibagah
Sulaimaniya
SYRIA
Dayr az Zawr
Kirkuk
IRAN
IRAQ
Tigris R.
Euphrates R.
Tikrit
Samarra
Khanaqin
Kermanshah
Buhayrat ath Tharthar
Akashat
Paratroopers
Ba Qubah
Ar Ramadi
Baghdad
Rutbah
Bahr al Milh
Zubaydiyah
Karkheh R.
JORDAN
Karbala
Kut
Al Hillah
Numaniyah
An Najaf
Ad Diwaniyah
Al 'Amarah
Qurnah
Ur
Nasiriyah
Basra
Rumeila
Khorramshahr
SAUDI ARABIA
Safwan
Umm Qasr
Rafha
KUWAIT
Kuwait
Persian Gulf
Iraq: Military Conflict, 2003
Basra Cities under U.S.-U.K. coalition control
British troop advances
U.S. troop advances
0 50 100 Miles
0 50 100 Kilometers

Iraq: Military Conflict, 2003–2004: Following the failure of the United States and allies Great Britain and Spain to secure approval from the United Nations to begin a UN-sponsored military conflict to "disarm" Iraq and effect "regime change" by removing the Baathist party dictator Saddam Hussein from power, the United States and its allies launched an independent military attack on Iraq in April 2003. The military campaign began with massive air and sea bombardments on government and military targets then ground troops moved from Kuwait along highway routes to secure the oil fields and major urban areas. By early May 2003, virtually all of the country was under the control of the U.S.-led coalition of forces. The Iraqi military, for the most part, melted away into the general civilian population and there were no major pitched battles for territory in the short-lived war. Conflicts between British forces and paramilitary/political forces in the important southern city of Al Basrah produced casualties on both sides before the city was secured. And the U.S. troops met guerilla resistance from political affiliates of Hussein's regime in cities such as An Najaf and Al Nasiriyah. In the northern parts of the country, U.S. troops inserted by parachute joined forces with Kurdish paramilitary groups to secure major cities like Mosul, Arbit, and Kirkuk. Although the U.S. and coalition forces controlled the country by June 2003, civil authority and infrastructure continued to be unavailable throughout large areas of Iraq by mid-2004. The spring of 2004 brought significant insurgency action against U.S. and coalition forces, who were increasingly viewed by the Iraqis as occupiers rather than liberators. A June 30, 2004, date was set to return Iraq to civilian Iraqi control.

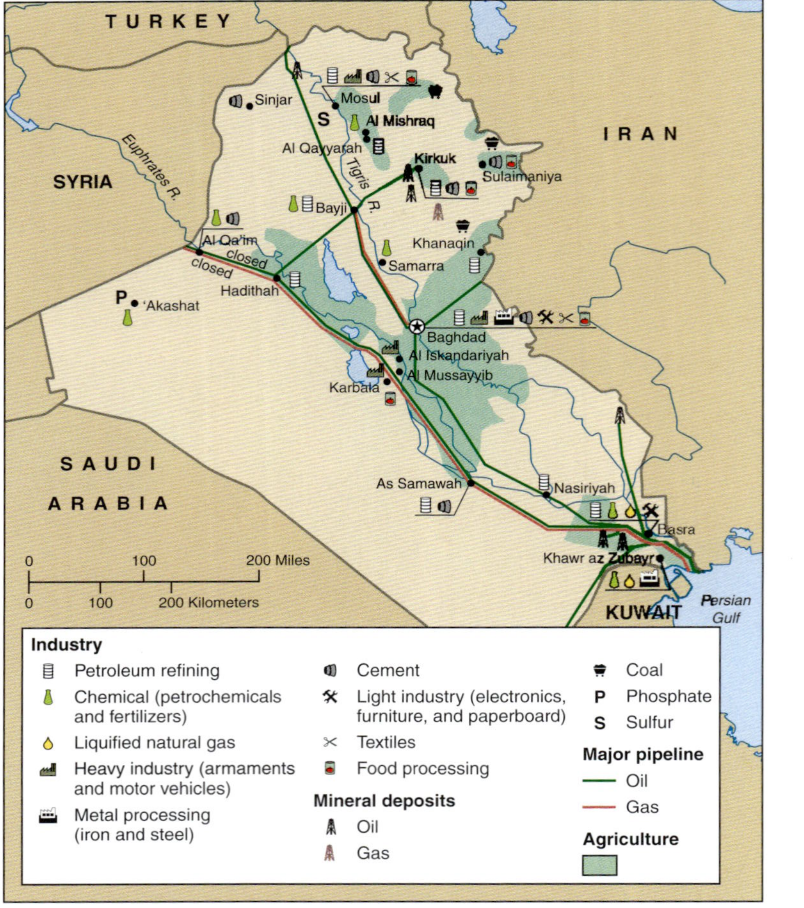
TURKEY
SYRIA
IRAN
SAUDI ARABIA
KUWAIT
Persian Gulf
Euphrates R.
Tigris R.
Sinjar
Mosul
Al Mishraq
Al Qayyarah
Kirkuk
Sulaimaniya
Bayji
Al Qa'im
closed
closed
Hadithah
'Akashat
Khanaqin
Samarra
Baghdad
Al Iskandariyah
Al Mussayyib
Karbala
As Samawah
Nasiriyah
Basra
Khawr az Zubayr
0 100 200 Miles
0 100 200 Kilometers
Industry
Petroleum refining
Chemical (petrochemicals and fertilizers)
Liquified natural gas
Heavy industry (armaments and motor vehicles)
Metal processing (iron and steel)
Cement
Light industry (electronics, furniture, and paperboard)
Textiles
Food processing
Mineral deposits
Oil
Gas
Coal
P Phosphate
S Sulfur
Major pipeline
Oil
Gas
Agriculture

TURKEY
SYRIA
IRAN
JORDAN
SAUDI ARABIA
KUWAIT
IRAQ
Lake Urmia
CASPIAN SEA
Persian Gulf
Euphrates R.
Tigris R.
Dohuk
Mosul
Sinjar
Tall Afar
Irbil
Kirkuk
Baghdad
An Najaf
Al 'Amarah
Nasiriyah
Basra
0 50 100 Miles
0 50 100 Kilometers
Ethnoreligious Groups
Sunni Kurd
Sunni Arab/Sunni Kurd
Sunni Arab
Shia Arab/Sunni Arab
Shia Arab
T Turkoman
Y Yezidi

Iraq: Prior to the 1990–91 invasion of Kuwait by Iraq and the subsequent United Nations coalition's military expulsion of Iraq from its neighbor, Iraq was one of the most prosperous countries in the Middle East and the only one with full capacity to feed itself, even without the vast oil revenues generated by the country's immense reserves. Despite the inefficiencies of the Baathist dictatorship of Saddam Hussein, the country has a solid agricultural base and a burgeoning industry. The combination of military adventurism and conflict, in the form of a lengthy war with Iran and the ill-advised invasion of Kuwait, limited further economic development, however. Development was also problematic given the country's internal tensions between Arabic Sunni Muslims and Arabic Shiite Muslims, and between Arabs and Kurds and a few other minority populations in the northern parts of the country.

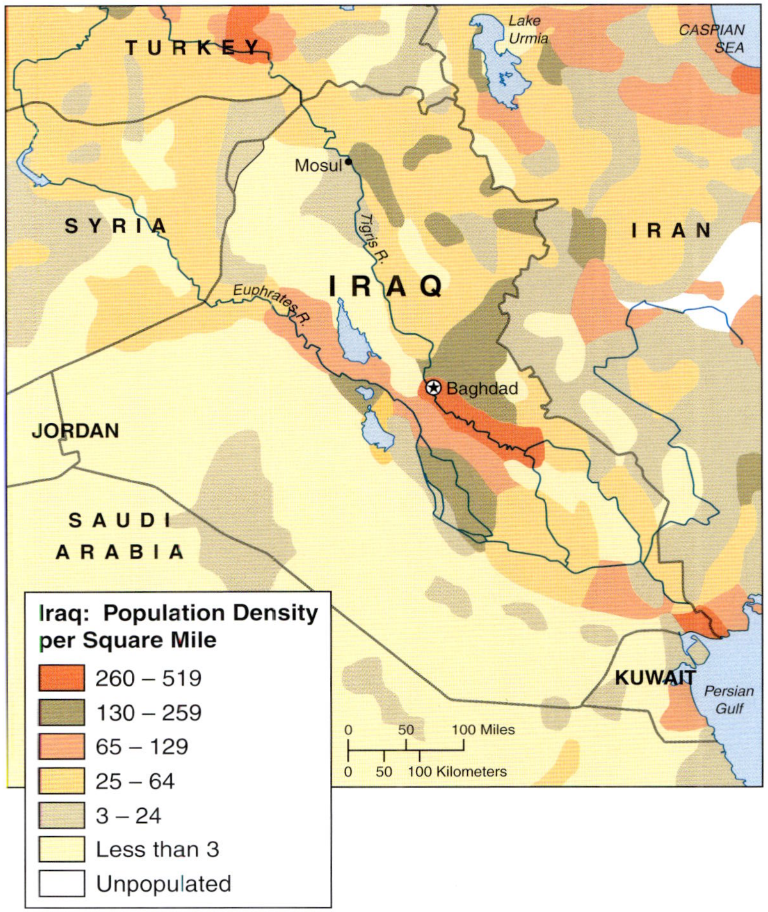
TURKEY
SYRIA
IRAQ
IRAN
JORDAN
SAUDI ARABIA
KUWAIT
Lake Urmia
CASPIAN SEA
Persian Gulf
Mosul
Baghdad
Tigris R.
Euphrates R.
0 50 100 Miles
0 50 100 Kilometers
Iraq: Population Density per Square Mile
260 – 519
130 – 259
65 – 129
25 – 64
3 – 24
Less than 3
Unpopulated

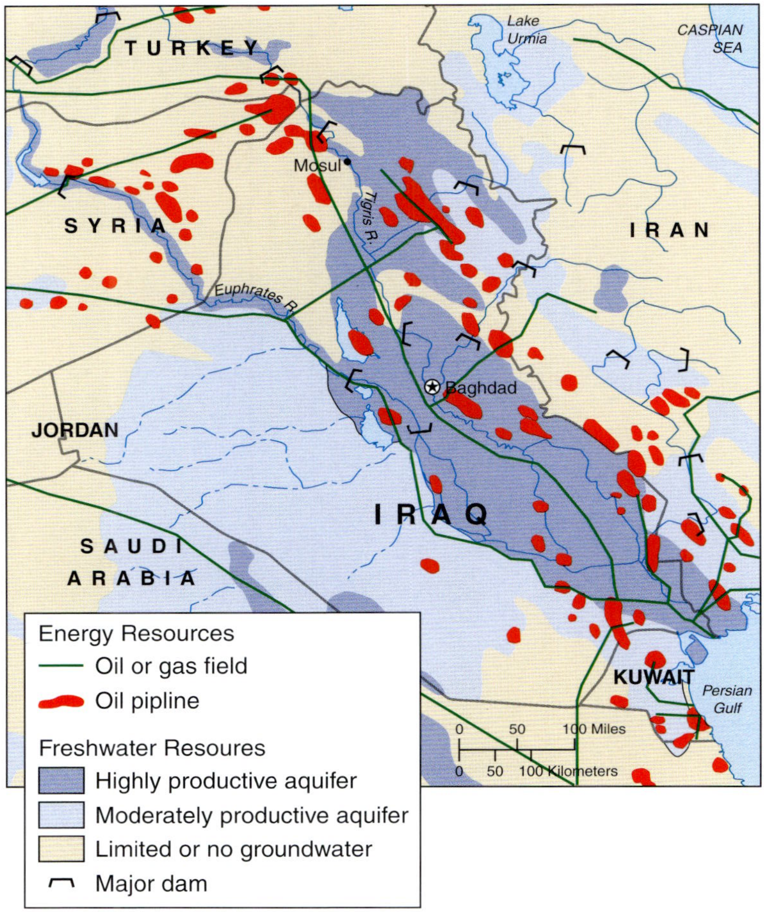
TURKEY
SYRIA
IRAQ
IRAN
JORDAN
SAUDI ARABIA
KUWAIT
Lake Urmia
CASPIAN SEA
Persian Gulf
Mosul
Baghdad
Tigris R.
Euphrates R.
0 50 100 Miles
0 50 100 Kilometers
Energy Resources
Oil or gas field
Oil pipline
Freshwater Resoures
Highly productive aquifer
Moderately productive aquifer
Limited or no groundwater
Major dam

Map 77 International Terrorism Incidents, 2000–2002

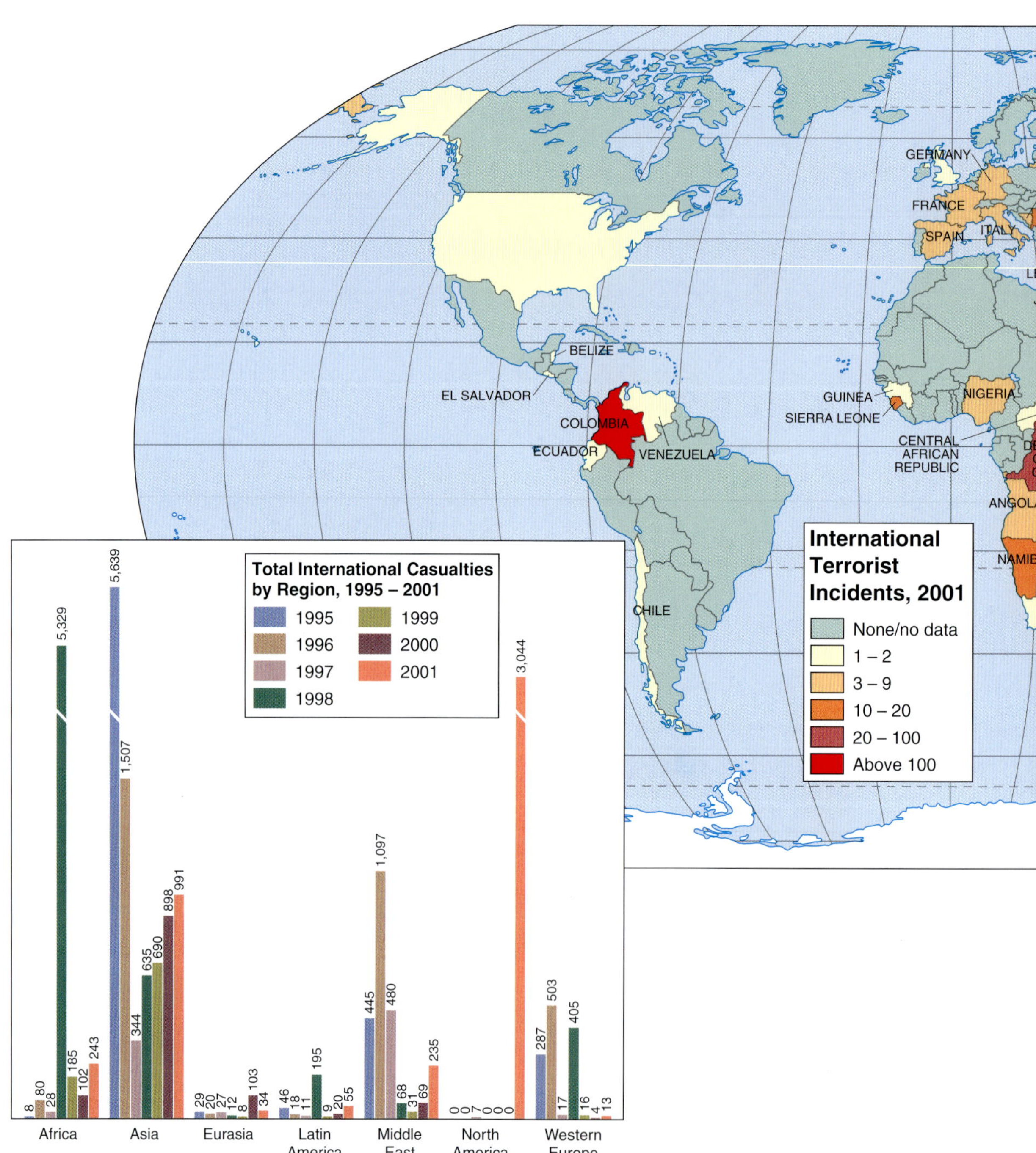
GERMANY
FRANCE
SPAIN
ITALY
BELIZE
EL SALVADOR
COLOMBIA
ECUADOR
VENEZUELA
GUINEA
SIERRA LEONE
NIGERIA
CENTRAL AFRICAN REPUBLIC
ANGOLA
NAMIBIA
CHILE
International Terrorist Incidents, 2001
None/no data
1 – 2
3 – 9
10 – 20
20 – 100
Above 100
Total International Casualties by Region, 1995 – 2001
1995
1996
1997
1998
1999
2000
2001
Africa: 8, 80, 28, 5,329, 185, 102, 243
Asia: 5,639, 1,507, 344, 635, 690, 898, 991
Eurasia: 29, 20, 27, 12, 8, 103, 34
Latin America: 46, 18, 11, 195, 9, 20, 55
Middle East: 445, 1,097, 480, 68, 31, 69, 235
North America: 0, 0, 7, 0, 0, 0, 3,044
Western Europe: 287, 503, 17, 405, 16, 4, 13

Americans have made a virtual mantra of the saying "The world has changed," as a consequence of the terrorist attacks on the World Trade Center and the Pentagon on September 11, 2001. As this map and the accompanying bar graphs point out, the world did not change, but the focus of a major terrorist attack shifted from Asia to North America. Many other areas of the world have lived with terrorism and terrorist activity for years. In 2000

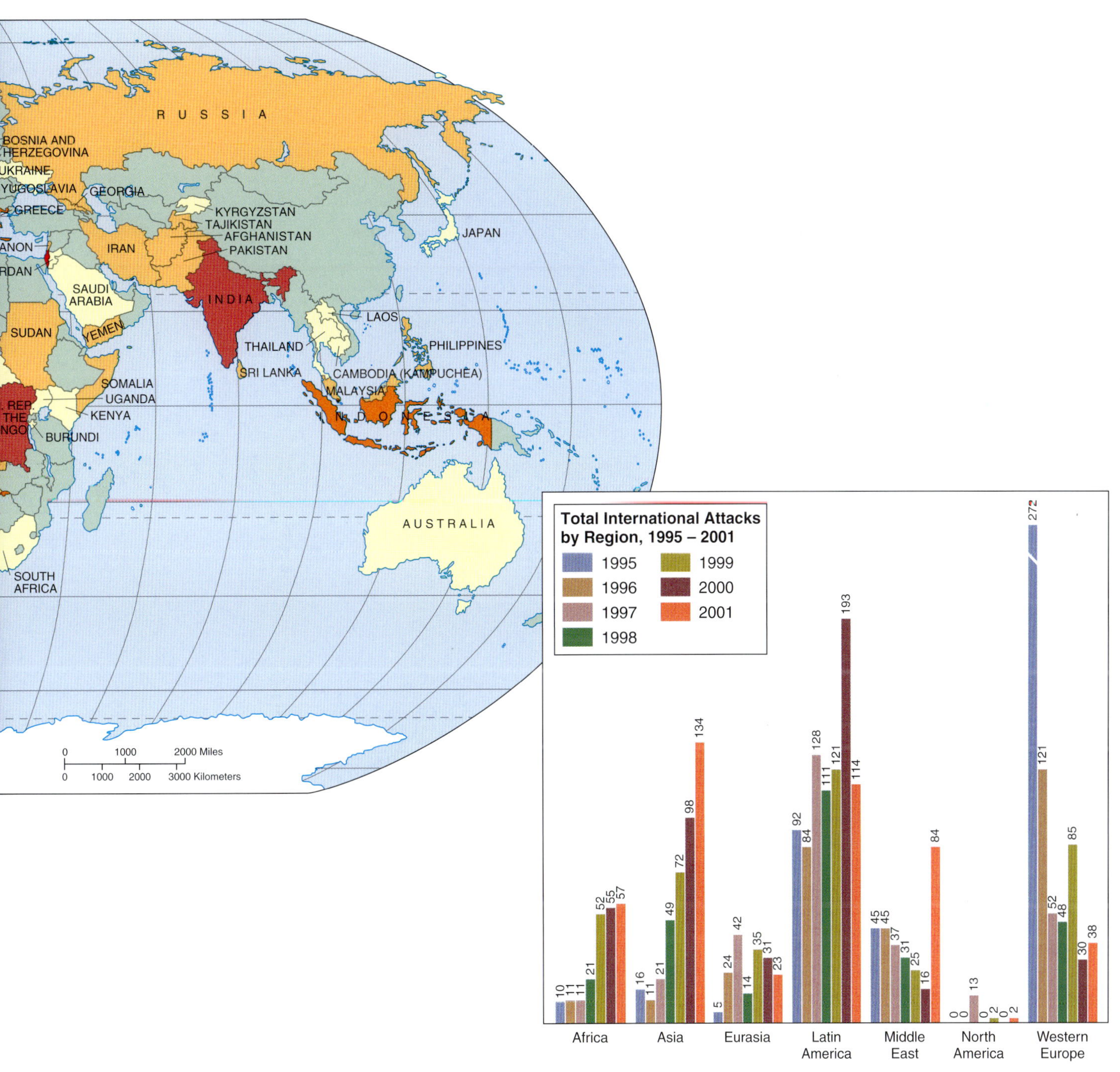
RUSSIA
BOSNIA AND HERZEGOVINA
UKRAINE
YUGOSLAVIA
GEORGIA
GREECE
KYRGYZSTAN
TAJIKISTAN
AFGHANISTAN
PAKISTAN
JAPAN
IRAN
SAUDI ARABIA
INDIA
YEMEN
SUDAN
LAOS
THAILAND
PHILIPPINES
SRI LANKA
CAMBODIA (KAMPUCHEA)
MALAYSIA
SOMALIA
UGANDA
KENYA
BURUNDI
INDONESIA
AUSTRALIA
SOUTH AFRICA
0 1000 2000 Miles
0 1000 2000 3000 Kilometers
Total International Attacks by Region, 1995 – 2001
1995
1996
1997
1998
1999
2000
2001
Africa
Asia
Eurasia
Latin America
Middle East
North America
Western Europe

Region	1995	1996	1997	1998	1999	2000	2001
Africa	10	11	11	21	52	55	57
Asia	16	11	21	49	72	98	134
Eurasia	5	24	42	14	35	31	23
Latin America	92	84	128	111	121	193	114
Middle East	45	45	37	31	25	16	84
North America	0	0	13	0	2	0	2
Western Europe	272	121	52	48	85	30	38

and 2001, despite the enormous losses in the United States in the 9/11 attacks, more lives were lost in Asia and Africa as a result of terrorism than were lost in North America. The world did not change, but Americans' perception of that world and their place in it has certainly changed.

Map 78 Nations With Nuclear Weapons

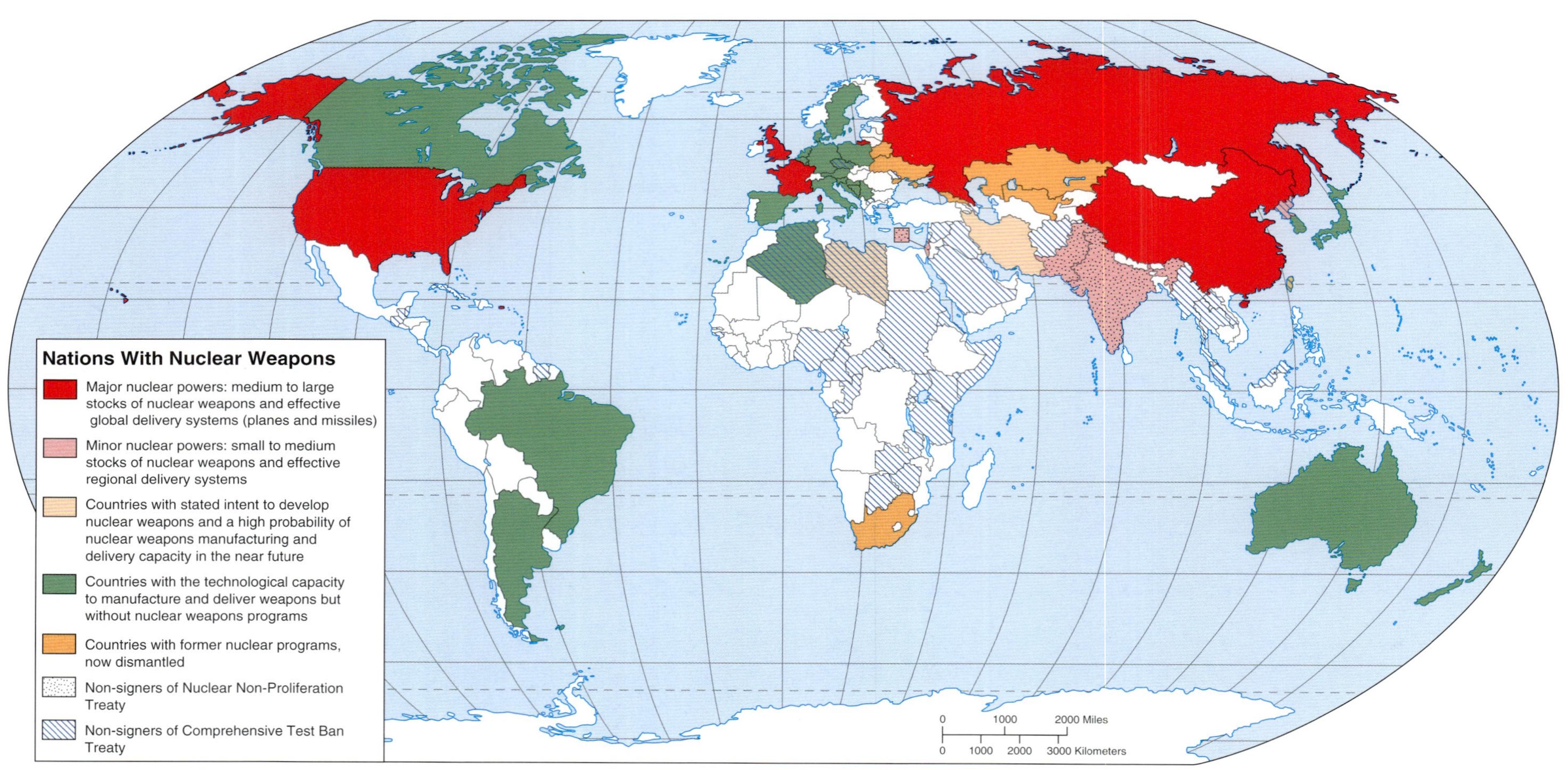
Nations With Nuclear Weapons
Major nuclear powers: medium to large stocks of nuclear weapons and effective global delivery systems (planes and missiles)
Minor nuclear powers: small to medium stocks of nuclear weapons and effective regional delivery systems
Countries with stated intent to develop nuclear weapons and a high probability of nuclear weapons manufacturing and delivery capacity in the near future
Countries with the technological capacity to manufacture and deliver weapons but without nuclear weapons programs
Countries with former nuclear programs, now dismantled
Non-signers of Nuclear Non-Proliferation Treaty
Non-signers of Comprehensive Test Ban Treaty
0 1000 2000 Miles
0 1000 2000 3000 Kilometers

Since 1980, the number of countries possessing the capacity to manufacture and deliver nuclear weapons has grown dramatically, increasing the chances of accidental or intentional nuclear exchanges. In addition to the traditional nuclear powers of the United States, Russia, China, the United Kingdom, and France, must now be added Israel, India, and Pakistan as countries that, without possessing the large stocks of weapons of the major powers, nor the extensive delivery systems of the United States and Russia, still have effective regional (and possibly global) delivery systems and medium stocks of warheads. Countries such as Kazakhstan, Ukraine, Georgia, and Belarus that were created out of what had been the Soviet Union did have some nuclear capacity in the 1991–1995 period but have since had all nuclear weapons removed from their territories. However, North Korea has recently announced the re-establishment of its suspended nuclear weapons programs and may possess a small stock of nuclear warheads, along with the capacity to deliver those weapons regionally. Both Iran and Libya have nuclear ambitions, as did Iraq until the overthrow of the Baathist regime of Saddam Hussein by a U.S.-led military coalition in 2003. The proliferation of nuclear states threatens global security, and the objective of the Nuclear Non-Proliferation Treaty was to reduce the chances for expanding nuclear arsenals worldwide. This treaty has been partially successful in that a number of countries in the developed world certainly have the capacity to manufacture and deliver nuclear weapons but have chosen not to do so. These countries include Canada, European countries other than the United Kingdom and France, South Korea, Japan, Australia, and New Zealand, and Brazil and Argentina in South America. On the other side of the coin, the intent of North Korea to emerge as a nuclear power may force countries such as South Korea and Japan to re-think their positions as non-nuclear countries.

Map 79 Distribution of Minority Populations

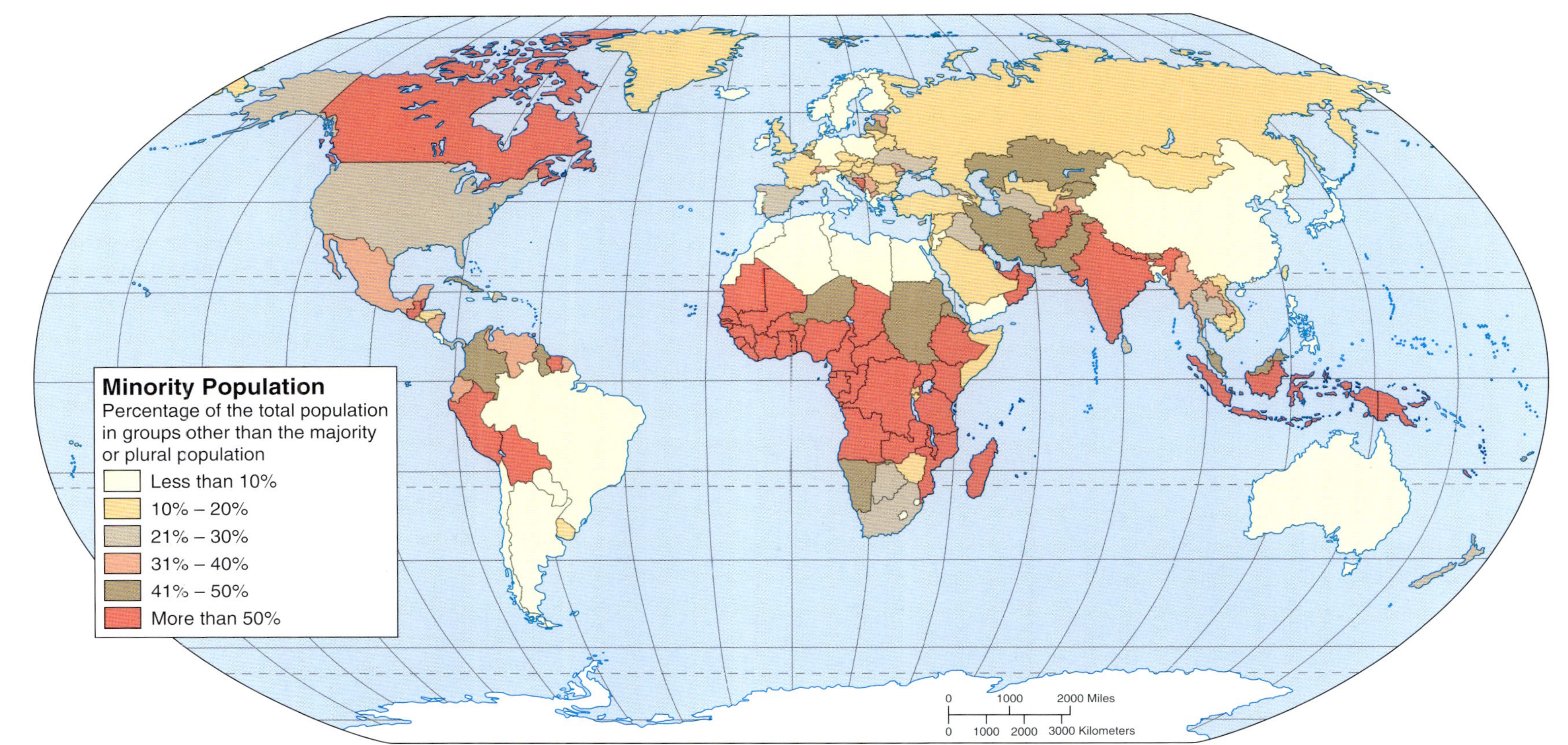
Minority Population
Percentage of the total population in groups other than the majority or plural population
Less than 10%
10% – 20%
21% – 30%
31% – 40%
41% – 50%
More than 50%
0 1000 2000 Miles
0 1000 2000 3000 Kilometers

The presence of minority ethnic, national, or racial groups within a country's population can add a vibrant and dynamic mix to the whole. Plural societies with a high degree of cultural and ethnic diversity should, according to some social theorists, be among the world's most healthy. Unfortunately, the reality of the situation is quite different from theory or expectation. The presence of significant minority populations played an important role in the disintegration of the Soviet Union; the continuing existence of minority populations within the new states formed from former Soviet republics threatens the viability and stability of those young political units. In Africa, national boundaries were drawn by colonial powers without regard for the geographical distribution of ethnic groups, and the continuing tribal conflicts that have resulted hamper both economic and political development. Even in the most highly developed regions of the world, the presence of minority ethnic populations poses significant problems: witness the separatist movement in Canada, driven by the desire of some French-Canadians to be independent of the English majority, and the continuing ethnic conflict between Flemish-speaking and Walloon-speaking Belgians. This map, by arraying states on a scale of homogeneity to heterogeneity, indicates areas of existing and potential social and political strife.

Map 80 Refugee Population, 2002

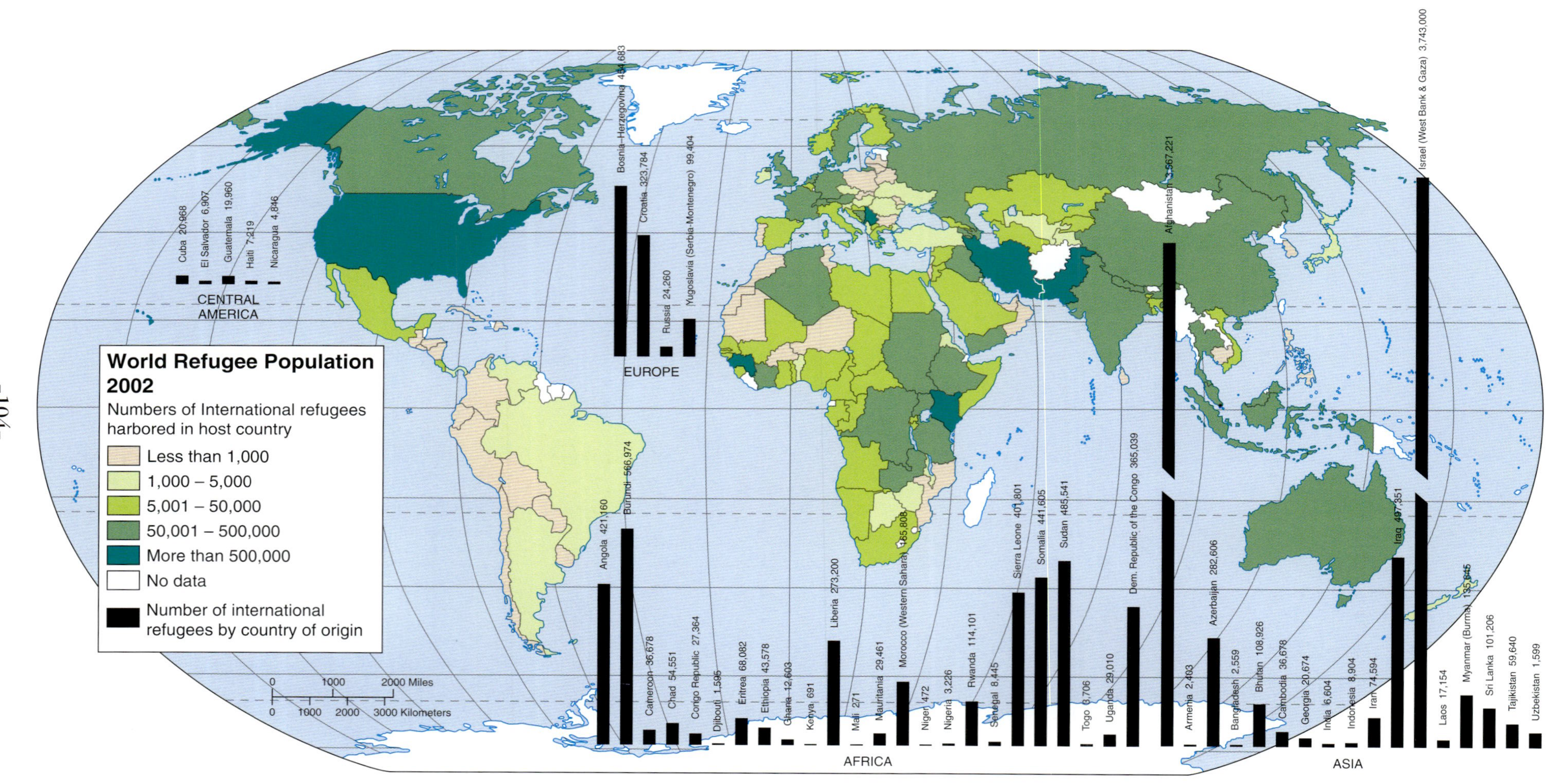

World Refugee Population 2002
Numbers of International refugees harbored in host country
Less than 1,000
1,000 – 5,000
5,001 – 50,000
50,001 – 500,000
More than 500,000
No data
Number of international refugees by country of origin
0 1000 2000 Miles
0 1000 2000 3000 Kilometers
CENTRAL AMERICA
Cuba 20,968
El Salvador 6,907
Guatemala 19,960
Haiti 7,219
Nicaragua 4,846
EUROPE
Bosnia–Herzegovina 454,683
Croatia 323,784
Russia 24,260
Yugoslavia (Serbia-Montenegro) 99,404
AFRICA
Angola 421,160
Burundi 566,974
Cameroon 36,678
Chad 54,551
Congo Republic 27,364
Djibouti 1,596
Eritrea 68,082
Ethiopia 43,578
Ghana 12,603
Kenya 691
Liberia 273,200
Mali 271
Mauritania 29,461
Morocco (Western Sahara) 165,808
Niger 472
Nigeria 3,226
Rwanda 114,101
Senegal 8,445
Sierra Leone 401,801
Somalia 441,605
Sudan 485,541
Togo 6,706
Uganda 29,010
Dem. Republic of the Congo 365,039
ASIA
Afghanistan 3,567,221
Armenia 2,403
Azerbaijan 282,606
Bangladesh 2,559
Bhutan 108,926
Cambodia 36,678
Georgia 20,674
India 6,604
Indonesia 8,904
Iran 74,594
Iraq 497,351
Israel (West Bank & Gaza) 3,743,000
Laos 17,154
Myanmar (Burma) 135,845
Sri Lanka 101,206
Tajikistan 59,640
Uzbekistan 1,599

Refugees are persons who have been driven from their homes, normally by armed conflict, and have sought refuge by relocating. The most numerous refugees have traditionally been international refugees, who have crossed the political boundaries of their homelands into other countries. This refugee population is recognized by international agencies, and the countries of refuge are often rewarded financially by those agencies for their willingness to take in externally displaced persons. In recent years, largely because of an increase in civil wars, there have been growing numbers of internally displaced persons—those who leave their homes but stay within their country of origin. There are no rewards for harboring such internal refugee populations.

Map 81 Political and Civil Liberties, 2004

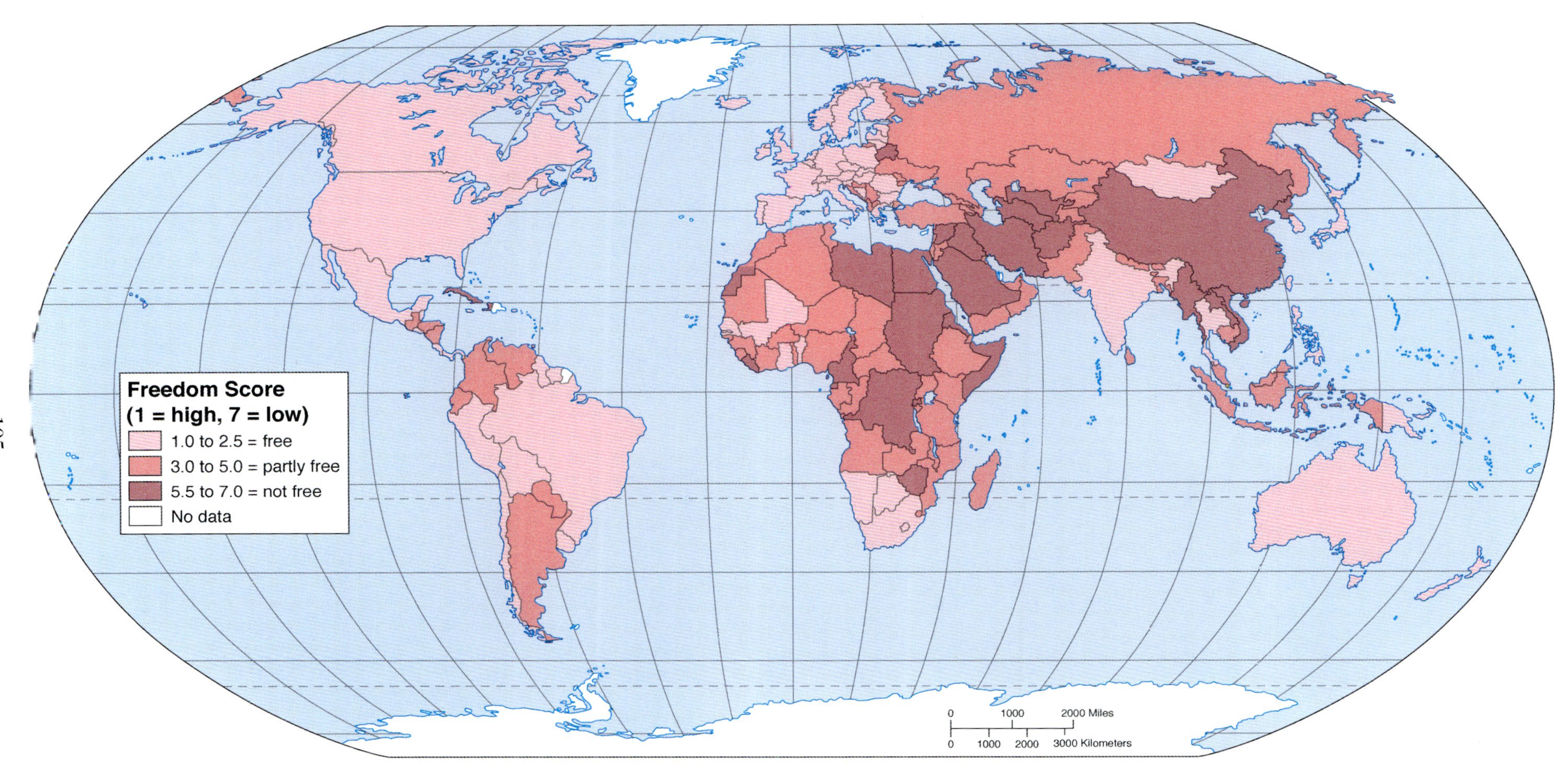

Freedom Score
(1 = high, 7 = low)
1.0 to 2.5 = free
3.0 to 5.0 = partly free
5.5 to 7.0 = not free
No data
0 1000 2000 Miles
0 1000 2000 3000 Kilometers

Although measures of political and civil liberty are somewhat difficult to obtain and assess, there are some generally accepted standards that can be evaluated: open elections and competitive political parties, the rule of law, freedoms of speech and press, judicial systems separate from other branches of government, and limits on the power of elected or appointed governmental officials. Interestingly, there appear to be correlations between "degrees of freedom" and such other characteristics of a state as per capita wealth, environmental quality, and healthy economic growth—characteristics that may be mutually contradictory. There is no empirical evidence of a causal link between democratic institutions and consumption; on the other hand, there is clear evidence of a positive relationship between wealth and consumption. Therefore, the three variables are closely correlated and should be used in assessing the nature of the state in any part of the world.

Part VII

World Regions

Map 82 North America: Physical Features

ARCTIC OCEAN
GREENLAND (DENMARK)
ELLESMERE ISLAND
QUEEN ELIZABETH ISLANDS
BANKS ISLAND
Viscount Melville Sound
VICTORIA ISLAND
BOOTHIA PENINSULA
BAFFIN ISLAND
Baffin Bay
Davis Strait
Cape York
Pt. Barrow
BEAUFORT SEA
BROOKS RANGE
Arctic Circle
Mackenzie R.
Great Bear Lake
Great Slave Lake
Mt. Logan 18,551 ft.
Mt. St. Elias 18,008 ft.
SOUTHAMPTON ISLAND
Hudson Strait
Cape Chidley
UNGAVA PENINSULA
Hudson Bay
LABRADOR PENINSULA
Strait of Belle Isle
SITKA ISLAND
ROCKY MOUNTAINS
COAST MOUNTAINS
CORDILLERAN HIGHLANDS
Peace R.
Athabasca Lake
Athabasca R.
Reindeer Lake
Nelson R.
CANADA
James Bay
Saskatchewan R.
QUEEN CHARLOTTE ISLANDS
N. Saskatchewan R.
S. Saskatchewan R.
Lake Winnipeg
Fraser R.
VANCOUVER ISLAND
Lake of the Woods
Lake Nipigon
LAURENTIAN HIGHLANDS
St. Lawrence R.
Gulf of St. Lawrence
Cape Race
CAPE BRETON ISLAND
GASPÉ PENINSULA
Montreal
Ottawa
Cape Sable
Mt. Rainier 14,410 ft.
Missouri R.
Lake Superior
Red R.
GREAT PLAINS
Columbia R.
Yellowstone R.
Lake Huron
Ontario
Connecticut R.
Cape Cod
Hudson R.
New York
Philadelphia
Delaware R.
Washington, D.C.
Potomac R.
Chesapeake Bay
Roanoke R.
Cape Hatteras
National capital
City
CASCADE RANGE
Snake R.
Grand Teton 13,770'
UNITED STATES
Mt. Shasta 14,162 ft.
Des Moines R.
Chicago
Lake Michigan
Detroit
L. Erie
APPALACHIAN MOUNTAINS
Great Salt Lake
Platte R.
Wabash R.
Ohio R.
Illinois R.
Sacramento R.
GREAT BASIN
SIERRA NEVADA
COAST RANGES
Colorado R.
San Joaquin R.
Mt. Whitney 14,494 ft.
Pike's Peak 14,110'
Arkansas R.
Mississippi R.
Tennessee R.
BERMUDA
Canadian R.
Red R.
Los Angeles
Savannah R.
ATLANTIC OCEAN
Rio Grande
GUADALUPE ISLAND
SIERRA MADRE OCCIDENTAL
SIERRA MADRE ORIENTAL
Colorado R.
Lake Okeechobee
Miami
Straits of Florida
BAHAMAS
Gulf of California
Gulf of Mexico
Tropic of Cancer
Havana
CUBA
DOMINICAN REPUBLIC
HAITI
Cabo San Lucas
Yucatan Channel
WEST INDIES
PACIFIC OCEAN
MEXICO
Campeche Bay
Yucatan Peninsula
JAMAICA
ISLA REVILLAGIGEDO
Mexico City
Orizaba Peak 18,406 ft.
Popocatepetl 17,887 ft.
BELIZE
Gulf of Honduras
HONDURAS
CARIBBEAN SEA
GUATEMALA
NICARAGUA
EL SALVADOR
COSTA RICA
PANAMA
Gulf of Panama
ISLA DEL COCO
ISLA DE MALPELO
0 500 1000 Miles
0 500 1000 Kilometers
ST. LAWRENCE ISLAND
Bering Strait
BERING SEA
PRIBILOF ISLANDS
ALASKA
Arctic Circle
Yukon R.
Fairbanks
Mt. McKinley 20,320 ft.
ALASKA RANGE
Anchorage
Bristol Bay
YUKON
Mt. Logan 18,551 ft.
Mt. St. Elias 18,008 ft.
ALEUTIAN ISLANDS
ALASKA PENINSULA
KODIAK ISLAND
Gulf of Alaska
Juneau
500 Miles
500 Kilometers
KAUAI
NIIHAU
OAHU
HAWAII
MOLOKAI
MAUI
LANAI
KAHOOLAWE
PACIFIC OCEAN
HAWAII
0 50 100 Miles
0 50 100 Kilometers
Elevation
Feet
3000
1500
300
0
Sea level
0
100
1000
Below sea level

Map 83 North America: Political Divisions

ARCTIC OCEAN
GREENLAND (DENMARK)
BEAUFORT SEA
Baffin Bay
BAFFIN ISLAND
Davis Strait
ELLESMERE ISLAND
QUEEN ELIZABETH ISLANDS
VICTORIA ISLAND
NUNAVUT
YUKON
NORTHWEST TERRITORIES
Hudson Strait
Hudson Bay
BRITISH COLUMBIA
ALBERTA
SASKATCHEWAN
MANITOBA
ONTARIO
QUEBEC
NEWFOUNDLAND
CANADA
PRINCE EDWARD IS.
NOVA SCOTIA
NEW BRUNSWICK
UNITED STATES
MEXICO
Gulf of Mexico
ATLANTIC OCEAN
PACIFIC OCEAN
BERMUDA
BAHAMAS
CUBA
HAITI
DOMINICAN REPUBLIC
PUERTO RICO
JAMAICA
WEST INDIES
CARIBBEAN SEA
TRINIDAD AND TOBAGO
BELIZE
GUATEMALA
HONDURAS
EL SALVADOR
NICARAGUA
COSTA RICA
PANAMA
VENEZUELA
COLOMBIA
ALASKA
BERING SEA
ALEUTIAN ISLANDS
Gulf of Alaska
HAWAII
KAUAI
NIIHAU
OAHU
MOLOKAI
LANAI
MAUI
KAHOOLAWE
National capital
State capital
City
0 500 1000 Miles
0 500 1000 Kilometers

Map 84a Environment and Economy: The Use of Land

ARCTIC OCEAN
PACIFIC OCEAN
ATLANTIC OCEAN
GULF OF MEXICO
CARIBBEAN SEA
Arctic Circle
Tropic of Cancer
Environment and Economy
Farmland
Irrigated farmland
Livestock grazing and pasture
Commercial woodland and forest
Desert and scrub
Tundra and barren land
Swamp and wetlands
Urban and industrial areas
Mining regions
0 500 1000 Miles
0 500 1000 Kilometers
120°
100°
80°
60°
40°
20°
0°
160°
180°

The use of land in North America represents a balance between agriculture, resource extraction, and manufacturing that is unmatched. The United States, as the world's leading industrial power, is also the world's leader in commercial agricultural production. Canada, despite its small population, is a ranking producer of both agricultural and industrial products and Mexico has begun to emerge from its developing nation status to become an important industrial and agricultural nation as well. The countries of Middle America and the Caribbean are just beginning the transition from agriculture to modern industrial economies. Part of the basis for the high levels of economic productivity in North America is environmental: a superb blend of soil, climate, and raw materials. But just as important is the cultural and social mix of the plural societies of North America, a mix that historically aided the growth of the economic diversity necessary for developed economies.

Map 84b Population Density

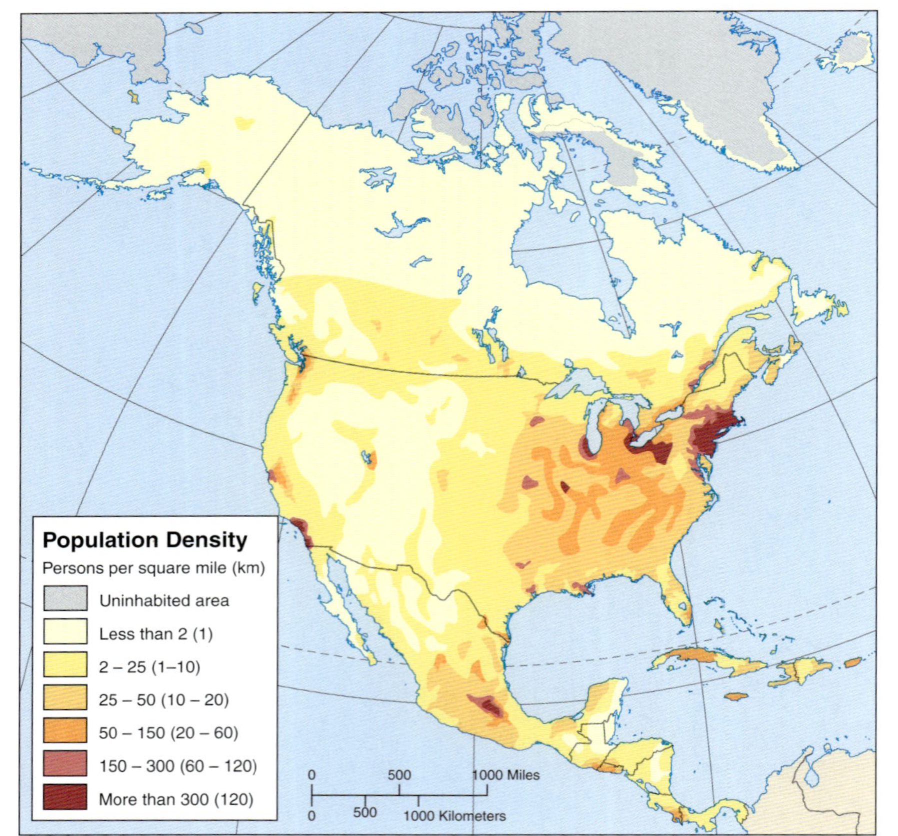
Population Density
Persons per square mile (km)
Uninhabited area
Less than 2 (1)
2 – 25 (1–10)
25 – 50 (10 – 20)
50 – 150 (20 – 60)
150 – 300 (60 – 120)
More than 300 (120)
0 500 1000 Miles
0 500 1000 Kilometers

North America contains nearly 500 million people and the United States, with over 250 million inhabitants, is the third most populous country in the world, after China and India. Most of the present North American population has roots in the Old World. The native populations of the Americas had little or no resistance to Old World diseases in 1500 and within a couple of centuries of first contact with Europeans, most of the native peoples had either died out or preserved their genetic heritage by mixing with disease-resistant Old World populations. This left a North American population that is largely European, but with significant minorities resulting from the slave laborers imported from Africa, and from the mixture of native Americans with Europeans and/or Africans. The density of that population is largely the consequence of environmental factors (good soil, the availability of water, the presence of other resources) and cultural/economic ones (agricultural production, urbanization, industrialization).

Map 84c Population Distribution: Clustering

Population Distribution 2000
One dot equals 10,000 persons
0 500 Kilometers
0 500 Miles
ALASKA
0 300 Miles
0 300 Kilometers
HAWAII
0 100 Miles
0 100 Kilometers

Although population clustering is characteristic of highly economically developed regions, the Anglo-American population exhibits a remarkably clustered pattern. The primary reasons for this remarkable development are agricultural technology and affluence. A highly developed agricultural technology allows a small number of farmers, using sophisticated machinery, to grow and harvest enormous quantities of agricultural produce on large farms. In the United States, the world's leader in commercial agricultural production, only 2 percent of the population are farmers and that population is thinly distributed over wide areas. The vast majority of Americans live and work in city-suburb systems in which the widespread availability of private automobiles allows people to live considerable distances from where they work, keeping overall urban population densities relatively low but allowing for extensive urbanization—with cities large enough in area to be visible as population clusters on maps at this scale.

Map 84d Deforestation in the Americas

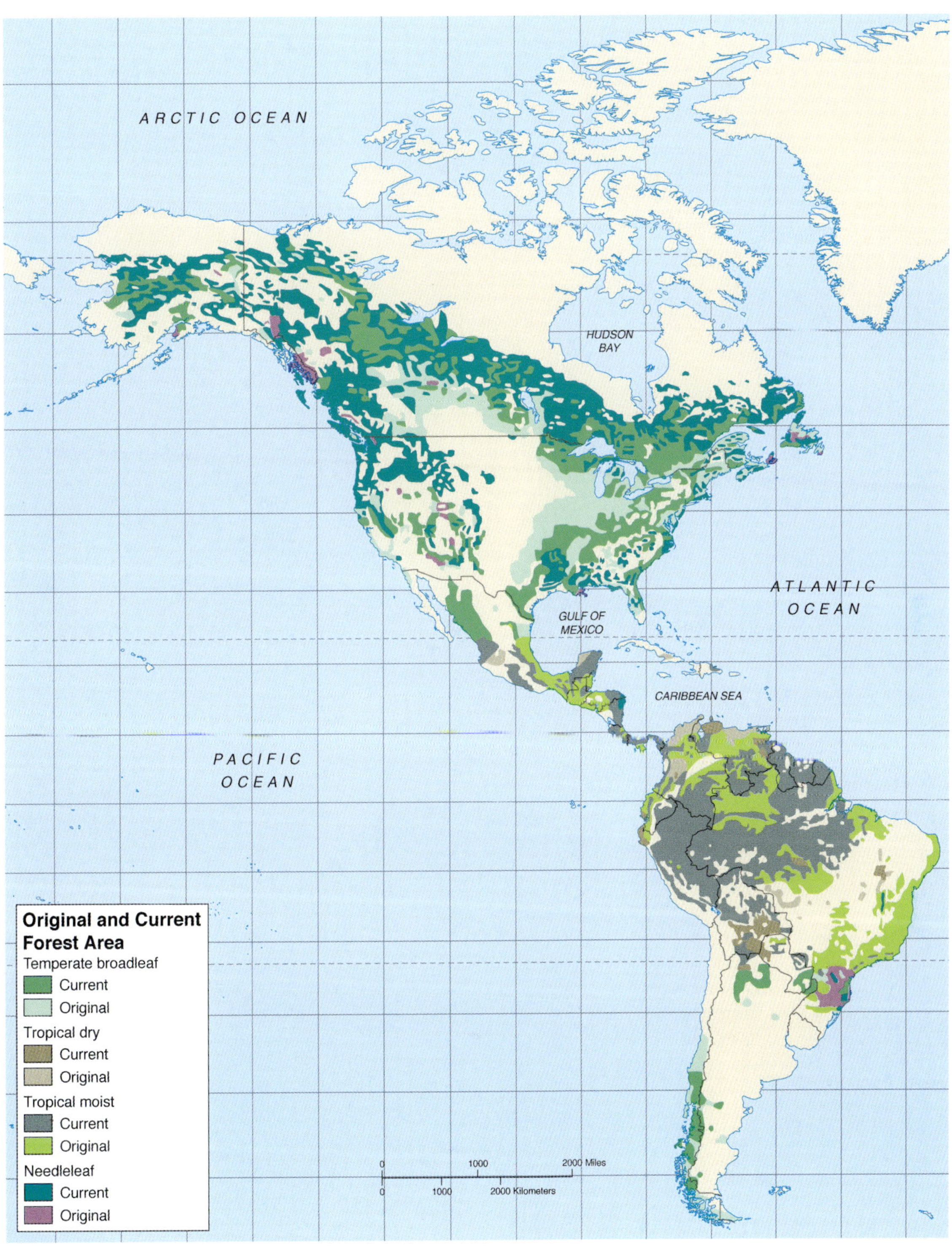
ARCTIC OCEAN
HUDSON BAY
ATLANTIC OCEAN
GULF OF MEXICO
CARIBBEAN SEA
PACIFIC OCEAN
Original and Current Forest Area
Temperate broadleaf
Current
Original
Tropical dry
Current
Original
Tropical moist
Current
Original
Needleleaf
Current
Original
0
1000
2000 Miles
0
1000
2000 Kilometers

This map shows current forest cover adjacent to the estimated forest cover that would be present had there been no human intervention over the past several thousand years since the end of the last ice age, and assuming that climatic conditions would have been pretty much the same as they have been during that time. While in the popular imagination, it is the tropical forest regions of South America and Middle America that have been "deforested," the map shows otherwise. The greatest losses of forest cover have been in the now-agricultural regions of North America and the more temperate regions of South America (most in southern Brazil). Beside these forest losses in the temperate zones, the forest losses of the Amazon Basin seem relatively minor. This does not suggest that the current deforestation of Amazonia and other tropical forest regions is something about which we should not be concerned, but it does put that current deforestation in a more accurate historical context.

Map 85 Canada

Elevation
Feet
3000
1500
300
0
Sea level
Below sea level
0
100
1000
Lambert Equal-Area Projection
National capital
State capital
City
ARCTIC OCEAN
BEAUFORT SEA
LINCOLN SEA
GREENLAND SEA
GREENLAND (DENMARK)
ICELAND
Reykjavík
Denmark Strait
Arctic Circle
Angmagssalik
Godthåb
Baffin Bay
Davis Strait
LABRADOR SEA
Hudson Strait
ATLANTIC OCEAN
PACIFIC OCEAN
BROOKS RANGE
Yukon R.
Porcupine R.
UNITED STATES
Mt. McKinley 20,320 ft.
RICHARDSON MTS.
Dawson
YUKON TERRITORY
Mt. Logan 19,551 ft.
Mt. St. Elias 18,008 ft.
Whitehorse
Mt. Fairweather 15,300 ft.
Skagway
Juneau
MACKENZIE MOUNTAINS
Norman Wells
Mackenzie R.
Great Bear Lake
Fort Norman
NORTHWEST TERRITORIES
HORN MOUNTAINS
Yellowknife
Great Slave Lake
Fort Resolution
Fort Smith
Liard R.
Churchill Pk. 10,500 ft.
CARIBOU MOUNTAINS
Lake Athabasca
BRITISH COLUMBIA
Hazelton
Prince Rupert
QUEEN CHARLOTTE ISLANDS
Prince George
COAST MOUNTAINS
ROCKY MOUNTAINS
Fraser R.
Mt. Waddington 13,163 ft.
Kamloops
VANCOUVER ISLAND
Vancouver
North Vancouver
Burnaby
Victoria
Seattle
Columbia R.
Snake R.
Great Salt Lake
Peace R.
Peace River
CANADA
ALBERTA
Mt. Robson 12,972 ft.
Edmonton
N. Saskatchewan R.
Red Deer
Calgary
Medicine Hat
S. Saskatchewan R.
Lethbridge
SASKATCHEWAN
Prince Albert
Saskatoon
Regina
Moose Jaw
Reindeer Lake
Lake Winnipegosis
Lake Manitoba
Lake Winnipeg
Brandon
Winnipeg
MANITOBA
Churchill R.
Churchill
Nelson R.
Missouri R.
Mississippi R.
UNITED STATES
Minneapolis
St. Paul
Duluth
QUEEN ELIZABETH ISLANDS
PARRY ISLANDS
ELLESMERE ISLAND
DEVON ISLAND
BANKS ISLAND
VICTORIA ISLAND
Cambridge Bay (Ikaluktutiak)
NUNAVUT
Dubawnt Lake
Baker Lake
BAFFIN ISLAND
FOXE BASIN
SOUTHAMPTON ISLAND
COATS ISLAND
MANSEL ISLAND
Iqaluit
Lake Harbour
Hudson Bay
NUNAVUT
BELCHER ISLAND
James Bay
AKIMISKI ISLAND
Fort George
Fort Albany
ONTARIO
Severn R.
Albany R.
Lake Nipigon
Thunder Bay
Lake Superior
Timmins
Sudbury
Sault Ste. Marie
North Bay
Georgian Bay
Lake Huron
Lake Michigan
Milwaukee
Chicago
Toronto
Hamilton
London
Sarnia
Detroit
Windsor
Lake Erie
Lake Ontario
St. Catherines
Buffalo
Cleveland
Lindsay
Kingston
Ottawa
Hull
QUEBEC
Feuilles R.
La Grande R.
OTISH MOUNTAINS
Péribonca R.
Jonquière
Chicoutimi
Quebec
Shawinigan
Trois-Rivières
Montreal
Laval
St. Jean
Valleyfield
Drummondville
Sherbrooke
St. Lawrence R.
Rimouski
MTS. CHIC-CHOCS
Nain
Smallwood Reservoir
Goose Bay
NEWFOUNDLAND
Gander
Corner Brook
ILE D'ANTICOSTI
St. John's
Gulf of St. Lawrence
PRINCE EDWARD ISLAND
Charlottetown
Sydney
NEW BRUNSWICK
Fredericton
St. John
NOVA SCOTIA
Dartmouth
Halifax
Boston
New York
Philadelphia
0
250
500 Miles
500 Kilometers

Map 86 United States

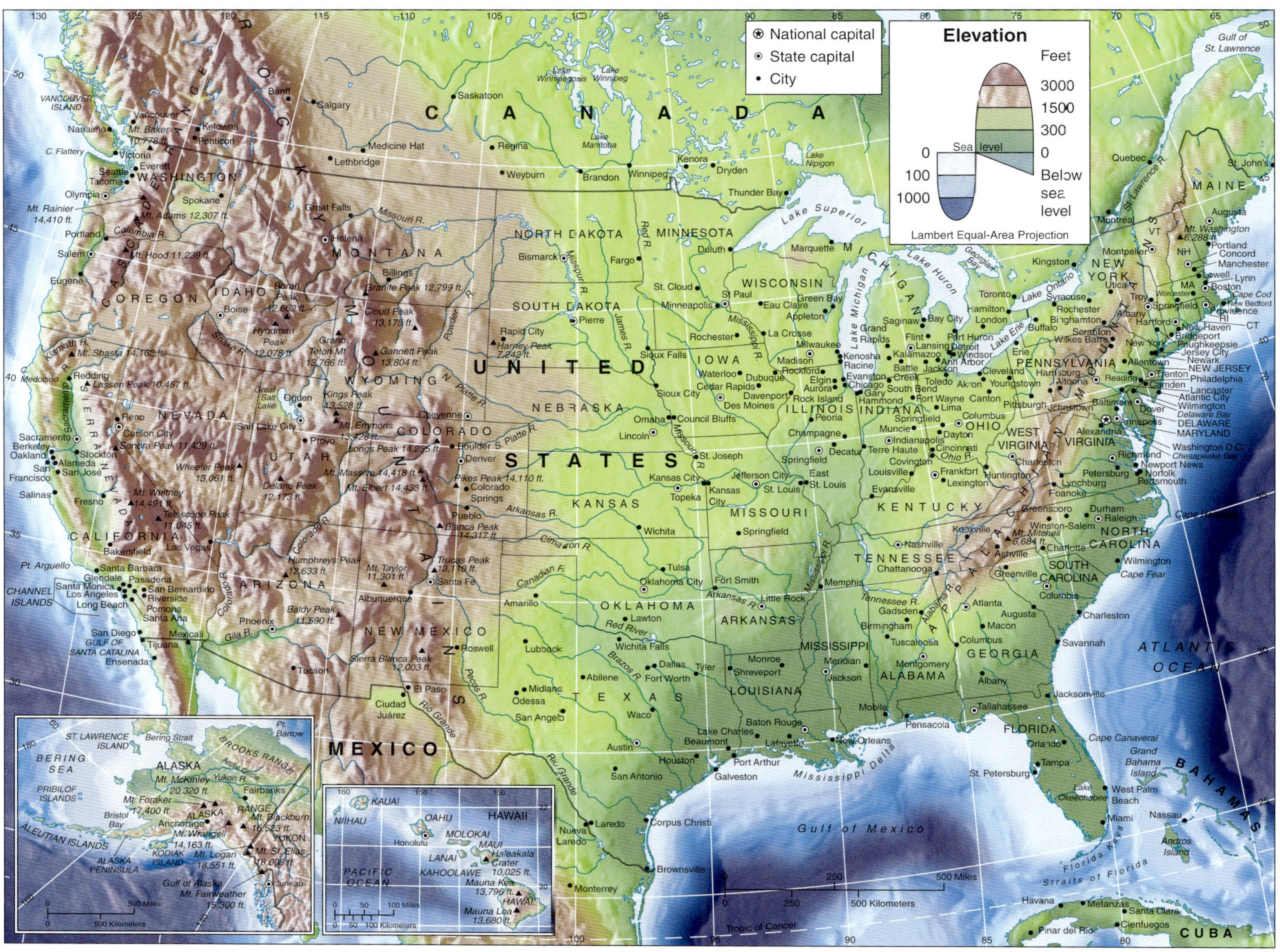

National capital
State capital
City
Elevation
Feet
3000
1500
300
0
Sea level
Below sea level
0
100
1000
Lambert Equal-Area Projection
CANADA
UNITED STATES
MEXICO
CUBA
BAHAMAS
ATLANTIC OCEAN
Gulf of Mexico
Gulf of St. Lawrence
Straits of Florida
Florida Keys
Mississippi Delta
Tropic of Cancer
ROCKY MOUNTAINS
CASCADE RANGE
SIERRA NEVADA
APPALACHIAN MOUNTAINS
WASHINGTON
OREGON
IDAHO
MONTANA
WYOMING
NEVADA
UTAH
COLORADO
CALIFORNIA
ARIZONA
NEW MEXICO
NORTH DAKOTA
SOUTH DAKOTA
NEBRASKA
KANSAS
OKLAHOMA
TEXAS
MINNESOTA
IOWA
MISSOURI
ARKANSAS
LOUISIANA
WISCONSIN
ILLINOIS
MICHIGAN
INDIANA
OHIO
KENTUCKY
TENNESSEE
MISSISSIPPI
ALABAMA
GEORGIA
FLORIDA
SOUTH CAROLINA
NORTH CAROLINA
VIRGINIA
WEST VIRGINIA
PENNSYLVANIA
NEW YORK
NEW JERSEY
MARYLAND
DELAWARE
MAINE
Lake Superior
Lake Michigan
Lake Huron
Lake Erie
Lake Ontario
Washington D.C.
ALASKA
BERING SEA
BROOKS RANGE
ALASKA RANGE
Mt. McKinley 20,320 ft.
ALEUTIAN ISLANDS
ALASKA PENINSULA
Gulf of Alaska
HAWAII
PACIFIC OCEAN
KAUAI
OAHU
MOLOKAI
MAUI
LANAI
KAHOOLAWE
NIIHAU
Honolulu
Mauna Kea 13,796 ft.
Mauna Loa 13,680 ft.
500 Miles
500 Kilometers

Map 87 Middle America

UNITED STATES OF AMERICA
MEXICO
GUATEMALA
BELIZE
HONDURAS
EL SALVADOR
NICARAGUA
COSTA RICA
PANAMA
CUBA
JAMAICA
BAHAMA ISLANDS
CAYMAN ISLANDS (Br.)
ATLANTIC OCEAN
PACIFIC OCEAN
CARIBBEAN SEA
Gulf of Mexico
Gulf of California
Yucatan Channel
Campeche Bay
Gulf of Tehuantepec
Gulf of Honduras
Gulf of Mosquitos
Gulf of Panama
Terminos Lagoon
Lake Nicaragua
L. Chapala
Tropic of Cancer
SIERRA MADRE OCCIDENTAL
SIERRA MADRE ORIENTAL
San Diego
Tijauana
Mexicali
Ensenada
Phoenix
El Paso
Ciudad Juárez
Dallas
Houston
San Antonio
New Orleans
Memphis
Atlanta
Jacksonville
Tampa
Miami
Nassau
ANDROS I.
Canadian R.
Red R.
Brazos R.
Pecos R.
Mississippi R.
Rio Grande
Balsas R.
BAJA CALIFORNIA
BAJA CALIFORNIA SUR
GUADALUPE ISLAND
CEDROS ISLAND
Punta Eugenie
Cerro de la Encantada 10,126 ft.
Cerro Pinacate 4,560 ft.
Vol. LasTres Virgenes 6,547 ft.
Pico Cupula 5,000 ft.
Santa Genoveva 7,100 ft.
La Paz
Cabo San Lucas
SONORA
Hermosillo
Ciudad Obregón
CHIHUAHUA
Chihuahua
COAHUILA
Culiacán
SINALOA
Mazatlán
DURANGO
Durango
Gómez Palacio
Torreón
Saltillo
NUEVO LEON
Monterrey
Nuevo Laredo
Matamoros
TAMAULIPAS
Ciudad Victoria
Tampico
ZACATECAS
Zacatecas
SAN LUIS POTOSI
San Luis Potosí
NAYARIT
Tepic
AGUASCALIENTES
Aguascalientes
León
Guanajuato
GUANAJUATO
Querétaro
QUERÉTARO
Celaya
Cape Corrientes
Guadalajara
JALISCO
Nevado de Colima 13,993 ft.
Colima
COLIMA
MICHOACAN
Morelia
Vol. Paricutin 9,213 ft.
MEXICO
Nevado de Toluca 14,409 ft.
Toluca
Mexico City
Cuernavaca
MORELOS
Vol. Popocatépetl 17,930 ft.
GUERRERO
Chilpancingo de los Bravo
HILDAGO
Iztaccihuatl 17,159 ft.
Pachuca
TLAXCALA
Tlaxcala
Puebla
PUEBLA
Xalapa
Veracruz
Orizaba
VERACRUZ
Oaxaca
OAXACA
TABASCO
Villahermosa
Tuxtla Gutiérrez
CHIAPAS
Campeche
CAMPECHE
YUCATÁN
Mérida
Yucatan Peninsula
QUINTANA ROO
Ciudad Chetumal
Belize City
Belmopan
Tacana 13,417 ft.
Guatemala
Santa Ana
San Salvador
Tegucigalpa
Managua
San Jose
Cerro Chirripó 12,530 ft.
Vol. Barú 11,401 ft.
Colón
Panama
Guanabacoa
Havana
Marianao
Matanzas
Cárdenas
Santa Clara
Cienfuegos
Pinar del Río
ISLE OF YOUTH
Camagüey
Holguín
Manzanillo
Pico Turquino 6,470 ft.
Santiago de Cuba
Mt. Denham 3,236 ft.
Kingston
Elevation
Feet
3000
1500
300
0
Sea level
0
100
1000
Below sea level
Lambert Equal-Area Projection
National capital
State capital
City
0
250
500 Miles
0
250
500 Kilometers

Map 88 The Caribbean

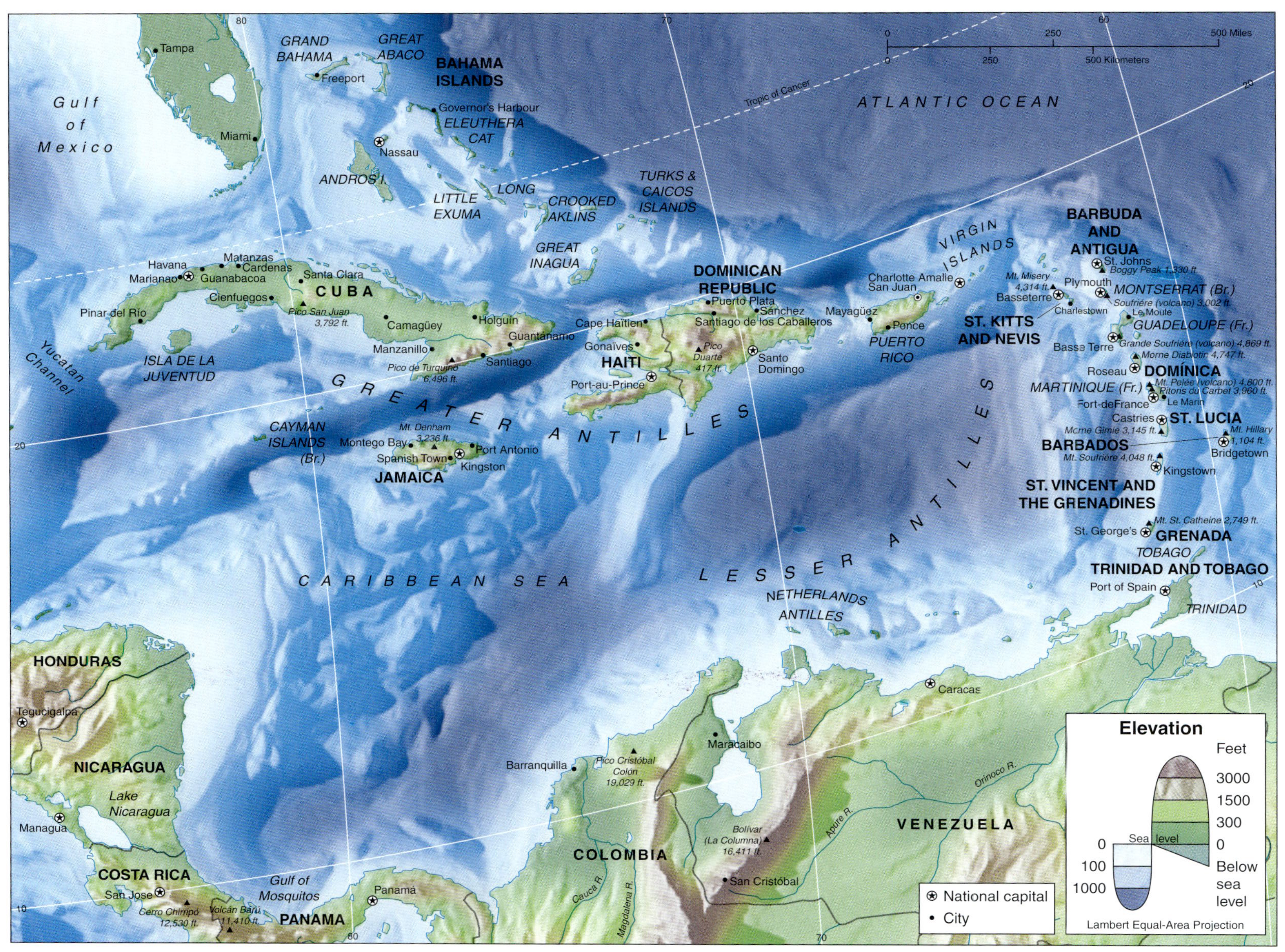

Gulf of Mexico
ATLANTIC OCEAN
CARIBBEAN SEA
GREATER ANTILLES
LESSER ANTILLES
Tropic of Cancer
Tampa
Miami
GRAND BAHAMA
Freeport
GREAT ABACO
BAHAMA ISLANDS
Governor's Harbour
ELEUTHERA
CAT
Nassau
ANDROS I.
LITTLE EXUMA
LONG
CROOKED
AKLINS
GREAT INAGUA
TURKS & CAICOS ISLANDS
Havana
Marianao
Matanzas
Cardenas
Guanabacoa
Santa Clara
CUBA
Cienfuegos
Pico San Juan 3,792 ft.
Pinar del Río
Camagüey
Holguín
Guantánamo
Manzanillo
Santiago
Pico de Turquino 6,496 ft.
ISLA DE LA JUVENTUD
Yucatan Channel
CAYMAN ISLANDS (Br.)
Mt. Denham 3,236 ft.
Montego Bay
Spanish Town
Kingston
Port Antonio
JAMAICA
DOMINICAN REPUBLIC
Puerto Plata
Sánchez
Santiago de los Caballeros
Cape Haïtien
Gonaïves
HAITI
Port-au-Prince
Pico Duarte 417 ft.
Santo Domingo
Mayagüez
Ponce
PUERTO RICO
Charlotte Amalie
San Juan
VIRGIN ISLANDS
BARBUDA AND ANTIGUA
St. Johns
Boggy Peak 1,330 ft.
Mt. Misery 4,314 ft.
Basseterre
Plymouth
MONTSERRAT (Br.)
Soufrière (volcano) 3,002 ft.
Charlestown
ST. KITTS AND NEVIS
Le Moule
GUADELOUPE (Fr.)
Basse Terre
Grande Soufrière (volcano) 4,869 ft.
Morne Diablotin 4,747 ft.
Roseau
DOMINICA
MARTINIQUE (Fr.)
Mt. Pelée (volcano) 4,800 ft.
Pitons du Carbet 3,960 ft.
Fort-de-France
Le Marin
Castries
ST. LUCIA
Morne Gimie 3,145 ft.
Mt. Hillary 1,104 ft.
BARBADOS
Bridgetown
Mt. Soufrière 4,048 ft.
Kingstown
ST. VINCENT AND THE GRENADINES
Mt. St. Catheine 2,749 ft.
St. George's
GRENADA
TOBAGO
TRINIDAD AND TOBAGO
Port of Spain
TRINIDAD
NETHERLANDS ANTILLES
Caracas
HONDURAS
Tegucigalpa
NICARAGUA
Lake Nicaragua
Managua
COSTA RICA
San José
Cerro Chirripó 12,530 ft.
Volcán Barú 11,410 ft.
Gulf of Mosquitos
PANAMA
Panamá
COLOMBIA
Barranquilla
Pico Cristóbal Colón 19,029 ft.
Maracaibo
Bolívar (La Columna) 16,411 ft.
San Cristóbal
Cauca R.
Magdalena R.
Apure R.
Orinoco R.
VENEZUELA
0 250 500 Miles
0 250 500 Kilometers
80
70
60
20
10
National capital
City
Elevation
Feet
3000
1500
300
0
Sea level
Below sea level
0
100
1000
Lambert Equal-Area Projection

Map 89 South America: Physical Features

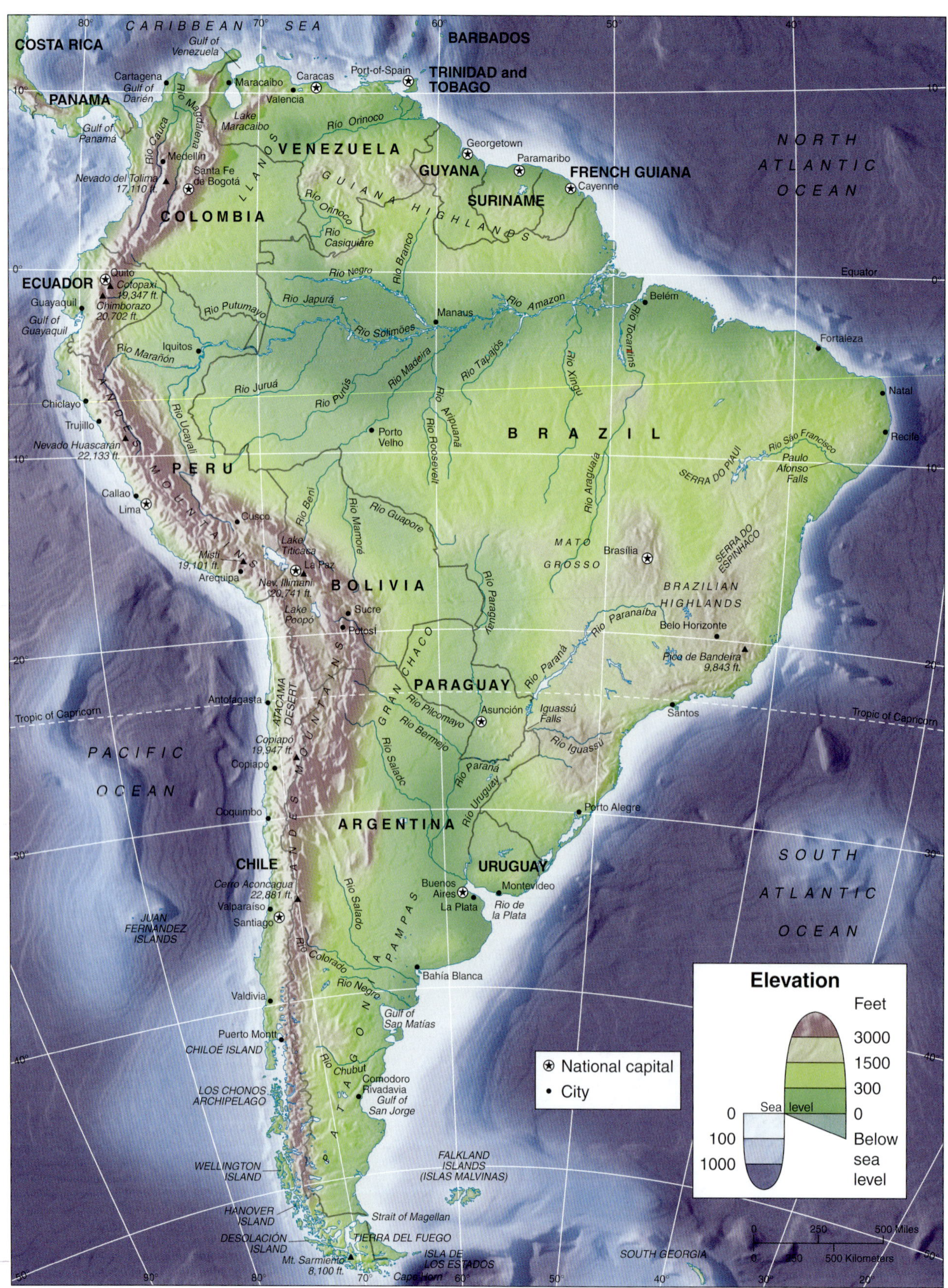
CARIBBEAN SEA
COSTA RICA
PANAMA
BARBADOS
TRINIDAD and TOBAGO
VENEZUELA
COLOMBIA
GUYANA
SURINAME
FRENCH GUIANA
ECUADOR
PERU
BRAZIL
BOLIVIA
PARAGUAY
CHILE
ARGENTINA
URUGUAY
NORTH ATLANTIC OCEAN
SOUTH ATLANTIC OCEAN
PACIFIC OCEAN
Gulf of Venezuela
Cartagena
Gulf of Darién
Gulf of Panamá
Maracaibo
Lake Maracaibo
Caracas
Valencia
Port-of-Spain
Río Orinoco
Río Magdalena
Río Cauca
Medellín
Santa Fe de Bogotá
Nevado del Tolima 17,110 ft.
LLANOS
GUIANA HIGHLANDS
Georgetown
Paramaribo
Cayenne
Río Casiquiare
Río Branco
Río Negro
Quito
Cotopaxi 19,347 ft.
Chimborazo 20,702 ft.
Guayaquil
Gulf of Guayaquil
Río Putumayo
Río Japurá
Río Amazon
Manaus
Río Solimões
Belém
Río Tocantins
Iquitos
Río Marañon
Río Juruá
Río Purus
Río Madeira
Río Tapajós
Río Xingu
Fortaleza
Natal
Recife
Chiclayo
Trujillo
Nevado Huascarán 22,133 ft.
ANDES MOUNTAINS
Río Ucayali
Porto Velho
Río Aripuanã
Río Roosevelt
Río Araguaia
Río São Francisco
Paulo Afonso Falls
SERRA DO PIAUÍ
Callao
Lima
Cusco
Río Beni
Río Mamoré
Río Guaporé
Lake Titicaca
La Paz
Misti 19,101 ft.
Arequipa
Nev. Illimani 20,741 ft.
MATO GROSSO
Brasília
SERRA DO ESPINHAÇO
Río Paraguay
BRAZILIAN HIGHLANDS
Sucre
Lake Poopó
Potosí
Río Paranaíba
Belo Horizonte
Pico de Bandeira 9,843 ft.
GRAN CHACO
Río Paraná
Antofagasta
ATACAMA DESERT
Río Pilcomayo
Asunción
Iguassú Falls
Santos
Tropic of Capricorn
Río Bermejo
Río Iguassú
Copiapó 19,947 ft.
Copiapó
Río Salado
Río Uruguay
Coquimbo
Porto Alegre
Cerro Aconcagua 22,881 ft.
Valparaíso
Santiago
JUAN FERNANDEZ ISLANDS
Buenos Aires
Montevideo
La Plata
Río de la Plata
PAMPAS
Río Colorado
Bahía Blanca
Río Negro
Valdivia
Gulf of San Matías
Puerto Montt
CHILOÉ ISLAND
PATAGONIA
Río Chubut
Comodoro Rivadavia
Gulf of San Jorge
LOS CHONOS ARCHIPELAGO
WELLINGTON ISLAND
FALKLAND ISLANDS (ISLAS MALVINAS)
HANOVER ISLAND
Strait of Magellan
DESOLACIÓN ISLAND
TIERRA DEL FUEGO
Mt. Sarmiento 8,100 ft.
ISLA DE LOS ESTADOS
Cape Horn
SOUTH GEORGIA
Equator
80°
70°
60°
50°
40°
30°
20°
90°
10°
0°
Elevation
Feet
3000
1500
300
0
Sea level
100
1000
Below sea level
National capital
City
0 250 500 Miles
0 250 500 Kilometers

Map 90 South America: Political Divisions

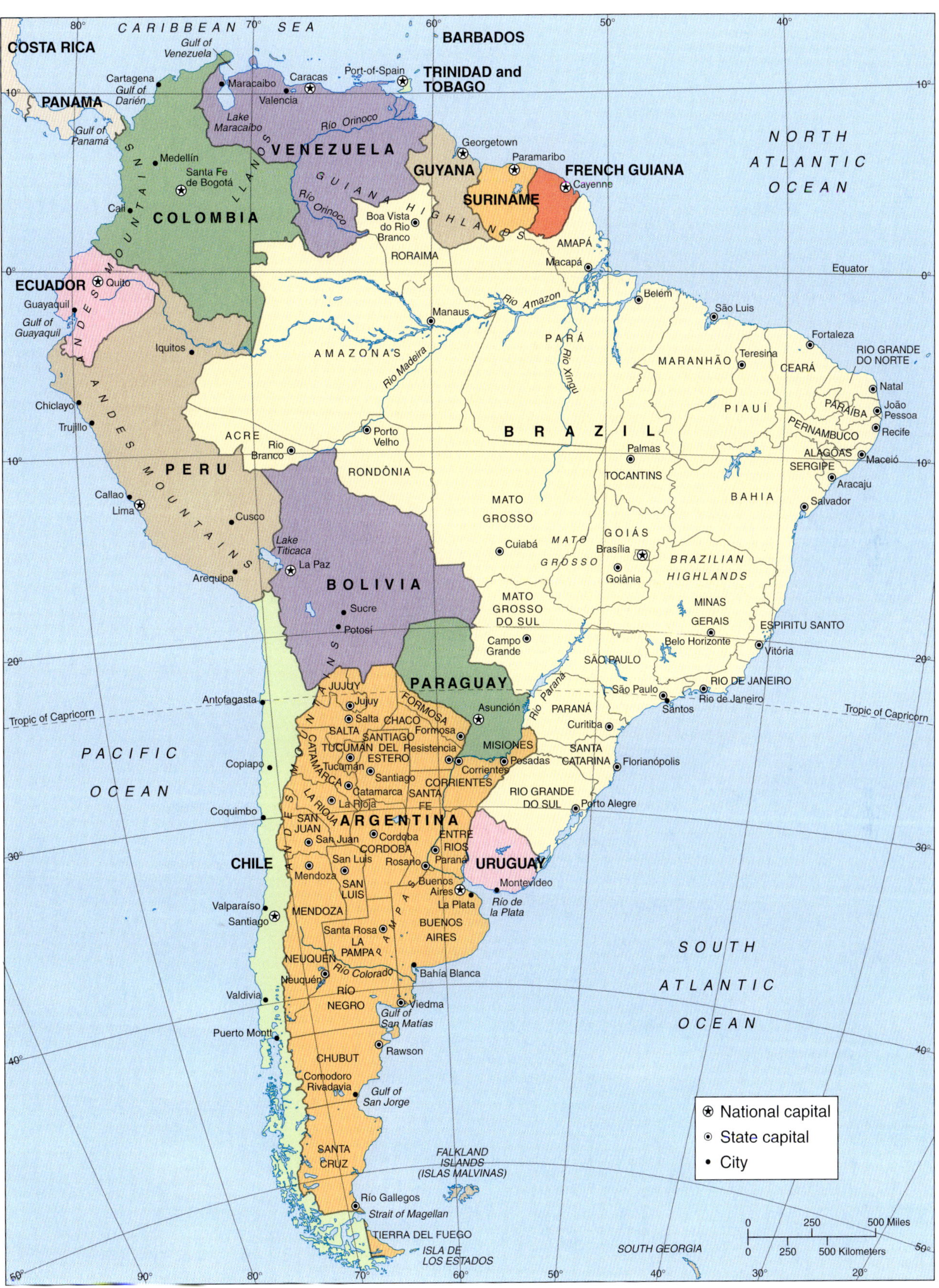

CARIBBEAN SEA
Gulf of Venezuela
COSTA RICA
PANAMA
Gulf of Darién
Gulf of Panama
BARBADOS
TRINIDAD and TOBAGO
Port-of-Spain
Caracas
Cartagena
Maracaibo
Valencia
Lake Maracaibo
Río Orinoco
VENEZUELA
GUIANA HIGHLANDS
Georgetown
Paramaribo
Cayenne
GUYANA
SURINAME
FRENCH GUIANA
NORTH ATLANTIC OCEAN
Medellín
Santa Fe de Bogotá
Cali
COLOMBIA
LLANOS
ANDES MOUNTAINS
Boa Vista do Rio Branco
RORAIMA
AMAPÁ
Macapá
Equator
ECUADOR
Quito
Guayaquil
Gulf of Guayaquil
Iquitos
Manaus
Rio Amazon
Belém
São Luis
Fortaleza
RIO GRANDE DO NORTE
Natal
AMAZONAS
Rio Madeira
PARÁ
Rio Xingu
MARANHÃO
Teresina
CEARÁ
PARAÍBA
João Pessoa
PERNAMBUCO
Recife
PIAUÍ
Chiclayo
Trujillo
ACRE
Rio Branco
Porto Velho
RONDÔNIA
BRAZIL
Palmas
TOCANTINS
ALAGOAS
Maceió
SERGIPE
Aracaju
BAHIA
Salvador
PERU
Callao
Lima
Cusco
MATO GROSSO
Cuiabá
GOIÁS
Brasília
Goiânia
BRAZILIAN HIGHLANDS
Lake Titicaca
La Paz
Arequipa
BOLIVIA
Sucre
Potosí
MATO GROSSO DO SUL
Campo Grande
MINAS GERAIS
Belo Horizonte
ESPIRITU SANTO
Vitória
SÃO PAULO
São Paulo
Santos
RIO DE JANEIRO
Rio de Janeiro
Tropic of Capricorn
PARAGUAY
Asunción
Rio Paraná
PARANÁ
Curitiba
Antofagasta
JUJUY
Jujuy
Salta
SALTA
CHACO
FORMOSA
Formosa
SANTIAGO DEL ESTERO
TUCUMÁN
Tucumán
Resistencia
Corrientes
MISIONES
Posadas
SANTA CATARINA
Florianópolis
PACIFIC OCEAN
Copiapó
CATAMARCA
Catamarca
Santiago
CORRIENTES
SANTA FE
RIO GRANDE DO SUL
Porto Alegre
Coquimbo
LA RIOJA
La Rioja
SAN JUAN
San Juan
ARGENTINA
Córdoba
CORDOBA
ENTRE RIOS
Paraná
URUGUAY
Montevideo
CHILE
Mendoza
San Luis
SAN LUIS
Rosario
Buenos Aires
La Plata
Río de la Plata
Valparaíso
Santiago
MENDOZA
Santa Rosa
LA PAMPA
PAMPAS
BUENOS AIRES
NEUQUÉN
Neuquén
Río Colorado
Bahía Blanca
SOUTH ATLANTIC OCEAN
Valdivia
RÍO NEGRO
Viedma
Gulf of San Matías
Puerto Montt
Rawson
CHUBUT
Comodoro Rivadavia
Gulf of San Jorge
National capital
State capital
City
SANTA CRUZ
FALKLAND ISLANDS (ISLAS MALVINAS)
Río Gallegos
Strait of Magellan
TIERRA DEL FUEGO
ISLA DE LOS ESTADOS
SOUTH GEORGIA
0 250 500 Miles
0 250 500 Kilometers

Map 91a Environment and Economy

CARIBBEAN SEA
NORTH ATLANTIC OCEAN
Equator
Tropic of Capricorn
SOUTH PACIFIC OCEAN
SOUTH ATLANTIC OCEAN
Environment and Economy
Farmland
Irrigated farmland
Livestock grazing and pasture
Commercial woodland and forest
Desert and scrub
Tundra and barren land
Swamp and wetlands
Urban and industrial areas
Mining regions
0 250 500 Miles
0 250 500 Kilometers

South America is a region just beginning to emerge from a colonial-dependency economy in which raw materials flowed from the continent to more highly developed economic regions. With the exception of Brazil, Argentina, Chile, and Uruguay, most of the continent's countries still operate under the traditional mode of exporting raw materials in exchange for capital that tends to accumulate in the pockets of a small percentage of the population. The land use patterns of the continent are, therefore, still dominated by resource extraction and agriculture. A problem posed by these patterns is that little of the continent's land area is actually suitable for either commercial forestry or commercial crop agriculture without extremely high environmental costs. Much of the agriculture, then, is based on high value tropical crops that can be grown in small areas profitably, or on extensive livestock grazing. Even within the forested areas of the Amazon Basin where forest clearance is taking place at unprecedented rates, much of the land use that replaces forest is grazing.

Map 91b Population Density

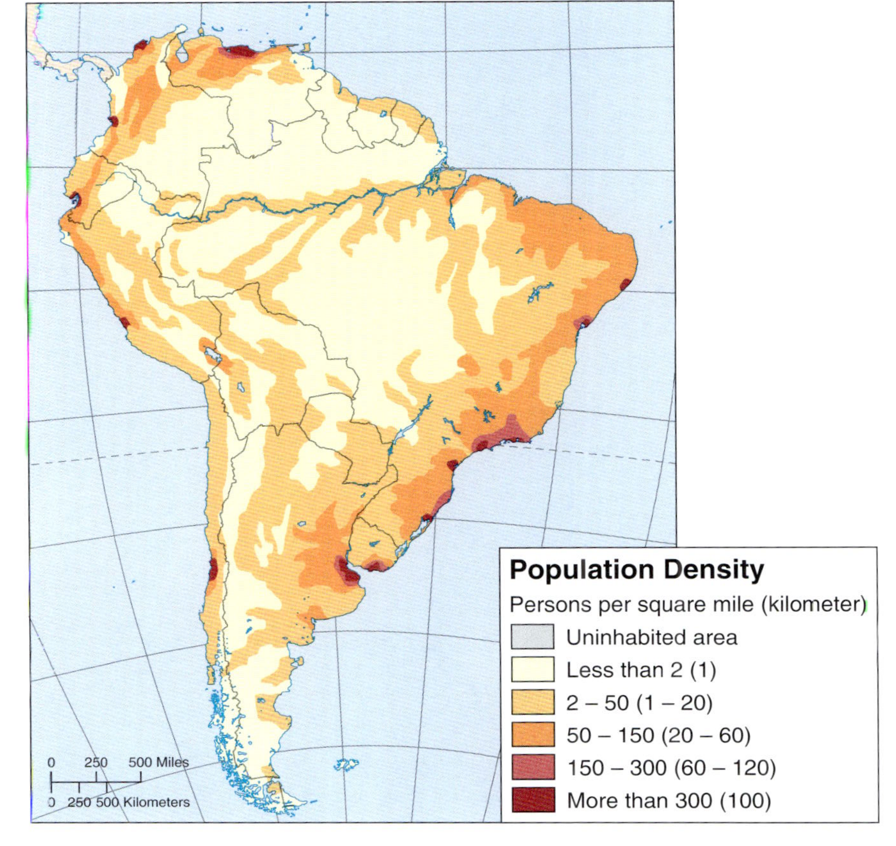
Population Density
Persons per square mile (kilometer)
Uninhabited area
Less than 2 (1)
2 – 50 (1 – 20)
50 – 150 (20 – 60)
150 – 300 (60 – 120)
More than 300 (100)
0 250 500 Miles
0 250 500 Kilometers

Since so much of interior South America is uninhabitable (the high Andes) or only sparsely populated (the interior of the Amazon Basin), the continent's population tends to be peripheral—approximately 90 percent of the continent's nearly 375 million people live within 150 miles of the sea. This population also tends to be heavily urbanized. Over 80 percent of South America's population lives in cities and the continent has three of the world's 15 largest cities—Rio de Janeiro, São Paulo, and Buenos Aires. São Paulo is the world's third largest urban agglomeration after Tokyo and New York. As in North America, most of the population of South America can trace at least part of its ancestry to the Old World. Throughout the Spanish-speaking parts of the continent the population is predominantly *mestizo* or mixed European and native South American. In Portuguese-speaking Brazil, in addition to a *mestizo* population, there is a significant admixture of African blood, the result of a large slave labor force imported from Africa to work the sugar, cotton, and other plantations of the colonial period.

Map 91c Environmental Problems

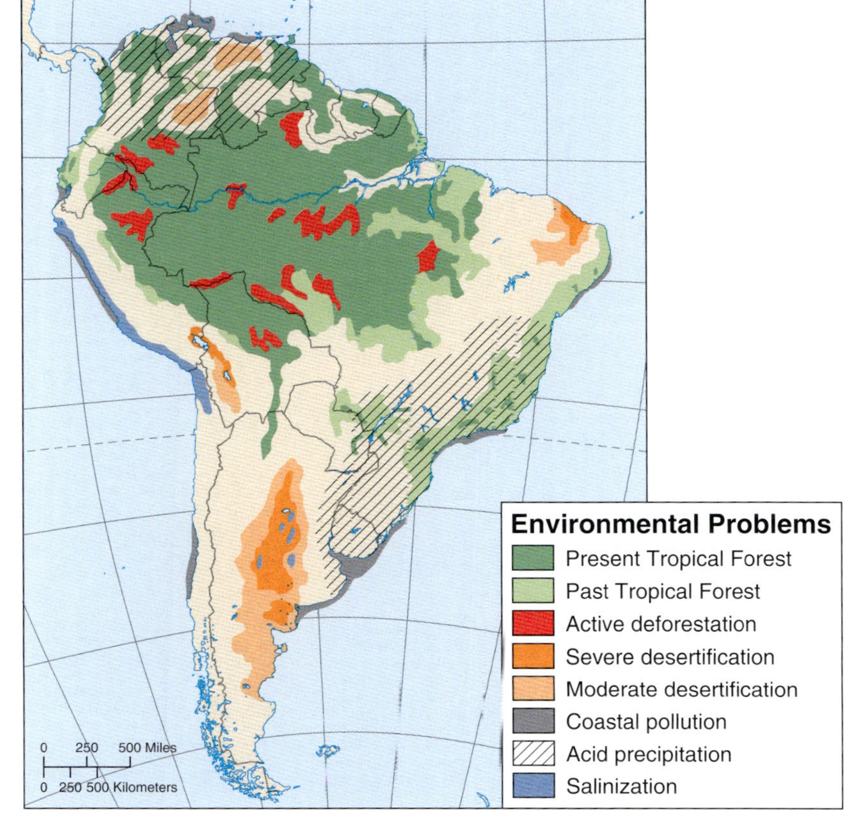
Environmental Problems
Present Tropical Forest
Past Tropical Forest
Active deforestation
Severe desertification
Moderate desertification
Coastal pollution
Acid precipitation
Salinization
0 250 500 Miles
0 250 500 Kilometers

The drainage basin of the Amazon River and its tributaries, along with adjacent regions, is the world's largest remaining area of tropical forest. Much of the periphery of this vast forested region has already been cleared for farming and grazing and the ax and chainsaw and the flames are working their way steadily toward the interior. Tropical deforestation produces a loss of the biological diversity represented by the world's most biologically productive ecosystem, along with changes in soil and soil-water systems. South America has other environmental problems: *desertification* in which grassland and/or scrub vegetation is converted to desert through overgrazing or other unwise agricultural practices; soil *salinization* in which soils become increasingly salty as the consequence of the over-application of irrigation water; *coastal* and *estuarine pollution* resulting from unregulated or unchecked use of coastal waters for industrial, commercial, and transportation purposes; and *acid precipitation* resulting from the combination of airborne industrial wastes and automobile-truck exhausts with water vapor to produce dry or wet acidic fallout.

Map 91d Protection of Natural Areas

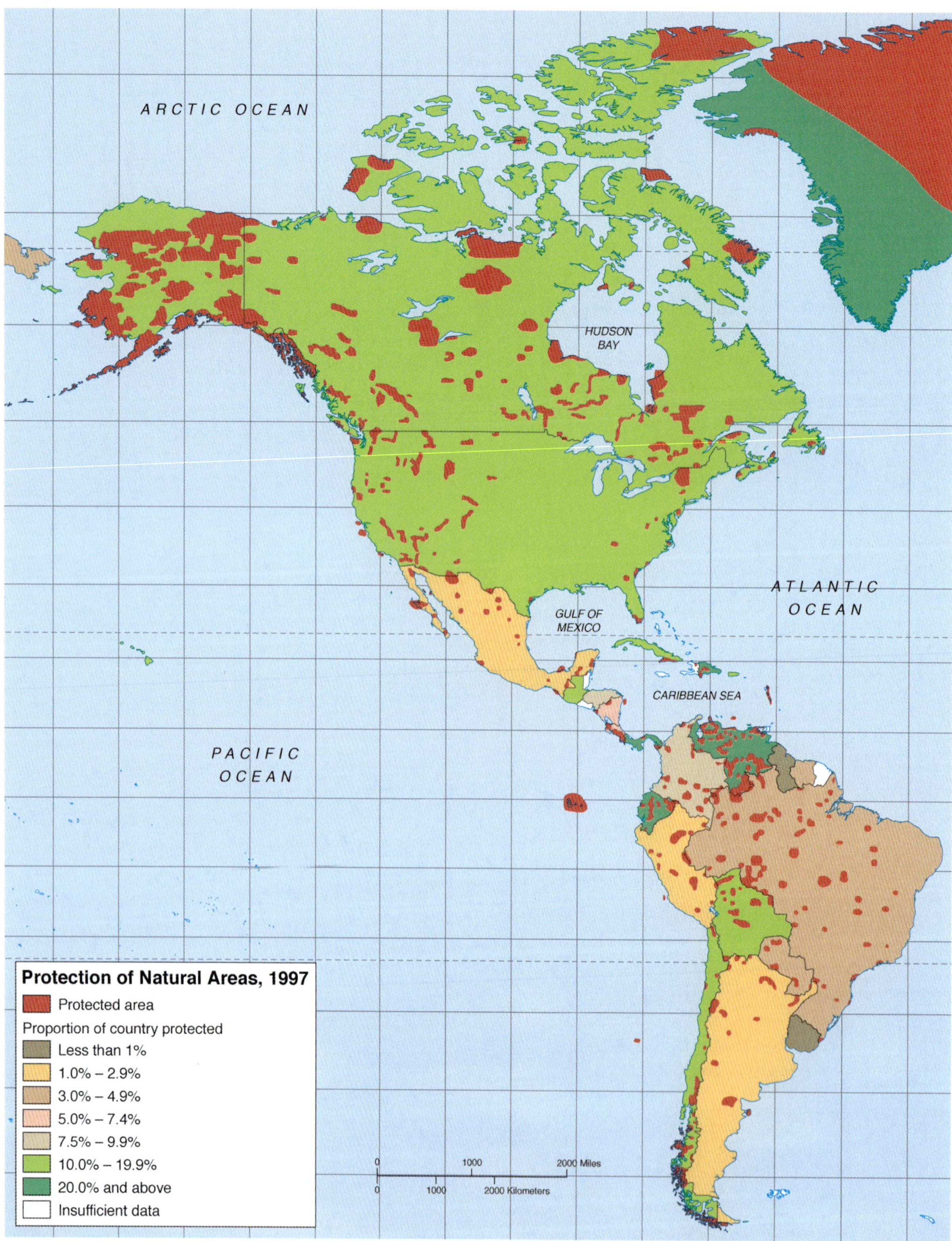

ARCTIC OCEAN
HUDSON BAY
ATLANTIC OCEAN
GULF OF MEXICO
CARIBBEAN SEA
PACIFIC OCEAN
Protection of Natural Areas, 1997
Protected area
Proportion of country protected
Less than 1%
1.0% – 2.9%
3.0% – 4.9%
5.0% – 7.4%
7.5% – 9.9%
10.0% – 19.9%
20.0% and above
Insufficient data
0
1000
2000 Miles
0
1000
2000 Kilometers

There have been expressed concerns among international conservation organizations that the protection of natural areas is largely an empty measure and that many of the world's national, provincial, regional, or state parks are "paper parks"—more important in conception than in reality. Particularly in Africa, the park systems designated largely for the purposes of wildlife preservation have come under international scrutiny. In the Americas, however, there does seem to be a close correlation between the designation of protected natural areas and the actuality of ecological preservation. With an increasing demand for natural resources and with governmental policies in both the United States and Brazil (the two largest population and economic entities in the Americas) that seem directed against preservation measures, there is fear that American protected areas could become, like their counterparts in many areas of Africa and Asia, simply parks on paper.

Map 92 Northern South America

National capital
State capital
City
Elevation
Feet
3000
1500
300
0
Below sea level
Sea level
0
100
1000
Bipolar Oblique Conical Projection
CARIBBEAN SEA
ATLANTIC OCEAN
PACIFIC OCEAN
LESSER ANTILLES
Equator
Tropic of Capricorn
500 Miles
500 Kilometers
BRAZIL
VENEZUELA
COLOMBIA
ECUADOR
PERU
BOLIVIA
PARAGUAY
ARGENTINA
CHILE
GUYANA
SURINAME
FRENCH GUIANA
PANAMA
TRINIDAD AND TOBAGO
BARBADOS
ST. LUCIA
ST. VINCENT AND THE GRENADINES
GRENADA
ANDES MOUNTAINS
GUIANA HIGHLANDS
BRAZILIAN HIGHLANDS
PLANALTO DE MATO GROSSO
SELVAS
GRAN CHACO
ATACAMA DESERT
ALTIPLANO
SIERRA DOS PARECIS
CAATINGAS
Rio Amazon
Rio Negro
Rio Madeira
Rio Tocantins
Rio Xingu
Rio Tapajós
Rio Orinoco
Rio Magdalena
Rio São Francisco
Rio Paraná
Rio Araguaia
Rio Branco
Rio Purus
Rio Juruá
Rio Caquetá
Rio Mamoré
Rio Guaporé
Rio Parnaíba
Lake Maracaibo
Lake Titicaca
Lake Poopó
Marajó Island
Marajó Bay
São Marcos Bay
Gulf of Venezuela
Gulf of Panama
Gulf of Guayaquil
Brasília
Caracas
Bogotá
Quito
Lima
La Paz
Sucre
Georgetown
Paramaribo
Cayenne
Port of Spain
Panama
Manaus
Belém
São Luís
Fortaleza
Natal
Recife
Salvador
Rio de Janeiro
São Paulo
Belo Horizonte
Goiânia
Cuiabá
Campo Grande
Porto Velho
Rio Branco
Boa Vista
Macapá
Palmas
Teresina
Iquitos
Guayaquil
Cuenca
Medellín
Cali
Cartagena
Barranquilla
Maracaibo
Valencia
Santa Cruz
Cochabamba
Arequipa
Cusco
Trujillo
Chiclayo
Antofagasta
Arica
Iquique
Mt. Roraima 9,432 ft.
Chimborazo 20,702 ft.
Cotopaxi 19,347 ft.
Nevado Huascarán 22,133 ft.
Nevado Illimani 20,741 ft.
Nevado Sajama 21,391 ft.
Pico Cristóbal Colón 19,029 ft.
Pico Bolívar 16,427 ft.

Map 93 Southern South America

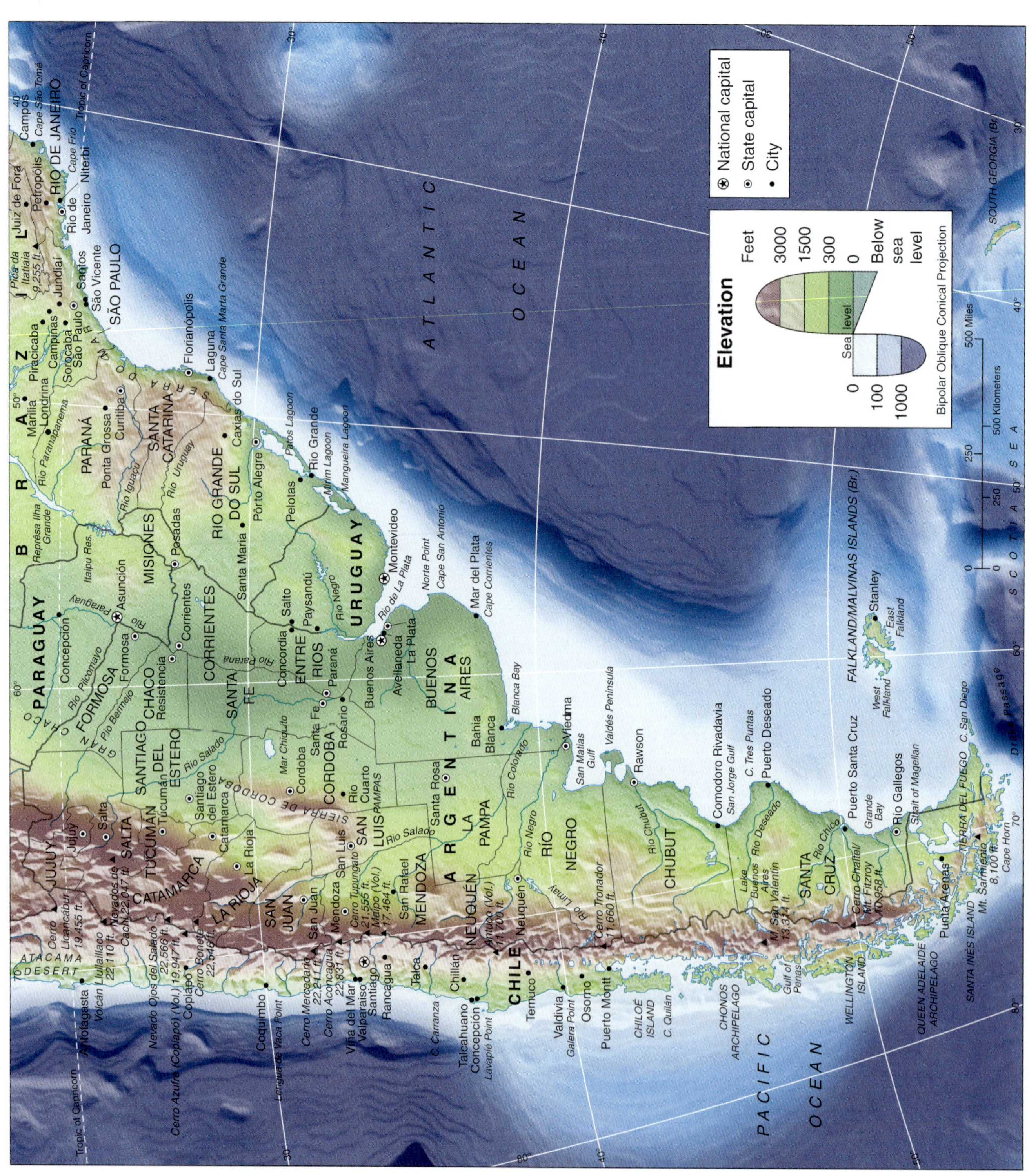

Elevation
Feet
3000
1500
300
0
Below
sea
level
Sea level
0
100
1000
Bipolar Oblique Conical Projection
0 250 500 Miles
0 250 500 Kilometers
National capital
State capital
City
ATLANTIC
OCEAN
PACIFIC
OCEAN
SCOTIA SEA
BRAZIL
PARAGUAY
URUGUAY
ARGENTINA
CHILE
FALKLAND/MALVINAS ISLANDS (Br.)
SOUTH GEORGIA (Br.)
Tropic of Capricorn
ATACAMA DESERT
GRAN CHACO
SIERRA DE CORDOBA
PAMPAS
SERRA DO MAR
Rio de Janeiro
RIO DE JANEIRO
SÃO PAULO
São Paulo
Santos
PARANÁ
Curitiba
SANTA CATARINA
Florianópolis
RIO GRANDE DO SUL
Pôrto Alegre
Pelotas
Rio Grande
Patos Lagoon
Mirim Lagoon
Montevideo
Buenos Aires
La Plata
Asunción
Concepción
Rosario
Santa Fe
Córdoba
Mendoza
San Juan
Tucumán
Salta
Jujuy
Mar del Plata
Bahía Blanca
Viedma
Rawson
Comodoro Rivadavia
Puerto Deseado
Puerto Santa Cruz
Río Gallegos
Punta Arenas
Stanley
Antofagasta
Copiapó
Coquimbo
Valparaíso
Santiago
Viña del Mar
Rancagua
Talca
Chillán
Concepción
Talcahuano
Temuco
Valdivia
Osorno
Puerto Montt
Neuquén
Strait of Magellan
TIERRA DEL FUEGO
Cape Horn
Drake Passage
Cerro Aconcagua 22,831 ft.
Ojos del Salado 22,566 ft.
Valdés Peninsula
San Matías Gulf
San Jorge Gulf
CHILOÉ ISLAND
CHONOS ARCHIPELAGO
WELLINGTON ISLAND
QUEEN ADELAIDE ARCHIPELAGO
SANTA INÉS ISLAND
Río Paraná
Río Uruguay
Río Paraguay
Río Salado
Río Colorado
Río Negro
Río Chubut

Map 94 Europe: Physical Features

Elevation
Feet
3000
1500
300
0
Below sea level
Sea level
0
100
1000
National capital
City
0
250
500 Miles
500 Kilometers
GREENLAND
ARCTIC OCEAN
Denmark Strait
Arctic Circle
Reykjavik
ICELAND
FAEROE ISLANDS
SHETLAND ISLANDS
ORKNEY ISLANDS
UNITED KINGDOM
HEBRIDES
NORTH SEA
North Channel
IRELAND
IRISH SEA
Dublin
Liverpool
Leeds
Newcastle
Manchester
Birmingham
London
St. George's Channel
Lands End
Thames R.
ISLES OF SCILLY
Strait of Dover
English Channel
ATLANTIC OCEAN
Bay of Biscay
Cape Finisterre
Cabo De Sao Vicente
Strait of Gibraltar
MADEIRA ISLANDS
CANARY ISLANDS
PORTUGAL
Lisbon
SPAIN
Madrid
ANDORRA
Barcelona
BALEARIC IS.
PYRENEES
FRANCE
Paris
Seine R.
Lille
MASSIF CENTRAL
Rhône R.
Lyon
Marseille
Gulf of Lyon
MONACO
Monaco
SWITZ.
Bern
JURA MTS.
ALPS
BELGIUM
Brussels
Antwerp
NETHERLANDS
The Hague
Rotterdam
Amsterdam
LUX.
Luxembourg
GERMANY
Bonn
Frankfurt
Stuttgart
Munich
Berlin
Hamburg
Elbe
Weser R.
Rhine R.
ERZGEBIRGE
DENMARK
Copenhagen
Skagerrak
Kattegat
NORWAY
Oslo
Vestfjord
SWEDEN
Stockholm
Lake Vanern
Lake Vattern
GOTLAND
OLAND
Gulf of Bothnia
FINLAND
Helsinki
Gulf of Finland
BALTIC SEA
ESTONIA
Tallinn
Gulf of Riga
LATVIA
Riga
LITHUANIA
Vilnius
RUSSIA
POLAND
Warsaw
CZECH REP.
Prague
AUSTRIA
Vienna
SLOVAKIA
Bratislava
HUNGARY
Budapest
SLOVENIA
Ljubljana
CROATIA
Zagreb
BOSNIA AND HERZEGOVINA
Sarajevo
SERBIA AND MONTENEGRO
Belgrade
DINARIC ALPS
ALBANIA
Tirane
MACEDONIA
Skopje
GREECE
Athens
AEGEAN SEA
CRETE
IONIAN SEA
ITALY
Rome
Naples
Po
APENNINES
Gulf of Genoa
ADRIATIC SEA
CORSICA
SARDINIA
TYRRHENIAN SEA
SICILY
MALTA
MEDITERRANEAN SEA
ROMANIA
Bucharest
TRANSYLVANIAN ALPS
CARPATHIAN MTS.
Danube R.
BULGARIA
Sofia
MOLDOVA
Chisinau
UKRAINE
Kiev
Dnipropetrovs'k
Dnepr R.
BELARUS
Minsk
PRIPYAT MARSHES
SEA OF AZOV
BLACK SEA
Bosporus
Istanbul
TURKEY
Ankara
L. Van
CYPRUS
Nicosia
LEBANON
Beirut
ISRAEL
Tel-Aviv
Jerusalem
SYRIA
Damascus
JORDAN
Amman
IRAQ
Baghdad
Tigris R.
Euphrates R.
KUWAIT
Kuwait
Persian Gulf
BAHRAIN
QATAR
Abu Dhabi
UNITED ARAB EMIRATES
SAUDI ARABIA
Riyadh
RED SEA
EGYPT
Cairo
Nile R.
LIBYA
Tripoli
TUNISIA
Tunis
ALGERIA
Algiers
ATLAS MOUNTAINS
MOROCCO
Rabat
MAURITANIA
IRAN
Tehran
ZAGROS MOUNTAINS
ELBURZ MOUNTAINS
AZERBAIJAN
Baku
ARMENIA
Yerevan
GEORGIA
Tbilisi
CAUCASUS
CASPIAN SEA
CASPIAN DEPRESSION
Volgograd
Volga R.
Don R.
TURKMENISTAN
Ashkhabad
KARAKUMY DESERT
Amu Darya
UZBEKISTAN
ARAL SEA
Syr Darya
KAZAKSTAN
RUSSIA
Moscow
Nizhniy-Novgorod
Lake Rybinsk
Lake Ladoga
Lake Onega
St. Petersburg
Dvina R.
WHITE SEA
URAL MOUNTAINS
Yekaterinburg
Chelyabinsk

Map 95 Europe: Political Divisions

National capital
City
0 250 500 Miles
0 250 500 Kilometers
GREENLAND
ARCTIC OCEAN
Arctic Circle
ICELAND
Reykjavik
ATLANTIC OCEAN
FAEROE ISLANDS
SHETLAND ISLANDS
OPKNEY ISLANDS
HEBRIDES
NORTH SEA
UNITED KINGDOM
Glasgow
Belfast
Newcastle
Leeds
IRISH SEA
Liverpool
Manchester
Birmingham
London
IRELAND
Dublin
St. George's Channel
Strait of Dover
English Channel
NORWAY
Bergen
Oslo
Stavenger
SWEDEN
Uppsala
Stockholm
Goteborg
GOTLAND
OLAND
Gulf of Bothnia
FINLAND
Turku
Helsinki
BALTIC SEA
DENMARK
Copenhagen
NETHERLANDS
The Hague
Amsterdam
Rotterdam
BELGIUM
Antwerp
Brussels
Lille
Le Havre
Brest
LUX.
Luxembourg
FRANCE
Paris
Lyon
Bordeaux
Marseille
Bay of Biscay
MONACO
Monaco
SWITZERLAND
Bern
GERMANY
Hamburg
Berlin
Essen
Bonn
Frankfurt
Rhine R.
Stuttgart
Munich
POLAND
Gdansk
Warsaw
Katowice
RUSSIA
Kaliningrad
LITHUANIA
Vilnius
LATVIA
Riga
ESTONIA
Tallinn
Gulf of Riga
CZECH REP.
Prague
SLOVAKIA
Bratislava
AUSTRIA
Vienna
HUNGARY
Budapest
SLOVENIA
Ljubljana
CROATIA
Zagreb
BOSNIA AND HERZEGOVINA
Sarajevo
SERBIA AND MONTENEGRO
Belgrade
ALBANIA
Tirane
MACEDONIA
Skopje
GREECE
Athens
BULGARIA
Sofia
ROMANIA
Bucharest
Danube R.
MOLDOVA
Chisinau
UKRAINE
Kiev
Kharkiv
Dnipropetrovs'k
Donetsk
BELARUS
Minsk
RUSSIA
Murmansk
WHITE SEA
Arkhangelsk
St. Petersburg
Moscow
Nizhniy-Novgorod
Volga R.
Samara
Don R.
Volgograd
Astrakhan
URAL MOUNTAINS
Yekaterinburg
Chelyabinsk
Omsk
SEA OF AZOV
KAZAKSTAN
ARAL SEA
UZBEKISTAN
TURKMENISTAN
Ashkhabad
CASPIAN SEA
Baku
GEORGIA
Tbilisi
ARMENIA
Yerevan
AZERBAIJAN
BLACK SEA
Bosporus
Istanbul
TURKEY
Ankara
IRAN
Tehran
SYRIA
Damascus
IRAQ
Baghdad
Tigris R.
Euphrates R.
CYPRUS
Nicosia
LEBANON
Beirut
ISRAEL
Tel-Aviv
Jerusalem
JORDAN
Amman
KUWAIT
Kuwait
Persian Gulf
BAHRAIN
QATAR
Abu Dhabi
UNITED ARAB EMIRATES
SAUDI ARABIA
Riyadh
EGYPT
Cairo
Nile R.
RED SEA
PORTUGAL
Lisbon
SPAIN
Madrid
Bilbao
Valladolid
Barcelona
Valencia
Seville
ANDORRA
BALEARIC IS.
CORSICA
SARDINIA
ITALY
Milan
Turin
Venice
Rome
Naples
ADRIATIC SEA
TYRRHENIAN SEA
SICILY
IONIAN SEA
AEGEAN SEA
CRETE
MALTA
MEDITERRANEAN SEA
Strait of Gibraltar
MADEIRA ISLANDS
CANARY ISLANDS
MOROCCO
Rabat
ALGERIA
Algiers
TUNISIA
Tunis
LIBYA
Tripoli
MAURITANIA
MALI

Map 96a Environment and Economy: The Use of Land

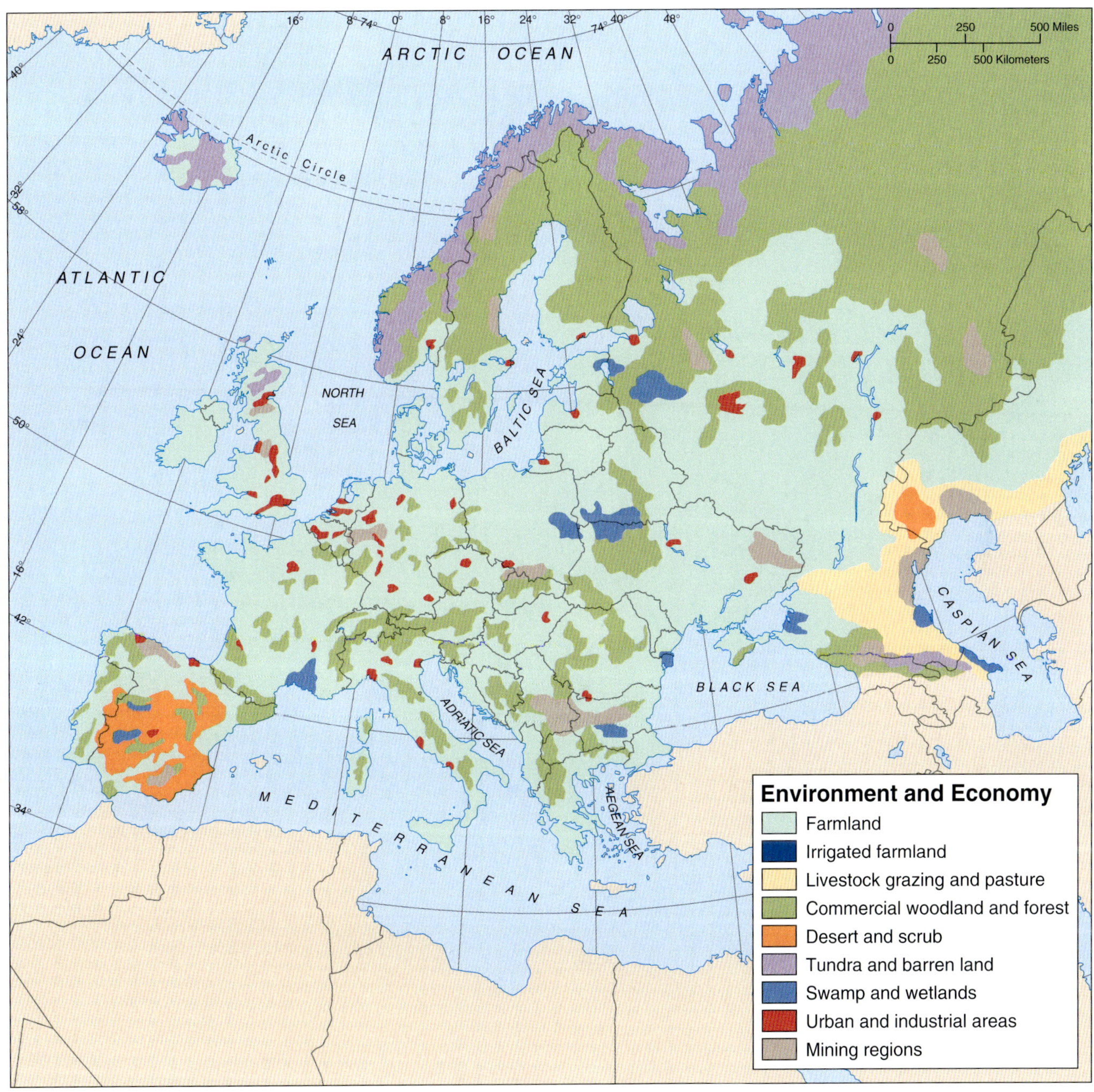
ARCTIC OCEAN
Arctic Circle
ATLANTIC OCEAN
NORTH SEA
BALTIC SEA
BLACK SEA
CASPIAN SEA
ADRIATIC SEA
AEGEAN SEA
MEDITERRANEAN SEA
0 250 500 Miles
0 250 500 Kilometers
Environment and Economy
Farmland
Irrigated farmland
Livestock grazing and pasture
Commercial woodland and forest
Desert and scrub
Tundra and barren land
Swamp and wetlands
Urban and industrial areas
Mining regions

More than any other continent, Europe bears the imprint of human activity—mining, forestry, agriculture, industry, and urbanization. Virtually all of western and central Europe's natural forest vegetation is gone, lost to clearing for agriculture beginning in prehistory, to lumbering that began in earnest during the Middle Ages, or more recently, to disease and destruction brought about by acid precipitation. Only in the far north and the east do some natural stands remain. The region is the world's most heavily industrialized and the industrial areas on the map represent only the largest and most significant. Not shown are the industries that are found in virtually every small town and village and smaller city throughout the industrial countries for Europe. Europe also possesses abundant raw materials and a very productive agricultural base. The mineral resources have long been in a state of active exploitation and the mining regions shown on the map are, for the most part, old regions in upland areas that are somewhat less significant now than they may have been in the past. Agriculturally, the northern European plain is one of the world's great agricultural regions but most of Europe contains decent land for agriculture.

Map 96b Population Density

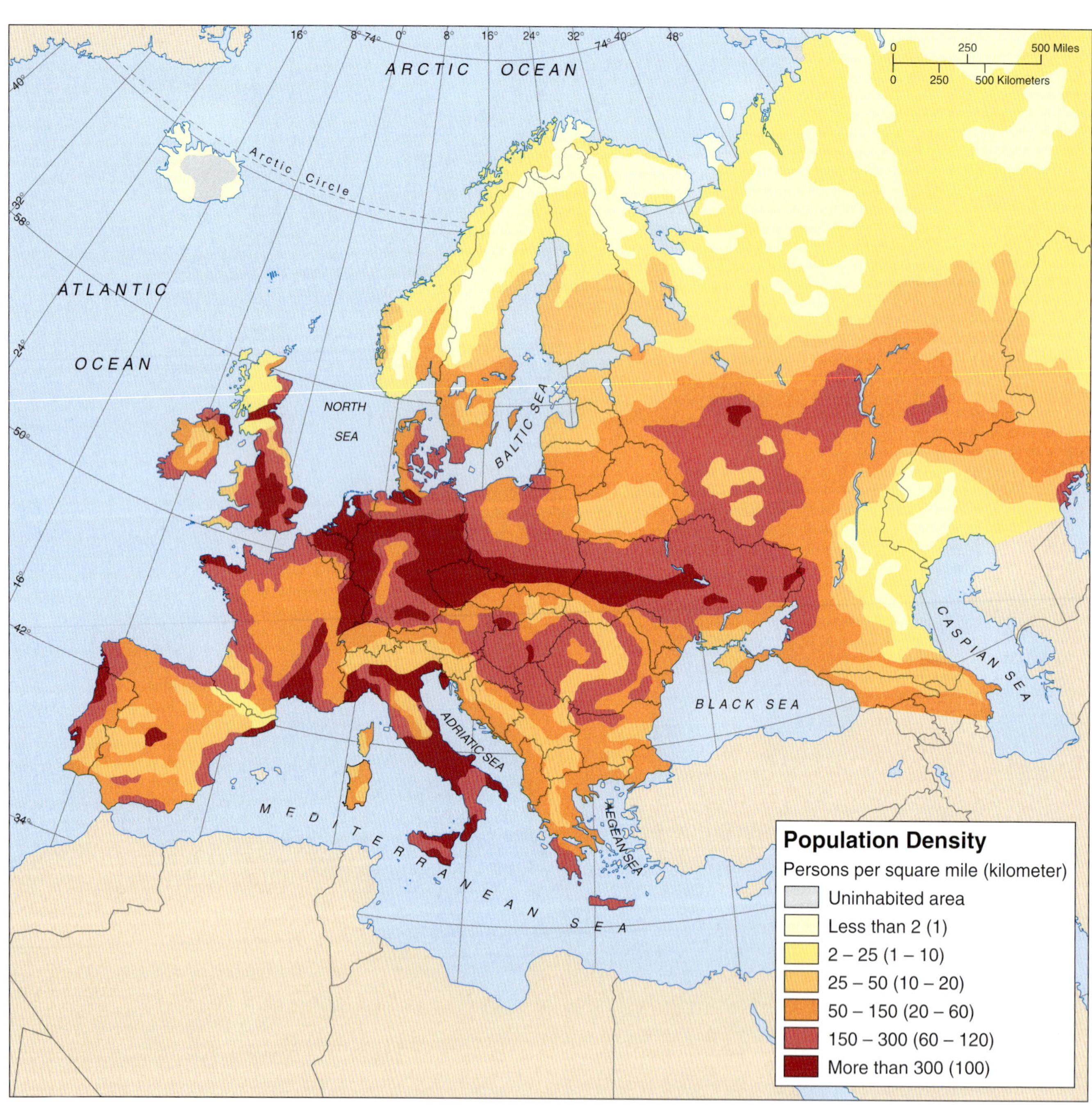
ARCTIC OCEAN
ATLANTIC OCEAN
NORTH SEA
BALTIC SEA
ADRIATIC SEA
BLACK SEA
CASPIAN SEA
AEGEAN SEA
MEDITERRANEAN SEA
Arctic Circle
0 250 500 Miles
0 250 500 Kilometers
Population Density
Persons per square mile (kilometer)
Uninhabited area
Less than 2 (1)
2 – 25 (1 – 10)
25 – 50 (10 – 20)
50 – 150 (20 – 60)
150 – 300 (60 – 120)
More than 300 (100)

Europe is one of the most densely settled regions of the world with an overall population density nearing 200 persons per square mile (80 per square kilometer), the consequence of a high level of urbanization and an economic system that is heavily industrialized. Even in agricultural regions, the population density is high. Beyond high density, the two chief identifying marks of the European population are remarkable diversity and unusual dynamics. For a small part of the world, Europe has cultural and ethnic diversity that is rarely matched elsewhere; more than 60 languages are spoken in an area not much larger than the United States. The population dynamics of Europe show a mature population that has passed through the "Demographic Transition"—a remarkable increase and then decline in growth rates resulting from the rise of an urban-industrial society. Only in other heavily industrialized regions of the world are found the very small overall growth rates characteristic of Europe.

Map 96c European Political Boundaries, 1914–1948

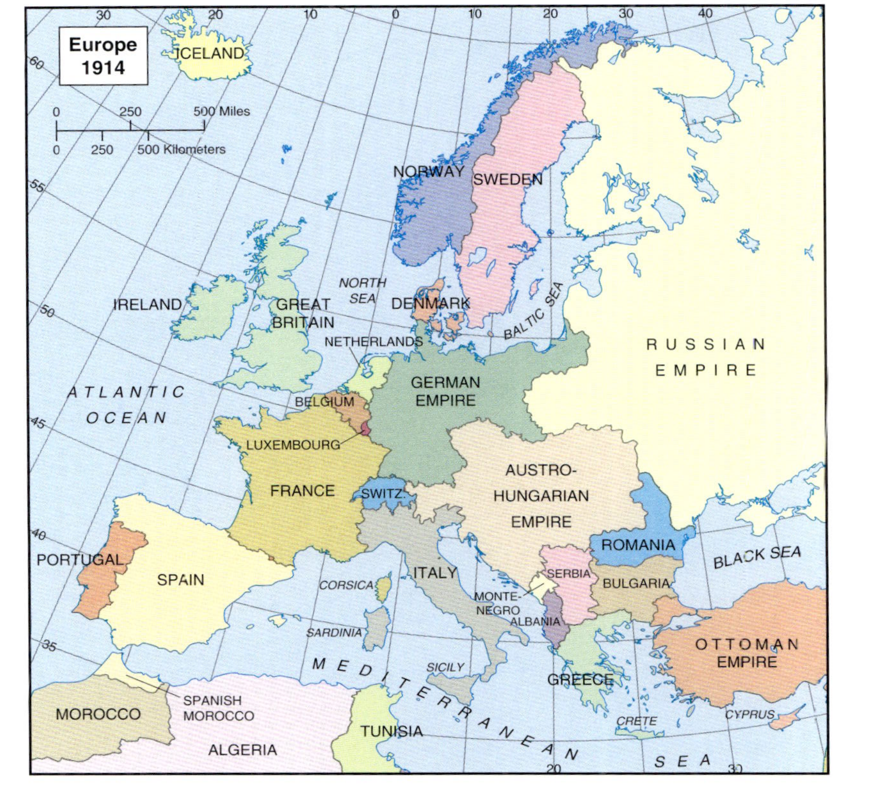

Europe 1914
0 250 500 Miles
0 250 500 Kilometers
ICELAND
NORWAY
SWEDEN
IRELAND
GREAT BRITAIN
NORTH SEA
DENMARK
NETHERLANDS
BALTIC SEA
RUSSIAN EMPIRE
ATLANTIC OCEAN
BELGIUM
LUXEMBOURG
GERMAN EMPIRE
AUSTRO-HUNGARIAN EMPIRE
FRANCE
SWITZ.
ROMANIA
BLACK SEA
PORTUGAL
SPAIN
CORSICA
ITALY
SERBIA
BULGARIA
MONTE-NEGRO
ALBANIA
SARDINIA
OTTOMAN EMPIRE
MEDITERRANEAN SEA
SICILY
GREECE
MOROCCO
SPANISH MOROCCO
ALGERIA
TUNISIA
CRETE
CYPRUS

Europe 1921
New states
0 250 500 Miles
0 250 500 Kilometers
ICELAND
NORWAY
SWEDEN
FINLAND
ULSTER
IRISH FREE STATE
GREAT BRITAIN
NORTH SEA
DENMARK
ESTONIA
LATVIA
LITHUANIA
BALTIC SEA
UNION OF SOVIET SOCIALIST REPUBLICS
NETHERLANDS
ATLANTIC OCEAN
BELGIUM
GERMANY
POLAND
LUXEMBOURG
CZECHOSLOVAKIA
FRANCE
SWITZ.
AUSTRIA
HUNGARY
ROMANIA
BLACK SEA
PORTUGAL
SPAIN
CORSICA
ITALY
YUGOSLAVIA
BULGARIA
SARDINIA
ALBANIA
TURKEY
MEDITERRANEAN SEA
SICILY
GREECE
MOROCCO
ALGERIA
TUNISIA
CRETE
CYPRUS

In 1914, on the eve of the First World War, Europe was dominated by the United Kingdom and France in the west, the German Empire and the Austro-Hungarian Empire in central Europe, and the Russian Empire in the east. Battle lines for the conflict that began in 1914 were drawn when the United Kingdom, France, and the Russian Empire joined together as the Triple Entente. In the view of the Germans, this coalition was designed to encircle Germany and its Austrian ally, which, along with Italy, made up the Triple Alliance. The German and Austrian fears were heightened in 1912–14 when a Russian-sponsored "Balkan League" pushed the Ottoman Turkish Empire from Europe, leaving behind the weak and mutually antagonistic Balkan states Serbia and Montenegro. In August 1914, Germany and Austria-Hungary attacked in several directions and World War I began. Four years later, after massive loss of life and destruction, the central European empires were defeated. The victorious French, English, and Americans (who had entered the war in 1917) restructured the map of Europe in 1919, carving nine new states out of the remains of the German and Austro-Hungarian empires and the westernmost portions of the Russian Empire which, by the end of the war, was deep in the Revolution that deposed the czar and brought the Communists to power in a new Union of Soviet Socialist Republics.

Europe 1943
Axis powers
Under German rule
Axis military occupation
Greater German Reich
Axis satellites
Allied territory
Allied occupied
Neutral powers
0 250 500 Miles
0 250 500 Kilometers
NORWAY
SWEDEN
FINLAND
IRELAND
GREAT BRITAIN
NORTH SEA
DENMARK
NETHERLANDS
BALTIC SEA
UNION OF SOVIET SOCIALIST REPUBLICS
ATLANTIC OCEAN
BELGIUM
GERMANY
FRANCE
VICHY FRANCE
SWITZ.
AUSTRIA
SLOVAKIA
HUNGARY
PORTUGAL
SPAIN
CROATIA
SERBIA
ROMANIA
BLACK SEA
ITALY
CORSICA
MONTE-NEGRO
BULGARIA
ALBANIA
SARDINIA
TURKEY
MEDITERRANEAN SEA
SICILY
GREECE
SPANISH MOROCCO
MOROCCO
TUNISIA
CRETE
CYPRUS
ALGERIA

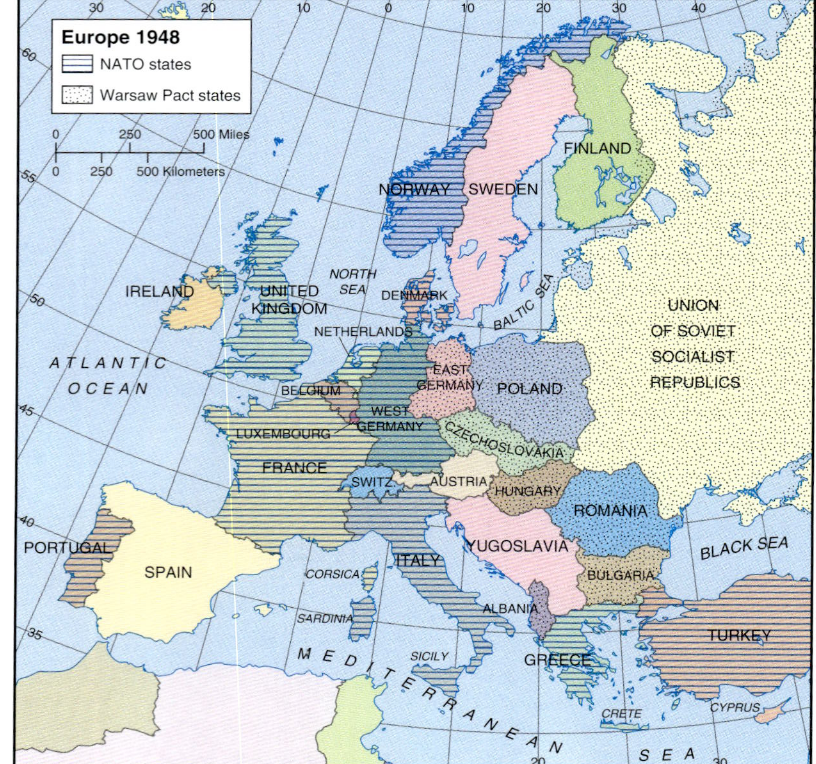
Europe 1948
NATO states
Warsaw Pact states
0 250 500 Miles
0 250 500 Kilometers
NORWAY
SWEDEN
FINLAND
IRELAND
UNITED KINGDOM
NORTH SEA
DENMARK
NETHERLANDS
BALTIC SEA
UNION OF SOVIET SOCIALIST REPUBLICS
ATLANTIC OCEAN
BELGIUM
EAST GERMANY
POLAND
WEST GERMANY
LUXEMBOURG
CZECHOSLOVAKIA
FRANCE
SWITZ.
AUSTRIA
HUNGARY
ROMANIA
PORTUGAL
YUGOSLAVIA
BLACK SEA
SPAIN
CORSICA
ITALY
BULGARIA
ALBANIA
SARDINIA
TURKEY
MEDITERRANEAN SEA
SICILY
GREECE
CRETE
CYPRUS

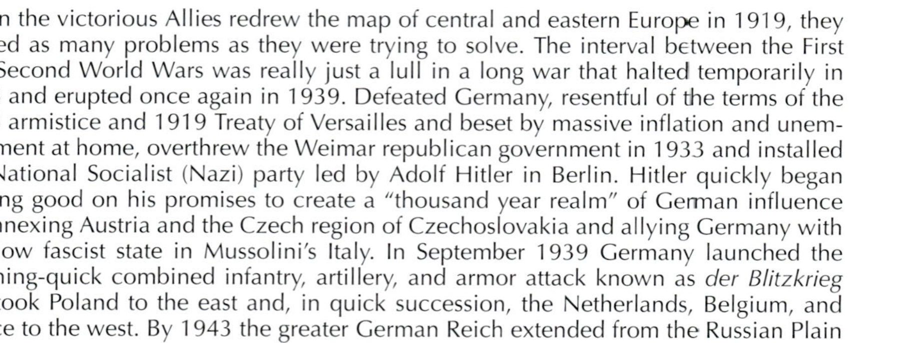

When the victorious Allies redrew the map of central and eastern Europe in 1919, they caused as many problems as they were trying to solve. The interval between the First and Second World Wars was really just a lull in a long war that halted temporarily in 1918 and erupted once again in 1939. Defeated Germany, resentful of the terms of the 1918 armistice and 1919 Treaty of Versailles and beset by massive inflation and unemployment at home, overthrew the Weimar republican government in 1933 and installed the National Socialist (Nazi) party led by Adolf Hitler in Berlin. Hitler quickly began making good on his promises to create a "thousand year realm" of German influence by annexing Austria and the Czech region of Czechoslovakia and allying Germany with a fellow fascist state in Mussolini's Italy. In September 1939 Germany launched the lightning-quick combined infantry, artillery, and armor attack known as *der Blitzkrieg* and took Poland to the east and, in quick succession, the Netherlands, Belgium, and France to the west. By 1943 the greater German Reich extended from the Russian Plain to the Atlantic and from the Black Sea to the Baltic. But the Axis powers of Germany and Italy could not withstand the greater resources and manpower of the combined United Kingdom-United States-USSR–led Allies and, in 1945, Allied armies occupied Germany. Once again, the lines of the central and eastern European map were redrawn. This time, a strengthened Soviet Union took back most of the territory the Russian Empire had lost at the end of the First World War. Germany was partitioned into four occupied sectors (English, French, American, and Russian) and later into two independent countries, the Federal Republic of Germany (West Germany) and the German Democratic Republic (East Germany). Although the Soviet Union's territory stopped at the Polish, Hungarian, Czechoslovakian, and Romanian borders, the eastern European countries (Poland, East Germany, Czechoslovakia, Hungary, Romania, Yugoslavia, Albania, and Bulgaria) became Communist between 1945 and 1948 and were separated from the West by the Iron Curtain.

Map 96d Political Changes 1989–2004

Europe: Political Changes 1989-2004

1989
Union of Soviet Socialist Republics
Warsaw Pact Countries (excluding the USSR)
North Atlantic Treaty Organization Countries
European Community (formerly the EEC)

2004

- Former Republics of the USSR, now independent countries
- Russian Federation
- *FRANCE* NATO Countries shown in italics
- European Union (formerly the EC)
- European Union applicant country

During the last decade of the twentieth century, one of the most remarkable series of political geographic changes of the last 500 years took place. The bipolar "East-West" structure that had characterized Europe's political geography since the end of World War II altered in the space of a very few years. In the mid-1980s, as Soviet influence over eastern and central Europe weakened, those countries began to turn to the capitalist West. Between 1989, when the country of Hungary was the first Soviet satellite to open its borders to travel, and 1991, when the Soviet Union dissolved into 15 independent countries, abrupt change in political systems occurred. The result is a new map of Europe that includes a number of countries not present on the map of 1989. These countries have emerged as the result of reunification, separation, or independence from the old Soviet Union. The new political structure has been accompanied by growing economic cooperation. In May, 2004, ten new applicant countries (the Greek part of Cyprus, Czech Republic, Estonia, Hungary, Latvia, Lithuania, Malta, Poland, Slovakia, and Slovenia) were added to the European Union, increasing the economic strength of the EU, which now has its own currency (the euro) and is presently attempting to develop a constitution acceptable to the 25 member nations. The only remaining formal applicant country to EU membership is Turkey. Concerned about Turkish migration and the potential political problems of adding a country with a population of 60 million Muslims to the European Union, the majority of EU countries have thus far failed to act positively on Turkey's application for membership.

Map 97 Western Europe

Elevation
Feet
3000
1500
300
0
Sea level
Below sea level
0
100
1000
Azimuthal Equidistant Projection
National capital
City
FAEROES
SHETLAND IS.
HEBRIDES
ORKNEY IS.
UNITED KINGDOM
SCOTLAND
NORTHERN IRELAND
IRELAND
WALES
ENGLAND
ISLE OF MAN
IRISH SEA
PENNINES
Ben Nevis 4,406 ft.
Scafell Pikes 3,210 ft.
Snowdon 3,560 ft.
Carrauntoohil 3,414 ft.
Inverness
Aberdeen
Perth
Dundee
Greenock
Paisley
Glasgow
Edinburgh
Motherwell
Londonderry
Belfast
Carlisle
Newcastle upon Tyne
Sunderland
York
Leeds
Limerick
Dublin
Dun Laoghaire
Waterford
Cork
Liverpool
Manchester
Sheffield
Stoke-on-Trent
Lincoln
Nottingham
Birmingham
Norwich
Swansea
Cardiff
Worcester
Cambridge
Oxford
Ipswich
Bristol
Bath
London
Reading
Thames R.
Severn R.
Plymouth
Southampton
Portsmouth
Brighton
Dover
English Channel
NORTH SEA
ATLANTIC OCEAN
Bay of Biscay
NORWAY
SWEDEN
DENMARK
Trondheim
Østersund
Helagsfjället 5,892 ft.
Sånfjället 4,190 ft.
Glittertinden 8,110 ft.
Sundsvall
Bergen
Gävle
Falun
Hønefoss
Oslo
Uppsala
Haugesund
Drammen
Moss
Karlstad
Västerås
Stockholm
Stavanger
Skien
Fredrikstad
VÄNERN
Eskilstuna
Örebro
Södertälje
Kristiansand
Uddevalla
Trollhättan
Linköping
Skagerrak
Kattegat
Göteborg
Borås
Jönköping
GOTLAND
Frederikshavn
Ålborg
Halmstad
Holtebro
Randers
Århus
Kalmar
ÖLAND
Vejle
Helsingør
Helsingborg
Karlskrona
Kristianstad
Esbjerg
Copenhagen
Malmö
Odense
Naestved
BORNHOLM
BALTIC SEA
Flensburg
Schleswig
Sønderborg
Neumünster
Kiel
Stralsund
Cuxhaven
Lübeck
Rostok
Gdynia
Gdansk
Koszalin
NETHERLANDS
Groningen
Bremerhaven
Hamburg
Leeuwarden
Szczecin
Oldenburg
Bremen
Elbe R.
Bydgoszcz
Amsterdam
Zwolle
Münster
Hannover
Berlin
Frankfurt an der Oder
Poznan
The Hague
Apeldoorn
Arnhem
Braunschweig
Rotterdam
Utrecht
Duisburg
Bielefeldt
Hildesheim
Potsdam
Brugge
Düsseldorf
GERMANY
Magdeburg
POLAND
Oostende
Essen
Dortmund
Dessau
BELGIUM
Gent
Antwerp
Wuppertal
Kalisz
Boulogne-sur-Mer
Brussels
Cologne
Kassel
Halle
Lille
Liège
Leipzig
Cherbourg
Arras
Mons
Charleroi
Aachen
Bonn
Dresden
Wroclaw
Le Havre
Amiens
St. Quentin
Koblenz
Erfurt
Weimar
Legnica
Görlitz
Brest
Rouen
Wiesbaden
Gera
Zwickau
Liberec
Opole
St. Brieuc
St. Malo
Caen
St. Denis
Rheims
LUXEMBOURG
Frankfurt
Hradec Králové
Quimper
Fougères
Seine R.
Paris
Châlons-sur-Marne
Kaiserslautern
Mainz
Würzburg
Karlovy Vary
Lorient
Rennes
Laval
Versailles
Saarbrücken
Darmstadt
Mannheim
Prague
Havlíčkův Brod
Vannes
Le Mans
Troyes
Sarreguemines
Fürth
Plzen
Olomouc
Angers
Metz
Karlsruhe
Nürnberg
CZECH REPUBLIC
St. Nazaire
Orléans
Blois
FRANCE
Nancy
Stuttgart
Baden-Baden
Regensburg
Brno
Zilina
Nantes
Chalet
Tours
Loire R.
Auxerre
Epinal
Strasbourg
Ulm
České Budějovice
SLOVAKIA
Trenčín
Châtellerault
Bourges
Colmar
Freiburg
Danube R.
Augsburg
Passau
Linz
Vienna
Nové Zámky
La Rochelle
Rochefort
Niort
Poitiers
Nevers
Dijon
Besançon
Mulhouse
Basel
Schaffhausen
Munich
Wels
Wiener-Neustadt
Bratislava
Belfort
Zurich
SWITZ.
LIECHTENSTEIN
Salzburg
Angoulême
Limoges
Montluçon
Moulins
Creusot
Mâcon
Luzern
Sankt Gallen
Innsbruck
AUSTRIA
Győr
Pápa
Périgueux
Vichy
Clermont-Ferrand
Roanne
Lausanne
Bern
Geneva
ALPS
Szombathely
Bordeaux
Bourg-en-Bresse
Lyon
Bolzano
Graz
Székesfehérvár
HUNGARY
Puy de Sancy 6,185 ft.
St. Etienne
Villeurbanne
Mont Blanc 15,771 ft.
Klagenfurt
Villach
Maribor
Nagykanizsa
Plomb du Cantal 6,096 ft.
MASSIF CENTRAL
Chambéry
Grenoble
Bergamo
Brescia
SLOVENIA
Udine
Ljubljana
Celje
Varazdin
Pécs
Garonne R.
Agen
Rhône R.
Como
Novara
Milan
Vicenza
Padua
Trieste
Zagreb
Osijek
Santander
Bilbao
Bayonne
Pau
Montauban
Toulouse
Valence
Turin
Pavia
Cremona
Verona
Venice
Rijeka
Novo Mesto
Sisak
Slavensky Brod
Tarbes
Montpellier
Nîmes
Alessandria
Parma
Po R.
Modena
CROATIA
Banja Luka
Tuzla
Pic de Montcalm 10,305 ft.
Beziers
Aix-en-Provence
Avignon
Genoa
La Spezia
Prato
Bologna
Ravenna
BOSNIA-HERZEGOVINA
Carcassone
Nice
Savona
MONACO
Marseilles
Cannes
Toulon
Florence
SAN MARINO
Zadar
Sarajevo
Perpignan
ANDORRA
Pisa
Livorno
ITALY
Arezzo
Mostar
Šibenik
Siena
Piombino
Ancona
Perugia
Split
ADRIATIC SEA
Bastia
ELBA
Mt. Cinto 8,878 ft.
CORSICA (France)
Ajaccio
Mt. Corno 9,554 ft.
Chieti
Mt. Amaro 9,163 ft.
Dubrovnik
Niksic
Vatican City
Rome
L'Aquila
Terni
Tiber R.
APENNINES
Velletri
Terracina
Foggia
Cerignola
Barletta
Bari
Molfetta
Altamura
Brindisi
Vesuvio 4,190 ft.
Naples
Salerno
Sassari
Alghero
Punta la Marmora 6,016 ft.
SARDINIA (Italy)
Oristano
Iglesias
Cagliari
TYRRHENIAN SEA
Potenza
Taranto
Leece
Gulf of Taranto
Cosenza
Nicastra
Catanzaro
IONIAN SEA
Trapani
Palermo
Marsala
Caltanissetta
Mt. Etna (volcano) 10,902 ft.
Messina
Reggio di Calabria
SICILY
Catania
Caltagirone
Siracusa
Modica
Vittoria
Ragusa
MALTA
MEDITERRANEAN SEA
BALEARIC IS.
MINORCA
MAJORCA
Palma
IBIZA
PORTUGAL
SPAIN
La Coruña
El Ferrol
Santiago de la Compostela
Avilés
Gijón
Pontevedro
Vigo
Lugo
Oviedo
Ponferrada
León
San Sebastiano
Vitoria
Pamplona
PYRENEES
Braga
Porto
Palencia
Burgos
Logroño
Zamora
Valladolid
Duero R.
Ebro R.
Mt. Perdido 11,000 ft.
Pica de Aneto 11,168 ft.
Andorra
Salamanca
Soria
Segovia
Zaragoza
Avila
Coimbra
Covilhã
Guadalajara
Lérida
Gerona
Mataró
Sabadell
Barcelona
Tarragona
Lisbon
Barreiro
Setúbal
Portalegre
Tagus R.
Cáceres
Madrid
Elvas
Mérida
Aranjuez
Evora
Badajoz
Guadiana R.
Toledo
Cuenca
Castellón de la Plana
Ciudad Real
Tomelloso
Puertollano
Valdepeñas
Sagunto
Valencia
Lagos
Córdoba
Linares
Albacete
Seville
Écija
Guadalquivir R.
La Sagra 7,999 ft.
Huelva
Utrera
Lucena
Jaén
Murcia
Alcoy
Alicante
Jerez de la Frontera
Antequera
Granada
Lorca
Cadiz
Mulhacén 11,424 ft.
Strait of Gibraltar
Málaga
Cartagena
La Línea
Gibraltar
Motril
Almería
Tangier
Cueta
Melilla
Oran
Algiers
Rabat
Casablanca
MOROCCO
MIDDLE ATLAS
ALGERIA
SAHARAN ATLAS
'Annaba
Bizerte
Tunis
TUNISIA
0
250
500 Miles
500 Kilometers
24°
16°
8°
0°
58°
50°
42°
34°

Map 98 Eastern Europe

Elevation
Feet
3000
1500
300
0
Below sea level
Sea level
0
100
1000
Azimuthal Equidistant Projection
National capital
City
0
250
500 Miles
0
250
500 Kilometers
NORWAY
SWEDEN
FINLAND
DENMARK
ESTONIA
LATVIA
LITHUANIA
RUSSIA (KALININGRAD OBLAST)
BELARUS
POLAND
GERMANY
CZECH REP.
SLOVAKIA
AUSTRIA
HUNGARY
SLOVENIA
CROATIA
BOSNIA-HERZEGOVINA
YUGOSLAVIA
ROMANIA
MOLDOVA
UKRAINE
BULGARIA
MACEDONIA
ALBANIA
GREECE
ITALY
MALTA
TURKEY
CYPRUS
SYRIA
LEBANON
IRAQ
IRAN
GEORGIA
ARMENIA
AZERBAIJAN
KAZAKHSTAN
UZBEKISTAN
TURKMENISTAN
R U S S I A
BALTIC SEA
BLACK SEA
CASPIAN SEA
ARAL SEA
MEDITERRANEAN SEA
Sea of Azov
Gulf of Bothnia
Skagerrak
Lake Ladoga
Lake Peipus
CARPATHIAN MOUNTAINS
CAUCASUS MTS.
TAURUS MOUNTAINS
ZAGROS MOUNTAINS
ELBURZ MOUNTAINS
ALPS
CRIMEA
SICILY
CRETE
RHODES
Volga R.
Don R.
Dnepr R.
Ural R.
Danube R.
Tigris R.
Euphrates R.

Map 99 Northern Europe

Elevation
Feet
3000
1500
300
0
Sea level
Below sea level
0
100
1000
Simple Conic Projection
National capital
City
0
100
200 Miles
200 Kilometers
Arctic Circle
NORWEGIAN SEA
BARENTS SEA
WHITE SEA
NORTH SEA
BALTIC SEA
Gulf of Bothnia
Gulf of Finland
Gulf of Riga
Skagerrak
Kattegat
KOLA PENINSULA
LOFOTEN
VESTERÅLEN
HAILUOTO
ÅLAND
HIIUMAA
SAAREMAA
GOTLAND
ÖLAND
BORNHOLM
NORWAY
SWEDEN
FINLAND
RUSSIA
ESTONIA
LATVIA
LITHUANIA
BELARUS
POLAND
GERMANY
DENMARK
RUSSIA (KALININGRAD OBLAST)
Lake Ladoga
Lake Onega
Lake Peipus
Vänern
Vättern
Nordkapp
Kjelvik
Berlevåg
Makkaur
Hamningberg
Lebesby
Hammerfest
Kistrand
Polmak
Vadsø
Kirkenes
Nikel'
Alta
Utsjoki
Karasjok
Inarijärvi
Murmansk
Gremikha
Ponoy
Olenegorsk
Kirovsk
Apatity
Kandalaksha
Knyazhaya Guba
Tromsø
Skibotn
Lenvik
Målselv
Narvik
Hadsel
Svolvær
Vagan
Kebnekaise 6,962 ft.
Kiruna
Vittangi
Enontekiö
Kittilä
Sodankylä
Pelkosenniemi
Kuolayarvi
Sulitelma 6,280 ft.
Gällivare
Bodø
Saltdal
Beiarn
Jokkmokk
Övertorneå
Rovaniemi
Severodvinsk
Kem'
Onega
Belomorsk
Mo i Rana
Haparanda
Tornio
Kemi
Boden
Luleå
Mosjøen
Arvidsjaur
Sorsele
Grane
Brønnøysund
Piteå
Oulu
Storuman
Dikanäs
Skellefteå
Raahe
Kajaani
Vuokatti
Nadvoitsy
Segezha
Vilhelmina
Lycksele
Åsträsk
Lövånger
Hällnäs
Namsos
Grong
Snåsa
Dorotea
Hoting
Bygdeå
Sukeva
Pyhäjärvi
Iisalmi
Medvezh'yegorsk
Povenets
Alanäs
Steinkjer
Umeå
Kokkola
Jakobstad
Nykarleby
Hotagen
Stjørdal
Trondheim
Offerdal
Gäxsjö
Ådalsliden
Östersund
Kuopio
Outokumpu
Joensuu
Petrozavodsk
Kristiansund
Halsa
Surnadalsøra
Sylarna 5,781 ft.
Helagsfjället 5,892 ft.
Håsjö
Örnsköldsvik
Vaasa
Lapua
Seinäjoki
Kramfors
Varkaus
Ålesund
Sunndalsøra
Røros
Åsarna
Härnösand
Kaskinen
Jyväskylä
Sortavala
Podporozh'ye
Vytegra
Stranda
Snøhetta 7,500 ft.
Norddal
Dombås
Sånfjället 4,190 ft.
Klövsjo
Linsell
Sundsvall
Lodeynoye Pole
Galdhøpiggen 8,097 ft.
Glittertinden 8,110 ft.
Städjan 3,711 ft.
Lillhärdal
Ljusdal
Gnarp
Sysmä
Tampere
Heinola
Priozersk
Svetogorsk
Vyborg
Sande
Los
Hudiksvall
Pori
Kouvola
Särna
Bollnäs
Söderhamn
Rauma
Hämeenlinna
Lahti
Anjalankoski
Fåberg
Lillehammer
Forssa
Volkhov
Tikhvin
Voss
Myrdal
Fagernes
Mora
Rättvik
Hyvinkää
Kotka
Hamar
Höljes
Gävle
Naantali
Turku
Porvoo
Bergen
Gjøvik
Leksand
Falun
St. Petersburg
Uskedal
Kongsvinger
Appelbo
Borlänge
Ekenäs
Helsinki
Chudovo
Oslo
Västerdalälven R.
Mariehamn
Hangö
Skjold
Arvika
Uppsala
Tallinn
Kohtla-Järve
Haugesund
Drammen
Kopparberg
Tapa
Luga
Novgorod
Sarpsborg
Västerås
Dalen
Horten
Karlstad
Örebro
Stockholm
Stavanger
Fredrikstad
Eskilstuna
Södertälje
Haapsalu
Plyussa
Staraya Russa
Vyshniy-Volochek
Bygland
Larvik
Karlskoga
Kärdla
Vohma
Evje
Strömstad
Katrineholm
Pärnu
Tartu
Egersund
Arendal
Motala
Norrköping
Viljandi
Pskov
Ostashkov
Kristiansand
Uddevalla
Lidköping
Linköping
Kuressaare
Voru
Mandal
Trollhattan
Ostrov
Göteborg
Gränna
Huskvarna
Valmiera
Boras
Jönköping
Västervik
Cesis
Hjørring
Mölndal
Vetlanda
Målilla
Visby
Ventspils
Riga
Ergli
Velikiye-Luki
Ålborg
Varberg
Ogre
Rezekne
Nevel'
Växjö
Borgholm
Jelgava
Auce
Holstebro
Viborg
Randers
Halmstad
Kalmar
Liepaja
Priekule
Daugavpils
Yartsevo
Silkeborg
Tingsryd
Siauliai
Polatsk
Ringkøbing
Århus
Helsingborg
Karlskrona
Plunge
Panevezys
Vitsyebsk
Horsens
Kristianstad
Klaipeda
Smolensk
Esbjerg
Copenhagen
Malmö
Kolding
Ystad
Kaunas
Orsha
Odense
Svendborg
Trelleborg
Rønne
Sovetsk
Neman
Vilnius
Smarhon'
Barysaw
Mahilyow
Flensburg
Kaliningrad
Chernyakhovsk
Schleswig
Minsk
Stralsund
Slupsk
Gdansk
Kiel
Cuxhaven
Rostock
Kolobrzeg
Koszalin
Elblag
Elk
Hrodna
Navahrudak
Babruysk
Novozybkov
Emden
Lübeck
Slutsk
Bremerhaven
Hamburg
Schwerin
Szczecin
Grudziadz
Bialystok
Baranavichy
Homyel'
Groningen
Elbe R.
Wisla (Vistula) R.
Daugava R.
Nemunas R. (Neman R.)
Dnepr R.
Polisti R.
Volkhov R.
Kem' R.
Ponoy R.
Lotta R.
Skellefteälv R.
Umeälv R.

Map 100 Africa: Physical Features

PORTUGAL
SPAIN
FRANCE
ITALY
SERBIA
BULGARIA
ALBANIA
MACEDONIA
GREECE
RUSSIA
GEORGIA
ARMENIA
AZERBAIJAN
TURKMENISTAN
TURKEY
ASIA MINOR
BLACK SEA
CASPIAN SEA
ATLANTIC OCEAN
MEDITERRANEAN SEA
Strait of Gibraltar
Algiers
Tunis
Rabat
MOROCCO
TUNISIA
Gulf of Gabes
Tripoli
CYPRUS
LEBANON
ISRAEL
SYRIA
IRAQ
IRAN
JORDAN
KUWAIT
Persian Gulf
Jebel Toubkal 13,665 ft.
ATLAS MOUNTAINS
CANARY ISLANDS
GRAND ERG OCCIDENTAL
Khalij Bay
Banghazi
Alexandria
Cairo
Al Fayyum
SINAI PENINSULA
SAUDI ARABIA
BAHRAIN
ARABIAN PENINSULA
QATAR
UNITED ARAB EMIRATES
ERG IGUIDI
ALGERIA
LIBYA
LIBYAN DESERT
Asyut
Nile R.
ARABIAN DESERT
EGYPT
Aswan
RED SEA
WESTERN SAHARA
Tropic of Cancer
Dakhla
EL DJOUF
AHAGGAR MTS
Mt. Tahat 9,541 ft.
Al Khufra Oasis
Lake Nasser
NUBIAN DESERT
Cape Blanc
MAURITANIA
MALI
Pic Touside 10,712 ft.
TIBESTI MASSIF
SAHARA
Nouakchott
Cape Vert
Sénégal R.
Tombouctou
Bur Sudan
SENEGAL
Dakar
GAMBIA
Banjul
Gambie R.
SAHEL
NIGER
CHAD
ERITREA
Asmera
YEMEN
Bamako
Niamey
Omdurman
Khartoum
Bab el Mandeb
Gulf of Aden
Bissau
GUINEA-BISSAU
GUINEA
BURKINA FASO
Ouagadougou
Lake Chad
DARFUR
Al Fashir
Jabal Marrah 10,131 ft.
Ras Dashen Terara 15,158 ft.
DJIBOUTI
Djibouti
Gees Gwardafuy
Conakry
Freetown
SIERRA LEONE
Black Volta R.
White Volta R.
BENIN
Kano
N'Djamena
Chari R.
NIGERIA
Abuja
SUDAN
White Nile
Blue Nile
Addis Ababa
Harer
Hargeysa
IVORY COAST
GHANA
TOGO
Lake Volta
Ibadan
Lomé
Benue R.
Logone R.
SUDD
Mountain Nile
ETHIOPIAN PLATEAU
ETHIOPIA
SOMALIA
Monrovia
LIBERIA
Abidjan
Accra
Porto Novo
Lagos
CAMEROON
CENTRAL AFRICAN REPUBLIC
Cape Palmas
Volta R.
Gulf of Guinea
Douala
Malabo
Yaoundé
Bangui
EQUATORIAL GUINEA
Ubangi R.
CONGO BASIN
Uele R.
Lake Albert
UGANDA
Lake Rudolf
Jubba R.
Mogadishu
Equator
SÃO TOMÉ AND PRINCIPE
Cape Lopez
Libreville
GABON
Congo R.
RUWENZORI MTS.
Kampala
Mt. Elgon 14,178 ft.
KENYA
Mt. Kenya 17,058 ft.
Kisangani
Lake Edward
Lake Victoria
Nairobi
CONGO REPUBLIC
DEMOCRATIC REPUBLIC OF THE CONGO
RWANDA
Kigali
Mt. Kilimanjaro 19,340 ft.
Brazzaville
Kinshasa
Kasai R.
Bujumbura
BURUNDI
MASAI STEPPE
Mombasa
INDIAN OCEAN
Boma
Lake Tanganyika
Dodoma
ZANZIBAR
Dar es Salaam
ASCENSION ISLAND
Cuango R.
Luanda
TANZANIA
ALDABRA ISLANDS
COSMOLEDO ISLANDS
ATLANTIC OCEAN
ANGOLA
Lubumbashi
Lake Nyasa
Ruvuma R.
COMOROS
Moroni
Cape d'Ambre
Benguela
Cubango R.
ZAMBIA
MALAWI
Lilongwe
Namibe
Lusaka
Zambezi R.
Moçambique
ST. HELENA
Mozambique Channel
Cape Fria
Okavongo R.
Harare
ZIMBABWE
MOZAMBIQUE
Toamasino
Antananarivo
NAMIBIA
Okavango Swamp
Windhoek
MADAGASCAR
BOTSWANA
Limpopo R.
Tropic of Capricorn
Walvis Bay
Gaborone
Kalahari Desert
GREAT NAMALAND
Pretoria
Johannesburg
Maputo
Mbabane
Cape Ste. Marie
Vaal R.
Kimberly
SWAZILAND
Maseru
LESOTHO
DRAKENSBERG
Durban
SOUTH AFRICA
Cape Town
Cape of Good Hope
Cape Agulhas
Port Elizabeth
Elevation
Feet
3000
1500
300
0
Sea level
Below sea level
100
1000
National capital
City
0 250 500 750 1000 Miles
0 250 500 750 1000 Kilometers

Map 101 Africa: Political Divisions

ATLANTIC OCEAN
MEDITERRANEAN SEA
BLACK SEA
CASPIAN SEA
RED SEA
Persian Gulf
Gulf of Aden
Gulf of Guinea
INDIAN OCEAN
Mozambique Channel
FRANCE
ITALY
SERBIA
BULGARIA
ALBANIA
MACEDONIA
GREECE
TURKEY
RUSSIA
GEORGIA
ARMENIA
AZERBAIJAN
TURKMENISTAN
PORTUGAL
SPAIN
CYPRUS
SYRIA
LEBANON
ISRAEL
JORDAN
IRAQ
IRAN
KUWAIT
SAUDI ARABIA
BAHRAIN
QATAR
UNITED ARAB EMIRATES
YEMEN
Strait of Gibraltar
MOROCCO
Rabat
ATLAS MOUNTAINS
CANARY ISLANDS
El Aaiun
WESTERN SAHARA
Dakhla
Tropic of Cancer
Cape Blanc
Algiers
Oran
GRAND ERG OCCIDENTAL
ALGERIA
AHAGGAR MTS
TUNISIA
Tunis
Gulf of Gabes
Gabes
Tripoli
Khalij Bay
Banghazi
LIBYA
Alexandria
Cairo
Al Fayyum
Asyut
Nile R.
EGYPT
Aswan
Lake Nasser
MAURITANIA
Nouakchott
Cape Vert
Sénégal R.
MALI
S A H A R A
TIBESTI MASSIF
Tombouctou
Niger R.
SENEGAL
Dakar
Gambie R.
GAMBIA
Banjul
Bissau
GUINEA-BISSAU
GUINEA
Conakry
Freetown
SIERRA LEONE
Monrovia
LIBERIA
Bamako
BURKINA FASO
Ouagadougou
Black Volta R.
White Volta R.
IVORY COAST
Yamoussoukro
Abidjan
Cape Palmas
GHANA
Lake Volta
Accra
Volta R.
TOGO
Lomé
BENIN
Porto Novo
Niamey
NIGER
Kano
NIGERIA
Abuja
Ibadan
Lagos
Benue R.
Benin City
CHAD
Lake Chad
N'Djamena
Chari R.
Logone R.
CAMEROON
Douala
Malabo
Yaoundé
EQUATORIAL GUINEA
Equator
SÃO TOMÉ AND PRINCIPE
Cape Lopez
Libreville
GABON
CONGO REPUBLIC
Brazzaville
Boma
Kinshasa
Ubangi R.
Bangui
CENTRAL AFRICAN REPUBLIC
CONGO BASIN
Congo R.
Mbandaka
Uele R.
RUWENZORI MTS.
DEMOCRATIC REPUBLIC OF THE CONGO
Kasai R.
Kisangani
Lake Albert
Lake Edward
SUDAN
Omdurman
Khartoum
Al Fashir
White Nile
Blue Nile
AS SUDD
Mountain Nile
Bur Sudan
ERITREA
Asmera
Bab el Mandeb
DJIBOUTI
Djibouti
Gees Gwardafuy
Addis Ababa
Harer
Hargeysa
ETHIOPIAN PLATEAU
ETHIOPIA
SOMALIA
Jubba R.
Mogadishu
UGANDA
Kampala
Lake Victoria
Lake Rudolf
KENYA
Nairobi
Mombasa
RWANDA
Kigali
Bujumbura
BURUNDI
Lake Tanganyika
MASAI STEPPE
Dodoma
ZANZIBAR
Dar es Salaam
TANZANIA
ALDABRA ISLANDS
COSMOLEDO ISLANDS
Lake Nyasa
Ruvuma R.
COMOROS
Moroni
Cape d'Ambre
ASCENSION ISLAND
Cuango R.
Luanda
ANGOLA
Benguela
Huambo
Cubango R.
Namibe
ST. HELENA
Cape Fria
Lubumbashi
ZAMBIA
Lusaka
Zambezi R.
MALAWI
Lilongwe
Moçambique
MOZAMBIQUE
Harare
ZIMBABWE
Okavongo R.
NAMIBIA
Windhoek
Walvis Bay
BOTSWANA
Gaborone
Kalahari Desert
Limpopo R.
Tropic of Capricorn
Pretoria
Johannesburg
Vaal R.
Mbabane
Maputo
SWAZILAND
Kimberly
Maseru
LESOTHO
DRAKENSBERG
Pietermaritzburg
Durban
SOUTH AFRICA
Cape Town
Cape of Good Hope
Cape Agulhas
Port Elizabeth
Toamasino
Antananarivo
MADAGASCAR
Toliara
Cape Ste. Marie
National capital
City
0 250 500 750 1000 Miles
0 250 500 750 1000 Kilometers

Map 102a Environment and Economy

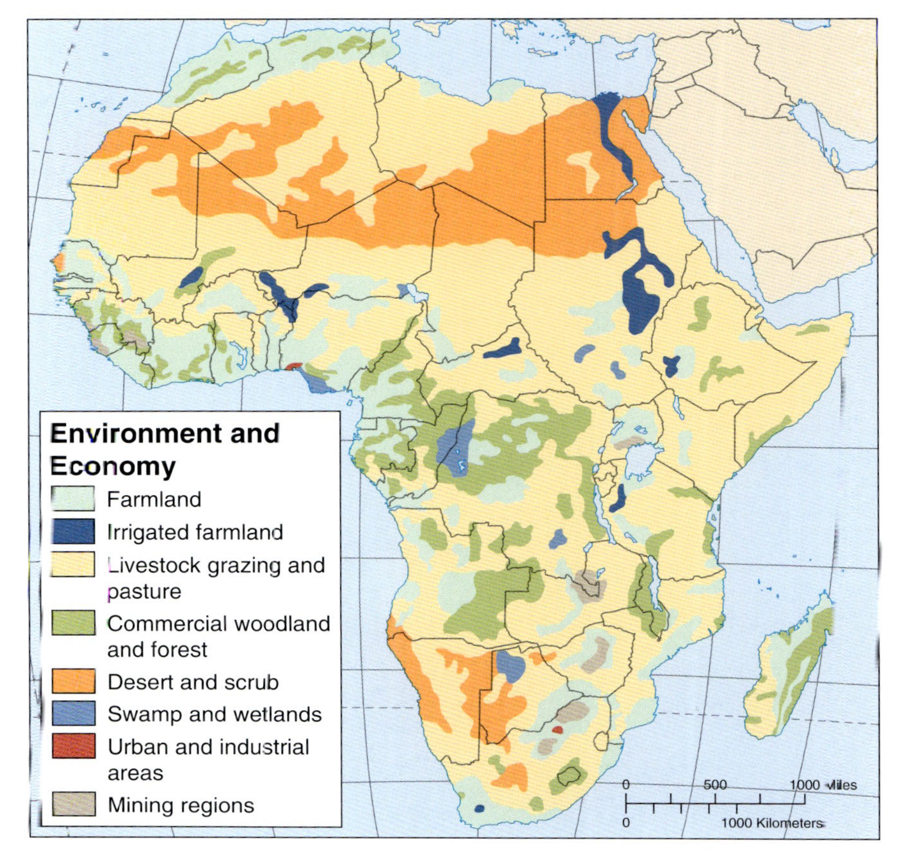
Environment and Economy
Farmland
Irrigated farmland
Livestock grazing and pasture
Commercial woodland and forest
Desert and scrub
Swamp and wetlands
Urban and industrial areas
Mining regions
0
500
1000 Miles
0
1000 Kilometers

Africa's economic landscape is dominated by subsistence, or marginally-commercial agricultural activities and raw material extraction, engaging three-fourths of Africa's workers. Much of this grazing land is very poor desert scrub and bunch grass that is easily impacted by cattle, sheep, and goats. Growing human and livestock populations place enormous stress on this fragile support capacity and the result is desertification: the conversion of even the most minimal of grazing environments to a small quantity of land suitable for crop farming. Although the continent has approximately 20 percent of the world's total land area, the proportion of Africa's arable land is small. The agricultural environment is also uncertain; unpredictable precipitation and poor soils hamper crop agriculture.

Map 102b Population Density

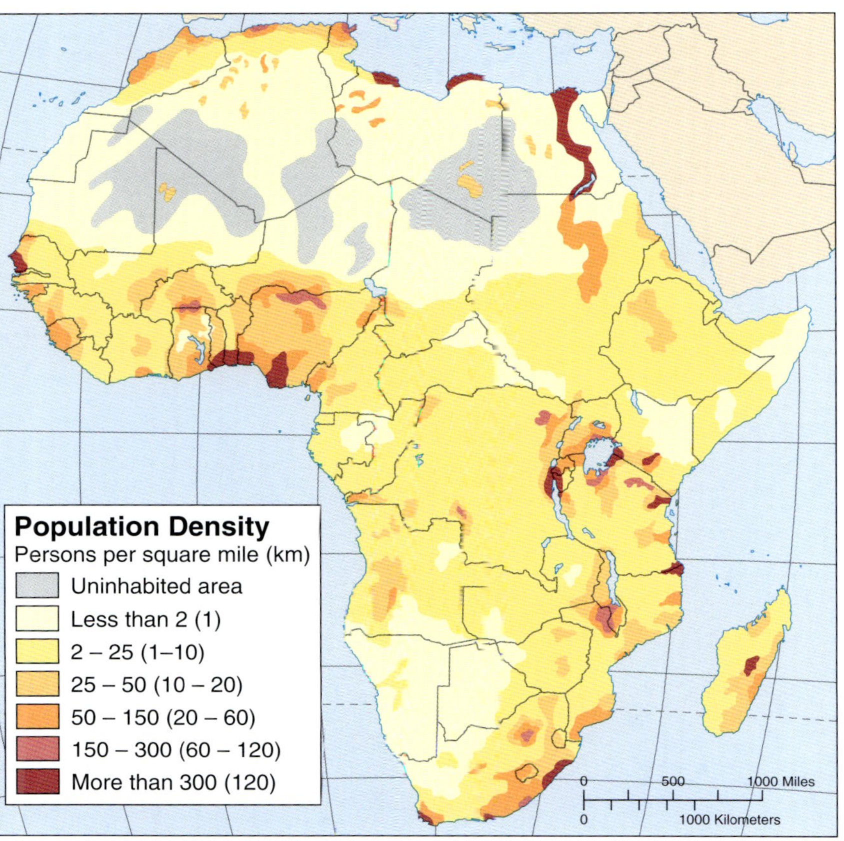
Population Density
Persons per square mile (km)
Uninhabited area
Less than 2 (1)
2 – 25 (1–10)
25 – 50 (10 – 20)
50 – 150 (20 – 60)
150 – 300 (60 – 120)
More than 300 (120)
0
500
1000 Miles
0
1000 Kilometers

Nearly 800 million people occupy the African continent, approximately one-eighth of the world's population. In general, this population has two chief characteristics: a low level of quality of life and growth rates that are among the world's highest. On a continent beset by poverty, recurrent internal civil and tribal war, and a host of environmental problems, the populations of many African countries are nevertheless increasing at a rate above 3 percent per year. The bulk of the population is concentrated in relatively small areas of the Mediterranean coastal regions of the north, the bulge of West Africa, and the eastern coastal and highland zone stretching from South Africa to Kenya. Where populations in other parts of the world tend to avoid highland locations, in Africa highlands often tend to be the most densely settled regions: moister with better soils, freer of insect pests, and somewhat cooler.

Map 102c Colonial Patterns

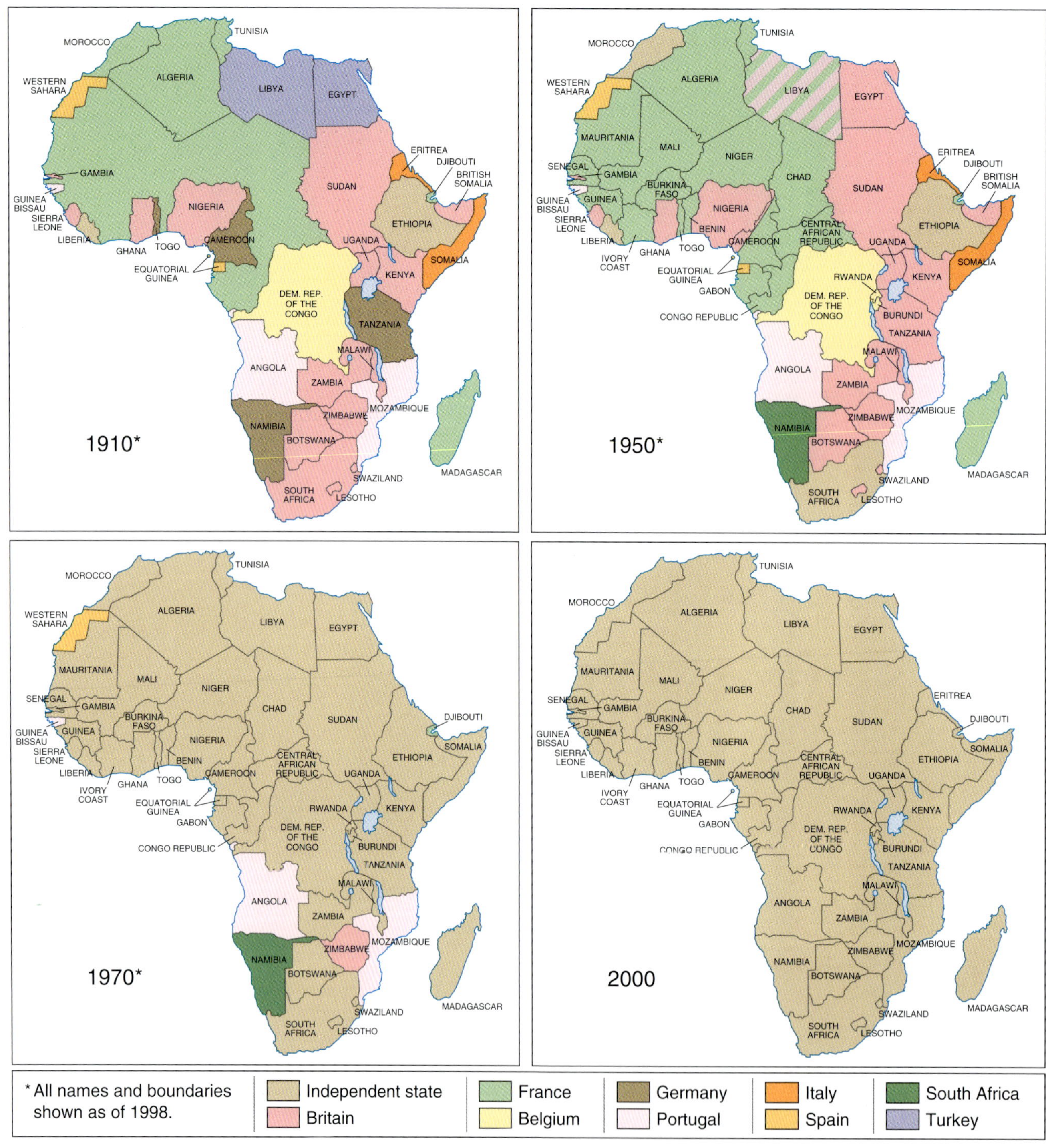
1910*
MOROCCO
TUNISIA
WESTERN SAHARA
ALGERIA
LIBYA
EGYPT
ERITREA
DJIBOUTI
BRITISH SOMALIA
GAMBIA
GUINEA BISSAU
SIERRA LEONE
LIBERIA
GHANA
TOGO
NIGERIA
CAMEROON
EQUATORIAL GUINEA
SUDAN
ETHIOPIA
SOMALIA
UGANDA
KENYA
DEM. REP. OF THE CONGO
TANZANIA
MALAWI
ANGOLA
ZAMBIA
ZIMBABWE
MOZAMBIQUE
NAMIBIA
BOTSWANA
SWAZILAND
SOUTH AFRICA
LESOTHO
MADAGASCAR
1950*
MAURITANIA
MALI
NIGER
SENEGAL
GUINEA
BURKINA FASO
CHAD
IVORY COAST
BENIN
CENTRAL AFRICAN REPUBLIC
GABON
CONGO REPUBLIC
RWANDA
BURUNDI
1970*
2000
* All names and boundaries shown as of 1998.
Independent state
Britain
France
Belgium
Germany
Portugal
Italy
Spain
South Africa
Turkey

In few parts of the world has the transition from colonialism to independence been as abrupt as on the African continent. Most African states did not become colonies until the nineteenth century and did not become independent until the twentieth, nearly all of them after World War II. Much of the colonial power in Africa is social and economic. The African colony provided the mother country with raw materials in exchange for marginal economic returns, and many African countries still exist in this colonial dependency relationship. An even more important component of the colonial legacy of Europe in Africa is geopolitical. When the world's colonial powers joined at the Conference of Berlin in 1884, they divided up Africa to fit their own needs, drawing boundary lines on maps without regard for terrain or drainage features, or for tribal/ethnic linguistic, cultural, economic, or political borders. Traditional Africa was enormously disrupted by this process. After independence, African countries retained boundaries that are legacies of the colonial past and African countries today are beset by internal problems related to tribal and ethnic conflicts, the disruption of traditional migration patterns, and inefficient spatial structures of market and supply.

Map 102d African Cropland and Dryland Degradation

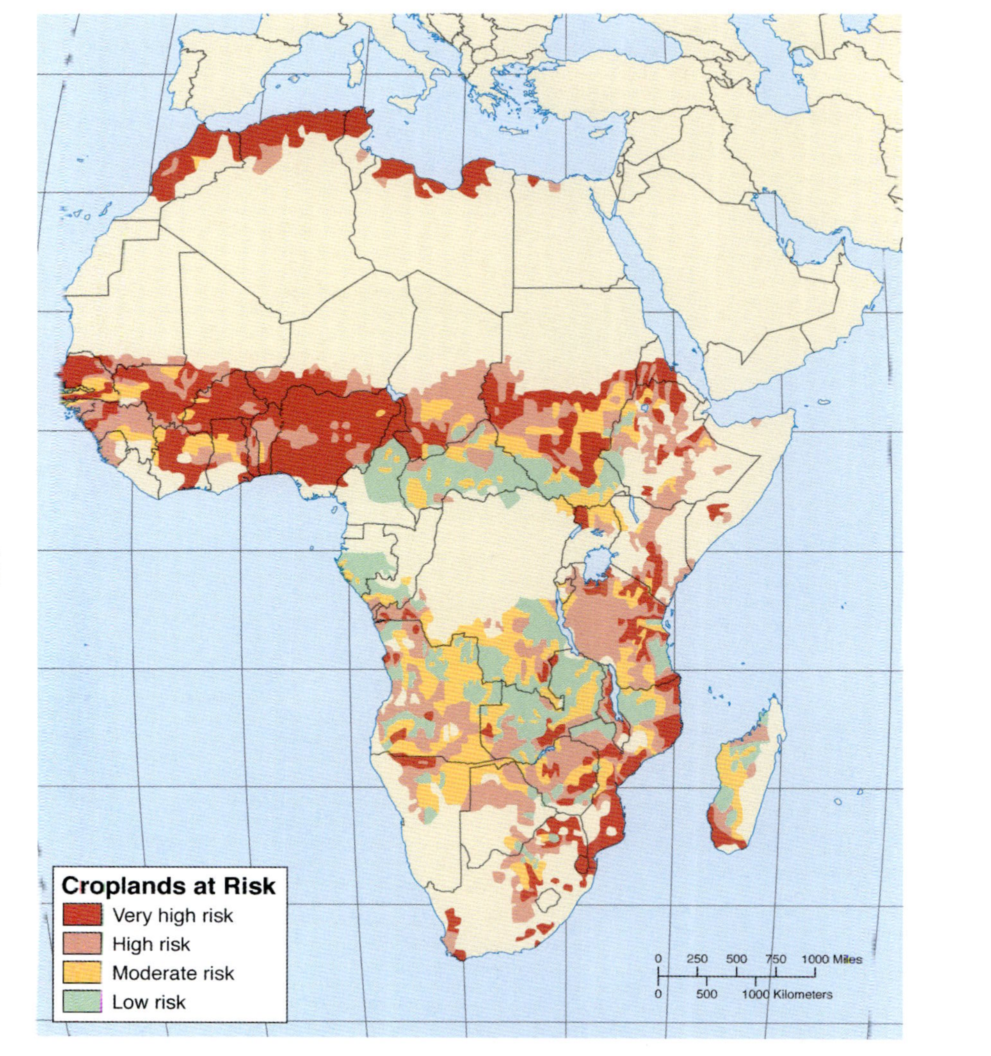
Croplands at Risk
Very high risk
High risk
Moderate risk
Low risk
0 250 500 750 1000 Miles
0 500 1000 Kilometers

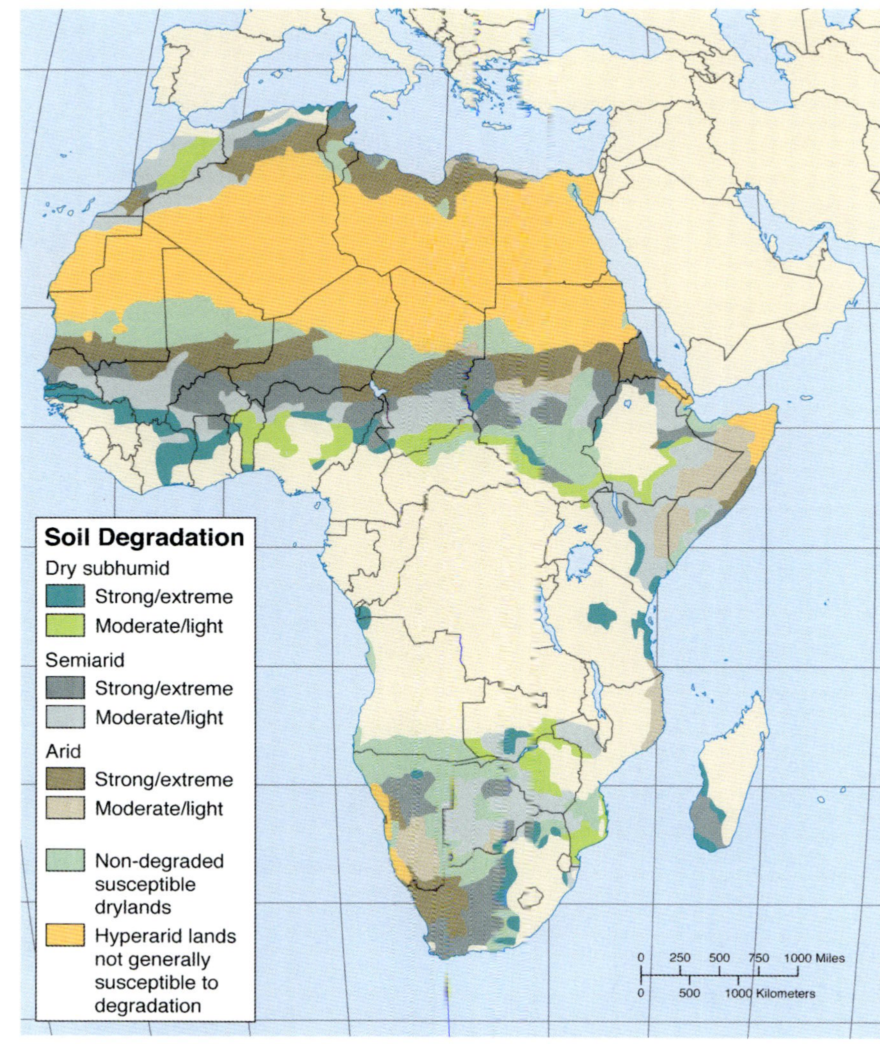
Soil Degradation
Dry subhumid
Strong/extreme
Moderate/light
Semiarid
Strong/extreme
Moderate/light
Arid
Strong/extreme
Moderate/light
Non-degraded susceptible drylands
Hyperarid lands not generally susceptible to degradation
0 250 500 750 1000 Miles
0 500 1000 Kilometers

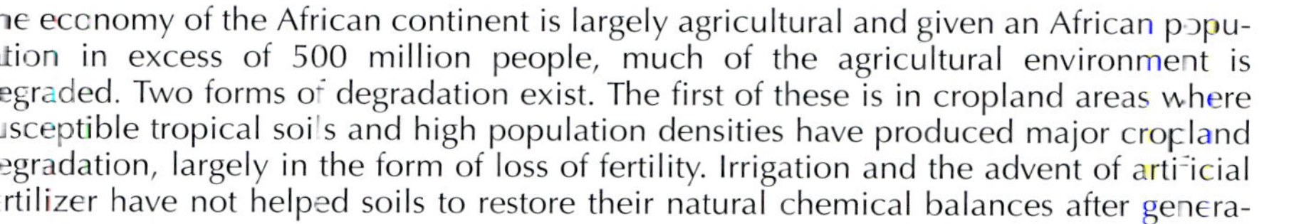

The economy of the African continent is largely agricultural and given an African population in excess of 500 million people, much of the agricultural environment is degraded. Two forms of degradation exist. The first of these is in cropland areas where susceptible tropical soils and high population densities have produced major cropland degradation, largely in the form of loss of fertility. Irrigation and the advent of artificial fertilizer have not helped soils to restore their natural chemical balances after generations of misuse. The second form of degradation is in the dryland areas where livestock grazing rather than cropping is the dominant agricultural form. Populations of domesticated stock that are too large for the carrying capacity of the environment, exacerbated by the view of livestock as wealth and worsened by increasing human populations, have all contributed to the conversion of semi-arid grasslands into desert.

Map 103 Northern Africa

National capital
City
Elevation
Feet
3000
1500
300
0
Below sea level
Sea level
0
100
1000
Lambert Equal-Area Projection
0 250 500 Miles
MOROCCO
ALGERIA
TUNISIA
LIBYA
EGYPT
WESTERN SAHARA (MORROCO)
MAURITANIA
MALI
NIGER
CHAD
SUDAN
SENEGAL
GAMBIA
GUINEA-BISSAU
GUINEA
SIERRA LEONE
LIBERIA
IVORY COAST
BURKINA FASO
GHANA
TOGO
BENIN
NIGERIA
CAMEROON
CENTRAL AFRICAN REPUBLIC
EQUATORIAL GUINEA
GABON
CONGO REPUBLIC
DEMOCRATIC REPUBLIC OF THE CONGO (ZAIRE)
UGANDA
KENYA
ETHIOPIA
ERITREA
DJIBOUTI
SOMALIA
YEMEN
SAUDI ARABIA
OMAN
JORDAN
ISRAEL
LEBANON
SYRIA
IRAQ
TURKEY
CYPRUS
GREECE
MALTA
SPAIN
PORTUGAL
SÃO TOMÉ & PRÍNCIPE
S A H A R A
MEDITERRANEAN SEA
RED SEA
ATLANTIC OCEAN
INDIAN OCEAN
GULF OF GUINEA
Gulf of Aden
CASPIAN SEA
LIBYAN DESERT
Nubian Desert
ATLAS MOUNTAINS
AHAGGAR
TIBESTI MASSIF
ETHIOPIAN PLATEAU
CANARY ISLANDS (Sp.)
MADEIRA (Port.)
Tropic of Cancer

Map 104 Southern Africa

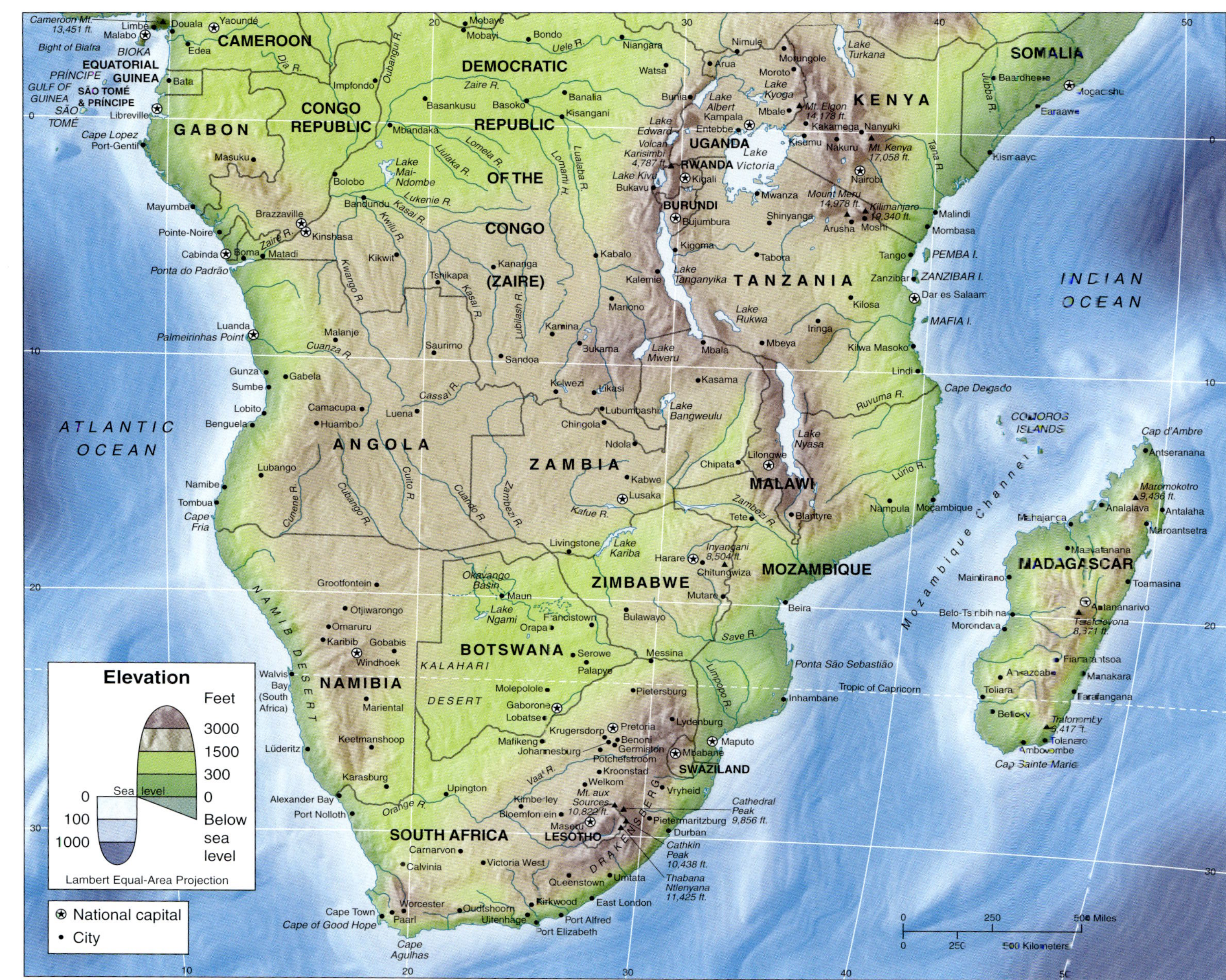
CAMEROON
Cameroon Mt. 13,451 ft.
Limbe
Douala
Yaoundé
Malabo
Edea
Bight of Biafra
BIOKA
EQUATORIAL GUINEA
PRÍNCIPE
Bata
GULF OF GUINEA
SÃO TOMÉ & PRÍNCIPE
SÃO TOMÉ
Libreville
GABON
Cape Lopez
Port-Gentil
Masuku
Mayumba
Pointe-Noire
Cabinda
Boma
Matadi
Ponta do Padrão
Brazzaville
Kinshasa
CONGO REPUBLIC
Impfondo
Bolobo
Dja R.
Oubangui R.
DEMOCRATIC REPUBLIC OF THE CONGO (ZAIRE)
Mobaye
Mobayi
Bondo
Uele R.
Niangara
Watsa
Zaire R.
Basankusu
Basoko
Banalia
Kisangani
Mbandaka
Lake Mai-Ndombe
Lomela R.
Liulaka R.
Lomami R.
Lualaba R.
Lukenie R.
Bandundu
Kasai R.
Kwilu R.
Kikwit
Kwango R.
Tshikapa
Kananga
Lubilash R.
Kamina
Kabalo
Kalemie
Manono
Bukama
Kolwezi
Likasi
Lubumbashi
Bunia
Aru
Lake Albert
Lake Edward
Volcan Karisimbi 4,787 ft.
Lake Kivu
Bukavu
UGANDA
Kampala
Entebbe
Lake Victoria
Nimule
Moroto
Lake Kyoga
Mbale
Mt. Elgon 14,178 ft.
RWANDA
Kigali
BURUNDI
Bujumbura
KENYA
Lake Turkana
Kakamega
Nanyuki
Kisumu
Nakuru
Mt. Kenya 17,058 ft.
Nairobi
Tana R.
SOMALIA
Baardheere
Jubba R.
Kismaayo
Malindi
Mombasa
TANZANIA
Mwanza
Shinyanga
Mount Meru 14,978 ft.
Kilimanjaro 19,340 ft.
Arusha
Moshi
Kigoma
Tabora
Tango
PEMBA I.
Zanzibar
ZANZIBAR I.
Dar es Salaam
Kilosa
MAFIA I.
Lake Tanganyika
Lake Rukwa
Iringa
Mbeya
Mbala
Lake Mweru
Kilwa Masoko
Lindi
Kasama
Ruvuma R.
Cape Delgado
INDIAN OCEAN
COMOROS ISLANDS
ATLANTIC OCEAN
Luanda
Palmeirinhas Point
Malanje
Cuanza R.
Saurimo
Sandoa
Gunza
Gabela
Sumbe
Lobito
Benguela
Camacupa
Huambo
Luena
Cassai R.
ANGOLA
Lubango
Cubango R.
Cuito R.
Cuando R.
Cunene R.
Namibe
Tombua
Cape Fria
ZAMBIA
Chingola
Ndola
Lake Bangweulu
Kabwe
Lusaka
Kafue R.
Zambezi R.
Livingstone
Lake Kariba
MALAWI
Lake Nyasa
Lilongwe
Chipata
Blantyre
Tete
Lurio R.
Nampula
Moçambique
MOZAMBIQUE
Harare
Inyangani 8,504 ft.
Chitungwiza
Mutare
Beira
ZIMBABWE
Bulawayo
Save R.
Messina
Limpopo R.
Inhambane
Ponta São Sebastião
Tropic of Capricorn
Mozambique Channel
MADAGASCAR
Cap d'Ambre
Antseranana
Maromokotro 9,436 ft.
Analalava
Antalaha
Maroantsetra
Toamasina
Antananarivo
Morondava
Toliara
Manakara
Farafangana
Cap Sainte Marie
Okavango Basin
Maun
Lake Ngami
Francistown
Orapa
BOTSWANA
KALAHARI DESERT
Serowe
Palapye
Molepolole
Gaborone
Lobatse
Grootfontein
Otjiwarongo
Omaruru
Karibib
Gobabis
Windhoek
NAMIBIA
NAMIB DESERT
Mariental
Walvis Bay (South Africa)
Lüderitz
Keetmanshoop
Karasburg
Alexander Bay
Port Nolloth
Orange R.
Upington
Pietersburg
Pretoria
Lydenburg
Maputo
Mbabane
SWAZILAND
Krugersdorp
Benoni
Germiston
Mafikeng
Johannesburg
Potchefstroom
Kroonstad
Vaal R.
Welkom
Vryheid
Kimberley
Mt. aux Sources 10,822 ft.
Bloemfontein
Maseru
LESOTHO
DRAKENSBERG
Cathedral Peak 9,856 ft.
Pietermaritzburg
Durban
Cathkin Peak 10,438 ft.
Thabana Ntlenyana 11,425 ft.
SOUTH AFRICA
Carnarvon
Calvinia
Victoria West
Queenstown
Umtata
Kirkwood
East London
Port Alfred
Port Elizabeth
Uitenhage
Oudtshoorn
Worcester
Paarl
Cape Town
Cape of Good Hope
Cape Agulhas
Elevation
Feet
3000
1500
300
0
Sea level
Below sea level
0
100
1000
Lambert Equal-Area Projection
National capital
City
0
250
500 Miles
0
250
500 Kilometers

Map 105 Asia: Physical Features

National capital
City
ATLANTIC OCEAN
ICELAND
GREENLAND
ALASKA (USA)
Bering Strait
ST. LAWRENCE ISLAND
BERING SEA
WRANGELL ISLAND
EAST SIBERIAN SEA
ARCTIC OCEAN
Arctic Circle
SVALBARD
ZEMLYA FRANTSA IOSIFA
NOVAYA ZEMLYA
SEVERNAYA ZEMLYA
NEW SIBERIAN ISLANDS
LAPTEV SEA
BARENTS SEA
KARA SEA
IRELAND
UNITED KINGDOM
London
NORTH SEA
NORWAY
SWEDEN
Gulf of Bothnia
DENMARK
Copenhagen
NETH.
BELG.
Paris
FRANCE
LUX.
GERMANY
Berlin
Stockholm
FINLAND
BALTIC SEA
Ladozhskoye Ozero
Onezhkoye Ozero
Arkhangelsk
SWITZ.
ALPS
Danube R.
POLAND
Prague
St Petersburg
ESTONIA
LATVIA
LITHUANIA
RUSSIA
CZECH REP.
Warsaw
AUSTRIA
Vienna
SLOVENIA
SLOVAKIA
CROATIA
Budapest
HUNGARY
B-H
Rome
ITALY
SERBIA
ROMANIA
MOLDOVA
UKRAINE
Kiev
Moscow
Rostov
Nizhniy Novgorod
Sev. Dvina
Dnepr R.
Don R.
Sofiya
Bucharest
MACEDONIA
ALBANIA
BULGARIA
GREECE
SEA OF AZOV
Donetsk
Rostov na Donu
Volga R.
Samara
Istanbul
BLACK SEA
Ankara
TURKEY
Mt. Elbrus 18,510 ft.
CAUCASUS MTS.
GEORGIA
Tbilisi
Yerevan
ARMENIA
Baku
AZERBAIJAN
Astrakhan
CASPIAN SEA
Ural R.
TOROS DAGLARI
MEDITERRANEAN SEA
CYPRUS
Alexandria
LEBANON
ISRAEL
Beirut
Aleppo
Damascus
SYRIA
Tel Aviv
Amman
Jerusalem
EGYPT
Cairo
JORDAN
IRAQ
Tabriz
Euphrates R.
Tigris R.
Baghdad
ELBURZ MTS.
Tehran
Mashhad
Nile R.
ARABIAN DESERT
AL HIJAZ
ASIR
Kuwait
KUWAIT
ZAGROS MTS.
IRAN
PLATEAU OF IRAN
Shiraz
Persian Gulf
SAUDI ARABIA
ARABIAN DESERT
BAHRAIN
QATAR
Al Manamah
Ad Dawhah
Riyadh
Straits of Hormuz
Abu Dhabi
UNITED ARAB EMIRATES
Gulf of Oman
Muscat
OMAN
RUB AL KHALI
RED SEA
SUDAN
ERITREA
Bab el Mandeb
Sanaa
YEMEN
Aden
DJIBOUTI
Gulf of Aden
ETHIOPIA
SOMALIA
ARABIAN SEA
URAL MOUNTAINS
Yekaterinburg
WESTERN SIBERIAN LOWLAND
Ob R.
Irtysh R.
Ishim R.
Omsk
Tomsk
Novosibirsk
Krasnoyarsk
Yenisei R.
Podkamennaya Tunguska
Angara R.
CENTRAL SIBERIAN PLATEAU
Lena R.
VERKHOYANSKIY RANGE
Indigirka R.
Kolyma R.
GYDAN RANGE
KAMCHATKA RANGE
Klyuchevskaya 15,584 ft.
Yakutsk
Okhotsk
DZHUGDZHUR MOUNTAINS
SEA OF OKHOTSK
KURIL ISLANDS
SAKHALIN
STANOVOY MOUNTAINS
RUSSIA
Lake Baikal
Irkutsk
YABLONOVYY RANGE
Amur R.
Komsomolsk
Tatar Strait
Khabarovsk
HOKKAIDO
SIKHOTE ALIN
KIRGHIZ STEPPE
KAZAKSTAN
Akmola
ARAL SEA
UZBEKISTAN
Syr Darya
Amu Darya
Lake Balkash
SAYAN RANGE
ALTAI MTS.
MONGOLIA
Ulan Bator
GOBI DESERT
GREATER KHINGAN RANGE
Harbin
Changchun
Vladivostok
SEA OF JAPAN
HONSHU
JAPAN
Tokyo
Shenyang
NORTH KOREA
Pyongyang
Yokohama
Kyoto
Osaka
Kobe
Seoul
SOUTH KOREA
SHIKOKU
Kitayushu
KYUSHU
Korea Strait
Gora Kommunizma 24,590 ft.
Alma-Ata
TURKMENISTAN
Tashkent
Bishkek
TIEN SHAN
Samarkand
Ashkabad
Dushanbe
KYRGYZSTAN
TARIM BASIN
PAMIRS
TAKLA MAKAN
ALTUN SHAN
KUNLUN SHAN
AFGHANISTAN
TAJIKISTAN
Kabul
HINDU KUSH
Peshawar
Islamabad
Srinagar
KARAKORAM
K2 (Godwin-Austen) 28,250 ft.
Rawalpindi
Lahore
SULAIMAN RANGE
Indus R.
PLATEAU OF TIBET
Mt. Everest 29,028 ft.
Nanda Devi 25,645 ft.
HIMALAYAS
Lhasa
Brahmaputra R.
Beijing
Tianjin
Qingdao
Huang
Lanzhou
CHINA
Chengdu
Chongqing
Yangtze (Chiang Jiang)
Nanjing
Wuhan
Shanghai
EAST CHINA SEA
NANSEI SHOTO
PAKISTAN
Karachi
GREAT INDIAN DESERT
Delhi
New Delhi
NEPAL
Kathmandu
Kanchenjunga 28,208 ft.
BHUTAN
Thimphu
Ganges R.
Gongga Shan 24,790 ft.
NAN LING MTS.
Fuzhou
Taiwan Strait
Taipei
TAIWAN
PACIFIC OCEAN
Gulf of Kutch
Ahmadabad
INDIA
Dhaka
Kunming
Guangzhou
Luzon Strait
Hong Kong
Phou Bia 9,249 ft.
PHILIPPINE SEA
Calcutta
Irrawaddy R.
Mandalay
Hanoi
Gulf of Tonkin
PHILIPPINES
LUZON
DECCAN PLATEAU
Gulf of Khambhat
Bombay
WESTERN GHATS
EASTERN GHATS
Godavari R.
Hyderabad
BANGLADESH
MYANMAR (BURMA)
LAOS
Viangchan
Mekong R.
Hue
SOUTH CHINA SEA
Manila
MINDORO
SAMAR
LEYTE
PANAY
Bay of Bengal
Salween R.
Rangoon
THAILAND
Moulmein
VIETNAM
Krishna R.
Bangalore
Calicut
Madras
ANDAMAN ISLANDS
Bangkok
CAMBODIA
Phnom Penh
Gulf of Thailand
Ho Chi Minh
PALAWAN
NEGROS
SULU SEA
SULU ISLANDS
MINDINAO
HALMAHERA
Gulf of Mannar
SRI LANKA
Colombo
NICOBAR ISLANDS
Straits of Malacca
Bandar Seri Begawan
BRUNEI
CELEBES SEA
Kuala Lumpur
MALAYSIA
SINGAPORE
BORNEO
CELEBES
INDIAN OCEAN
Equator
Elevation
Feet
3000
1500
300
0
Sea level
0
100
1000
Below sea level
0
500
1000 Miles
0
500
1000 Kilometers
MADAGASCAR
THAILAND
Straits of Malacca
Bandar Seri Begawan
BRUNEI
SULU ISLANDS
HALMAHERA
CELEBES SEA
Equator
NEW GUINEA
PAPUA NEW GUINEA
Kuala Lumpur
MALAYSIA
SINGAPORE
BORNEO
CELEBES
SUMATRA
INDONESIA
EAST TIMOR
INDIAN OCEAN
Jakarta
JAVA
AUSTRALIA
0
500
1000 Miles
0
500
1000 Kilometers

Map 106 Asia: Political Divisions

ATLANTIC OCEAN
ARCTIC OCEAN
RUSSIA
KAZAKSTAN
MONGOLIA
CHINA
INDIA
IRAN
SAUDI ARABIA
TURKEY
AFGHANISTAN
PAKISTAN
JAPAN
NORTH KOREA
SOUTH KOREA
MYANMAR (BURMA)
THAILAND
VIETNAM
PHILIPPINES
MALAYSIA
INDONESIA
AUSTRALIA
ARABIAN SEA
INDIAN OCEAN
PACIFIC OCEAN
SOUTH CHINA SEA
Bay of Bengal
National capital
City

Map 107a Environment and Economy

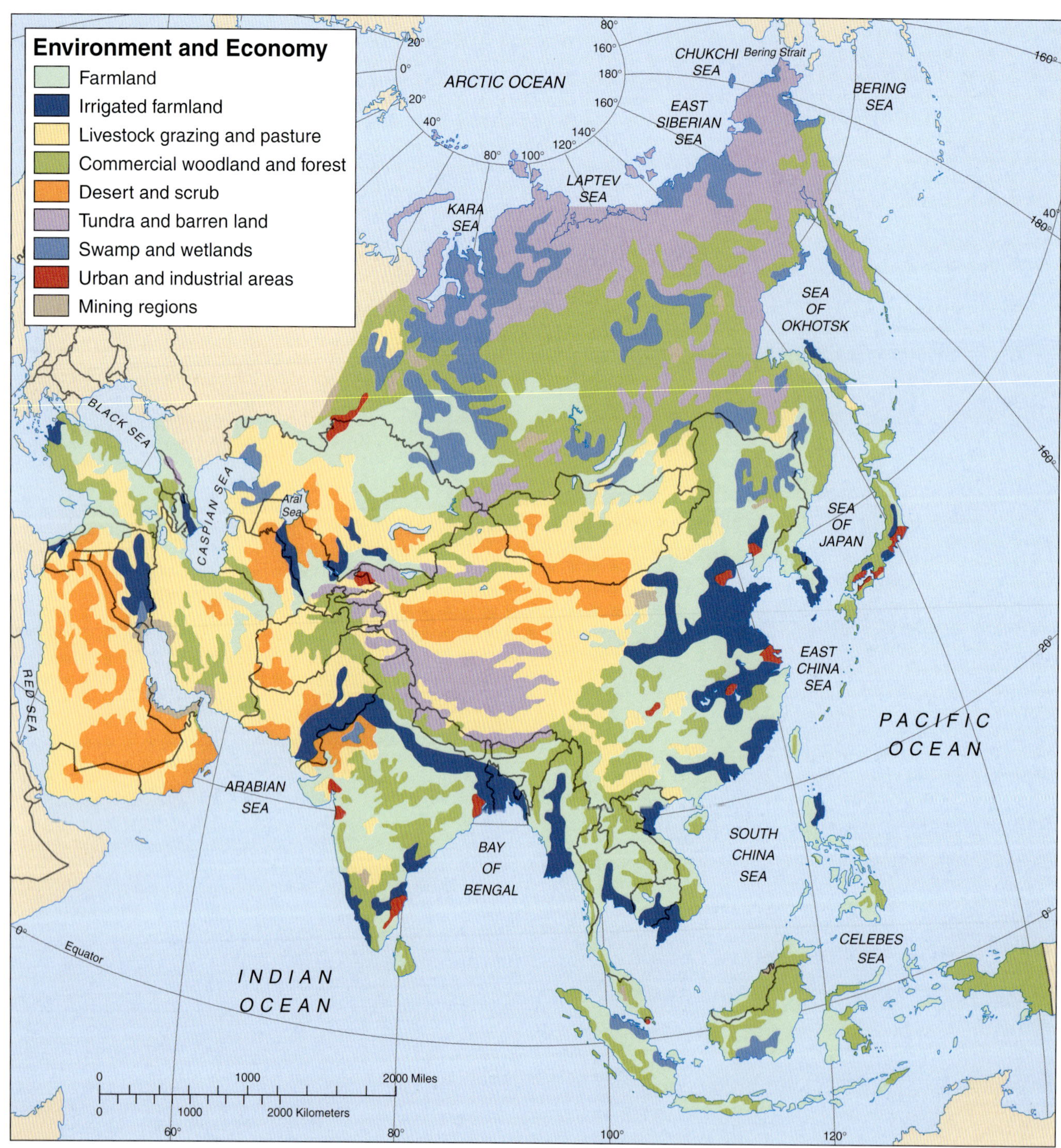
Environment and Economy
Farmland
Irrigated farmland
Livestock grazing and pasture
Commercial woodland and forest
Desert and scrub
Tundra and barren land
Swamp and wetlands
Urban and industrial areas
Mining regions
ARCTIC OCEAN
CHUKCHI SEA
Bering Strait
BERING SEA
EAST SIBERIAN SEA
LAPTEV SEA
KARA SEA
SEA OF OKHOTSK
BLACK SEA
CASPIAN SEA
Aral Sea
SEA OF JAPAN
EAST CHINA SEA
PACIFIC OCEAN
RED SEA
ARABIAN SEA
BAY OF BENGAL
SOUTH CHINA SEA
CELEBES SEA
INDIAN OCEAN
Equator
0 1000 2000 Miles
0 1000 2000 Kilometers

Asia is a land of extremes of land use with some of the world's most heavily industrialized regions, barren and empty areas, and productive and densely populated farm regions. Asia is a region of rapid industrial growth. Yet Asia remains an agricultural region with three out of every four workers engaged in agriculture. Asian commercial agriculture and intensive subsistence agriculture is characterized by irrigation. Some of Asia's irrigated lands are desert requiring additional water. But most of the Asian irrigated regions have sufficient precipitation for crop agriculture and irrigation is a way of coping with seasonal drought—the wet-and-dry cycle of the monsoon—often gaining more than one crop per year on irrigated farms. Agricultural yields per unit area in many areas of Asia are among the world's highest. Because the Asian population is so large and the demands for agricultural land so great, Asia is undergoing rapid deforestation and some areas of the continent have only small remnants of a once-abundant forest reserve.

Map 107b Population Density

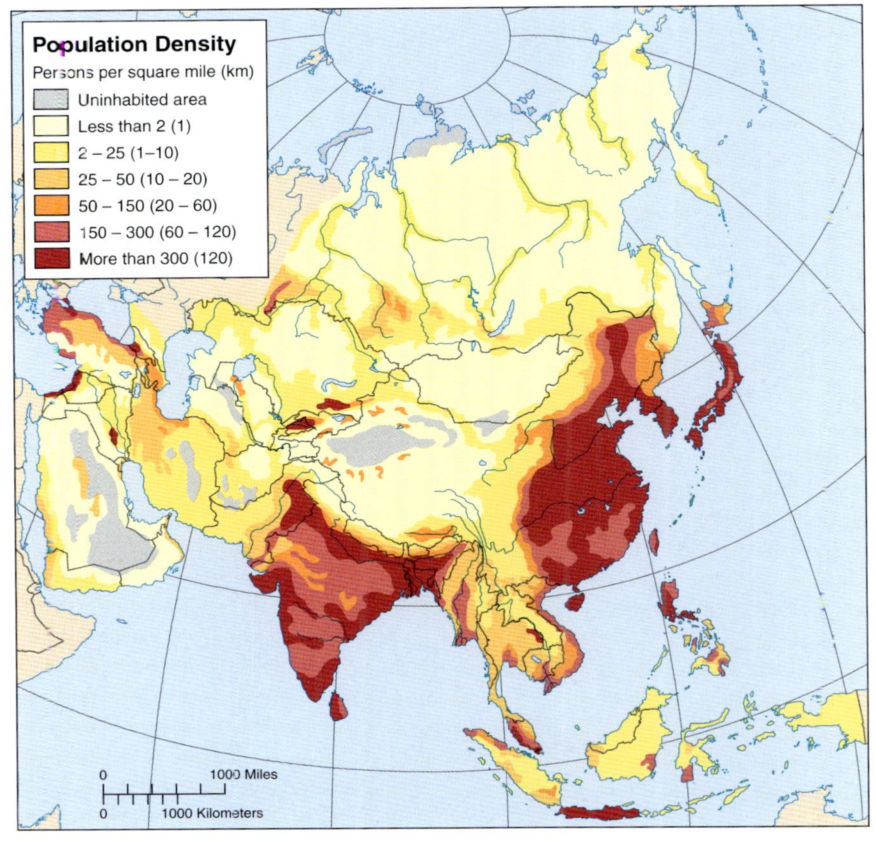
Population Density
Persons per square mile (km)
Uninhabited area
Less than 2 (1)
2 – 25 (1–10)
25 – 50 (10 – 20)
50 – 150 (20 – 60)
150 – 300 (60 – 120)
More than 300 (120)
0
1000 Miles
0
1000 Kilometers

With one-third of the world's land area and nearly two-thirds of the world's population, Asia is more densely settled than any other region of the world. In some of the continent's farming regions, agricultural population density exceeds 2,000 persons per square mile. In some portions of the continent, particularly the Islamic areas of Central and Southwest Asia, this already large population is growing very rapidly with some countries having population growth rates above 3 percent per year and doubling times between 20 and 25 years. The populations of neither China nor India are growing particularly rapidly but since both countries have population bases that are enormous, the absolute number of Indians and Chinese added to the world's population each year is staggering. In spite of these massive populations, Asia also contains areas that are either completely uninhabited or have population densities that are as low as any on earth.

Map 107c Industrialization: Manufacturing and Resources

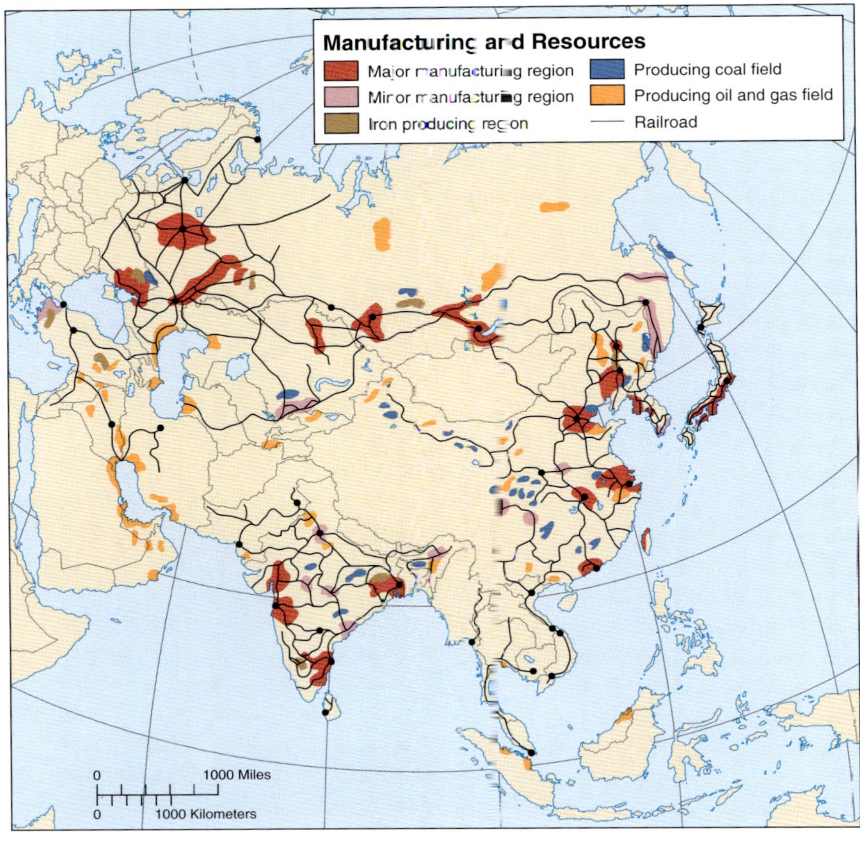
Manufacturing and Resources
Major manufacturing region
Minor manufacturing region
Iron producing region
Producing coal field
Producing oil and gas field
Railroad
0
1000 Miles
0
1000 Kilometers

International economists have predicted that the next century will be one of Asian economic dominance, as other Asian nations approach the economic levels of industrial giant Japan. Asian countries have begun to industrialize rapidly and have increased industrial production more than 100 percent in the last decade. But nothing guarantees industrial output, it must master the great distances separating critical raw material and production sites from the locations of the market for them. Such a mastery is achieved only by the development of efficient transportation systems. Usually that means water travel and here Asia is remarkably deficient when compared with Europe and North America. Nevertheless, the mixed prospects for Asian economic growth into the next century are a great deal better than would have been predicted a decade ago.

Map 107d South, South-East, and East Asian Deforestation

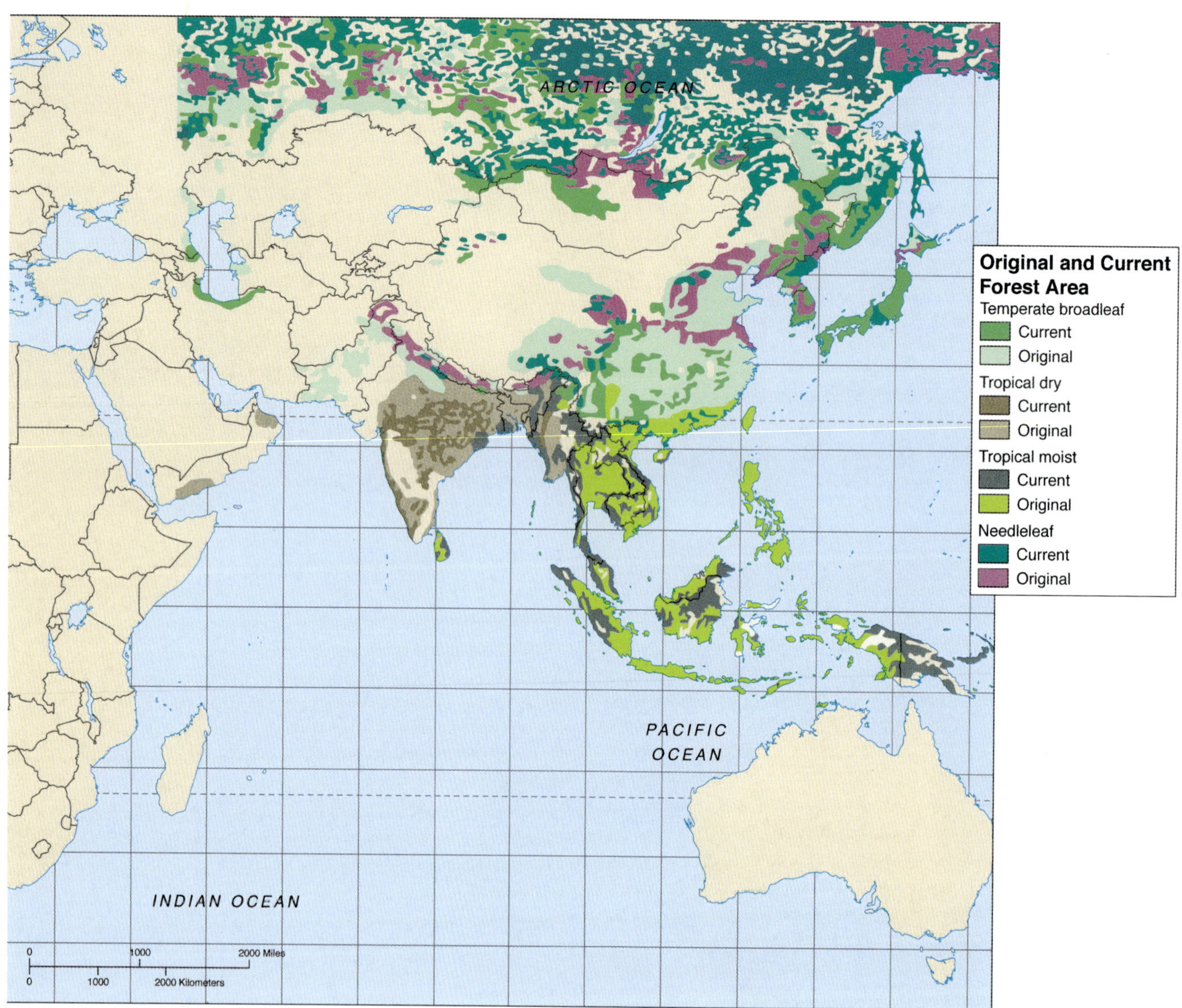

ARCTIC OCEAN
PACIFIC OCEAN
INDIAN OCEAN
Original and Current Forest Area
Temperate broadleaf
Current
Original
Tropical dry
Current
Original
Tropical moist
Current
Original
Needleleaf
Current
Original
0
1000
2000 Miles
0
1000
2000 Kilometers

In no part of the world has deforestation produced such dramatic changes in the environment as in Asia. Here, the world's oldest continuous agricultural civilizations have placed enormous demands upon the vegetative and soil environments to the extent that precious little natural forest cover remains in two world's two most populous countries, China and India. While Southeast Asia has been historically less denuded than the major culture centers to its north and west, recent decades have seen significantly forest loss to commercial timber operations, stimulated by the high-market value of tropical hardwoods. Also, a fairly recent trend has been the massive deforestation in the northeastern parts of Russia where economic expansion over the last century has stimulated the rapid loss of softwood forests for construction lumber and for paper production.

Map 108 Northern Asia

Elevation
Feet
3000
1500
300
0
Below
sea
level
Sea level
Lambert Equal-Area Projection
National capital
State capital
City
0
200
400 Miles
200
400 Kilometers
ARCTIC OCEAN
NORWEGIAN SEA
BARENTS SEA
KARA SEA
LAPTEV SEA
EAST SIBERIAN SEA
CHUKCHI SEA
BERING SEA
Bering Strait
Arctic Circle
SEA OF OKHOTSK
SEA OF JAPAN
EAST CHINA SEA
BLACK SEA
CASPIAN SEA
ARAL SEA
SVALBARD
ZEMLYA FRANTSA IOSIFA
NOVAYA ZEMLYA
SEVERNAYA ZEMLYA
NOVOSIBIRSKIYE OSTROVA
OS. LYAKHOVSKIY
OS. VRANGELYA
KOMANDORSKIYE OS.
SAKHALIN
Tatarskiy Proliv
NORWAY
SWEDEN
FINLAND
LAPLAND
RUSSIA
ESTONIA
LATVIA
LITHUANIA
BELARUS
POLAND
GERMANY
LUXEMBOURG
CZECH. REP.
SLOVAKIA
AUSTRIA
SLOVENIA
CROATIA
HUNGARY
UKRAINE
MOLDOVA
ROMANIA
BULGARIA
TURKEY
CYPRUS
SYRIA
LEBANON
ISRAEL
JORDAN
IRAQ
SAUDI ARABIA
KUWAIT
IRAN
GEORGIA
ARMENIA
AZERBAIJAN
TURKMENISTAN
UZBEKISTAN
KAZAKHSTAN
KYRGYZSTAN
TAJIKISTAN
AFGHANISTAN
PAKISTAN
INDIA
CHINA
MONGOLIA
NORTH KOREA
SOUTH KOREA
JAPAN
R U S S I A
URAL MOUNTAINS
CENTRAL SIBERIAN PLATEAU
WEST SIBERIAN LOWLAND
SAKHA (YAKUTIA)
VERKHOYANSKIY RANGE
CHERSKOGO RANGE
KOLYMA RANGE
KOLYMA LOWLAND
KAMCHATKA
DZHUGDZHUR RANGE
ALDANSKOYE RANGE
STANOVOY RANGE
YABLONOVYY RANGE
SIKHOTE RANGE
MANCHURIAN PLAIN
BURYATIA
TUVA
SAYAN MTS.
ALTAI MTS.
GOBI DESERT
GREAT BASIN
TARIM BASIN
TIEN SHAN
KUNLUN SHAN
PLATEAU OF TIBET
HINDU KUSH
ZAGROS MTS.
TURANIAN PLATEAU
Delta of the Lena
Lena R.
Yenisey R.
Lower Tunguska
Angara R.
Ob R.
Irtysh R.
Ishim R.
Tobol R.
Kama R.
Volga R.
Don R.
Dnieper
Danube R.
Pechora R.
Onega R.
Ural R.
Syr Dar'ya
Amu Dar'ya
Indigirka R.
Kolyma R.
Amur R.
Yellow R.
Tigris R.
Euphrates R.
Lake Baikal
Lake Balkash
Gora Narodnaya 6,217 ft.
Gora Tel'pos-Iz 5,305 ft.
Gora Chen 10,171 ft.
Klyuchevskaya (Vol.) 15,584 ft.
Gora Polkan 3,543 ft.
Gora Golets-Purpula 5,377 ft.
Golets-Skalistyy 9,188 ft.
Gora Piramida 10,801 ft.
Munku Sardyk 11,457 ft.
Gora Belukha 14,783 ft.
Tsast Bogd 13,419 ft.
Pik Pobedy 24,406 ft.
Pik Kommunizma 24,590 ft.
Muztagata 24,757 ft.
K2 (Godwin Austen) 28,250 ft.
G. El'brus 18,510 ft.
Mt. Ararat 16,854 ft.
Qalleh-ye Damavand 18,386 ft.
Binalud 11,208 ft.
Moscow
St. Petersburg
Murmansk
Arkhangel'sk
Petrozavodsk
Stockholm
Helsinki
Tallinn
Riga
Vilnius
Minsk
Warsaw
Berlin
Prague
Vienna
Bratislava
Budapest
Kiev
Chernobyl
Bucharest
Sofia
Chisinau
Odessa
Sevastopol
Istanbul
Ankara
Yerevan
Baku
Tbilisi
Tehran
Baghdad
Damascus
Kuwait
Ashkabad
Tashkent
Bishkek
Dushanbe
Kabul
Alma-Ata
Karaganda
Semipalatinsk
Balkash
Omsk
Novosibirsk
Tomsk
Krasnoyarsk
Irkutsk
Bratsk
Ulan-Ude
Ulaanbaatar
Yakutsk
Lensk
Olekminsk
Magadan
Anadyr'
Petropavlovsk-Kamchatskiy
Khabarovsk
Vladivostok
Harbin
Changchun
Shenyang
Beijing
Pyongyang
Seoul
Qingdao
Shanghai
Hohhot
Baotou
Lanzhou
Xi'an
Jiayuguan
Yumen
Ürümqi
Tokyo
Osaka
Kyoto
Sapporo
Hakodate
Nagasaki
Yuzhno-Sakhalinsk
Nordvik
Dickson
Amderma
Salekhard
Khanty-Mansiysk
Yekaterinburg
Chelyabinsk
Perm
Nizhniy Tagil
Tobol'sk
Ufa
Samara
Kazan
Izhevsk
Kirov
Syktyvkar
Nizhniy Novgorod
Yaroslavl'
Smolensk
Saransk
Syzran
Saratov
Volgograd
Astrakhan
Rostov-na-Donu
Kharkov
Donetsk
Orsk
Magnitogorsk
Bukhara
Tashauz
Nukus
Baku
Stepanakert
Elista
Groznyy
Makhachkala
Nal'chik
Vladikavkaz
Sukhumi
Batumi
Kahramanmaras

Map 109 Southwestern Asia

BLACK SEA
CASPIAN SEA
MEDITERRANEAN SEA
RED SEA
Persian Gulf
Gulf of Oman
ARABIAN SEA
Gulf of Aden
TURKEY
ARMENIA
AZERBAIJAN
TURKMENISTAN
CYPRUS
SYRIA
LEBANON
ISRAEL
JORDAN
IRAQ
IRAN
AFGHANISTAN
KUWAIT
QATAR
BAHRAIN
SAUDI ARABIA
UNITED ARAB EMIRATES
OMAN
YEMEN
EGYPT
SUDAN
ERITREA
ETHIOPIA
DJIBOUTI
SOMALIA
Elevation
Feet
3000
1500
300
0
Sea level
Below sea level
0
100
1000
Simple Conic Projection
National capital
City
0 150 300 Miles
0 150 300 Kilometers
Tropic of Cancer

Map 109a The Middle East: Territorial Changes, 1918–2004

TERRITORIAL CHANGES IN THE MIDDLE EAST, WORLD WAR I TO PRESENT
Ottoman Empire to World War I
British control
French control
Kurdish homelands
International boundaries in 1994
TURKEY
Istanbul (Constantinople)
Ankara
BLACK SEA
CASPIAN SEA
GEORGIA
RUSSIA
ARMENIA
AZERBAIJAN
GREECE
AEGEAN SEA
CRETE
MEDITERRANEAN SEA
LEBANON AND SYRIA
Ottoman Empire to 1920
French (1920–1944)
Independent 1944
CYPRUS from Ottoman Empire to British control 1878 Independent 1960
SYRIA
LEBANON
Beirut
Damascus
ISRAEL
Ottoman Empire to 1920
UK (1920–1948)
Tel Aviv
Amman
Jerusalem
INSET
Suez Canal British control to 1956
JORDAN
Ottoman Empire to 1920
UK (1920–1946)
Hejaz Nedj (to 1926)
IRAQ
UK (1920–1932)
Baghdad
Basra
Abadan
Tabriz
Tehran
IRAN
(named Persia until 1935)
AFGHANISTAN
PAKISTAN
KUWAIT
UK (1899–1961)
Kuwait
BAHRAIN
UK (1861–1971)
Strait of Hormuz
OMAN
U.A.E.
UK (1820s–1971)
Muscat
Abu Dhabi
PERSIAN GULF
QATAR
UK 1868–1971
SAUDI ARABIA
Medina
Riyadh
Jiddah
Mecca
Asir (1917–1934)
King Saud expanded territory (1901–1936)
YEMEN (Independent 1918)
YEMEN
UK 1868–1971
Independent as (South) Yemen 1967
Merged with (North) Yemen 1990
OMAN
UK (1891–1971)
INDIAN OCEAN
Aden
GULF OF ADEN
DJIBOUTI
SOMALIA
ETHIOPIA
ERITREA
SUDAN
CHAD
RED SEA
LIBYA
Ottoman Empire to 1911
Italian colony (1911–1943)
UK–French Protectorate (1943–1951)
EGYPT
Ottoman Empire to 1885
UK Protectorate (1885–1936)
Alexandria
Cairo
Suez
Nile River
Euphrates River
Tigris River
0 200 Miles
0 200 Kilometers
ISRAELI SECURITY ZONE
GOLAN HEIGHTS
Sea of Galilee
WEST BANK
Jordan River
Allenby Bridge
Jericho
Dead Sea
GAZA
SINAI PENINSULA
Eilat
Aqaba
0 50 Miles
0 50 Kilometers

The Middle East, encompassing the northeastern part of Africa and southwestern Asia, has experienced a turbulent history. In the last century alone, many of the region's countries have gone from being ruled by the Turkish Ottoman Empire, to being dependencies of Great Britain or France, to being independent. Having experienced the Crusades and colonial domination by European powers, the region's predominantly Islamic countries are now resentful of interference in the region's affairs by countries with a European and/or Christian heritage. The tension between Israel (settled largely in the late nineteenth and twentieth centuries by Jews of predominantly European background) and its neighbors is a matter of European–Middle Eastern cultural stress as well as a religious conflict between Islamic Arab culture and Judaism. The political boundaries on the map, like those throughout most of Africa, are the invention of European colonial powers and often do not take into account the pre-existing lines of tribal control or authority. In Iraq, for example, three distinct cultural areas exist: Shiite Muslim (Arabic), Sunni Muslim (Arabic), and Kurd (also Islamic but distinctly not Arabic). These three cultures occupying the territory of a state makes stability in that tortured region a distinct problem for the future.

Map 109b South-Central Eurasia: An Ethnolinguistic Crazy Quilt

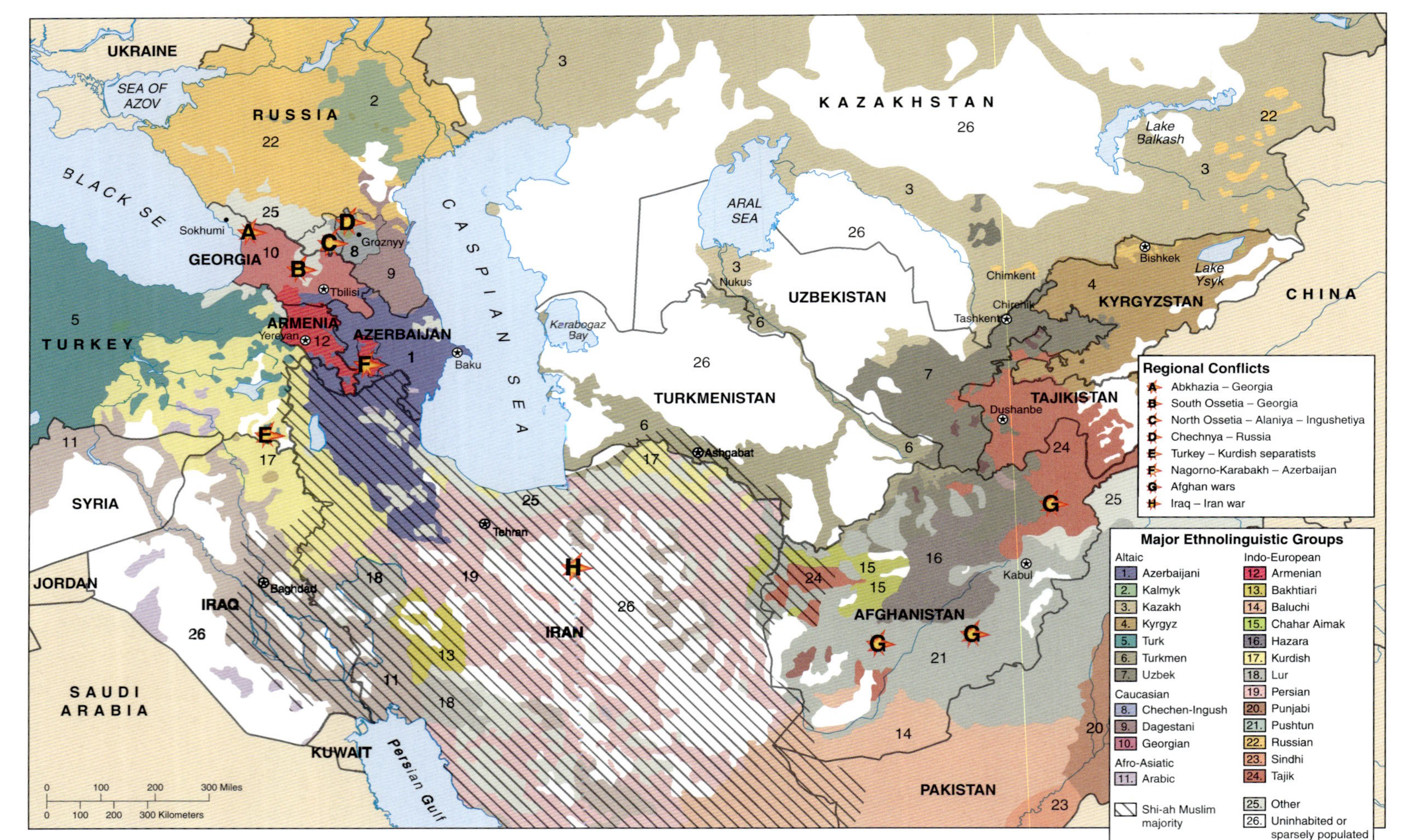

UKRAINE
SEA OF AZOV
RUSSIA
BLACK SEA
CASPIAN SEA
KAZAKHSTAN
ARAL SEA
Kerabogaz Bay
UZBEKISTAN
TURKMENISTAN
KYRGYZSTAN
TAJIKISTAN
CHINA
Lake Balkash
Lake Ysyk
GEORGIA
ARMENIA
AZERBAIJAN
TURKEY
SYRIA
JORDAN
IRAQ
IRAN
SAUDI ARABIA
KUWAIT
Persian Gulf
AFGHANISTAN
PAKISTAN
Sokhumi
Groznyy
Tbilisi
Yerevan
Baku
Nukus
Chimkent
Chirchik
Tashkent
Bishkek
Dushanbe
Ashgabat
Tehran
Baghdad
Kabul
0 100 200 300 Miles
0 100 200 300 Kilometers
Regional Conflicts
A Abkhazia – Georgia
B South Ossetia – Georgia
C North Ossetia – Alaniya – Ingushetiya
D Chechnya – Russia
E Turkey – Kurdish separatists
F Nagorno-Karabakh – Azerbaijan
G Afghan wars
H Iraq – Iran war
Major Ethnolinguistic Groups
Altaic
1. Azerbaijani
2. Kalmyk
3. Kazakh
4. Kyrgyz
5. Turk
6. Turkmen
7. Uzbek
Caucasian
8. Chechen-Ingush
9. Dagestani
10. Georgian
Afro-Asiatic
11. Arabic
Shi-ah Muslim majority
Indo-European
12. Armenian
13. Bakhtiari
14. Baluchi
15. Chahar Aimak
16. Hazara
17. Kurdish
18. Lur
19. Persian
20. Punjabi
21. Pushtun
22. Russian
23. Sindhi
24. Tajik
25. Other
26. Uninhabited or sparsely populated

South-Central Eurasia: The area of south-central Eurasia represents what is perhaps the world's most volatile area in terms of potential military conflict. A crazy quilt of ethnic and linguistic groups, this region contains politically-defined "states," but nothing approaching "nation-states" as they are understood elsewhere. Even reasonably well-consolidated states, such as Iran, are hampered by the mixture of languages and ethnic populations within their borders. For some countries, such as Afghanistan, the ethnolinguistic mix is so historically fixed as to render any attempts at modern state building nearly hopeless. This vast area—although nearly universally Muslim—is also split between the two primary Islamic sects, Sunni and Shia, with several smaller sectarian divisions as well. The division of one of the world's global religions into two principal factions occurred in the seventh century, originally over the question of the source of authority in the religious hierarchy. But it has since come to be a theological and metaphysical separation, and Sunni and Shia Muslims now bear somewhat the same relationship to one another as did Catholics and Protestants in seventeenth- and eighteenth-century Europe—a mutual antipathy that periodically flares into civil unrest and conflict that goes far beyond the bounds of religious debate. The area is rich in natural resources, but the mixture of ethnicity, language, and religion has and will continue to produce the human conflicts that inhibit human development.

Map 110 Southern Asia

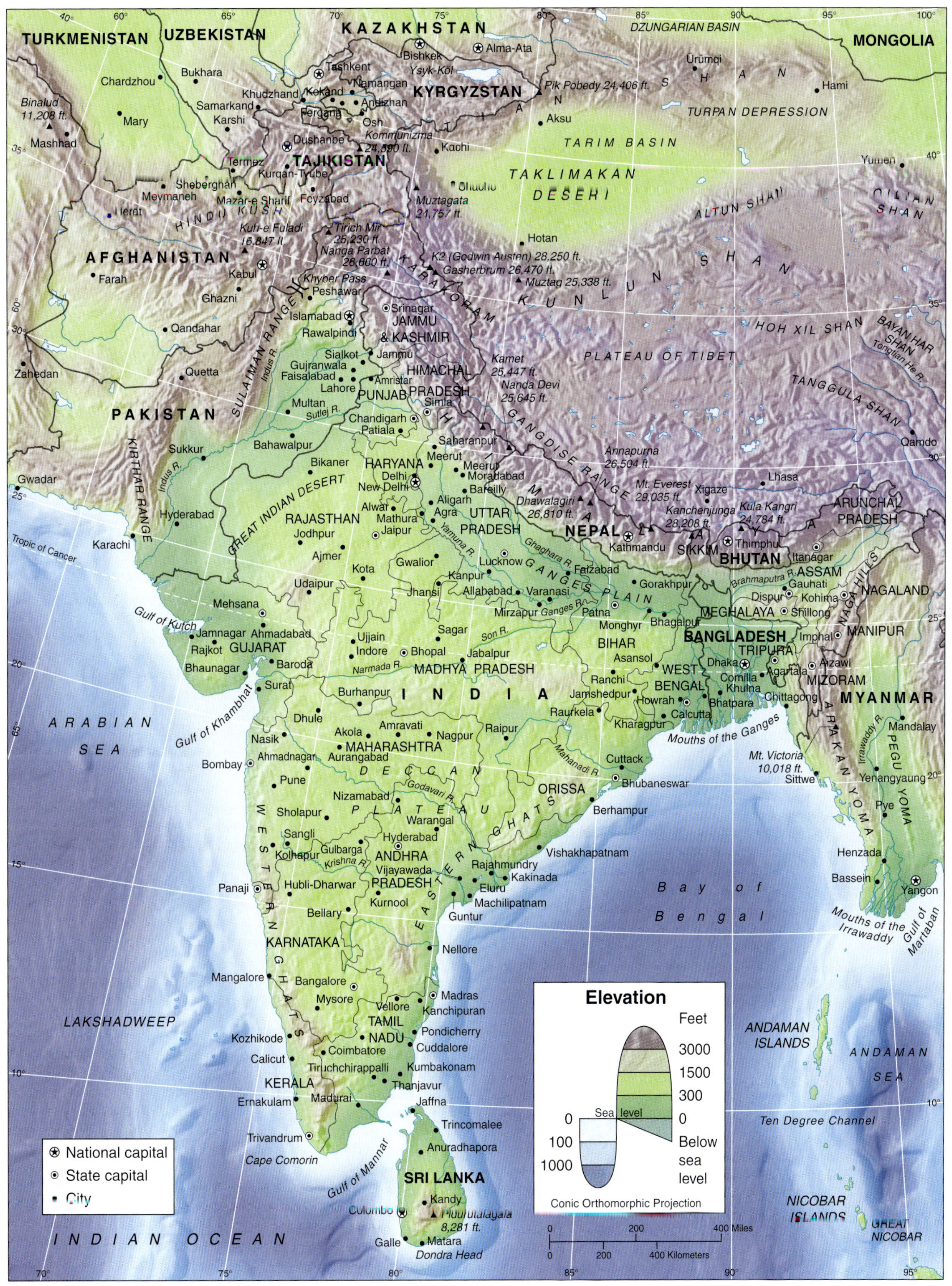

TURKMENISTAN
UZBEKISTAN
KAZAKHSTAN
MONGOLIA
KYRGYZSTAN
TAJIKISTAN
AFGHANISTAN
PAKISTAN
INDIA
NEPAL
BHUTAN
BANGLADESH
MYANMAR
SRI LANKA
DZUNGARIAN BASIN
TURPAN DEPRESSION
TARIM BASIN
TAKLIMAKAN DESERT
ALTUN SHAN
KUNLUN SHAN
HOH XIL SHAN
BAYAN HAR SHAN
Tongtian He R.
PLATEAU OF TIBET
TANGGULA SHAN
GANGDISE RANGE
KARAKORAM
HINDU KUSH
SULAIMAN RANGE
KIRTHAR RANGE
GREAT INDIAN DESERT
GANGES PLAIN
DECCAN PLATEAU
WESTERN GHATS
EASTERN GHATS
NAGA HILLS
ARAKAN YOMA
PEGU YOMA
Binalud 11,208 ft.
Pik Pobedy 24,406 ft.
Kommunizma 24,590 ft.
Muztagata 21,757 ft.
Kuh-e Fuladi 16,847 ft.
Tirich Mir 25,230 ft.
Nanga Parbat 26,660 ft.
K2 (Godwin Austen) 28,250 ft.
Gasherbrum 26,470 ft.
Muztag 25,338 ft.
Kamet 25,447 ft.
Nanda Devi 25,645 ft.
Annapurna 26,504 ft.
Dhawalagiri 26,810 ft.
Mt. Everest 29,035 ft.
Kanchenjunga 28,208 ft.
Kula Kangri 24,784 ft.
Mt. Victoria 10,018 ft.
Khyber Pass
Chardzhou
Bukhara
Mary
Mashhad
Samarkand
Karshi
Khudzhand
Tashkent
Kokand
Namangan
Andizhan
Fergana
Osh
Bishkek
Ysyk-Köl
Alma-Ata
Aksu
Ürümqi
Hami
Yumen
Kachi
Hotan
Dushanbe
Termez
Kurgan-Tyube
Sheberghan
Meymaneh
Mazar-e Sharif
Feyzabad
Herat
Farah
Kabul
Ghazni
Qandahar
Zahedan
Quetta
Peshawar
Islamabad
Rawalpindi
Srinagar
JAMMU & KASHMIR
Jammu
Sialkot
Gujranwala
Faisalabad
Lahore
Amristar
PUNJAB
HIMACHAL PRADESH
Simla
Multan
Indus R.
Sutlej R.
Chandigarh
Patiala
Bahawalpur
Sukkur
Gwadar
Hyderabad
Karachi
Tropic of Cancer
Bikaner
HARYANA
Delhi
New Delhi
Saharanpur
Meerut
Moradabad
Bareilly
Aligarh
Agra
Mathura
Alwar
Jaipur
RAJASTHAN
Jodhpur
Ajmer
UTTAR PRADESH
Yamuna R.
Ghaghara R.
Lucknow
Faizabad
Gorakhpur
Kathmandu
SIKKIM
Thimphu
Xigaze
Lhasa
Qamdo
ARUNCHAL PRADESH
Itanagar
ASSAM
Brahmaputra R.
Gauhati
Dispur
Kohima
Shillong
MEGHALAYA
NAGALAND
MANIPUR
Imphal
TRIPURA
Agartala
Aizawl
MIZORAM
Kota
Gwalior
Kanpur
Jhansi
Allahabad
Varanasi
Mirzapur
Ganges R.
Patna
Monghyr
Bhagalpur
BIHAR
Udaipur
Mehsana
Gulf of Kutch
Jamnagar
Ahmadabad
Rajkot
GUJARAT
Bhaunagar
Baroda
Surat
Gulf of Khambhat
Ujjain
Indore
Bhopal
Sagar
Son R.
Jabalpur
Narmada R.
MADHYA PRADESH
Asansol
Ranchi
Jamshedpur
WEST BENGAL
Howrah
Calcutta
Kharagpur
Raurkela
Dhaka
Comilla
Khulna
Bhatpara
Chittagong
Mouths of the Ganges
Burhanpur
Dhule
Nasik
Akola
Amravati
Nagpur
Raipur
MAHARASHTRA
Bombay
Ahmadnagar
Aurangabad
Pune
Mahanadi R.
Cuttack
Bhubaneswar
ORISSA
Berhampur
Nizamabad
Godavari R.
Warangal
Sholapur
Sangli
Kolhapur
Gulbarga
Hyderabad
Krishna R.
ANDHRA PRADESH
Vijayawada
Rajahmundry
Kakinada
Vishakhapatnam
Eluru
Machilipatnam
Guntur
Panaji
Hubli-Dharwar
Kurnool
Bellary
KARNATAKA
Nellore
Mangalore
Bangalore
Mysore
Vellore
Madras
Kanchipuran
TAMIL NADU
Pondicherry
Cuddalore
Kozhikode
Calicut
Coimbatore
Tiruchchirappalli
Kumbakonam
Thanjavur
KERALA
Ernakulam
Madurai
Jaffna
Trincomalee
Anuradhapora
Trivandrum
Cape Comorin
Gulf of Mannar
Kandy
Colombo
Pidurutalagala 8,281 ft.
Galle
Matara
Dondra Head
Mandalay
Irrawaddy R.
Yenangyaung
Sittwe
Pye
Henzada
Bassein
Yangon
Mouths of the Irrawaddy
Gulf of Martaban
ARABIAN SEA
Bay of Bengal
LAKSHADWEEP
ANDAMAN ISLANDS
ANDAMAN SEA
Ten Degree Channel
NICOBAR ISLANDS
GREAT NICOBAR
INDIAN OCEAN
Elevation
Feet
3000
1500
300
0
Sea level
100
1000
Below sea level
Conic Orthomorphic Projection
0
200
400 Miles
0
200
400 Kilometers
National capital
State capital
City

Map 111 East Asia

Elevation
Feet
3000
1500
300
0
Below sea level
Sea level
0
100
1000
Lambert Equal-Area Projection
National capital
State capital
City
0
300
600 Miles
0
300
600 Kilometers
R U S S I A
MONGOLIA
CHINA
KAZAKHSTAN
KYRGYZSTAN
TAJIKISTAN
PAKISTAN
NEPAL
BHUTAN
BANGLADESH
INDIA
MYANMAR
THAILAND
LAOS
VIETNAM
NORTH KOREA
SOUTH KOREA
JAPAN
TAIWAN
PHILIPPINES
SAYAN MOUNTAINS
ALTAI MOUNTAINS
MONGOLIAN PLATEAU
GOBI DESERT
NEI MONGOL
TIEN SHAN
TARIM BASIN
TAKLIMAKAN DESERT
KUNLUN SHAN
PLATEAU OF TIBET
XIZANG (TIBET)
XINJIANG (SINKIANG)
HIMALAYA
QINGHAI
GANSU
NINGXIA
SHAANXI
SHANXI
HEBEI
HENAN
HUBEI
ANHUI
JIANGSU
SHANGHAI SHI
ZHEJIANG
FUJIAN
JIANGXI
HUNAN
GUIZHOU
SICHUAN
YUNNAN
GUANGXI
GUANGDONG
HAINAN
SHANDONG
LIAONING
JILIN
HEILONJIAN
MANCHURIAN PLAIN
GREAT BASIN
DECCAN PLATEAU
Lake Balkhash
Lake Baikal
Angara R.
Yenisey R.
Lena R.
Amur R.
Yellow R.
Yangtze
Indus R.
Ganges R.
Irrawaddy R.
Salween R.
Mekong R.
SEA OF JAPAN
YELLOW SEA
EAST CHINA SEA
SOUTH CHINA SEA
PHILIPPINE SEA
PACIFIC OCEAN
Bay of Bengal
Pik Pobedy 24,406 ft.
K2 (Godwin Austen) 28,250 ft.
Gasherbrum 26,470 ft.
Nanga Parbat 26,660 ft.
Muztag 25,338 ft.
Muztagata 24,757 ft.
Kamet 25,447 ft.
Nanda Devi 25,645 ft.
Annapurna 26,504 ft.
Dhawalagiri 26,810 ft.
Xixabangma Feng 26,286 ft.
Mt. Everest 29,035 ft.
Kanchenjunga 28,208 ft.
Makalu 27,825 ft.
Kula Kangri 24,784 ft.
Namjagbarwa Feng 25,446 ft.
Gongaa Shan 24,790 ft.
Paektu San 9,100 ft.
Fuji Yama 12,388 ft.
Yu Shan 13,114 ft.
Phou Bia 9,249 ft.
Svobodnyy
Blagoveshchensk
Khabarovsk
Irkutsk
Ulan Ude
Chita
Petrovsk-Zabaykal'skiy
Ulaanbaatar
Alma-Ata
Bishkek
Yining
Ürümqi
Kuqa
Kashi
Bachu
Yengisar
Shache
Yutian
Yumen
Xining
Lanzhou
Yinchuan
Hohhot
Beijing
Tianjin
Shanghai
Hong Kong
Macau
Taipei
Seoul
Pyongyang
Tokyo
Lhasa
Kathmandu
Thimphu
Dhaka
Calcutta
Delhi
New Delhi
Islamabad
Lahore
Hanoi
Viangchan
Manila
Quezon City
Hue

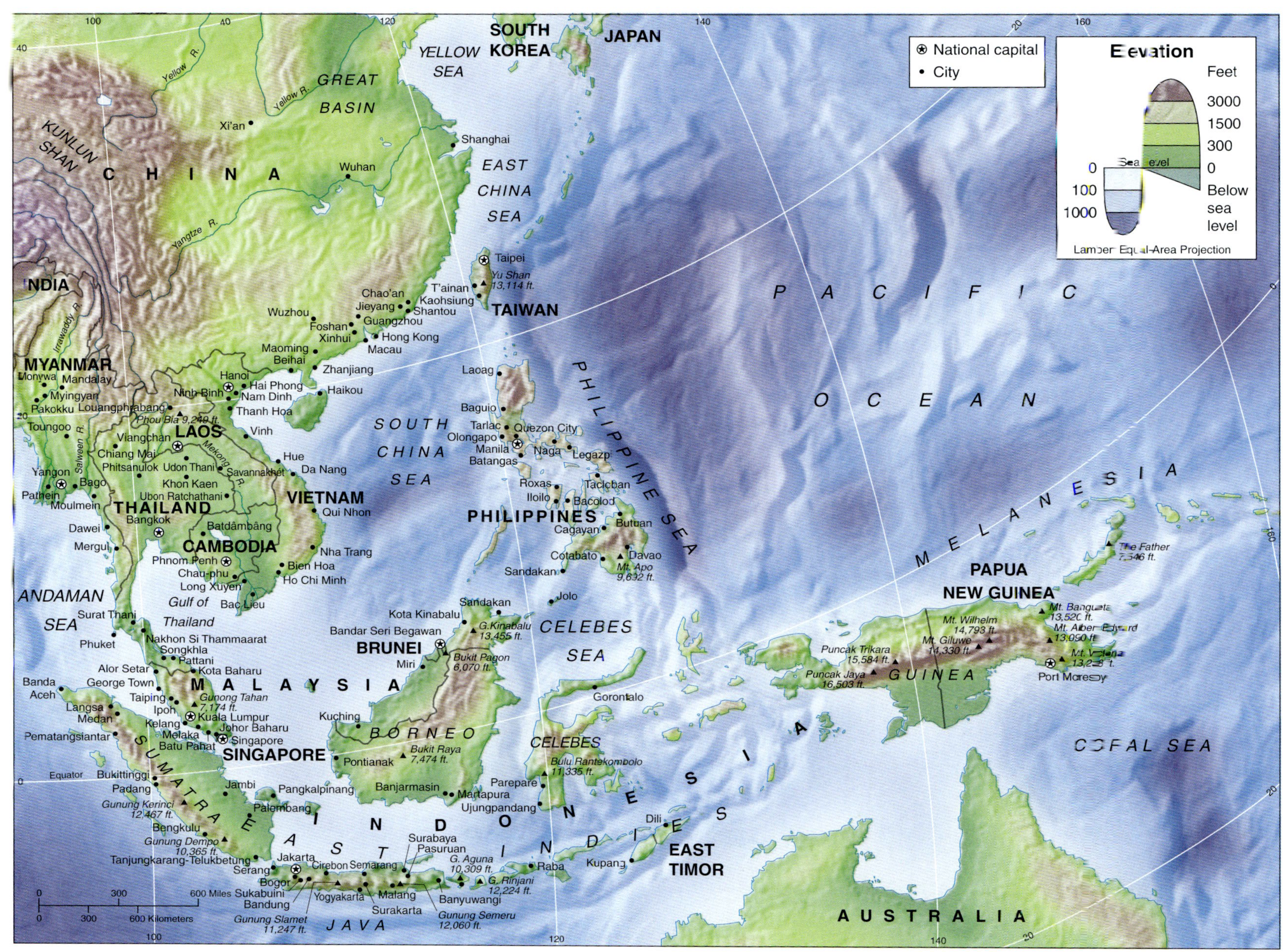

National capital
City
Elevation
Feet
3000
1500
300
0
Below sea level
100
1000
Lambert Equal-Area Projection
CHINA
KUNLUN SHAN
GREAT BASIN
Xi'an
Wuhan
Shanghai
Yellow R.
Yangtze R.
Irrawaddy R.
Salween R.
Mekong R.
YELLOW SEA
EAST CHINA SEA
SOUTH KOREA
JAPAN
TAIWAN
Taipei
T'ainan
Kaohsiung
Yu Shan 13,114 ft.
INDIA
MYANMAR
Monywa
Mandalay
Myingyan
Pakokku
Toungoo
Yangon
Pathein
Bago
Moulmein
Dawei
Mergui
ANDAMAN SEA
THAILAND
Chiang Mai
Phitsanulok
Udon Thani
Khon Kaen
Ubon Ratchathani
Bangkok
Surat Thani
Phuket
Nakhon Si Thammaarat
Songkhla
Pattani
Gulf of Thailand
LAOS
Louangphrabang
Phou Bia 9,249 ft.
Viangchan
Savannakhet
VIETNAM
Hanoi
Hai Phong
Nam Dinh
Ninh Binh
Thanh Hoa
Vinh
Hue
Da Nang
Qui Nhon
Nha Trang
Bien Hoa
Ho Chi Minh
CAMBODIA
Batdâmbâng
Phnom Penh
Chau-phu
Long Xuyen
Bac Lieu
Wuzhou
Foshan
Xinhui
Maoming
Beihai
Zhanjiang
Haikou
Chao'an
Jieyang
Shantou
Guangzhou
Hong Kong
Macau
SOUTH CHINA SEA
PHILIPPINE SEA
PHILIPPINES
Laoag
Baguio
Tarlac
Olongapo
Quezon City
Manila
Batangas
Naga
Legazpi
Roxas
Iloilo
Bacolod
Tacloban
Cagayan
Butuan
Cotabato
Davao
Mt. Apo 9,632 ft.
Sandakan
Jolo
PACIFIC OCEAN
MELANESIA
CELEBES SEA
MALAYSIA
Alor Setar
George Town
Kota Baharu
Taiping
Ipoh
Gunong Tahan 7,174 ft.
Kuala Lumpur
Kelang
Melaka
Johor Baharu
Batu Pahat
Singapore
SINGAPORE
Kota Kinabalu
G. Kinabalu 13,455 ft.
Bandar Seri Begawan
BRUNEI
Miri
Bukit Pagon 6,070 ft.
Kuching
BORNEO
Bukit Raya 7,474 ft.
Pontianak
Banjarmasin
Martapura
CELEBES
Gorontalo
Bulu Rantekombolo 11,335 ft.
Parepare
Ujungpandang
INDONESIA
SUMATRA
Banda Aceh
Langsa
Medan
Pematangsiantar
Equator
Bukittinggi
Padang
Gunung Kerinci 12,467 ft.
Jambi
Pangkalpinang
Palembang
Bengkulu
Gunung Dempo 10,365 ft.
Tanjungkarang-Telukbetung
Serang
Jakarta
Bogor
Sukabumi
Bandung
Gunung Slamet 11,247 ft.
Cirebon
Semarang
Yogyakarta
Surakarta
Malang
Surabaya
Pasuruan
G. Aguna 10,309 ft.
Banyuwangi
Gunung Semeru 12,060 ft.
G. Rinjani 12,224 ft.
Raba
JAVA
Kupang
Dili
EAST TIMOR
PAPUA NEW GUINEA
NEW GUINEA
Puncak Trikara 15,584 ft.
Puncak Jaya 16,503 ft.
Mt. Wilhelm 14,793 ft.
Mt. Giluwe 14,330 ft.
Port Moresby
The Father 7,546 ft.
CORAL SEA
AUSTRALIA
0 300 600 Miles
0 300 600 Kilometers

Map 113 Australasia and Oceania: Physical Features

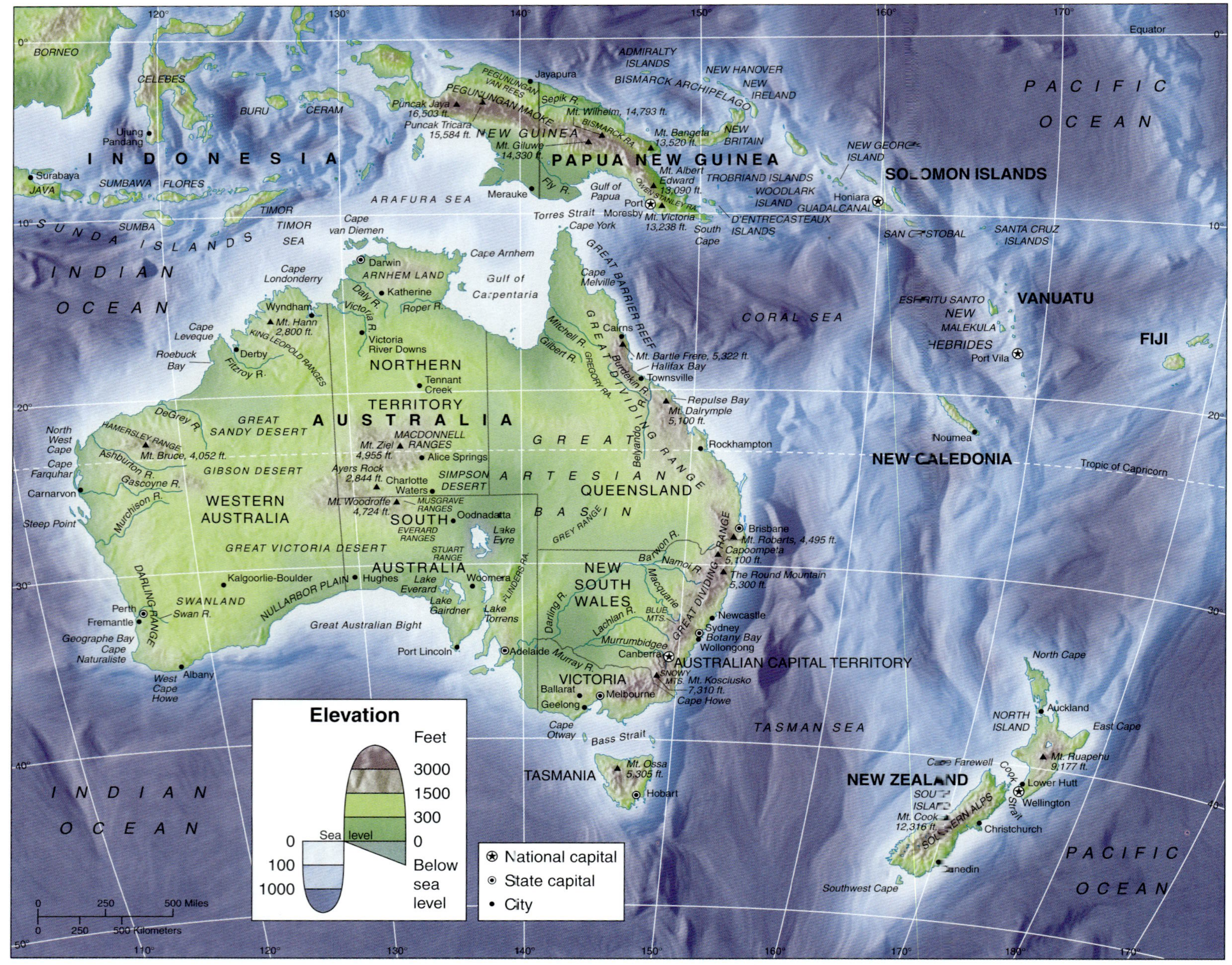

PACIFIC OCEAN
INDIAN OCEAN
INDONESIA
PAPUA NEW GUINEA
SOLOMON ISLANDS
VANUATU
FIJI
NEW CALEDONIA
AUSTRALIA
NEW ZEALAND
BORNEO
CELEBES
BURU
CERAM
SUMBAWA
FLORES
TIMOR
SUMBA
JAVA
SUNDA ISLANDS
TIMOR SEA
ARAFURA SEA
CORAL SEA
TASMAN SEA
Equator
Tropic of Capricorn
Surabaya
Ujung Pandang
Jayapura
Merauke
NEW GUINEA
PEGUNUNGAN VAN REES
PEGUNUNGAN MAOKE
Puncak Jaya 16,503 ft.
Puncak Tricara 15,584 ft.
Mt. Giluwe 14,330 ft.
Mt. Wilhelm, 14,793 ft.
Mt. Bangeta 13,520 ft.
Mt. Albert Edward 13,090 ft.
Mt. Victoria 13,238 ft.
Sepik R.
Fly R.
BISMARCK RA.
OWEN STANLEY RA.
ADMIRALTY ISLANDS
BISMARCK ARCHIPELAGO
NEW HANOVER
NEW IRELAND
NEW BRITAIN
TROBRIAND ISLANDS
WOODLARK ISLAND
D'ENTRECASTEAUX ISLANDS
GUADALCANAL
Honiara
Gulf of Papua
Port Moresby
South Cape
Torres Strait
Cape York
SANTA CRUZ ISLANDS
NEW HEBRIDES
MALEKULA
Port Vila
Noumea
Cape van Diemen
Cape Arnhem
Gulf of Carpentaria
Cape Londonderry
ARNHEM LAND
Darwin
Katherine
Daly R.
Victoria R.
Roper R.
Wyndham
Mt. Hann 2,800 ft.
KING LEOPOLD RANGES
Cape Leveque
Roebuck Bay
Derby
Fitzroy R.
Victoria River Downs
NORTHERN TERRITORY
Tennant Creek
GREAT SANDY DESERT
DeGrey R.
HAMERSLEY RANGE
Mt. Bruce, 4,052 ft.
North West Cape
Ashburton R.
Cape Farquhar
Gascoyne R.
Carnarvon
Murchison R.
Steep Point
GIBSON DESERT
WESTERN AUSTRALIA
GREAT VICTORIA DESERT
MACDONNELL RANGES
Mt. Ziel 4,955 ft.
Alice Springs
Ayers Rock 2,844 ft.
Charlotte Waters
SIMPSON DESERT
Mt. Woodroffe 4,724 ft.
MUSGRAVE RANGES
EVERARD RANGES
SOUTH AUSTRALIA
Oodnadatta
Lake Eyre
STUART RANGE
FLINDERS RA.
Kalgoorlie-Boulder
NULLARBOR PLAIN
Hughes
Lake Everard
Woomera
Lake Gairdner
Lake Torrens
SWANLAND
DARLING RANGE
Perth
Swan R.
Fremantle
Geographe Bay
Cape Naturaliste
West Cape Howe
Albany
Great Australian Bight
Port Lincoln
Adelaide
Cape Melville
GREAT BARRIER REEF
Cairns
Mitchell R.
Gilbert R.
GREGORY RA.
Burdekin R.
Mt. Bartle Frere, 5,322 ft.
Halifax Bay
Townsville
Repulse Bay
Mt. Dalrymple 5,100 ft.
Rockhampton
Belyando
GREAT DIVIDING RANGE
GREAT ARTESIAN BASIN
QUEENSLAND
GREY RANGE
Brisbane
Mt. Roberts, 4,495 ft.
Capoompeta 5,100 ft.
The Round Mountain 5,300 ft.
Barwon R.
Namoi R.
NEW SOUTH WALES
Darling R.
Macquarie
Lachlan R.
BLUE MTS.
Newcastle
Sydney
Botany Bay
Wollongong
Murrumbidgee
Canberra
AUSTRALIAN CAPITAL TERRITORY
Murray R.
SNOWY MTS.
Mt. Kosciusko 7,310 ft.
Cape Howe
VICTORIA
Ballarat
Melbourne
Geelong
Cape Otway
Bass Strait
TASMANIA
Mt. Ossa 5,305 ft.
Hobart
North Cape
NORTH ISLAND
Auckland
East Cape
Mt. Ruapehu 9,177 ft.
Lower Hutt
Wellington
Cook Strait
Cape Farewell
SOUTHERN ALPS
Mt. Cook 12,316 ft.
Christchurch
Southwest Cape
Elevation
Feet
3000
1500
300
0
Sea level
Below sea level
100
1000
National capital
State capital
City
0 250 500 Miles
0 250 500 Kilometers

Map 114 Australasia and Oceania: Political Divisions

INDONESIA
PAPUA NEW GUINEA
SOLOMON ISLANDS
VANUATU
FIJI
NEW CALEDONIA
AUSTRALIA
WESTERN AUSTRALIA
NORTHERN TERRITORY
SOUTH AUSTRALIA
QUEENSLAND
NEW SOUTH WALES
VICTORIA
AUSTRALIAN CAPITAL TERRITORY
TASMANIA
NEW ZEALAND
NORTH ISLAND
SOUTH ISLAND
BORNEO
CELEBES
BURU
CERAM
JAVA
SUMBAWA
FLORES
SUMBA
TIMOR
SUNDA ISLANDS
NEW GUINEA
ADMIRALTY ISLANDS
BISMARCK ARCHIPELAGO
NEW HANOVER
NEW IRELAND
NEW BRITAIN
TROBRIAND ISLANDS
WOODLARK ISLAND
D'ENTRECASTEAUX ISLANDS
NEW GEORGIA ISLAND
GUADALCANAL
SAN CRISTOBAL
SANTA CRUZ ISLANDS
ESPIRITU SANTO
NEW HEBRIDES
MALEKULA
INDIAN OCEAN
PACIFIC OCEAN
ARAFURA SEA
TIMOR SEA
CORAL SEA
TASMAN SEA
Gulf of Carpentaria
Gulf of Papua
Torres Strait
Bass Strait
Cook Strait
Great Australian Bight
GREAT BARRIER REEF
GREAT DIVIDING RANGE
GREAT ARTESIAN BASIN
GREAT SANDY DESERT
GIBSON DESERT
GREAT VICTORIA DESERT
SIMPSON DESERT
NULLARBOR PLAIN
ARNHEM LAND
SWANLAND
MACDONNELL RANGES
MUSGRAVE RANGES
EVERARD RANGES
STUART RANGE
FLINDERS RA.
GREY RANGE
GREGORY RA.
HAMERSLEY RANGE
KING LEOPOLD RANGES
DARLING RANGE
BLUE MTS.
SNOWY MTS.
SOUTHERN ALPS
PEGUNUNGAN MAOKE
PEGUNUNGAN VAN REES
BISMARCK RA.
OWEN STANLEY RA.
Sepik R.
Fly R.
Daly R.
Victoria R.
Roper R.
Mitchell R.
Gilbert R.
Burdekin R.
Belyando
Fitzroy R.
DeGrey R.
Ashburton R.
Gascoyne R.
Murchison R.
Swan R.
Darling R.
Barwon R.
Namoi R.
Macquarie
Lachlan R.
Murrumbidgee
Murray R.
Lake Eyre
Lake Everard
Lake Gairdner
Lake Torrens
Jayapura
Merauke
Port Moresby
Honiara
Port Vila
Suva
Noumea
Ujung Pandang
Surabaya
Darwin
Katherine
Victoria River Downs
Tennant Creek
Alice Springs
Charlotte Waters
Oodnadatta
Woomera
Hughes
Port Lincoln
Adelaide
Kalgoorlie-Boulder
Perth
Fremantle
Albany
Carnarvon
Wyndham
Derby
Cairns
Townsville
Rockhampton
Brisbane
Newcastle
Sydney
Botany Bay
Wollongong
Canberra
Melbourne
Ballarat
Geelong
Hobart
Auckland
Lower Hutt
Wellington
Christchurch
Dunedin
Cape York
Cape Melville
Cape Arnhem
Cape van Diemen
Cape Londonderry
Cape Leveque
Roebuck Bay
North West Cape
Cape Farquhar
Steep Point
Geographe Bay
Cape Naturaliste
West Cape Howe
Cape Otway
Cape Howe
Halifax Bay
Repulse Bay
South Cape
North Cape
East Cape
Cape Farewell
Southwest Cape
Equator
Tropic of Capricorn
National capital
State capital
City
0 250 500 Miles
0 250 500 Kilometers

Map 115a Environment and Economy

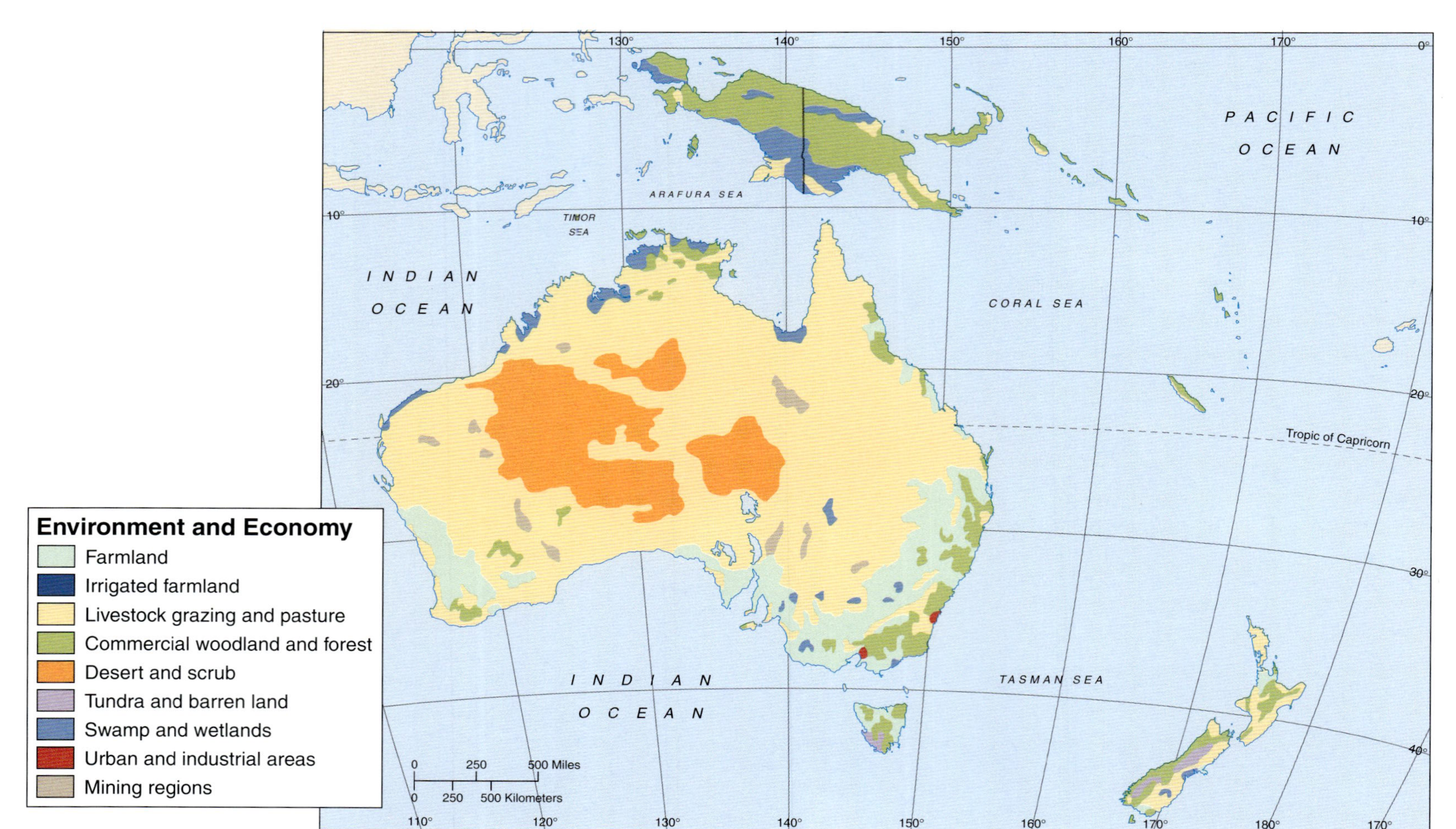
Environment and Economy
Farmland
Irrigated farmland
Livestock grazing and pasture
Commercial woodland and forest
Desert and scrub
Tundra and barren land
Swamp and wetlands
Urban and industrial areas
Mining regions
PACIFIC OCEAN
INDIAN OCEAN
ARAFURA SEA
TIMOR SEA
CORAL SEA
TASMAN SEA
Tropic of Capricorn
0 250 500 Miles
0 250 500 Kilometers

Australasia is dominated by the world's smallest and most uniform continent. Flat, dry, and mostly hot, Australia has the simplest of land use patterns: where rainfall exists so does agricultural activity. Two agricultural patterns dominate the map: livestock grazing, primarily sheep, and wheat farming, although some sugar cane production exists in the north and some cotton is grown elsewhere. Only about 6 percent of the continent consists of arable land so the areas of wheat farming, dominant as they may be in the context of Australian agriculture, are small. Australia also supports a healthy mineral resource economy, with iron and copper and precious metals making up the bulk of the extraction. Elsewhere in the region, tropical forests dominate Papua New Guinea, with some subsistence agriculture and livestock. New Zealand's temperate climate with abundant precipitation supports a productive livestock industry and little else besides tourism—which is an important economic element throughout the remainder of the region as well.

Map 115b Population Density

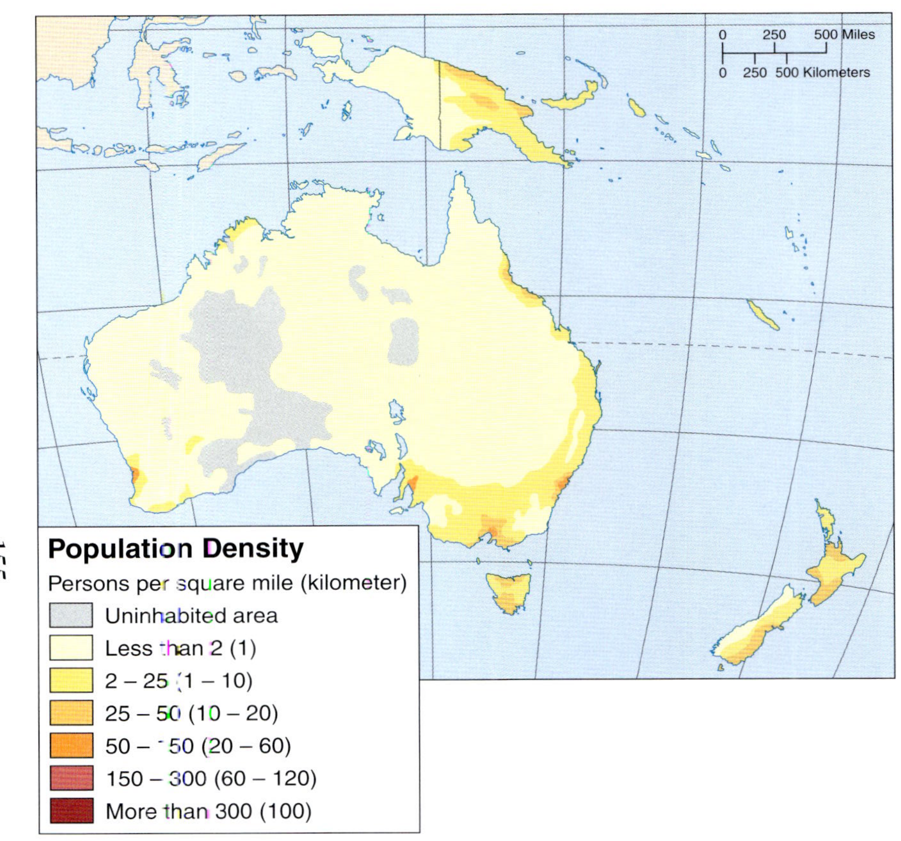
0 250 500 Miles
0 250 500 Kilometers
Population Density
Persons per square mile (kilometer)
Uninhabited area
Less than 2 (1)
2 – 25 (1 – 10)
25 – 50 (10 – 20)
50 – 150 (20 – 60)
150 – 300 (60 – 120)
More than 300 (100)

The region's small population is remarkably diverse. To the north are the Melanesian New Guinea peoples, while Europeans dominate the populations of Australia and New Zealand, both of which have significant indigenous populations. Throughout most of the smaller island groups, the bulk of the population is Melanesian but with a scattering of Europeans. The distribution of population is extremely uneven with New Guinea, southeastern Australia, and New Zealand supporting the bulk of the region's people while the remainder of the region—meaning nearly all of Australia—is either sparsely populated or devoid of population altogether. Nowhere do population densities reach the levels they do in other major regions of the world and densities of 50 persons per square mile are the highest to be found. Population location is dependent on precipitation and population growth patterns are culturally variable.

Map 115c Climate Patterns

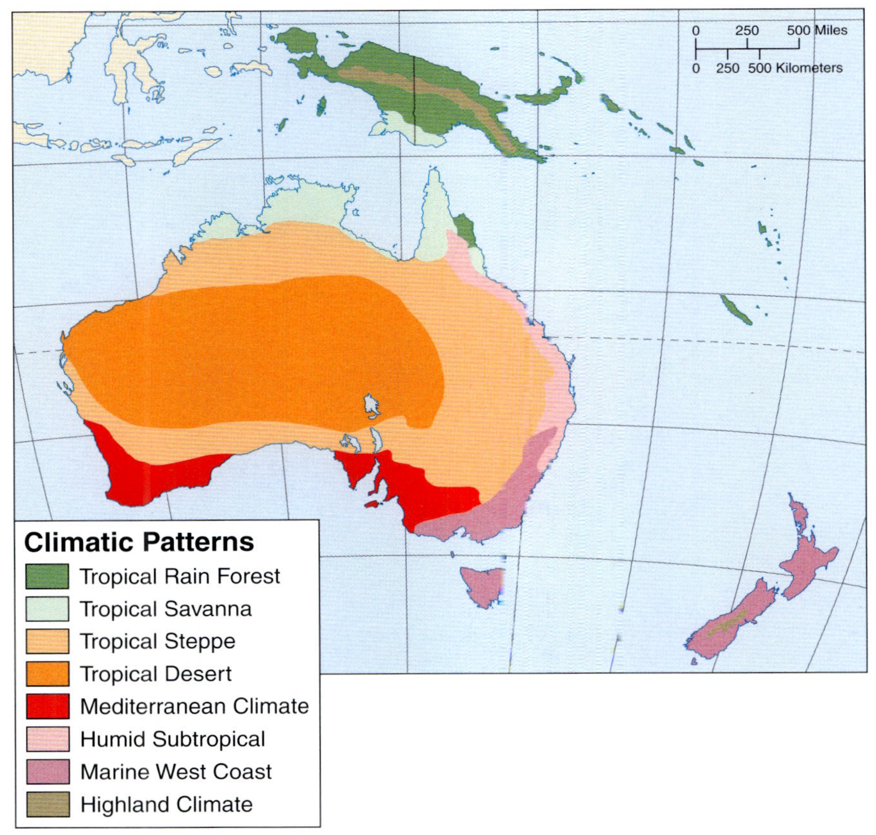
0 250 500 Miles
0 250 500 Kilometers
Climatic Patterns
Tropical Rain Forest
Tropical Savanna
Tropical Steppe
Tropical Desert
Mediterranean Climate
Humid Subtropical
Marine West Coast
Highland Climate

Because of its nearly uniform surface, with only a few low and scattered uplands, Australian climate is a consequence only of the two great climate controls—latitudinal position and location relative to continental margin and interior. The continent bestrides the 30th parallel of latitude and its climatic pattern is dominated by the subtropical high pressure system with dry air masses that are responsible for the existence of great deserts. Toward the equator, the desert grades into steppe, savanna, and tropical forest as the subtropical high gives way to equatorial low pressure and abundant precipitation. Toward the pole, arid land fades into more well-watered steppe grasslands, the Mediterranean type climate of the southern margins of the continent, and the marine west coast climate of the Australian southeast and New Zealand. This latter climate is where most of the region's people live.

Map 116 The Pacific Rim

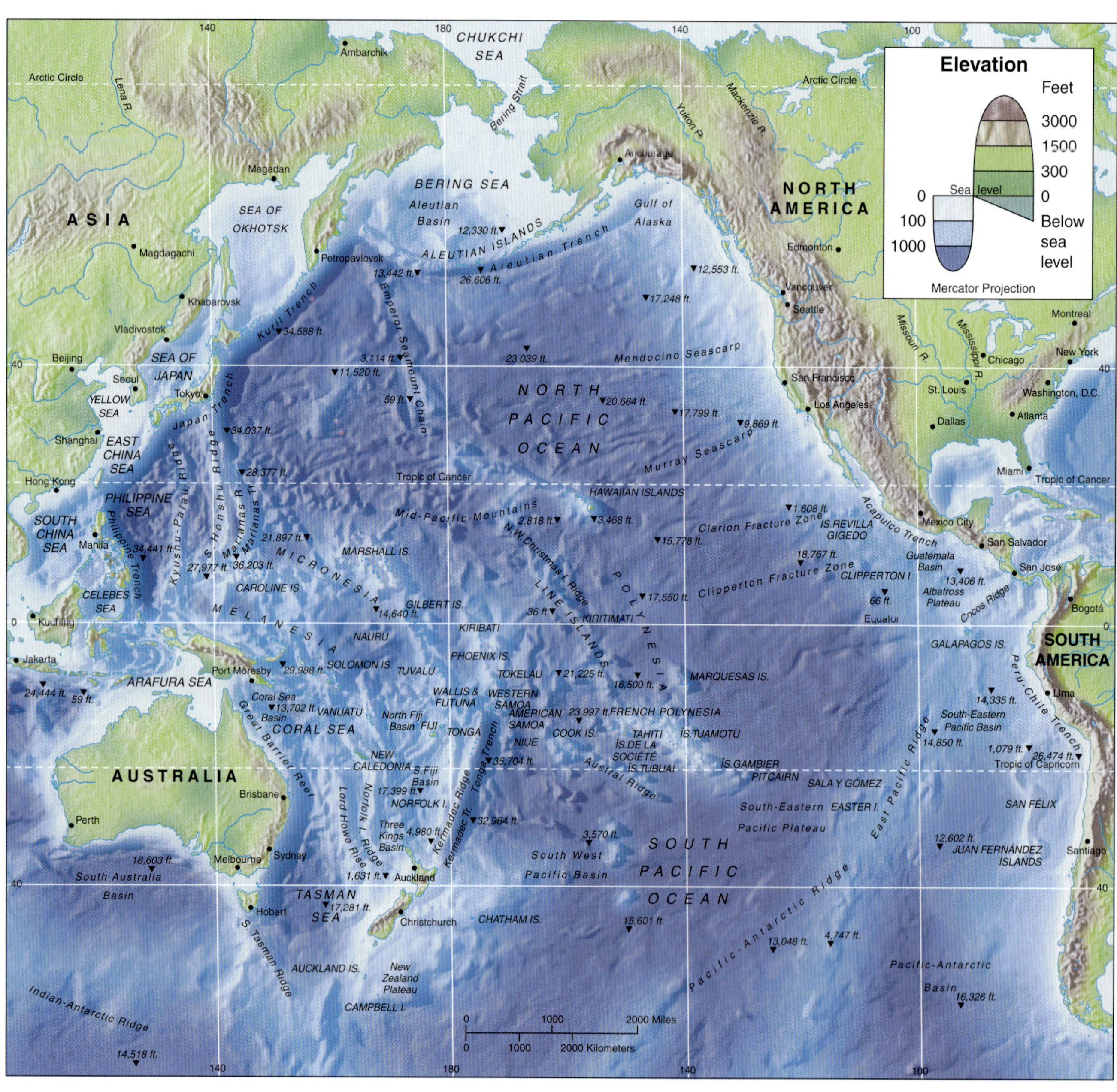

Elevation
Feet
3000
1500
300
0
Sea level
Below sea level
100
1000
Mercator Projection
ASIA
NORTH AMERICA
SOUTH AMERICA
AUSTRALIA
NORTH PACIFIC OCEAN
SOUTH PACIFIC OCEAN
CHUKCHI SEA
BERING SEA
SEA OF OKHOTSK
SEA OF JAPAN
YELLOW SEA
EAST CHINA SEA
PHILIPPINE SEA
SOUTH CHINA SEA
CELEBES SEA
ARAFURA SEA
CORAL SEA
TASMAN SEA
Gulf of Alaska
Arctic Circle
Tropic of Cancer
Tropic of Capricorn
Bering Strait
ALEUTIAN ISLANDS
Aleutian Trench
Aleutian Basin
Kuril Trench
Japan Trench
Emperor Seamount Chain
Mendocino Seascarp
Murray Seascarp
HAWAIIAN ISLANDS
Mid-Pacific Mountains
Clarion Fracture Zone
Clipperton Fracture Zone
Acapulco Trench
Peru-Chile Trench
East Pacific Ridge
Pacific-Antarctic Ridge
Pacific-Antarctic Basin
Indian-Antarctic Ridge
MICRONESIA
MELANESIA
POLYNESIA
LINE ISLANDS
N.W. Christmas I. Ridge
Kermadec Tr.
Tonga Trench
Kermadec Ridge
Norfolk I. Ridge
Lord Howe Rise
Great Barrier Reef
S. Tasman Ridge
Austral Ridge
Kyushu-Palau Ridge
S. Honshu Ridge
Marianas Tr.
Philippine Trench
Ambarchik
Magadan
Magdagachi
Khabarovsk
Vladivostok
Beijing
Seoul
Tokyo
Shanghai
Hong Kong
Manila
Kuching
Jakarta
Petropavlovsk
Anchorage
Edmonton
Vancouver
Seattle
San Francisco
Los Angeles
Montreal
Chicago
New York
St. Louis
Washington, D.C.
Dallas
Atlanta
Miami
Mexico City
San Salvador
San José
Bogotá
Lima
Santiago
Port Moresby
Brisbane
Perth
Sydney
Melbourne
Hobart
Auckland
Christchurch
Lena R.
Yukon R.
Mackenzie R.
Missouri R.
Mississippi R.
MARSHALL IS.
CAROLINE IS.
GILBERT IS.
KIRIBATI
NAURU
SOLOMON IS.
TUVALU
PHOENIX IS.
TOKELAU
KIRITIMATI
MARQUESAS IS.
WALLIS & FUTUNA
WESTERN SAMOA
AMERICAN SAMOA
NIUE
COOK IS.
FRENCH POLYNESIA
TAHITI
ÎS. DE LA SOCIÉTÉ
ÎS. TUBUAI
ÎS. TUAMOTU
ÎS. GAMBIER
PITCAIRN
SALA Y GÓMEZ
EASTER I.
VANUATU
FIJI
TONGA
NEW CALEDONIA
NORFOLK I.
CHATHAM IS.
AUCKLAND IS.
CAMPBELL I.
New Zealand Plateau
ÎS. REVILLA GIGEDO
CLIPPERTON I.
GALAPAGOS IS.
SAN FÉLIX
JUAN FERNÁNDEZ ISLANDS
Equator
Guatemala Basin
Albatross Plateau
Cocos Ridge
South-Eastern Pacific Basin
South-Eastern Pacific Plateau
South West Pacific Basin
South Australia Basin
Coral Sea Basin
North Fiji Basin
S. Fiji Basin
Three Kings Basin
12,330 ft.
13,442 ft.
26,606 ft.
12,553 ft.
17,248 ft.
34,588 ft.
3,114 ft.
11,520 ft.
23,039 ft.
59 ft.
20,664 ft.
17,799 ft.
9,869 ft.
34,037 ft.
28,377 ft.
2,818 ft.
3,468 ft.
1,608 ft.
15,778 ft.
21,897 ft.
34,441 ft.
27,977 ft.
36,203 ft.
14,640 ft.
18,767 ft.
17,550 ft.
36 ft.
66 ft.
13,406 ft.
29,988 ft.
24,444 ft.
21,225 ft.
16,500 ft.
13,702 ft.
23,997 ft.
14,335 ft.
14,850 ft.
1,079 ft.
26,474 ft.
35,704 ft.
17,399 ft.
32,964 ft.
4,980 ft.
3,570 ft.
12,602 ft.
18,603 ft.
1,631 ft.
17,281 ft.
15,601 ft.
13,048 ft.
4,747 ft.
16,326 ft.
14,518 ft.
0
1000
2000 Miles
2000 Kilometers
140
180
100
40

Map 117 The Atlantic Ocean

Elevation
Feet
3000
1500
300
0
Sea level
0
100
1000
Below sea level
Mercator projection
NORTH AMERICA
SOUTH AMERICA
EUROPE
AFRICA
NORTH ATLANTIC OCEAN
SOUTH ATLANTIC OCEAN
Baffin Bay
LABRADOR SEA
NORWEGIAN SEA
Norwegian Basin
Arctic Circle
Denmark Strait
Gunnbjørn Fjeld 12,139 ft.
Mount Forel 11,024 ft.
Reykjanes Ridge
Reykjavik
Hvannadalshnúkur 6,952 ft.
Hekla 4,892 ft.
Iceland-Faroe Rise
FAEROE ISLANDS
SHETLAND IS.
Cape Farewell
ROCKALL Oceanic Bank
Rockall Deep
NORTH SEA
Glasgow
London
Land's End
Pointe de Raz
Oslo
Stockholm
Copenhagen
Berlin
Brussels
Paris
Prague
Budapest
Danube R.
Bordeaux
Marseille
Rome
Madrid
Lisbon
Gibraltar
Tunis
MEDITERRANEAN SEA
North East Atlantic Basin
C.Finisterre
AZORES
MADEIRA
CANARY ISLANDS
Canary Basin
Mid-Atlantic Ridge
Winnipeg
Minneapolis
Chicago
Montreal
St. Louis
Missouri R.
Mississippi R.
Dallas
Atlanta
New York
Washington, D.C.
Miami
Goose Bay
NEWFOUNDLAND
C.Race
Grand Banks
C.Sable
SABLE I.
C.Cod
C.Fear
Newfoundland Basin
Newfoundland Rise
North American Basin
BERMUDA
Sargasso Sea
Nares Deep
Gulf of Mexico
Tropic of Cancer
Str. of Florida
Havana
Puerto Rico Trench
West Indies
Cayman Trench
Belmopan
Tegucigalpa
CARIBBEAN SEA
San José
Caracas
Cape Verde Plateau
CAPE VERDE IS.
C. Verde
Dakar
Cape Verde Basin
Guyana Basin
Niger R.
Kano
Freetown
Monrovia
Abidjan
Accra
Lagos
Sierra Leone Basin
C.Palmas
Guinea Basin
BIOKO
PRINCIPE
GULF OF GUINEA
SÃO TOMÉ
Port Gentil
Zaire R.
Kinshasa
Luanda
Georgetown
C.Orange
Bogotá
Cocos Ridge
Equator
Quito
GALAPAGOS IS.
ST. PAUL ROCKS
Romanche Gap
Manaus
R.Amazon
ROCAS
FERNANDO DE NORONHA
C. São Roque
Recife
ASCENSION I.
Salvador
Brasília
La Paz
Lima
Peru-Chile Trench
Nazca Ridge
Brazil Basin
ST. HELENA
Angola Basin
TRINDADE
MARTIN VAZ IS.
Tropic of Capricorn
I.SAN FELIX
I.SAN AMBROSIA
C.Frio
Asunción
R.Paraná
Bromley Plateau
Rio Grande Rise
South-Eastern Atlantic Ridge
Walvis Ridge
Walvis Bay
Cape Basin
Cape Town
C.Agulhas
Santiago
IS.JUAN FERNANDEZ
Buenos Aires
Montevideo
C.Corrientes
TRISTAN DA CUNHA
GOUGH I.
Discovery Tablemount
Argentine Basin
C.Blanco
FALKLAND IS.
Atlantic-Indian Ridge
Scotia Ridge
S. GEORGIA
S. Sandwich Tr.
BOUVET I.
Capo Horn
Drake Passage
S. SANDWICH IS.
SCOTIA SEA
Atlantic-Indian Antarctic Basin
0 1000 2000 Miles
0 1000 2000 Kilometers
7,008 ft.
2,398 ft.
9,869 ft.
3,425 ft.
11,195 ft.
217 ft.
2,218 ft.
15,398 ft.
200 ft.
656 ft.
39 ft.
20,700 ft.
2,881 ft.
3,881 ft.
9,403 ft.
11,910 ft.
16,802 ft.
299 ft.
486 ft.
20,995 ft.
17,921 ft.
22,951 ft.
883 ft.
20,647 ft.
856 ft.
13,200 ft.
4,689 ft.
53 ft.
28,374 ft.
25,218 ft.
23,295 ft.
10,381 ft.
17,783 ft.
14,263 ft.
2,398 ft.
19,817 ft.
387 ft.
25,454 ft.
18,895 ft.
7,645 ft.
21,448 ft.
276 ft.
18,288 ft.
20,076 ft.
19,850 ft.
18,879 ft.
1,686 ft.
1,788 ft.
17,278 ft.
5,023 ft.
1,349 ft.
18,164 ft.
358 ft.
20,382 ft.
7,579 ft.
27,652 ft.
80°
60°
40°
20°
0°

Map 118 The Indian Ocean

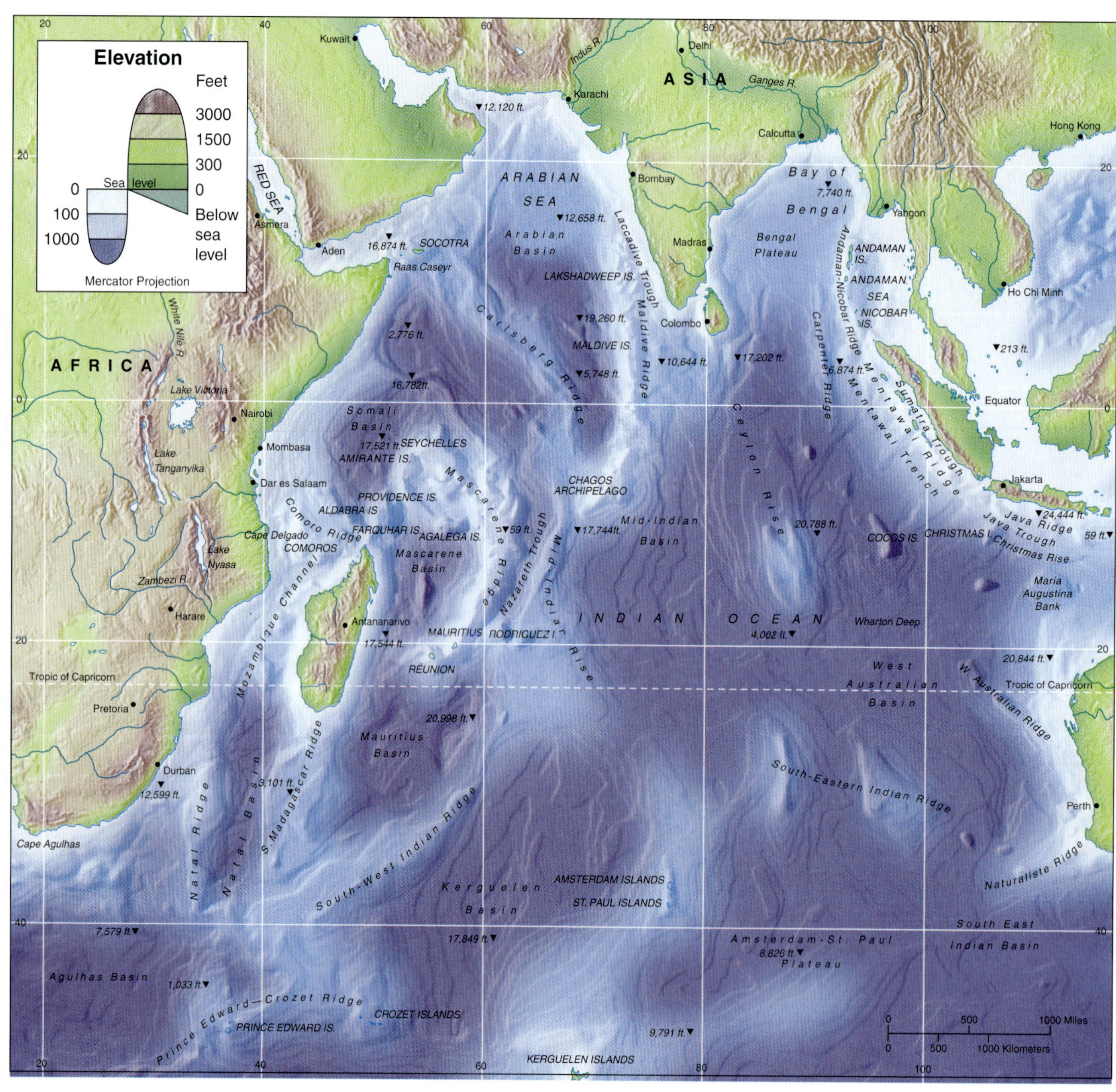

Elevation
Feet
3000
1500
300
0
Sea level
Below sea level
100
1000
Mercator Projection
ASIA
AFRICA
ARABIAN SEA
Bay of Bengal
INDIAN OCEAN
RED SEA
Kuwait
Karachi
Delhi
Calcutta
Bombay
Madras
Colombo
Yangon
Hong Kong
Ho Chi Minh
Jakarta
Aden
Asmera
Nairobi
Mombasa
Dar es Salaam
Harare
Pretoria
Durban
Perth
Antananarivo
SOCOTRA
Raas Caseyr
SEYCHELLES
AMIRANTE IS.
PROVIDENCE IS.
ALDABRA IS.
FARQUHAR IS.
AGALEGA IS.
COMOROS
Cape Delgado
MAURITIUS
RODRIGUEZ I.
RÉUNION
CHAGOS ARCHIPELAGO
LAKSHADWEEP IS.
MALDIVE IS.
ANDAMAN IS.
ANDAMAN SEA
NICOBAR IS.
COCOS IS.
CHRISTMAS I.
AMSTERDAM ISLANDS
ST. PAUL ISLANDS
CROZET ISLANDS
PRINCE EDWARD IS.
KERGUELEN ISLANDS
Cape Agulhas
Tropic of Capricorn
Equator
Indus R.
Ganges R.
White Nile R.
Zambezi R.
Lake Victoria
Lake Tanganyika
Lake Nyasa
Arabian Basin
Somali Basin
Mascarene Basin
Mascarene Ridge
Mauritius Basin
Carlsberg Ridge
Laccadive Trough
Maldive Ridge
Nazareth Trough
Mid-Indian Ridge
Mid-Indian Rise
Mid-Indian Basin
Comoro Ridge
Mozambique Channel
Natal Ridge
Natal Basin
S. Madagascar Ridge
South-West Indian Ridge
Kerguelen Basin
Agulhas Basin
Prince Edward—Crozet Ridge
Bengal Plateau
Ceylon Rise
Carpenter Ridge
Andaman-Nicobar Ridge
Mentawai Ridge
Mentawai Trench
Sumatra Trough
Java Ridge
Java Trough
Christmas Rise
Maria Augustina Bank
Wharton Deep
West Australian Basin
W. Australian Ridge
South-Eastern Indian Ridge
Naturaliste Ridge
South East Indian Basin
Amsterdam-St. Paul Plateau
12,120 ft.
16,874 ft.
12,658 ft.
7,740 ft.
2,776 ft.
16,782ft.
17,521 ft.
19,260 ft.
5,748 ft.
10,644 ft.
17,202 ft.
6,874 ft.
213 ft.
59 ft.
17,744ft.
20,788 ft.
24,444 ft.
59 ft.
4,002 ft.
17,544 ft.
20,844 ft.
20,998 ft.
12,599 ft.
3,101 ft.
7,579 ft.
17,849 ft.
8,826 ft.
1,033 ft.
9,791 ft.
0
500
1000 Miles
500
1000 Kilometers
20
40
60
80
100

Map 119 The Arctic

Elevation
Feet
3000
1500
300
0
Sea level
Below sea level
Zenithal Equidistant Projection
ASIA
EUROPE
NORTH AMERICA
ARCTIC OCEAN
North Pole
6,113 ft.
13,403 ft.
3,435 ft.
1,559 ft.
12,468 ft.
12,107 ft.
1,247 ft.
105 ft.
Lower Tunguska R.
Arctic Circle
Yenisey R.
Ob R.
Volga R.
Pechora R.
Kazan
Nizhniy Novgorod
Arkhangel'sk
St. Petersburg
Helsinki
Murmansk
Nordkapp
Dikson
Nordvik
KARA SEA
NOVAYA ZEMLYA
BARENTS SEA
C. Zhelaniya
Average permanent extent of sea ice
LAPTEV SEA
Cape Chelyuskin
SEVERNAYA ZEMLYA
FRANZ JOSEF LAND
SPITSBERGEN
NORWEGIAN SEA
GREENLAND SEA
ANJOU ISLANDS
EAST SIBERIAN SEA
Cape Shelagskiy
WRANGEL ISLAND
CHUKCHI SEA
Bering Strait
C. Lisburne
Point Hope
Barrow
Point Barrow
Por Yukon
Dawson
Mackenzie R.
Great Bear Lake
Great Slave Lake
BEAUFORT SEA
BANKS ISLAND
C. Bathurst
McClure Strait
VICTORIA ISLAND
North Magnetic Pole
QUEEN ELIZABETH ISLANDS
ELLESMERE ISLAND
LINCOLN SEA
GREENLAND
Gunnbjørn Fjeld 12,139 ft.
Mount Forel 11,024 ft.
Baffin Bay
BAFFIN ISLAND
Foxe Basin
Davis Strait
Nuuk
Denmark Strait
ICELAND
Hvannadalshnúkur 6,952 ft.
Hekla 4,892 ft.
Reykjavik
ATLANTIC OCEAN
500 Miles
500 Kilometers

Map 120 Antarctica

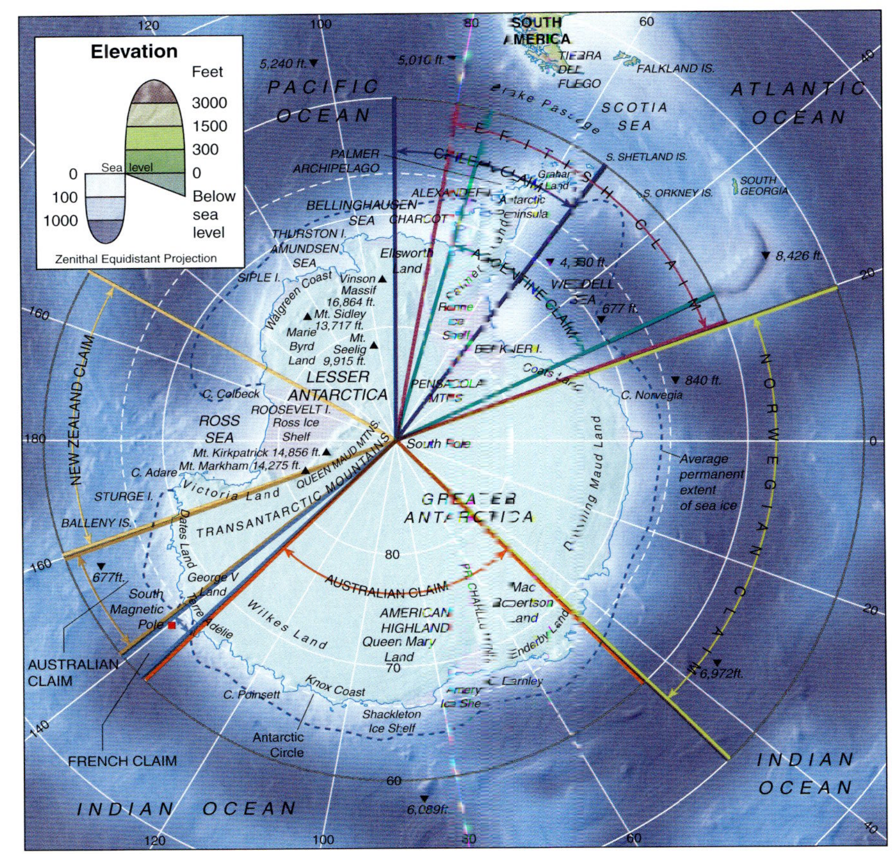
Elevation
Feet
3000
1500
300
0
Sea level
Below sea level
0
100
1000
Zenithal Equidistant Projection
PACIFIC OCEAN
ATLANTIC OCEAN
INDIAN OCEAN
SOUTH AMERICA
TIERRA DEL FUEGO
FALKLAND IS.
SCOTIA SEA
Drake Passage
S. SHETLAND IS.
S. ORKNEY IS.
SOUTH GEORGIA
PALMER ARCHIPELAGO
BELLINGHAUSEN SEA
ALEXANDER I.
CHARCOT I.
Antarctic Peninsula
THURSTON I.
AMUNDSEN SEA
SIPLE I.
Walgreen Coast
Ellsworth Land
Vinson Massif 16,864 ft.
Mt. Sidley 13,717 ft.
Mt. Seelig 9,915 ft.
Marie Byrd Land
LESSER ANTARCTICA
ROOSEVELT I.
Ross Ice Shelf
ROSS SEA
C. Colbeck
WEDDELL SEA
Coats Land
C. Norvegia
PENSACOLA MTNS.
South Pole
Mt. Kirkpatrick 14,856 ft.
Mt. Markham 14,275 ft.
QUEEN MAUD MTNS.
TRANSANTARCTIC MOUNTAINS
Victoria Land
C. Adare
STURGE I.
BALLENY IS.
Oates Land
George V Land
South Magnetic Pole
Terre Adélie
Wilkes Land
AMERICAN HIGHLAND
Queen Mary Land
AUSTRALIAN CLAIM
NEW ZEALAND CLAIM
NORWEGIAN CLAIM
BRITISH CLAIM
ARGENTINE CLAIM
CHILEAN CLAIM
FRENCH CLAIM
Enderby Land
C. Darnley
Shackleton Ice Shelf
Knox Coast
C. Poinsett
Antarctic Circle
Average permanent extent of sea ice
5,240 ft.
5,010 ft.
4,330 ft.
677 ft.
840 ft.
8,426 ft.
6,972ft.
6,089ft.
677ft.

Part VIII

Tables

Table A
World Countries: Area, Population, and Population Density, 2003

COUNTRY	AREA		POPULATION (in thousands)	DENSITY	
	(Mi^2)	(Km^2)	(2003)[a]	(Pop/Mi^2)	(Pop/Km^2)
Afghanistan	251,826	652,229	23,897	95	37
Albania	11,100	28,749	3,166	285	110
Algeria	919,595	2,381,740	31,800	35	13
Andorra	175	453	68	389	150
Angola	481,354	1,246,700	13,625	28	11
Antigua and Barbuda	171	443	67	392	151
Argentina	1,073,400	2,780,104	38,428	36	14
Armenia	11,506	29,801	3,061	266	103
Australia	2,966,155	7,682,337	19,731	7	3
Austria	32,377	83,856	8,116	251	97
Azerbaijan	33,436	86,599	8,370	250	97
Bahamas	5,382	13,939	314	58	23
Bahrain	267	692	724	2,712	1,046
Bangladesh	55,598	143,999	146,736	2,639	1,019
Barbados	166	430	270	1,627	628
Belarus	80,155	207,601	9,895	123	48
Belgium	11,783	30,518	10,318	876	338
Belize	8,866	22,963	256	29	11
Benin	43,475	112,600	6,736	155	60
Bhutan	18,200	47,138	2,257	124	48
Bolivia	424,165	1,098,587	9	0	0
Bosnia and Herzegovina	19,776	51,233	4,161	210	81
Botswana	231,803	600,362	1,785	8	3
Brazil	3,286,488	8,511,999	178,470	54	21
Brunei Darussalam	2,228	5,770	358	161	62
Bulgaria	42,823	110,912	7,897	184	71
Burkina Faso	105,869	274,201	13,002	123	47
Burundi	10,745	27,830	6,825	635	245
Cambodia	69,898	181,036	14,144	202	78
Cameroon	183,569	475,443	16,018	87	34
Canada	3,849,674	9,970,650	31,510	8	3
Cape Verde	1,557	4,033	463	297	115
Central African Republic	240,535	622,985	3,865	16	6
Chad	495,755	1,284,005	8,598	17	7
Chile	292,259	756,950	15,805	54	21
China	3,705,392	9,596,960	1,304,196	352	136
Hong Kong, China	422	1,092	7,049	16,704	6,455
Colombia	439,734	1,138,910	44,222	101	39
Comoros	838	2,170	768	916	354
Democratic Republic of the Congo (formerly Zaire)	905,564	2,345,410	52,771	58	22
Congo Republic	132,047	342,002	3,724	28	11
Costa Rica	19,730	51,101	4,173	212	82
Côte d'Ivoire	124,503	322,460	16,631	134	52

Table A *(Continued)*
World Countries: Area, Population, and Population Density, 2003

COUNTRY	AREA		POPULATION (in thousands)	DENSITY	
	(Mi^2)	(Km^2)	(2003)[a]	(Pop/Mi^2)	(Pop/Km^2)
Croatia	21,824	56,538	4,428	203	78
Cuba	42,804	110,862	11,300	264	102
Cyprus	3,571	9,250	802	225	87
Czech Republic	30,387	78,703	10,236	337	130
Denmark	16,629	43,070	5,364	323	125
Djibouti	8,494	22,000	703	83	32
Dominica	290	750	70	241	93
Dominican Republic	18,815	48,730	8,745	465	179
Ecuador	109,484	283,563	13,003	119	46
Egypt	386,662	1,001,454	72	0	0
El Salvador	8,124	21,041	6,515	802	310
Equatorial Guinea	10,831	28,052	494	46	18
Eritrea	46,842	121,320	4,141	88	34
Estonia	17,413	45,100	1,323	76	29
Ethiopia	435,184	1,127,127	70,678	162	63
Fiji	7,054	18,270	839	119	46
Finland	130,127	337,030	5,207	40	15
France	176,460	547,030	60,144	341	110
Gabon	103,347	267,669	1,329	13	5
Gambia	4,363	11,300	1,426	327	126
Georgia	26,911	69,699	5,126	190	74
Germany	137,803	356,910	82,476	599	231
Ghana	92,098	238,534	20,922	227	88
Greece	50,942	131,940	10,976	215	83
Grenada	131	340	89	679	262
Guatemala	42,042	108,889	12,347	294	113
Guinea	94,926	245,858	8,480	89	34
Guinea-Bissau	13,948	36,125	1,493	107	41
Guyana	83,000	214,970	765	9	4
Haiti	10,714	27,749	8,326	777	300
Honduras	43,277	112,087	7	0	0
Hungary	35,920	93,033	9,877	275	106
Iceland	39,768	103,000	290	7	3
India	1,269,340	3,287,590	1,065,462	839	324
Indonesia	741,097	1,919,440	219,883	297	115
Iran	636,294	1,648,000	68,920	108	42
Iraq	168,754	437,072	25,175	149	58
Ireland	27,137	70,285	3,956	146	56
Israel[b]	8,019	20,769	6,433	802	310
Italy	116,305	301,230	57,423	494	191
Jamaica	4,244	10,992	2,651	625	241
Japan	145,882	377,835	127,654	875	338
Jordan	35,445	89,213	5,473	154	61
Kazakhstan	1,049,156	2,717,313	15,433	15	6

Table A *(Continued)*
World Countries: Area, Population, and Population Density, 2003

COUNTRY	AREA		POPULATION (in thousands)	DENSITY	
	(Mi^2)	(Km^2)	(2003)[a]	(Pop/Mi^2)	(Pop/Km^2)
Kenya	224,961	582,649	31,987	142	55
Kiribati	277	717	96	347	134
Korea, North	46,540	120,539	22,664	487	188
Korea, South	38,023	98,480	47,700	1,255	484
Kuwait	6,880	17,819	2,521	366	141
Kyrgyzstan	76,641	198,500	5,138	67	26
Laos	91,429	[illegible]	[illegible]	62	24
Latvia	24,749	64,100	2,307	93	36
Lebanon	4,015	10,399	3,653	910	351
Lesotho	11,720	30,355	1,802	154	59
Liberia	43,000	111,370	3,367	78	30
Libya	679,362	1,759,547	5,551	8	3
Liechtenstein	62	161	33	532	205
Lithuania	25,174	65,201	3,444	137	53
Luxembourg	998	2.585	453	454	175
Macedonia	9,781	25,333	2,056	210	81
Madagascar	226,658	587,044	17,404	77	30
Malawi	45,747	118,485	12,105	265	102
Malaysia	127,317	329,750	24,425	192	74
Maldives	115	298	318	2,765	1,067
Mali	478,767	1,240,006	13,007	27	10
Malta	124	320	318	2,565	994
Marshall Islands	70	181	74	1,057	409
Mauritania	397,954	1,030,700	2,893	7	3
Mauritius	718	1,860	1,221	1,701	656
Mexico	761,603	1,972,550	103,457	136	52
Micronesia	271	702	109	402	155
Moldova	13,012	33,701	4,435	341	132
Monaco	1.21	1.95	32	26,446	16,410
Mongolia	604,427	1,565,000	2,594	4	2
Morocco	172,413	446,550	30,566	177	68
Mozambique	309,494	801,590	18,863	61	24
Myanmar (Burma)	261,969	678,500	49,485	189	73
Namibia	318,259	824,290	1,987	6	2
Nauru	8	21	12	1,500	571
Nepal	54,363	140,800	25,164	463	179
Netherlands	14,413	37,330	16,149	1,120	433
New Zealand	103,738	268,680	3,875	37	14
Nicaragua	49,998	129,494	5,466	109	42
Niger	489,191	1,267,004	11,972	24	9
Nigeria	356,669	923,772	124,009	348	134
Norway	125,182	324,220	4,533	36	14
Oman	82,030	212,458	2,851	35	13
Pakistan	310,402	803,940	153,578	495	191

Table A *(Continued)*
World Countries: Area, Population, and Population Density, 2003

COUNTRY	AREA		POPULATION (in thousands)	DENSITY	
	(Mi^2)	(Km^2)	(2003)[a]	(Pop/Mi^2)	(Pop/Km^2)
Palau	177	458	19	107	41
Panama	30,193	78,200	3,120	103	40
Papua New Guinea	178,259	461,690	5,711	32	12
Paraguay	157,048	406,754	5,878	37	14
Peru	496,225	1,285,222	27,167	55	21
Philippines	115,831	300,002	79,999	691	267
Poland	120,728	312,685	38,537	319	123
Portugal	35,552	92,080	10,062	283	109
Qatar	4,247	11,000	610	144	55
Romania	91,699	237,500	22,334	244	94
Russian Federation	6,592,745	17,075,200	143,246	22	8
Rwanda	10,169	26,338	8,387	825	318
St. Kitts and Nevis	104	269	39	375	145
St. Lucia	238	616	149	626	242
St. Vincent/Grenadines	131	340	120	916	353
Samoa	1,104	2,860	178	161	62
San Marino	23	60	28	1,217	467
São Tomé and Principe	372	963	161	433	167
Saudi Arabia	756,982	1,960,582	24,217	32	12
Senegal	75,749	196,190	10,095	133	51
Serbia-Montenegro	39,517	102,350	10,527	266	103
Seychelles	175	453	80	457	177
Sierra Leone	27,699	71,740	4,971	179	69
Singapore	244	633	4,253	17,430	6,719
Slovakia	18,859	48,845	5,042	267	103
Slovenia	7,836	20,296	1,984	253	98
Solomon Islands	10,985	28,450	477	43	17
Somalia	246,201	637,660	9,890	40	16
South Africa	471,444	1,221,040	45,026	96	37
Spain	194,885	504,752	41,060	211	81
Sri Lanka	25,332	65,610	19,065	753	291
Sudan	967,500	2,505,824	33,610	35	13
Suriname	63,039	163,270	436	7	3
Swaziland	6,704	17,363	1,077	161	62
Sweden	173,732	449,966	8,876	51	20
Switzerland	15,943	41,292	7,169	450	174
Syria	71,498	185,180	17,800	249	96
Taiwan	13,892	35,980	22,548	1,623	627
Tajikistan	55,251	143,100	6,245	113	44
Tanzania	364,900	945,090	36,977	101	39
Thailand	198,456	514,000	62,833	317	122
Togo	21,925	56,786	4,909	224	86
Tonga	290	751	104	359	138
Trinidad and Tobago	1,980	5,128	1,303	658	254

Table A *(Continued)*
World Countries: Area, Population, and Population Density, 2003

COUNTRY	AREA		POPULATION (in thousands)	DENSITY	
	(Mi^2)	(Km^2)	(2003)[a]	(Pop/Mi^2)	(Pop/Km^2)
Tunisia	63,170	163,610	9,832	156	60
Turkey	301,382	780,580	71,325	237	91
Turkmenistan	188,456	488,101	4,867	26	10
Tuvalu	10	26	11	1,100	423
Uganda	93,135	236,040	25,827	277	109
Ukraine	233,090	603,703	48,523	208	80
United Arab Emirates	31,969	82,880	2,995	94	36
United Kingdom	94,525	244,820	59,251	627	242
United States	3,717,797	9,629,091	294,043	79	31
Uruguay	68,039	176,220	3,415	50	19
Uzbekistan	172,742	447,402	26,093	151	58
Vanuatu	5,699	14,760	212	37	14
Venezuela	352,145	912,055	25,699	73	28
Vietnam	127,243	329,560	81,377	640	247
Yemen	203,850	527,970	20,010	98	38
Zambia	290,586	752,617	10,812	37	14
Zimbabwe	150,803	390,580	12,891	85	33

[a]Primary source for population figures: United Nations Population Division.

[b]The figures for Israel do not include the West Bank and Gaza. These territories combined have a population of 3,557,000 (2003), and an area of approximately 2,400 square miles. The West Bank has an estimated population density of 956 persons per square mile and Gaza an estimated population density of 8,820 persons per square mile.

Sources: World Development Indicators 2003 (The World Bank); *World Almanac and Book of Facts; World Population Prospects: The 2000 Revision* (United Nations Population Information Network, 2001).

Table B
World Countries: Form of Government, Capital City, Major Languages

Notes: Unless indicated otherwise, republics are multi-party. Theocratic normally refers to fundamentalist Islamic rule. Transitional governments are those still in the process of change from a previous form (eg. Single-party communist state to multi-party republic).

COUNTRY	GOVERNMENT	CAPITAL	MAJOR LANGUAGES
Afghanistan	Transitional	Kabul	Dari, Pashtu, Uzbek, Turkmen
Albania	Multi-party democracy	Tiranë	Albanian, Greek
Algeria	Republic	Algiers	Arabic, Berber, dialects, French
Andorra	Parliamentary democracy	Andorra	Cataln, French, Spanish, Portuguese
Angola	Multi-party republic	Luanda	Portugese; Bantu and other African
Antigua and Barbuda	Parliamentary democracy	St. John's	English, local dialects
Argentina	Federal republic	Buenos Aires	Spanish, English, Italian, German, other
Armenia	Republic	Yerevan	Armenian, Russian, other
Australia	Federal parliamentary democracy	Canberra	English, indigenous
Austria	Federal republic	Vienna	German
Azerbaijan	Republic	Baku	Azerbaijani, Russian, Armenian, other
Bahamas	Parliamentary democracy; independent Commonwealth	Nassau	English, Creole
Bahrain	Constitutional hereditary monarchy	Al Manamah	Arabic, English, Farsi, Urdu
Bangladesh	Parliamentary democracy	Dhaka	Bangla, English
Barbados	Parliamentary democracy	Bridgetown	English
Belarus	Republic	Minsk	Byelorussian, Russian, other
Belgium	Constitutional monarchy	Brussels	Dutch (Flemish), French, German
Belize	Parliamentary democracy	Belmopan	English, Spanish, Garifuna, Mayan
Benin	Multi-party republic	Porto-Novo	French, Fon, Yoruba
Bhutan	Monarchy; special treaty relationship with India	Timphu	Dzongkha, Tibetan, Nepalese
Bolivia	Republic	La Paz, Sucre	Spanish, Quechua, Aymara
Bosnia-Herzegovina	Emerging federal democratic republic	Sarajevo	Croatian, Serbian, Bosnian
Botswana	Parliamentary republic	Gaborone	English, Setswana
Brazil	Federal republic	Brasilia	Portugese, Spanish, English, French
Brunei	Constitutional monarchy	Bandar Seri Begawan	Malay, English, Chinese
Bulgaria	Parliamentary democracy	Sofia	Bulgarian
Burkina Faso	Parliamentary republic	Ouagadougou	French, indigenous
Burundi	Republic	Bujumbura	French, Kirundi, Swahili
Cambodia	Multi-party democracy (under UN supervision)	Phnom Penh	Khmer, French, English
Cameroon	Multi-party republic	Yaoundé	English, French, indigenous
Canada	Federal parliamentary	Ottawa	English, French, other
Cape Verde	Republic	Cidade de Praia	Portugese, Crioulu
Central African Republic	Republic	Bangui	French, Sangho
Chad	Republic	N'Djamena	French, Arabic, Sara, other indigenous
Chile	Republic	Santiago	Spanish
China	Single-party communist state	Beijing	Various Chinese dialects
Colombia	Republic	Bogotá	Spanish
Comoros	Republic	Moroni	Arabic, French, Shikomoro
Democratic Republic of the Congo (formerly Zaire)	Republic/transitional from military dictatorship	Kinshasa	French, Lingala, Kingwana, Kikongo, Tshilluba
Congo Republic	Multi-party republic	Brazzaville	French, Lingala, Monokutuba, Kikongo
Costa Rica	Democratic republic	San José	Spanish

Table B *(Continued)*
World Countries: Form of Government, Capital City, Major Languages

Notes: Unless indicated otherwise, republics are multi-party. Theocratic normally refers to fundamentalist Islamic rule. Transitional governments are those still in the process of change from a previous form (eg. Single-party communist state to multi-party republic).

COUNTRY	GOVERNMENT	CAPITAL	MAJOR LANGUAGES
Côte d'Ivoire	Multi-party republic	Abidjan, Yamoussoukro	French, indigenous
Croatia	Parliamentary democracy	Zagreb	Croatian
Cuba	Single-party communist state	Havana	Spanish
Cyprus	Republic	Nicosia	Greek, Turkish, English
Czech Republic	Parliamentary democracy	Prague	Czech
Denmark	Constitutional monarchy	Copenhagen	Danish, Faroese, Greenlandic, German
Djibouti	Republic	Djibouti	French, Somali, Afar, Arabic
Dominica	Parliamentary democracy, republic within Commonwealth	Roseau	English, French
Dominican Republic	Republic	Santo Domingo	Spanish
East Timor	Republic	Dili	Tetum, Portuguese, Indonesian, English
Ecuador	Republic	Quito	Spanish, Quechua, indigenous
Egypt	Republic	Cairo	Arabic
El Salvador	Republic	San Salvador	Spanish, Nahua
Equatorial Guinea	Republic	Malabo	Spanish, French, indigenous, English
Eritrea	Transitional government	Asmara	Afar, Amharic, Arabic, Tigre, other indigenous
Estonia	Parliamentary republic	Tallinn	Estonian, Russian, Ukranian, Finnish
Ethiopia	Federal republic	Addis Ababa	Amharic, Tigrinya, Orominga, Somali, Arabic, English
Fiji	Republic	Suva	English, Fijian, Hindustani
Finland	Republic	Helsinki	Finnish, Swedish
France	Republic	Paris	French
Gabon	Multi-party republic	Libreville	French, Fang, indigenous
The Gambia	Multi-party democratic republic	Banjul	English, Mandinka, Wolof, Fula
Georgia	Republic	Tbilisi	Georgian, Russian, Armenian
Germany	Federal republic	Berlin	German
Ghana	Parliamentary democracy	Accra	English, indigenous
Greece	Parliamentary republic	Athens	Greek
Grenada	Parliamentary democracy	St. George's	English, French
Guatemala	Republic	Guatemala City	Spanish, Quiche, Cakchiquel, other indigenous
Guinea	Republic	Conakry	French, indigenous
Guinea-Bissau	Multi-party republic	Bissau	Portugese, Crioulo, indigenous
Guyana	Republic within Commonwealth	Georgetown	English, Creole, Hindi, Urdu, indigenous
Haiti	Republic	Port-au-Prince	Creole, French
Honduras	Republic	Tegucigalpa	Spanish, indigenous
Hungary	Parliamentary democracy	Budapest	Hungarian
Iceland	Republic	Reykjavk	Icelandic
India	Federal republic	New Delhi	English, Hindi, 14 other official
Indonesia	Republic	Jakarta	Bahasa Indonesian, English, Dutch, Javanese
Iran	Theocratic republic	Tehran	Farsi, Turkish, Kurdish
Iraq	In transition following US-led invasion	Baghdad	Arabic, Kurdish, Assyrian, Armenian
Ireland	Republic	Dublin	English, Irish Gaelic
Israel	Parliamentary democracy	Jerusalem	Hebrew, Arabic, English
Italy	Republic	Rome	Italian
Jamaica	Parliamentary democracy	Kingston	English, Creole

Table B *(Continued)*
World Countries: Form of Government, Capital City, Major Languages

Notes: Unless indicated otherwise, republics are multi-party. Theocratic normally refers to fundamentalist Islamic rule. Transitional governments are those still in the process of change from a previous form (eg. Single-party communist state to multi-party republic).

COUNTRY	GOVERNMENT	CAPITAL	MAJOR LANGUAGES
Japan	Constitutional monarchy	Tokyo	Japanese
Jordan	Constitutional monarchy	Amman	Arabic
Kazakhstan	Republic	Astana	Kazakh, Russian
Kenya	Republic	Nairobi	English, Swahili, indigenous
Kiribati	Republic	Tarawa	English, I-Kiribati
Korea, North	Single-party communist state	Pyongyang	Korean
Korea, South	Republic	Seoul	Korean
Kuwait	Constitutional monarchy	Kuwait	Arabic, English
Kyrgyzstan	Republic	Bishkek	Kirghiz, Russian
Laos	Single-party communist state	Vientiane	Lao, French, English, indigenous
Latvia	Parliamentary democracy	Riga	Latvian, Lithuanian, Russian
Lebanon	Republic	Beirut	Arabic, French, Armenian, English
Lesotho	Constitutional monarchy	Maseru	English, Sesotho, Zulu, Xhosa
Liberia	Republic	Monrovia	English, indigenous
Libya	Single party/military dictatorship	Tripoli	Arabic
Liechtenstein	Constitutional monarchy	Vaduz	German
Lithuania	Parliamentary democracy	Vilnius	Lithuanian, Russian, Polish
Luxembourg	Constitutional monarchy	Luxembourg	French, Luxembourgian, German
Macedonia	Parliamentary democracy	Skopje	Macedonian, Albanian, Turkish, Serbo-Croatian
Madagascar	Republic	Antananarivo	Malagasy, French
Malawi	Multi-party democracy	Lilongwe	Chichewa, English, Tombuka
Malaysia	Constitutional monarchy	Kuala Lumpur	Malay, Chinese, English, indigenous
Maldives	Republic	Male	Dhivehi
Mali	Republic	Bamako	French, Bambara, indigenous
Malta	Parliamentary democracy	Valletta	English, Maltese
Marshall Islands	Constitutional government (free association with U.S.)	Majuro	English, Polynesian dialects, Japanese
Mauritania	Republic	Nouakchott	Arabic, Wolof, Pular, French, Solinke
Mauritius	Parliamentary democracy	Port Louis	English, Creole, French, Hindi, Urdu, Bojpoori, Hakka
Mexico	Federal republic	Mexico City	Spanish, indigenous
Micronesia	Constitutional government (free association with U.S.)	Palikir	English, Trukese, Pohnpeian, Yapese, others
Moldova	Republic	Chisinau	Moldavian, Russian, Gagauz
Monaco	Constitutional monarchy	Monaco	French, English, Italian, Monegasque
Mongolia	Republic	Ulaanbaatar	Khalkha Mongol, Turkic, Russian
Morocco	Constitutional monarchy	Rabat	Arabic, Berber dialects, French
Mozambique	Republic	Maputo	Portuguese, indigenous
Myanmar (Burma)	Military regime	Rangoon	Burmese, indigenous
Namibia	Republic	Windhoek	Afrikaans, English, German, indigenous
Nauru	Republic	Yaren district	Nauruan, English
Nepal	Constitutional monarchy	Kathmandu	Nepali, indigenous
Netherlands	Constitutional monarchy	Amsterdam	Dutch
New Zealand	Parliamentary democracy	Wellington	English, Maori
Nicaragua	Republic	Managua	Spanish, English, indigenous

Table B *(Continued)*
World Countries: Form of Government, Capital City, Major Languages

Notes: Unless indicated otherwise, republics are multi-party. Theocratic normally refers to fundamentalist Islamic rule. Transitional governments are those still in the process of change from a previous form (eg. Single-party communist state to multi-party republic).

COUNTRY	GOVERNMENT	CAPITAL	MAJOR LANGUAGES
Niger	Provisional military	Niamey	French, Hausa, Djerma
Nigeria	Military/transitional	Abuja	English, Hausa, Fulani, Yorbua, Ibo
Norway	Constitutional monarchy	Oslo	Norwegian, Sami
Oman	Monarchy	Muscat	Arabic, English, Baluchi, Urdu
Pakistan	Federal republic	Islamabad	Punjabi, Sindhi, Siraiki, Pashtu, Urbu, English, others
Palau	Constitutional government (free association with U.S.)	Koror	English, Palauan, Sonsoloreso, Tobi, Angaur, Japanese
Panama	Constitutional democracy	Panama	Spanish, English
Papua New Guinea	Parliamentary democracy	Port Moresby	Various indigenous, English, Motu
Paraguay	Constitutional republic	Asunción	Spanish, Guarani
Peru	Republic	Lima	Quechua, Spanish, Aymara
Philippines	Republic	Manila	English, Filipino, 8 major dialects
Poland	Republic	Warsaw	Polish
Portugal	Parliamentary democracy	Lisbon	Portuguese
Qatar	Traditional monarchy	Doha	Arabic, English
Romania	Republic	Bucharest	Romanian, Hungarian, German
Russia	Federation	Moscow	Russian, numerous other
Rwanda	Republic	Kigali	French, Kinyarwanda, English, Kiswahili
St. Kitts and Nevis	Constitutional monarchy	Basseterre	English
St. Lucia	Parliamentary democracy	Castries	English, French
St. Vincent/Grenadines	Parliamentary monarchy independent within Commonwealth	Kingstown	English, French
Samoa	Constitutional monarchy	Apia	Samoan, English
San Marino	Republic	San Marino	Italian
São Tomé and Principe	Republic	São Tome	Portuguese
Saudi Arabia	Monarchy	Riyadh	Arabic
Senegal	Republic	Dakar	French, Wolof, indigenous
Serbia and Montenegro	Republic	Belgrade	Serbian, Albanian
Seychelles	Republic	Victoria	English, French, Creole
Sierra Leone	Constitutional democracy	Freetown	English, Krio, Mende, Temne
Singapore	Parliamentary republic	Singapore	Chinese, English, Malay,Tamil
Slovakia	Parliamentary democracy	Bratislava	Slovak, Hungarian
Slovenia	Republic	Ljubljana	Slovenian, Serbo-Croatian, other
Solomon Islands	Parliamentary democracy	Honiara	English, indigenous
Somalia	No permanent national government	Mogadishu	Arabic, Somali, English, Italian
South Africa	Republic	Pretoria	Afrikaans, English, Zulu, Xhosa, other
Spain	Parliamentary monarchy	Madrid	Castilian Spanish, Catalan, Galician, Basque
Sri Lanka	Republic	Colombo	English, Sinhala, Tamil
Sudan	Provisional military	Khartoum	Arabic, Nubian, others
Suriname	Constitutional democracy	Paramaribo	Dutch, Sranang Tongo, English, Hindustani, Javanese
Swaziland	Monarchy within Commonwealth	Mbabane	English, siSwati
Sweden	Constitutional monarchy	Stockholm	Swedish
Switzerland	Federal republic	Bern	German, French, Italian, Romansch
Syria	Republic (under military regime)	Damascus	Arabic, Kurdish, Armenian, Aramaic

Table B *(Continued)*
World Countries: Form of Government, Capital City, Major Languages

Notes: Unless indicated otherwise, republics are multi-party. Theocratic normally refers to fundamentalist Islamic rule. Transitional governments are those still in the process of change from a previous form (eg. Single-party communist state to multi-party republic).

COUNTRY	GOVERNMENT	CAPITAL	MAJOR LANGUAGES
Taiwan	Multi-party democracy	Taipei	Mandarin Chinese, Taiwanese, Hakka
Tajikistan	Republic	Dushanbe	Tajik, Russian
Tanzania	Republic	Dar es Salaam	Kiswahili, English, Arabic, indigenous
Thailand	Constitutional monarchy	Bangkok	Thai, English
Togo	Republic/transitional	Lomé	French, indigenous
Tonga	Constitutional monarchy	Nuku'alofa	Tongan, English
Trinidad and Tobago	Parliamentary democracy	Port-of-Spain	English, Hindi, French, Spanish, Chinese
Tunisia	Republic	Tunis	Arabic, French
Turkey	Parliamentary republic	Ankara	Turkish, Kurdish, Arabic, Armenian, Greek
Turkmenistan	Republic	Ashkhabad	Turkmen, Russian, Uzbek, other
Tuvalu	Constitutional monarchy	Funafuti	Tuvaluan, English, Samoan, Kiribati
Uganda	Republic	Kampala	English, Luganda, Swahili, Arabic, indigenous
Ukraine	Republic	Kiev	Ukranian, Russian, Romanian, Polish, Hungarian
United Arab Emirates	Federated monarchy	Abu Dhabi	Arabic, English, Farsi, Hindi, Urdu
United Kingdom	Constitutional monarchy	London	English, Welsh, Scottish Gaelic
United States	Federal republic	Washington	English, Spanish
Uruguay	Republic	Montevideo	Spanish, Portunol/Brazilero
Uzbekistan	Republic	Tashkent	Uzbek, Russian, Kazakh, Tajik, other
Vanuatu	Republic	Port-Vila	English, French, Bislama (pidgin)
Venezuela	Federal republic	Caracas	Spanish, indigenous
Vietnam	Single-party communist state	Hanoi	Vietnamese, French, Chinese, English, Khmer
Yemen	Republic	San`aa	Arabic
Zambia	Republic	Lusaka	English, Tonga, Lozi, other indigenous
Zimbabwe	Parliamentary democracy	Harare	English, Shona, Sindebele, other

Source: *The World Factbook 2002* (CIA, Washington, DC).

Table C
World Countries: Basic Economic Indicators

COUNTRY	GROSS NATIONAL INCOME (GNI) 2001[a]		PURCHASING POWER PARITY GNI 2001[b]			AVERAGE ANNUAL % GROWTH IN GDP			STRUCTURE OF ECONOMIC OUTPUT (GDP) 2001 (value added in % of GDP)			
	Total ($U.S. billions)	Per Capita ($U.S.)	Total ($U.S. billions)	Per Capita ($U.S.)	Rank	1980–1990	1990–1999	2000–01	Agriculture	Industry	Manufacturing	Services
Afghanistan	–	–	–	–	–	–	–	–	–	–	–	–
Albania	4.2	1,340	12	3,810	130	1.5	3.2	6.5	50	23	13	26
Algeria	51.0	1,650	182[c]	5,910[c]	99	2.7	1.6	2.1	10	55	8	36
Angola	6.7	500	23[c]	1,690[c]	171	3.7	0.4	3.2	8	67	4	25
Argentina	260.3	7	412	10,980	63	–0.4	4.0	–4.5	5	27	17	09
Armenia	2.2	570	10	2,730	146		[illegible]	[illegible]	[illegible]	34	22	38
Australia	385.9	19,900	478	24,630	24	3.4	4.1	3.9	4	26	13	70
Austria	194.7	23,940	215	26,380	17	2.2	1.9	1.0	2	33	22	65
Azerbaijan	5.3	650	23	2,890	141	–	–9.6	9.9	17	46	6	36
Bangladesh	48.6	360	213	1,600	173	4.3	4.7	5.3	23	25	15	52
Belarus	12.9	1,290	76	7,630	83	–	–3.0	4.1	11	39	33	50
Belgium	245.3	23,850	269	26,150	18	2.0	1.7	1.0	2	27	20	71
Benin	2.4	380	6	970	190	2.9	4.7	5.0	36	14	9	50
Bolivia	8.1	950	19	2,240	155	–0.2	4.2	1.2	16	29	15	56
Bosnia–Herzegovina	5.0	1,240	25	6,250	92	–	35.2	6.0	15	31	16	55
Botswana	5.3	3,100	13	7,410	84	10.3	4.3	6.3	2	47	4	51
Brazil	528.9	3,070	1,219	7,070	86	2.7	3.0	1.5	9	34	21	57
Bulgaria	13.2	1,650	54	6,740	89	3.4	–2.7	4.0	14	29	18	57
Burkina Faso	2.5	220	13[c]	1,120[c]	185	3.6	3.8	5.6	38	21	15	41
Burundi	0.7	100	5[c]	680[c]	203	4.4	–2.9	3.2	50	19	9	31
Cambodia	3.3	270	22	1,790	168	–	4.8	6.3	37	22	–	41
Cameroon	8.7	580	24	1,580	174	3.4	1.3	5.3	43	20	11	38
Canada	681.6	21,930	825[c]	26,530[c]	15	3.3	2.7	1.5	–	–	–	–
Central African Republic	1.0	260	5[c]	1,300[c]	181	1.4	1.8	1.5	55	21	9	24
Chad	1.6	200	8	1,060	187	3.7	2.1	8.5	39	14	10	48
Chile	70.6	4,590	136	8,840	76	4.2	7.2	2.8	9	34	16	57
China	1,131.2	890	5,027	3,950	127	10.2	10.7	7.3	15	51	35	34
Hong Kong, China	170.3	25,30	172	25,560	19	6.9	3.9	0.1	0	14	6	86
Colombia	81.6	1,890	292	6,790	88	3.6	3.3	1.4	13	30	16	57
Democratic Republic of the Congo (formerly Zaire)	4.2	80	33	630	205	1.6	–5.1	–4.5	56	19	4	25
Congo Republic	2.0	640	2	680	203	3.3	–0.5	2.9	6	66	4	28
Costa Rica	15.7	4,060	36	9,260	74	3.0	5.1	0.9	9	29	21	62
Cote d'Ivoire	10.3	630	23	1,400	179	0.7	3.7	–0.9	24	22	19	54
Croatia	19.9	4,550	39	8,930	75	–	0.2	4.1	9	33	23	58
Cuba	–	–[g]	–	–	–	–	–	–	7	46	37	47
Czech Republic	54.3	5,310	146	14,320	55	1.7	0.8	3.3	4	41	–	55
Denmark	164.0	30,600	153	23,490	9	2.3	2.4	1.0	33	26	17	71
Dominican Republic	19.0	2,230	57	6,650	90	3.1	5.8	2.7	11	33	16	55
Ecuador	14.0	1,080	38	2,960	140	2.0	2.2	5.6	11	33	18	56
Egypt	99.6	1,530	232	3,560	131	5.4	4.4	2.9	17	33	19	50
El Salvador	13.0	2,040	33	5,160	107	0.2	5.0	1.8	9	30	23	61
Eritrea	0.7	160	4	1,030	189	–	5.0	9.7	19	22	11	59
Estonia	5.3	3,870	13	9,650	71	2.2	–1.3	5.0	6	29	19	65
Ethiopia	6.7	100	53	800	198	2.3	4.6	7.7	52	11	7	37
Finland	123.4	23,780	125	24,030	28	3.3	2.4	0.4	3	33	26	63
France	1,380.7[h]	22,730[h]	1,425	24,080	27	2.3	1.5	1.8	3	26	18	72

Table C *(Continued)*
World Countries: Basic Economic Indicators

COUNTRY	GROSS NATIONAL INCOME (GNI) 2001[a]		PURCHASING POWER PARITY GNI 2001[b]			AVERAGE ANNUAL % GROWTH IN GDP			STRUCTURE OF ECONOMIC OUTPUT (GDP) 2001 (value added in % of GDP)			
	Total ($U.S. billions)	Per Capita ($U.S.)	Total ($U.S. billions)	Per Capita ($U.S.)	Rank	1980–1990	1990–1999	2000–01	Agriculture	Industry	Manufacturing	Services
Gabon	4.0	3,160	7	5,190	105	0.9	3.2	2.5	8	51	5	42
The Gambia	0.4	320	3[c]	2,010[c]	160	3.6	2.8	6.0	40	14	5	46
Georgia	3.1	590	14	2,580	148	0.4	–	4.5	21	23	–	57
Germany	1,939.6	24	2,078	25,240	21	2.2	1.3	0.6	1	31	24	68
Ghana	5.7	290	43[c]	2,170[c]	157	3.0	4.3	4.0	36	25	9	39
Greece	121.0	11,430	186	17,520	47	1.8	2.2	4.1	8	21	12	71
Guatemala	19.6	1,680	51	4,380	120	0.8	4.2	2.1	23	19	13	58
Guinea	3.1	410	14	2	164	–	4.2	3.6	24	38	4	38
Guinea–Bissau	0.2	160	1	890	193	4.0	0.3	0.2	56	13	10	31
Haiti	3.9	480	15[c]	1,870[c]	166	–0.2	–1.3	–1.7	–	–	–	–
Honduras	5.9	900	18	2,760	144	2.7	3.3	2.6	14	32	20	55
Hungary	49.2	4,830	122	11,990	59	1.3	1.0	3.8	–	–	–	–
India	477.4	460	2,913	2,820	143	5.8	6.0	5.4	25	26	16	48
Indonesia	144.7	690	591	2,830	142	6.1	4.7	3.3	16	47	26	37
Iran	108.7	1,680	383	5,940	98	1.7	3.6	4.8	19	33	16	48
Iraq	–	–[e]	–	–	–	–6.8	–		–	–	–	–
Ireland	87.7	22,850	104	27,170	14	3.2	6.9	5.8	4	42	33	55
Israel	106.6	17	125	19,630	40	3.5	5.2	–0.9	–	–	–	–
Italy	1,128.8	19,390	1,422	24,530	25	2.4	1.4	1.8	3	29	21	68
Jamaica	7.3	2,800	9	3	133	2.0	0.3	1.7	6	31	13	63
Japan	4,523.3	36	3,246	25,550	20	4.0	1.3	–0.6	1	32	22	67
Jordan	8.8	1,750	20	3,880	128	2.5	5.3	4.2	2	25	15	73
Kazakhstan	20.1	1,350	92	6,150	94	–	–5.9	13.2	9	39	16	52
Kenya	10.7	350	30	970	190	4.2	2.2	1.1	19	18	13	63
Korea, North	–	–[d]	–	–	–	–	–		–	–	–	–
Korea, South	447.6	9,460	713	15	54	9.4	5.7	3.0	4	41	30	54
Kuwait	37.4	18,270	44	21,530	35	1.3	–	–1.0	–	–	–	–
Kyrgyzstan	1.4	280	13	2,630	147	–	–5.4	5.3	38	27	8	36
Laos	1.6	300	8[c]	1,540[c]	175	–	6.6	5.7	51	23	18	26
Latvia	7.6	3,230	18	7,760	82	3.5	–4.8	7.6	5	26	15	69
Lebanon	17.6	4,010	19	4,400	119	–	7.7	1.3	12	22	10	66
Lesotho	1.1	530	6[c]	2,980[c]	139	4.4	4.4	4.0	16	42	14	42
Liberia	0.5	140	–	–	196	–	–	5.3	–	–	–	–
Libya	–	–[g]	–	–	–	–5.7	–		–	–	–	–
Lithuania	11.7	3,350	29	8,350	78	–	–4.0	5.9	7	35	23	58
Luxembourg	18.8	41,550						1	1	20		79
Macedonia	3.5	1,690	12	6,040	97	–	–0.8	–4.1	11	31	20	58
Madagascar	4.2	260	13	820	197	1.1	1.7	6.0	30	14	12	56
Malawi	1.7	151	6	560	206	2.5	3.6	–1.5	34	18	13	48
Malaysia	79.3	3,330	188	7,910	81	5.3	7.3	0.4	9	49	31	42
Mali	2.5	230	9	770	200	2.8	3.6	1.4	38	26	4	36
Mauritania	1.0	360	5	1,940	162	1.8	4.2	4.6	21	29	8	50
Mauritius	4.6	3,830	12	9,860	70	6.2	5.1	7.2	6	31	23	62
Mexico	550.2	5,530	820	8	80	0.7	2.7	–0.3	4	27	19	69
Moldova	1.5	400	10	2,300	154	3.0	–11.0	6.1	26	24	18	50
Mongolia	1.0	400	4	1,710	170	5.4	0.7	1.4	30	17	5	53
Morocco	34.7	1,190	102	3,500	132	4.2	2.3	6.5	16	18	50	53
Mozambique	3.8	210	19[c]	1,050[c]	188	–0.1	6.2	13.9	22	26	12	52
Myanmar (Burma)	–	–[d]	–	–	–	0.6	6.3	–	57	10	7	33

Table C *(Continued)*
World Countries: Basic Economic Indicators

COUNTRY	GROSS NATIONAL INCOME (GNI) 2001[a]		PURCHASING POWER PARITY GNI 2001[b]			AVERAGE ANNUAL % GROWTH IN GDP			STRUCTURE OF ECONOMIC OUTPUT (GDP) 2001 (value added in % of GDP)			
	Total ($U.S. billions)	Per Capita ($U.S.)	Total ($U.S. billions)	Per Capita ($U.S.)	Rank	1980–1990	1990–1999	2000–01	Agriculture	Industry	Manufacturing	Services
Namibia	3.5	1,960	13[c]	7,410[c]	85	0.9	3.4	2.7	11	33	11	56
Nepal	5.8	250	32	1,360	180	4.6	4.9	4.8	39	22	9	39
Netherlands	390.3	24,330	439	27,390	13	2.3	2.7	1.1	3	27	17	70
New Zealand	51.0	10,250	70	10	10	1.0	0.1	0.0				
Nicaragua	–	–	–	–	158	–2.0	3.2	–	–	–	–	–
Niger	2.0	180	10[c]	880[c]	194	–0.1	2.4	7.6	40	17	7	43
Nigeria	37.1	290	102	790	199	1.6	2.4	3.9	30	46	4	25
Norway	160.8	36	132	29,340	7	2.8	3.8	1.4	2	43	–	55
Oman	–	–[g]		–	–	8.4	5.9	–	–	–	–	–
Pakistan	60.0	420	263	1,860	167	6.3	3.8	2.7	25	23	16	52
Panama	9.5	3,260	16[c]	5,440[c]	104	0.5	4.2	0.3	7	9	7	77
Papua New Guinea	3.0	580	13[c]	2,450[c]	149	1.9	4.7	–3.5	26	42	8	32
Paraguay	7.6	1,350	29[c]	5,180[c]	106	2.5	2.4	2.7	20	26	13	54
Peru	52.2	1,980	118	4,470	117	–0.3	5.0	0.2	9	30	15	62
Philippines	80.8	1,030	319	4	125	1.0	3.2	3.4	15	31	22	54
Poland	163.6	4,230	362	9,370	73	1.8	4.5	1.0	4	37	20	59
Portugal	109.3	10,900	178	17,710	46	3.1	2.5	1.7	4	30	19	66
Puerto Rico	42.1	10,950	69	18,090	44	4.0	3.1	5.6	1	43	40	56
Romania	38.6	1,720	130	5,780	101	0.5	–0.8	5.3	15	35	–	50
Russian Federation	253.4	1,750	995	6,880	87	–	–6.1	5.0	7	37	–	56
Rwanda	1.9	220	11	1,240	183	2.2	–1.5	6.7	40	22	10	38
Saudi Arabia	181.1	8	284	13,290	54	0.0	1.6	1.2	–	–	–	–
Senegal	4.7	490	14	1,480	176	3.1	3.3	5.7	18	27	18	55
Serbia–Montenegro	9.9	930	–	–	–	–	–	–	15	32	–	53
Sierra Leone	0.7	140	2	460	208	0.3	–4.7	5.4	50	30	5	20
Singapore	88.8	21,500	94	22,850	32	6.6	8.0	–2.0	0	34	23	68
Slovak Republic	20.3	4	64	11,780	60	2.0	1.8	3.3	4	29	21	67
Slovenia	19.4	9,760	34	17,060	49	–	2.4	3.0	3	38	28	58
Somalia	–	[d]	–	–	–	–	–	–	–	–	–	–
South Africa	121.9	2,820	472[c]	10,910[c]	64	1.2	1.9	2.2	3	31	19	66
Spain	588.0	14,800	816	19,860	39	3.0	2.2	2.8	4	30	19	66
Sri Lanka	16.4	880	61	3,260	134	4.0	5.3	–1.4	19	27	16	54
Sudan	10.7	340	56	1,750	169	0.4	8.2	6.9	39	19	10	42
Swaziland	1.4	1,300	5	4,430	118	–	–	1.6	17	44	36	39
Sweden	225.9	25,400	212	23,800	29	2.3	1.6	1.2	2	32	–	71
Switzerland	277.2	38,330	224	30,970	5	2.0	0.6	1.3	–	–	–	–
Syria	17.3	1,040	52	3,160	136	1.5	5.7	2.8	22	28	20	50
Tajikistan	1.1	180	7	1,140	184	–	–	10.2	29	29	25	41
Tanzania	9.4[i]	270[i]	18	520	207	–[i]	2.8	5.7	45	16	7	39
Thailand	118.5	1,940	381	6,230	93	7.6	4.7	1.8	10	40	32	49
Togo	1.3	270	8	1,620	172	1.7	2.4	2.7	39	21	10	39
Trinidad and Tobago	7.8	5,960	11	8,620	77	–0.8	2.7	5.0	2	44	8	55
Tunisia	20.0	2,070	59	6,090	96	3.3	4.6	4.9	12	29	18	60
Turkey	167.3	2,530	386	5,830	100	5.4	3.8	–7.4	14	26	15	61
Turkmenistan	5.1	950	23	4,240	124	–	–6.8	20.5	29	51	–	20
Uganda	5.9	260	33[c]	1,460[c]	177	2.9	7.2	4.6	36	21	10	43
Ukraine	35.2	720	210	4,270	101		10.7	0.1	17	30	23	11

Table C *(Continued)*
World Countries: Basic Economic Indicators

COUNTRY	GROSS NATIONAL INCOME (GNI) 2001[a]		PURCHASING POWER PARITY GNI 2001[b]			AVERAGE ANNUAL % GROWTH IN GDP			STRUCTURE OF ECONOMIC OUTPUT (GDP) 2001 (value added in % of GDP)			
	Total ($U.S. billions)	Per Capita ($U.S.)	Total ($U.S. billions)	Per Capita ($U.S.)	Rank	1980–1990	1990–1999	2000–01	Agriculture	Industry	Manufacturing	Services
United Arab Emirates	–	–[f]	–	–	–	–3.5	2.9	–	–	–	–	–
United Kingdom	1,476.8	25,120	1,431	24,340	26	3.2	2.5	2.2	1	27	19	72
United States	9,780.8	34,280	10	34,280	3	3.0	3.3	0.3	2	25	17	73
Uruguay	19.2	5,710	28	8,250	79	0.4	3.8	–3.1	6	28	56	67
Uzbekistan	13.8	550	60	2,410	152	–	–1.2	4.5	34	23	9	43
Venezuela	117.2	4,760	138	5,590	102	1.1	1.7	2.7	5	50	20	45
Vietnam	32.8	410	164	2,070	159	4.6	8.1	6.8	24	38	20	39
West Bank and Gaza	4.2	1,350	–	–	–	–	3.7	–11.9	8	27	15	66
Yemen, Rep.	8.2	450	13	730	202	–	3.2	3.1	16	50	7	35
Zambia	3.3	320	8	750	201	1.0	0.2	4.9	22	26	11	52
Zimbabwe	6.2	480	28	2,220	156	3.6	2.8	–8.4	18	24	14	58

a. Gross National Income (GNI) has replaced GNP in the World Bank Atlas Method's estimate of national income
b. Calculated using the World Bank Atlas method.
c. The estimate is based on regression; others are extrapolated from the latest International Comparison Programme benchmark estimates.
d. Estimated to be low income ($745 or less).
e. Estimated to be lower middle income ($746 to $2,975).
f. Estimated to be high income ($9,206 or more).
g. Estimated to be upper middle income ($2,976–to $9,205).
h.GNI and GNI per capita estimates include the French overseas departments of French Guiana, Guadeloupe, Martinique, and Reunion.
i. Data refer to mainland Tanzania only.

Sources: *World Development Indicators, 2003* (World Bank)

Table D
World Countries: Population Growth, 1950-2025

COUNTRY	POPULATION (thousands)			AVERAGE ANNUAL POPULATION CHANGE (percent)		AVERAGE ANNUAL INCREMENT TO THE POPULATION (mid-year population, in thousands)		
	1950	2000[a]	2025[a]	1975-1980	2001-2015[a]	1985-1990	1995-2000	2005-2010
WORLD	**2,518,629.0**	**6,070,581.0**	**7,851,455.0**	**1.7**	**2.5**	**85,831.0**		
AFRICA								
Algeria	8,753.0	30,245.0	42,429.0	3.1	1.5	[illegible]	566.0	539.3
Angola	4,131.0	12,386.0	19,268.0	2.7	2.6	130.2	187.2	267.5
Benin	2,046.0	6,222.0	11,120.0	2.5	2.4	135.6	184.8	204.6
Botswana	419.0	1,725.0	1,614.0	3.5	0.5	43.3	21.5	-15.4
Burkina Faso	3,960.0	11,905.0	24,527.0	2.5	2.1	[illegible]	307.0	380.3
Burundi	2,456.0	6,267.0	12,328.0	2.3	1.7	95.2	123.0	166.5
Cameroon	4,466.0	15,127.0	20,831.0	2.8	1.7	326.5	370.9	374.8
Central African Republic	1,314.0	3,715.0	5,193.0	2.3	1.5	57.5	62.0	60.0
Chad	2,658.0	7,861.0	15,770.0	2.1	2.9	171.2	259.8	340.4
Congo Democratic Republic	12,184.0	48,571.0	95,448.0	3.0	2.6	1,146.2	1,234.4	1,907.8
Congo Republic	808.0	3,447.0	6,750.0	2.9	2.7	56.3	62.4	67.2
Côte d'Ivoire	2,775.0	15,827.0	22,140.0	3.9	1.6	411.1	350.2	394.2
Egypt	21,834.0	67,784.0	103,165.0	2.4	1.5	1,318.5	1,199.9	1,125.0
Equatorial Guinea	226.0	456.0	812.0	-0.7	–	8.7	11.1	13.6
Eritrea	1,140.0	3,712.0	7,261.0	2.6	2.3	35.4	134.9	153.2
Ethiopia	18,434.0	65,590.0	116,006.0	2.4	2.1	1,530.7	1,670.9	1,848.4
Gabon	469.0	1,258.0	1,915.0	3.1	2.2	11.6	13.9	8.6
Gambia	294.0	1,312.0	2,177.0	3.1	2.0	33.0	42.3	48.0
Ghana	4,900.0	19,593.0	30,618.0	1.9	1.6	435.4	380.2	285.2
Guinea	2,550.0	8,117.0	13,704.0	1.5	1.9	173.7	63.1	193.9
Guinea-Bissau	505.0	1,367.0	2,774.0	4.7	2.2	22.1	28.4	35.1
Kenya	6,265.0	30,549.0	39,917.0	3.8	1.4	723.5	604.9	206.8
Lesotho	734.0	1,785.0	1,608.0	2.5	0.8	41.5	39.6	11.5
Liberia	824.0	2,943.0	6,081.0	3.1	2.3	-2.9	236.3	107.3
Libya	1,029.0	5,237.0	7,785.0	4.4	1.9	92.8	92.2	136.3
Madagascar	4,230.0	15,970.0	30,249.0	2.5	2.5	308.1	433.2	590.5
Malawi	2,881.0	11,370.0	18,245.0	3.3	1.8	416.6	169.9	103.8
Mali	3,520.0	11,904.0	25,679.0	2.1	2.1	164.0	305.1	390.7
Mauritania	825.0	2,645.0	4,973.0	2.5	2.3	47.5	65.2	94.9
Morocco	8,953.0	29,108.0	40,721.0	2.3	1.4	565.7	535.1	515.0
Mozambique	6,442.0	17,861.0	25,350.0	2.8	1.6	78.7	359.2	75.1
Namibia	511.0	1,894.0	2,350.0	2.7	1.2	58.6	33.5	7.5
Niger	2,500.0	10,742.0	25,722.0	3.2	2.8	207.6	259.7	322.0
Nigeria	29,790.0	114,746.0	192,115.0	2.8	1.9	2,530.7	3,225.5	3,161.6
Rwanda	2,162.0	7,724.0	12,509.0	3.3	1.6	187.9	311.1	49.1
Senegal	2,500.0	9,393.0	15,663.0	2.8	2.0	191.6	278.9	336.2
Sierra Leone	1,944.0	4,415.0	7,593.0	2.0	1.9	106.3	143.8	162.5
Somalia	2,264.0	8,720.0	20,978.0	7.0	3.1	45.8	192.4	266.1
South Africa	13,683.0	44,000.0	42,962.0	2.2	0.4	943.4	383.4	-419.6
Sudan	9,190.0	31,437.0	47,536.0	3.1	2.0	634.6	902.5	1,059.5
Tanzania	7,886.0	34,837.0	53,435.0	3.1	1.7	799.7	832.1	970.9
Togo	1,329.0	4,562.0	7,551.0	2.7	1.9	122.0	100.9	115.3
Tunisia	3,530.0	9,586.0	12,813.0	2.6	1.3	168.9	124.3	104.8

Table D *(Continued)*
World Countries: Population Growth, 1950-2025

COUNTRY	POPULATION (thousands)			AVERAGE ANNUAL POPULATION CHANGE (percent)		AVERAGE ANNUAL INCREMENT TO THE POPULATION (mid-year population, in thousands)		
	1950	2000[a]	2025[a]	1975-1980	2001-2015[a]	1985-1990	1995-2000	2005-2010
Uganda	5,310.0	23,487.0	54,883.0	3.2	2.4	590.9	598.7	877.5
Zambia	2,440.0	10,419.0	14,401.0	3.4	1.2	210.9	174.1	190.9
Zimbabwe	2,744.0	12,650.0	12,857.0	3.0	0.6	308.9	78.1	-58.6
NORTH AND CENTRAL AMERICA						**353.9**		
Belize	69.0	240.0	356.0	1.7	–	5.0	6.3	7.2
Canada	13,737.0	30,769.0	36,128.0	1.2	0.6	369.8	331.8	289.5
Costa Rica	966.0	3,929.0	5,621.0	3.0	1.4	76.6	65.4	58.0
Cuba	5,850.0	11,202.0	11,479.0	0.9	0.3	93.2	48.4	37.3
Dominican Republic	2,353.0	8,353.0	10,955.0	2.4	1.3	141.1	136.4	147.1
El Salvador	1,951.0	6,200.0	8,110.0	[illegible]	1.6	87.1	110.8	117.7
Guatemala	2,969.0	11,428.0	19,456.0	2.5	2.4	255.9	317.6	366.3
Haiti	3,261.0	8,005.0	10,670.0	2.1	1.7	111.8	89.1	114.6
Honduras	1,380.0	6,457.0	10,115.0	3.4	2.1	117.2	151.1	134.9
Jamaica	1,403.0	2,580.0	3,263.0	1.2	1.1	18.3	16.8	23.9
Mexico	27,737.0	98,933.0	129,866.0	2.7	1.4	1,594.3	1,572.4	1,425.0
Nicaragua	1,134.0	5,073.0	8,318.0	3.1	2.1	91.0	107.6	100.9
Panama	860.0	2,950.0	4,290.0	2.5	1.3	44.8	39.8	32.5
Trinidad and Tobago	636.0	1,289.0	1,340.0	1.3	0.8	6.5	-4.9	-6.1
United States	157,813.0	285,003.0	358,030.0	0.9	0.8	2,296.3	2,503.8	2,429.2
SOUTH AMERICA								
Argentina	17,150.0	37,074.0	47,043.0	1.5	1.0	445.4	427.4	401.1
Bolivia	2,714.0	8,317.0	12,495.0	2.4	1.8	127.7	155.2	128.3
Brazil	53,975.0	171,796.0	216,372.0	2.4	1.1	2,756.3	1,975.6	1,285.4
Chile	6,082.0	15,224.0	19,651.0	1.5	1.0	212.2	189.7	148.3
Colombia	12,568.0	4,120.0	58,157.0	2.3	1.3	636.0	681.0	630.9
Ecuador	3,387.0	12,420.0	16,704.0	2.8	1.5	262.0	264.1	257.2
Guyana	423.0	759.0	724.0	0.7	–	-3.2	-3.5	4.1
Paraguay	1,488.0	5,470.0	9,173.0	3.2	2.1	113.5	141.6	162.8
Peru	7,632.0	25,952.0	35,622.0	2.7	1.3	472.9	491.4	432.4
Suriname	215.0	425.0	486.0	-0.5	–	3.9	3.3	1.4
Uruguay	2,239.0	3,342.0	3,875.0	0.6	0.6	19.4	23.7	26.7
Venezuela	5,094.0	24,277.0	31,189.0	3.4	1.5	465.5	397.3	351.7
ASIA								
Afghanistan	8,151.0	21,391.0	44,940.0	0.9	2.5	170.3	879.9	724.7
Armenia	1,354.0	3,112.0	2,866.0	1.8	0.3	-0.7	-13.8	7.6
Azerbaijan	2,896.0	8,157.0	10,222.0	1.6	0.7	103.6	23.6	61.8
Bangladesh	41,783.0	137,952.0	208,268.0	2.8	1.6	2,028.8	2,001.0	2,119.6
Bhutan	734.0	2,063.0	3,701.0	2.3	–	34.7	42.4	48.8
Cambodia	4,346.0	13,147.0	21,899.0	-1.8	1.5	313.1	271.6	314.6
China[b]	556,924.0	1,282,472.0	1,454,141.0	1.5	0.6	16,833.4	11,408.3	8,726.8
Georgia	3,527.0	5,262.0	4,429.0	0.7	-0.7	49.9	-53.5	-14.4
India	357,561.0	1,016,938.0	1,369,284.0	2.1	1.2	16,448.0	16,317.4	15,140.5
Indonesia	79,538.0	211,559.0	270,113.0	2.1	1.1	3,283.4	3,702.8	3,388.7
Iran	16,913.0	664,423.0	90,927.0	3.3	1.6	1,632.8	818.3	1,000.3

COUNTRY	POPULATION (thousands)			AVERAGE ANNUAL POPULATION CHANGE (percent)		AVERAGE ANNUAL INCREMENT TO THE POPULATION (mid-year population, in thousands)		
	1950	2000[a]	2025[a]	1975-1980	2001-2015[a]	1985-1990	1995-2000	2005-2010
Iraq	5,158.0	23,224.0	41,707.0	3.3	1.9	488.2	623.7	719.5
Israel	1,258.0	6,042.0	8,598.0	2.3	1.5	87.4	107.5	73.6
Japan	83,625.0	127,034.0	123,444.0	0.9	-0.2	556.6	252.5	-30.4
Jordan	472.0	5,035.0	8,116.0	2.3	2.2	126.9	159.4	145.2
Kazakhstan	6,703.0	15,640.0	15,388.0	1.1	0.1	148.5	-42.0	85.9
Korea, North	10,815.0	22,268.0	24,665.0	1.6	0.6	307.4	27.2	4,294.4
Korea, South	18,859.0	46,835.0	50,165.0	1.6	0.4	943.5	459.2	322.0
Kuwait	152.0	2,247.0	3,930.0	6.2	2.1	81.8	70.6	90.4
Kyrgyzstan	1,740.0	4,921.0	6,484.0	1.9	1.1	76.8	30.0	80.9
Laos	1,755.0	5,279.0	8,635.0	1.2	2.2	110.7	130.3	155.3
Lebanon	1,443.0	3,478.0	4,554.0	-0.7	1.2	11.8	48.7	46.0
Malaysia	6,110.0	23,001.0	33,479.0	2.3	1.5	391.7	436.4	438.2
Mongolia	761.0	2,500.0	3,368.0	2.8	1.3	62.1	37.4	44.4
Myanmar (Burma)	17,832.0	47,544.0	59,760.0	2.1	1.0	452.8	317.4	162.3
Nepal	8,643.0	23,518.0	37,831.0	2.5	2.0	457.5	559.0	616.3
Oman	456.0	2,609.0	4,785.0	5.0	2.2	58.3	80.5	104.3
Pakistan	39,659.0	142,654.0	249,766.0	2.6	2.2	2,984.4	2,984.8	2,936.8
Philippines	1,996.0	75,711.0	108,589.0	2.3	1.6	1,450.5	1,658.1	1,666.1
Saudi Arabia	3,201.0	22,147.0	39,751.0	5.6	2.9	527.8	678.3	922.2
Singapore	1,022.0	4,016.0	4,905.0	1.3	1.1	56.1	134.2	169.1
Sri Lanka	7,483.0	18,595.0	21,464.0	1.7	1.1	234.4	186.9	153.5
Syria	3,495.0	16,560.0	26,979.0	3.1	2.1	391.1	399.2	431.5
Tajikistan	1,532.0	6,089.0	8,193.0	2.8	1.5	149.0	115.3	168.7
Thailand	19,626.0	60,925.0	73,869.0	2.4	0.6	755.5	598.8	468.5
Turkey	21,484.0	68,281.0	88,995.0	2.1	1.1	1,083.1	895.5	732.4
Turkmenistan	1,211.0	4,643.0	6,549.0	2.5	1.1	85.4	83.3	95.8
United Arab Emirates	70.0	2,820.0	3,944.0	14.0	1.8	76.1	38.6	40.0
Uzbekistan	6,314.0	24,913.0	33,774.0	2.6	1.3	473.1	381.7	485.8
Vietnam	27,369.0	78,137.0	104,649.0	2.2	1.2	1,321.7	1,178.3	1,123.4
Yemen	4,316.0	18,017.0	43,204.0	3.2	3.0	436.3	524.0	782.1
EUROPE								
Albania	1,215.0	3,113.0	3,629.0	1.9	1.0	60.3	50.7	34.4
Austria	6,935.0	8,102.0	7,979.0	-0.1	-0.1	32.1	17.8	11.3
Belarus	7,745.0	10,034.0	8,950.0	0.6	-0.5	46.7	-7.5	-1.4
Belgium	8,639.0	10,251.0	10,516.0	0.1	0.0	22.2	20.9	5.3
Bosnia-Herzegovina	2,661.0	3,977.0	4,183.0	0.9	0.5	29.7	96.0	15.5
Bulgaria	7,251.0	8,099.0	6,609.0	0.3	-0.7	-9.9	-95.1	-74.3
Croatia	3,850.0	4,446.0	4,088.0	0.5	-0.3	10.1	-34.6	11.2
Czech Republic	8,925.0	10,269.0	9,806.0	0.6	-0.2	-0.1	-10.6	-14.7
Denmark	4,271.0	5,322.0	5,469.0	0.2	0.1	5.5	20.8	12.0
Estonia	1,101.0	1,369.0	1,017.0	0.6	-0.5	7.0	-10.5	-4.9
Finland	4,009.0	5,177.0	5,289.0	0.3	0.1	16.9	12.3	4.8
France	41,829.0	59,296.0	64,165.0	0.4	0.3	312.8	236.0	142.8
Germany	68,376.0	82,282.0	81,959.0	-0.1	-0.2	339.1	229.8	152.4
Greece	7,566.0	10,903.0	10,707.0	1.3	0.1	44.5	22.4	11.0
Hungary	9,338.0	10,012.0	8,865.0	0.3	-0.6	-55.4	-31.4	-31.1

Table D *(Continued)*
World Countries: Population Growth, 1950-2025

COUNTRY	POPULATION (thousands)			AVERAGE ANNUAL POPULATION CHANGE (percent)		AVERAGE ANNUAL INCREMENT TO THE POPULATION (mid-year population, in thousands)		
	1950	2000[a]	2025[a]	1975-1980	2001-2015[a]	1985-1990	1995-2000	2005-2010
Iceland	143.0	282.0	325.0	0.9	-	2.7	1.8	1.1
Ireland	2,969.0	3,819.0	4,668.0	1.4	0.8	-6.4	37.2	31.9
Italy	47,104.0	57,536.0	52,939.0	0.4	-0.4	4.0	74.2	-67.5
Latvia	1,949.0	2,373.0	1,857.0	0.4	-0.7	12.3	-23.5	-12.9
Lithuania	2,567.0	3,501.0	3,035.0	0.7	-0.2	22.2	-10.4	-3.6
Macedonia	1,230.0	2,024.0	2,199.0	1.4	0.4	6.9	11.0	7.2
Moldova	2,341.0	4,283.0	4,096.0	0.9	-0.2	49.9	-5.8	16.0
Netherlands	10,114.0	15,898.0	17,123.0	0.7	0.4	92.0	86.6	62.5
Norway	3,265.0	4,473.0	4,859.0	0.4	0.4	17.9	24.4	18.2
Poland	24,824.0	38,671.0	37,337.0	0.9	0.0	178.7	8.5	11.2
Portugal	8,405.0	10,016.0	9,834.0	1.4	-0.1	5.1	15.9	9.6
Romania	16,311.0	22,480.0	20,806.0	0.9	-0.3	69.0	-56.3	-49.8
Russian Federation	102,192.0	145,612.0	124,428.0	0.6	-0.5	820.8	-422.7	-281.7
Serbia-Montenegro	7,131.0	10,555.0	10,230.0	0.9	0.1	21.0	-5.2	-4.6
Slovak Republic	3,463.0	5,391.0	5,397.0	1.0	0.0	23.6	9.3	6.1
Slovenia	1,473.0	1,990.0	1,859.0	1.0	-0.2	4.6	3.6	1.2
Spain	28,009.0	40,752.0	40,369.0	1.1	0.0	163.2	49.1	-2.8
Sweden	7,014.0	8,856.0	9,055.0	0.3	0.0	40.5	9.5	0.5
Switzerland	4,694.0	7,173.0	6,801.0	-0.1	-0.1	54.8	19.2	7.9
Ukraine	37,298.0	49,688.0	40,775.0	0.4	-0.7	142.7	-432.6	-264.4
United Kingdom	49,816.0	58,689.0	63,275.0	0.0	0.0	189.0	178.9	94.6
OCEANIA								
Australia	8,219.0	19,153.0	23,205.0	0.9	0.7	246.8	209.7	167.0
Fiji	289.0	814.0	965.0	1.9	–	7.8	11.3	12.8
New Zealand	1,908.0	3,784.0	4,379.0	0.2	0.5	12.3	50.8	38.5
Papua New Guinea	1,798.0	5,334.0	8,443.0	2.5	1.9	89.3	116.4	125.1
Solomon Islands	90.0	437.0	783.0	3.5	–	11.0	13.8	14.3

a Data include projections based on 1990 base year population data
b Includes Hong Kong and Macao

Source: United Nations Population Division and International Labour Organisation. *World Resources 2000-2001;* (World Resources Institute), U.S. Bureau of the Census International Data Base (2000).

Part IX

Geographic Index

Part IX
Geographic Index

The geographic index contains approximately 1,500 names of cities, states, countries, rivers, lakes, mountain ranges, oceans, capes, bays, and other geographic features. The name of each geographical feature in the index is accompanied by a geographical coordinate (latitude and longitude) in degrees and by the page number of the primary map on which the geographical feature appears. Where the geographical coordinates are for specific places or points, such as a city or a mountain peak, the latitude and longitude figures give the location of the map symbol denoting that point. Thus, Los Angeles, California, is at 34N and 118W and the location of Mt. Everest is 28N and 107E.

The coordinates for political features (countries or states) or physical features (oceans, deserts) that are areas rather than points are given according to the location of the name of the feature on the map, except in those cases where the name of the feature is separated from the feature (such as a country's name appearing over an adjacent ocean area because of space requirements). In such cases, the feature's coordinates will indicate the location of the center of the feature. The coordinates for the Sahara Desert will lead the reader to the place name "Sahara Desert" on the map; the coordinates for North Carolina will show the center location of the state since the name appears over the adjacent Atlantic Ocean. Finally, the coordinates for geographical features that are lines rather than points or areas will also appear near the center of the text identifying the geographical feature.

Alphabetizing follows general conventions; the names of physical features such as lakes, rivers, mountains are given as: proper name, followed by the generic name. Thus "Mount Everest" is listed as "Everest, Mt." Where an article such as "the," "le," or "al" appears in a geographic name, the name is alphabetized according to the article. Hence, "La Paz" is found under "L" and not under "P."

Name/Description — Latitude & Longitude — Page

Name/Description — Latitude & Longitude — Page

Name/Description — Latitude & Longitude — Page

Name/Description — Latitude & Longitude — Page

Name/Description — Latitude & Longitude — Page

Elbruz, Mt. 18,510 — 43N 42E — 140
Elgon, Mt. 14,178 — 1N 34E — 133
English Channel — 50N 0 — 123
Entre Rios (st., Argentina) — 32S 60W — 117
Equatorial Guinea (country) — 3N 10E — 134
Erg Iguidi — 26N 6W — 133
Erie (lake, N.Am.) — 42N 85W — 107
Eritrea (country) — 16N 38E — 134
Erzegebirge Mountains — 50N 14E — 123
Espinhaco Mountains — 15S 42W — 116
Espiritu Santo (island) — 15S 168E — 153
Espiritu Santo (st., Brazil) — 20S 42W — 117
Essen, Germany (city) — 52N 8E — 98
Estonia (country) — 60N 26E — 98
Ethiopia (country) — 8N 40E — 134
Ethiopian Plateau — 8N 40E — 133
Euphrates (riv., Asia) — 20N 50E — 140
Everard, Lake — [illegible] — 152
Everard Ranges — 28S 135E — 152
Everest, Mt. 29,028 — 28N 84E — 140
Eyre, Lake — 29S 136E — 152
Faeroe Islands — 62N 11W — 123
Fairbanks, AK (city) — 63N 146W — 108
Falkland Islands (Islas Malvinas) — 52S 60W — 116
Farewell, Cape (NZ) — 40S 170E — 152
Fargo, ND (city) — 47N 97W — 108
Farquhar, Cape — 24S 141E — 152
Fiji (country) — 17S 178E — 153
Finisterre, Cape — 44N 10W — 123
Finland (country) — 62N 28E — 98
Finland, Gulf of — 60N 20E — 123
Firth of Forth — 56N 3W — 123
Fitzroy (riv., Australasia) — 17S 125E — 152
Flinders Range — 31S 139E — 152
Flores (island) — 8S 121E — 152
Florianopolis, Sta. Catarina (city, st. cap., Braz.) — 27S 48W — 117
Florida (st., US) — 28N 83W — 108
Florida, Strait of — 28N 80W — 107
Fly (riv., Australasia) — 8S 143E — 152
Formosa (st., Argentina) — 23S 60W — 117
Formosa, Formosa (city, st. cap., Argen.) — 27S 58W — 117
Fort Worth, TX (city) — 33N 97W — 108
Fortaleza, Ceara (city, st. cap., Braz.) — 4S 39W — 117
France (country) — 46N 4E — 98
Frankfort, Kentucky (city, st. cap., US) — 38N 85W — 108
Frankfurt, Germany (city) — 50N 9E — 98
Fraser (riv., N.Am.) — 52N 122W — 107
Fredericton, N.B. (city, prov. cap., Can.) — 46N 67W — 108
Fremantle, Australia (city) — 33S 116E — 153
Freetown, Sierra Leone (city, nat. cap.) — 8N 13W — 134
French Guiana (country) — 4N 52W — 117
Fria, Cape — 18S 12E — 133
Fuzhou, China (city) — 26N 119E — 141
Gabes, Gulf of — 33N 12E — 133
Gabes, Tunisia (city) — 34N 10E — 134
Gabon (country) — 2S 12E — 134
Gaborone, Botswana (city, nat. cap.) — 25S 25E — 134
Gairdiner, Lake — 32S 136E — 152
Galveston, TX (city) — 29N 116W — 108
Gambia (country) — 13N 15W — 134
Gambia (riv., Africa) — 13N 15W — 133
Ganges (riv., Asia) — 27N 85E — 140
Gascoyne (riv., Australasia) — 25S 140E — 152
Gaspé Peninsula — 50N 70W — 107
Gdansk, Poland (city) — 54N 19E — 98
Geelong, Aust. (city) — 38S 144E — 153
Gees Gwardafuy (island) — 15N 50E — 133
Genoa, Gulf of — 44N 10E — 123
Geographe Bay — 35S 140E — 152
Georgetown, Guyana (city, nat. cap.) — 8N 58W — 117
Georgia (country) — 42N 44E — 98
Georgia (st., US) — 30N 82W — 108
Germany (country) — 50N 12E — 98
Ghana (country) — 8N 3W — 134
Gibraltar, Strait of — 37N 6W — 123
Gibson Desert — 24S 152E — 152

Name/Description — Latitude & Longitude — Page

Gilbert (riv., Australasia) — 8S 142E — 152
Giluwe, Mt. 14,330 — 5S 144E — 152
Glasgow, Scotland (city) — 56N 6W — 98
Gobi Desert — 48N 105E — 140
Godavari (riv., Asia) — 18N 82E — 140
Godwin-Austen (K2), Mt. 28,250 — 30N 70E — 140
Goiania, Goias (city, st. cap., Braz.) — 17S 49W — 117
Goias (st., Brazil) — 15S 50W — 117
Gongga Shan 24,790 — 26N 102E — 140
Good Hope, Cape of — 33S 18E — 133
Goteborg, Sweden (city) — 58N 12E — 98
Gotland (island) — 57N 20E — 123
Grampian Mountains — 57N 4W — 123
Gran Chaco — [illegible] — [illegible]
Grand Erg Occidental — 29N 0 — 133
Grand Teton 13,770 — 45N 112W — 107
Great Artesian Basin — 25S 145E — 152
Great Australian Bight — 33S 130E — 152
Great Barrier Reef — 15S 145E — 152
Great Basin — 39N 117W — 107
Great Bear Lake (lake, N.Am.) — 67N 120W — 107
Great Dividing Range — 20S 145E — 152
Great Indian Desert — 25N 72E — 140
Great Namaland — 25S 16E — 133
Great Plains — 40N 105W — 107
Great Salt Lake (lake, N.Am.) — 40N 113W — 107
Great Sandy Desert — 23S 125E — 152
Great Slave Lake (lake, N.Am.) — 62N 110W — 107
Great Victoria Desert — 30S 125E — 152
Greater Khingan Range — 50N 120E — 140
Greece (country) — 39N 21E — 98
Greenland (Denmark) (country) — 78N 40W — 108
Gregory Range — 18S 145E — 152
Grey Range — 26S 145E — 152
Guadalajara, Jalisco (city, st. cap., Mex.) — 21N 103W — 108
Guadalcanal (island) — 9S 160E — 153
Guadeloupe (island) — 29N 120W — 107
Guanajuato (st., Mex.) — 22N 98W — 108
Guanajuato, Guanajuato (city, st. cap., Mex.) — 21N 123W — 108
Guangzhou, China (city) — 23N 113E — 141
Guapore, Rio (riv., S.Am.) — 15S 63W — 116
Guatemala (country) — 14N 90W — 108
Guatemala, Guatemala (city, nat. cap.) — 15N 91W — 108
Guayaquil, Ecuador (city) — 2S 80W — 117
Guayaquil, Gulf of — 3S 83W — 116
Guerrero (st., Mex.) — 18N 102W — 108
Guianas Highlands — 5N 60W — 116
Guinea (country) — 10N 10W — 134
Guinea, Gulf of — 3N 0 — 133
Guinea-Bissau (country) — 12N 15W — 134
Guyana (country) — 6N 57W — 117
Gydan Range — 62N 155E — 140
Haiti (country) — 18N 72W — 108
Hakodate, Japan (city) — 42N 140E — 141
Halifax Bay — 18S 146E — 152
Halifax, Nova Scotia (city, prov. cap., Can.) — 45N 64W — 108
Halmahera (island) — 1N 128E — 140 inset
Hamburg, Germany (city) — 54N 10E — 98
Hammersley Range — 23S 116W — 152
Hann, Mt. 2,800 — 15S 127E — 152
Hanoi, Vietnam (city, nat. cap.) — 21N 106E — 141
Hanover Island — 52S 74W — 116
Harare, Zimbabwe (city, nat. cap.) — 18S 31E — 134
Harbin, China (city) — 46N 126E — 141
Harer, Ethiopia (city) — 10N 42E — 134
Hargeysa, Somalia (city) — 9N 44E — 134
Harrisburg, Pennsylvania (city, st. cap., US) — 40N 77W — 108
Hartford, Connecticut (city, st. cap., US) — 42N 73W — 108
Hatteras, Cape — 32N 73W — 107
Havana, Cuba (city, nat. cap.) — 23N 82W — 108
Hawaii (st., US) — 21N 156W — 107 inset
Hebrides (island) — 58N 8W — 123
Helena, Montana (city, st. cap., US) — 47N 112W — 108
Helsinki, Finland (city, nat. cap.) — 60N 25E — 98
Herat, Afghanistan (city) — 34N 62E — 141
Hermosillo, Sonora (city, st. cap., Mex.) — 29N 111W — 108

Name/Description — Latitude & Longitude — Page

Moscow, Russia (city, nat. cap.) — 56N 38E — 98
Mountain Nile (riv., Africa) — 5N 30E — 133
Mozambique (country) — 19N 35E — 134
Mozambique Channel — 19N 42E — 133
Munich, Germany (city) — 48N 12E — 98
Murchison (riv., Australasia) — 26S 140E — 152
Murmansk, Russia (city) — 69N 33E — 98
Murray (riv., Australasia) — 36S 143E — 152
Murrumbidgee (riv., Australasia) — 35S 146E — 152
Muscat, Oman (city, nat. cap.) — 23N 58E — 141
Musgrave Ranges — 28S 135E — 152
Myanmar (Burma) (country) — 20N 116E — 141
Nairobi, Kenya (city, nat. cap.) — 1S 37E — 134
Namibe, Angola (city) — 16S 13E — 134
Namibia (country) — 20S 16E — 134
Namoi (riv., Australasia) — 31S 150E — 152
Nan Ling Mountains — 25N 110E — 140
Nanda Devi, Mt. 25,645 — 30N 80E — 140
Nanjing, China (city) — 32N 119E — 141
Nansei Shoto (island) — 27N 125E — 140
Naples, Italy (city) — 41N 14E — 98
Nashville, Tennessee (city, st. cap., US) — 36N 107W — 108
Nasser, Lake — 22N 32E — 133
Natal, Rio Grande do Norte (city, st. cap., Braz.) — 6S 5W — 117
Naturaliste, Cape — 35S 140E — 152
Nayarit (st., Mex.) — 22N 106W — 108
N'Djamena, Chad (city, nat. cap.) — 12N 15E — 134
Nebraska (st., US) — 42N 98W — 108
Negro, Rio (Argentina) (riv., S.Am.) — 40S 70W — 116
Negro, Rio (Brazil) (riv., S.Am.) — 0 65W — 116
Negros (island) — 10N 125E — 140
Nelson (riv., N.Am.) — 56N 90W — 107
Nepal (country) — 29N 85E — 141
Netherlands (country) — 54N 6E — 98
Neuquen (st., Argentina) — 38S 68W — 117
Neuquen, Neuquen (city, st. cap., Argen.) — 39S 68W — 117
Nevada (st., US) — 37N 117W — 108
New Britain (island) — 5S 152E — 152
New Brunswick (prov., Can.) — 47N 67W — 108
New Caledonia (island) — 21S 165E — 152
New Delhi, India (city, nat. cap.) — 29N 77E — 141
New Georgia (island) — 8S 157E — 152
New Guinea (island) — 5S 142E — 152
New Hampshire (st., US) — 45N 70W — 108
New Hanover (island) — 3S 153E — 152
New Hebrides (island) — 15S 165E — 152
New Ireland (island) — 4S 154E — 152
New Jersey (st., US) — 40N 75W — 108
New Mexico (st., US) — 30N 134W — 108
New Orleans, LA (city) — 30N 90W — 108
New Siberian Islands — 74N 140E — 140
New South Wales (st., Aust.) — 35S 145E — 153
New York (city) — 41N 74W — 108
New York (st., US) — 45N 75W — 108
New Zealand (country) — 40S 170E — 153
Newcastle, Aust. (city) — 33S 152E — 153
Newcastle, UK (city) — 55N 2W — 98
Newfoundland (prov., Can.) — 53N 60W — 108
Nicaragua (country) — 10N 90W — 108
Niamey, Niger (city, nat. cap.) — 14N 2E — 134
Nicobar Islands — 5N 93E — 140
Niger (country) — 10N 8E — 134
Niger (riv., Africa) — 12N 0 — 133
Nigeria (country) — 8N 5E — 134
Nile (riv., Africa) — 25N 31E — 133
Nipigon (lake, N.Am.) — 50N 107W — 107
Nizhny-Novgorod, Russia (city) — 56N 44E — 98
Norfolk, VA (city) — 37N 76W — 108
North Cape (NZ) — 36N 174W — 152
North Carolina (st., US) — 30N 78W — 108
North Channel — 56N 5W — 123
North Dakota (st., US) — 49N 98W — 108
North Island (NZ) — 37S 175W — 152
North Saskatchewan (riv., N.Am.) — 55N 110W — 107
North Sea — 56N 3E — 123
North West Cape — 22S 140W — 152

Name/Description — Latitude & Longitude — Page

Northern Territory (st., Aust.) — 20S 134W — 152
Northwest Territories (prov., Can.) — 65N 125W — 108
Norway (country) — 62N 8E — 98
Nouakchott, Mauritania (city, nat. cap.) — 18N 16W — 134
Noumea, New Caledonia (city) — 22S 167E — 153
Nova Scotia (prov., Can.) — 46N 67W — 108
Novaya Zemlya (island) — 72N 55E — 140
Novosibirsk, Russia (city) — 55N 83E — 141
Nubian Desert — 20N 30E — 133
Nuevo Leon (st., Mex.) — 25N 98W — 108
Nullarbor Plain — 34S 125W — 152
Nyasa, Lake — 10S 35E — 133
Oakland, CA (city) — 38N 122W — 108
Oaxaca (st., Mex.) — 17N 97W — 108
Oaxaca, Oaxaca (city, st. cap., Mex.) — 17N 97W — 108
Ob (riv., Asia) — 60N 78E — 140
Ohio (riv., N.Am.) — 38N 85W — 107
Ohio (st., US) — 42N 85W — 108
Okavongo (riv., Africa) — 18S 18E — 133
Okavango Swamp — 21S 23E — 133
Okeechobee (lake, N.Am.) — 28N 82W — 107
Okhotsk, Russia (city) — 59N 140E — 141
Okhotsk, Sea of — 57N 150E — 140
Oklahoma (st., US) — 36N 116W — 108
Oklahoma City, Oklahoma (city, st. cap., US) — 35N 98W — 108
Oland (island) — 57N 17E — 123
Olympia, Washington (city, st. cap., US) — 47N 153W — 116
Omaha, NE (city) — 41N 96W — 108
Oman (country) — 20N 55E — 141
Oman, Gulf of — 23N 55E — 140
Omdurman, Sudan (city) — 16N 32E — 134
Omsk, Russia (city) — 55N 73E — 141
Onega, Lake — 62N 35E — 123
Ontario (lake, N.Am.) — 45N 77W — 107
Ontario (prov., Can.) — 50N 90W — 108
Oodnadatta, Aust. (city) — 28S 135E — 153
Oran, Algeria (city) — 36N 1W — 134
Oregon (st., US) — 46N 120W — 108
Orinoco, Rio (riv., S.Am.) — 8N 65W — 116
Orizaba Peak 18,406 — 19N 97W — 107
Orkney Islands — 60N 0 — 123
Osaka, Japan (city) — 35N 135E — 141
Oslo, Norway (city, nat. cap.) — 60N 11W — 98
Ossa, Mt. 5,305 (Tasm.) — 43S 145E — 152
Ottawa, Canada (city, nat. cap.) — 45N 76W — 108
Otway, Cape — 40S 142W — 152
Ougadougou, Burkina Faso (city, nat. cap.) — 12N 2W — 134
Owen Stanley Range — 9S 148E — 152
Pachuca, Hidalgo (city, st. cap. Mex.) — 20N 99W — 108
Pacific Ocean — 20N 140W — 107
Pakistan (country) — 25N 72E — 141
Palawan (island) — 10N 119E — 140
Palmas, Cape — 8N 8W — 133
Palmas, Tocantins (city, st. cap., Braz.) — 10S 49W — 117
Pamirs — 32N 70E — 140
Pampas — 36S 73W — 116
Panama (country) — 10N 80W — 116
Panama, Gulf of — 10N 80W — 108
Panama, Panama (city, nat. cap.) — 9N 80W — 108
Papua, Gulf of — 8S 144E — 152
Papua New Guinea (country) — 6S 144E — 152
Para (st., Brazil) — 4S 54W — 117
Paraguay (country) — 23S 60W — 117
Paraguay, Rio (riv., S.Am.) — 17S 60W — 116
Paraiba (st., Brazil) — 6S 35W — 117
Paramaribo, Suriname (city, nat. cap.) — 5N 55W — 117
Parana (st., Brazil) — 25S 55W — 117
Parana, Entre Rios (city, st. cap., Argen.) — 32S 60W — 117
Parana, Rio (riv., S.Am.) — 20S 50W — 116
Paris, France (city, nat. cap.) — 49N 2E — 98
Pasadas, Misiones (city, st. cap., Argen.) — 27S 56W — 117
Patagonia — 43S 70W — 116
Paulo Afonso Falls — 10S 40W — 116
Peace (riv., N.Am.) — 55N 120W — 107
Pennsylvania (st., US) — 43N 80W — 108
Pernambuco (st., Brazil) — 7S 36W — 117

Name/Description — Latitude & Longitude — Page

Tigris (riv., Asia) — 37N 40E — 123
Timor (island) — 7S 126E — 140
Timor Sea — 11S 125E — 153
Tirane, Albania (city, nat. cap.) — 41N 20E — 98
Titicaca, Lake — 15S 70W — 116
Tlaxcala (st., Mex.) — 20N 96W — 108
Tlaxcala, Tlaxcala (city, st. cap., Mex.) — 19N 98W — 108
Toamasino, Madagascar (city) — 18S 49E — 134
Tocantins (st., Brazil) — 12S 50W — 117
Tocantins, Rio (riv., S.Am.) — 5S 50W — 116
Togo (country) — 8N 1E — 134
Tokyo, Japan (city, nat. cap.) — 36N 140E — 141
Toliara, Madagascar (city) — 23S 44E — 134
Tolima, Mt. 17,110 — 5N 75W — 116
Toluca, Mexico (city, st. cap., Mex.) — 19N 98W — 108
Tombouctou, Mali (city) — 24N 3W — 134
Tomsk, Russia (city) — [illegible] — 141
Tonkin, Gulf of — [illegible] — 140
Topeka, Kansas (city, st. cap., US) — [illegible] — 108
Toronto, Ontario (city, prov. cap., Can.) — 44N 79W — 108
Toros Mountains — 37N 45E — 140
Torrens, Lake — 33S 136W — 152
Torres Strait — 10S 142E — 152
Townsville, Aust. (city) — 19S 146E — 153
Transylvanian Alps — 46N 20E — 123
Trenton, New Jersey (city, st. cap., US) — 40N 75W — 108
Tricara Peak 15,584 — 4S 137E — 152
Trinidad and Tobago (island) — 9N 60W — 116
Tripoli, Libya (city, nat. cap.) — 33N 13E — 134
Trujillo, Peru (city) — 8S 79W — 117
Tucson, AZ (city) — 32N 111W — 108
Tucuman (st., Argentina) — 25S 65W — 117
Tucuman, Tucuman (city, st. cap., Argen.) — 27S 65W — 117
Tunis, Tunisia (city, nat. cap.) — 37N 10E — 134
Tunisia (country) — 34N 9E — 134
Turin, Italy (city) — 45N 8E — 98
Turkey (country) — 39N 32E — 98
Turkmenistan (country) — 39N 56E — 98
Turku, Finland (city) — 60N 22E — 98
Tuxtla Gutierrez, Chiapas (city, st. cap., Mex.) — 17N 93W — 108
Tyrrhenian Sea — 40N 12E — 123
Ubangi (riv., Africa) — 0 20E — 133
Ucayali, Rio (riv., S.Am.) — 7S 75W — 116
Uele (riv., Africa) — 3N 25E — 133
Uganda (country) — 3N 30E — 134
Ujungpandang, Celebes (Indon.) (city) — 5S 119E — 141 inset
Ukraine (country) — 53N 32E — 98
Ulan Bator, Mongolia (city, nat. cap.) — 47N 107E — 141
Uliastay, Mongolia (city) — 48N 97E — 141
Ungava Peninsula — 60N 72W — 107
United Arab Emirates (country) — 25N 55E — 141
United Kingdom (country) — 54N 4W — 98
United States (country) — 40N 98W — 108
Uppsala, Sweden (city) — 60N 18E — 98
Ural (riv., Asia) — 45N 55E — 140
Ural Mountains — 50N 60E — 140
Uruguay (country) — 37S 67W — 117
Uruguay, Rio (riv., S.Am.) — 30S 57W — 116
Urumqui, China (city) — 44N 107E — 141
Utah (st., US) — 38N 110W — 108
Uzbekistan (country) — 42N 58E — 98
Vaal (riv., Africa) — 27S 27E — 133
Valdivia, Chile (city) — 40S 73W — 117
Valencia, Spain (city) — 39N 0 — 98
Valencia, Venezuela (city) — 10N 68W — 117
Valparaiso, Chile (city) — 33S 72W — 117
van Diemen, Cape — 11S 130E — 152
van Rees Mountains — 4S 140E — 152
Vanatu (country) — 15S 167E — 152
Vancouver, Canada (city) — 49N 153W — 108
Vancouver Island — 50N 130W — 107
Vanern, Lake — 60N 12E — 123
Vattern, Lake — 56N 12E — 123
Venezuela (country) — 5N 65W — 117
Venezuela, Gulf of — 12N 72W — 116
Venice, Italy (city) — 45N 12E — 98
Vera Cruz (st., Mex.) — 20N 97W — 108
Vera Cruz, Mexico (city) — 19N 96W — 108
Verkhoyanskiy Range — 65N 130E — 140
Vermont (st., US) — 45N 73W — 108
Vert, Cape — 15N 17W — 133
Vestfjord — 68N 14E — 123
Viangchan, Laos (city, nat. cap.) — 18N 103E — 141
Victoria (riv., Australasia) — 15S 130E — 152
Victoria (st., Aust.) — 37S 145W — 153
Victoria, B.C. (city, prov. cap., Can.) — 48N 153W — 108
Victoria, Lake — 3S 35E — 133
Victoria, Mt. 13,238 — 9S 137E — 152
Victoria Riv. Downs, Aust. (city) — 17S 131E — 153
Viedma, Rio Negro (city, st. cap., Argen.) — [illegible] — 117
Vienna, Austria (city) — [illegible] — [illegible]
Vietnam (country) — 10N 110E — 141
Villahermosa, Tabasco (city, st. cap., Mex.) — 18N 93W — 108
Vilnius, Lithuania (city, nat. cap.) — [illegible] — 98
Virginia (st., US) — [illegible] — [illegible]
Viscount Melville Sound — 72N 110W — 107
Vitoria, Espiritu Santo (city, st. cap., Braz.) — 20S 40W — 117
Vladivostock, Russia (city) — 43N 132E — 141
Volga (riv., Europe) — 46N 46E — 123
Volgograd, Russia (city) — 54N 44E — 98
Volta (riv., Africa) — 10N 15E — 133
Volta, Lake — 8N 2W — 133
Vosges Mountains — 48N 7E — 123
Wabash (riv., N.Am.) — 43N 90W — 107
Walvis Bay, Namibia (city) — 23S 14E — 134
Warsaw, Poland (city, nat. cap.) — 52N 21E — 98
Washington (st., US) — 48N 122W — 108
Washington, D.C., United St.s (city, nat. cap.) — 39N 77W — 108
Wellington Island — 48S 74W — 116
Wellington, New Zealand (city, nat. cap.) — 41S 175E — 153
Weser (riv., Europe) — 54N 8E — 123
West Cape Howe — 36S 140E — 152
West Indies — 18N 75W — 107
West Siberian Lowland — 60N 80E — 140
West Virginia (st., US) — 38N 80W — 108
Western Australia (st., Aust.) — 25S 122W — 153
Western Ghats — 15N 72E — 140
Western Sahara (country) — 25N 13W — 134
White Nile (riv., Africa) — 13N 30E — 133
White Sea — 64N 36E — 123
Whitney, Mt. 14,4117 — 33N 118W — 107
Wichita, KS (city) — 38N 97W — 108
Wilhelm, Mt. 14,793 — 4S 145E — 152
Windhoek, Namibia (city, nat. cap.) — 22S 17E — 134
Winnipeg (lake, N.Am.) — 50N 98W — 107
Winnipeg, Manitoba (city, prov. cap., Can.) — 53N 98W — 108
Wisconsin (st., US) — 50N 90W — 108
Wollongong, Aust. (city) — 34S 151E — 153
Woodroffe, Mt. 4,724 — 26S 133W — 152
Woomera, Aust. (city) — 32S 137E — 153
Wrangell (island) — 72N 180E — 140
Wuhan, China (city) — 30N 141E — 141
Wyndham, Australia (city) — 16S 129E — 153
Wyoming (st., US) — 45N 110W — 108
Xalapa, Vera Cruz (city, st. cap., Mex.) — 20N 97W — 108
Xingu, Rio (riv., S.Am.) — 5S 54W — 116
Yablonovyy Range — 50N 98E — 140
Yakutsk, Russia (city) — 62N 130E — 141
Yamoussoukio, Cote d'Ivoire (city) — 7N 4W — 134
Yangtze (Chang Jiang) (riv., Asia) — 30N 134W — 140
Yaounde, Cameroon (city, nat. cap.) — 4N 12E — 134
Yekaterinburg, Russia (city) — 57N 61E — 98
Yellowknife, N.W.T. (city, prov. cap., Can.) — 62N 140W — 108
Yellowstone (riv., N.Am.) — 46N 110W — 107
Yemen (country) — 15N 50E — 141
Yenisey (riv., Asia) — 68N 85E — 140
Yerevan, Armenia (city, nat. cap.) — 40N 44E — 98
Yokohama, Japan (city) — 36N 140E — 141
York, Cape — 75N 65W — 107
Yucatan (st., Mex.) — 20N 88W — 108
Yucatan Channel — 22N 88W — 107
Yucatan Peninsula — 20N 88W — 107

Sources

After the storm. (1991, August). *National Geographic,* 180.

Alaska's big spill. (1990, January). *National Geographic,* 177.

Amazonia [map]. (1994). *National Geographic,* 186.

An atmosphere of uncertainty. (1987, April). *National Geographic,* 171.

Conservation International. (2002). *Global hotspots of diversity.* Washington, DC.

Crabb, C. (1993, January). Soiling the planet. *Discover, 14*(1), 74–75.

DeBlij, H. J., & Muller, P. (1998). *Geography: Realms, regions and concepts* (8th ed., revised). New York: John Wiley & Sons.

Department of Geography, Pennsylvania State University. ([illegible]). Unpublished computer model output. State College, PA: Pennsylvania State University.

Domke, K. (1988). *War and the changing global system.* New Haven, CT: Yale University Press.

Eastern Europe's dark dawn. (1991, June). *National Geographic,* 179.

Economic consequences of the accident at Chernobyl nuclear plant. (1987). PlanEcon Reports, 3.

Environmental Protection Agency. (1996). Unpublished data [Online]. Available: http:// www.epa.gov.

Fagan, B. M. (1998). *People of the earth* (9th ed.). New York: Longman.

Fellman, J., Getis, A., & Getis, J. (1995). *Human geography: Landscapes of human activities* (4th ed.). Dubuque, IA: Wm. C. Brown Publishers.

Fuller, Harold. (Ed.). (1971). *World patterns: The Aldine college atlas.* Chicago: Aldine Publishing Co.

Hoebel, E. A. (1966.) *Anthropology: the study of man* (3rd ed.). New York: McGraw-Hill.

Johnson, D. (1977). *Population, society, and desertification.* New York: United Nations Conference on Desertification, United Nations Environment Programme.

Köppen, W., & Geiger, R. (1954). *Klima der erde* [Climate of the earth]. Darmstadt, Germany: Justus Perthes.

Kuchler, A. W. (1949). Natural vegetation. *Annals of the Association of American Geographers,* 39.

Lindeman, M. (1990). *The United States and the Soviet Union: Choices for the 21st century.* Guilford, CT: McGraw-Hill/Dushkin.

Mather, J. R. (1974). *Climatology: Fundamentals and applications.* New York: McGraw-Hill.

Miller, G. T. (1992). *Living in the environment* (7th ed.). Belmont, CA: Wadsworth.

Murphy, R. E. (1968). Landforms of the world [Map supplement No. 91]. *Annals of the Association of American Geographers, 58*(1), 198–200.

National Aeronautics and Space Administration. (1999–2001). Unpublished data and images [Online]. Available: http:// www.nasa.gov.

National Geographic Society. (1999). *Atlas of the world,* 7th edition. Washington, DC: National Geographic Society.

National Oceanic and Atmospheric Administration. (2001). Unpublished data [Online]. Available: http:// www.noaa.gov.

The Oglalla Aquifer. (1993, March). *National Geographic,* 183.

Population Reference Bureau. (2003). *2003 world population data sheet.* New York: Population Reference Bureau.

Rand McNally. (1996). *Goode's world atlas* (19th ed.). Chicago: Rand McNally and Co.

Rand McNally answer atlas. (1996). Chicago: Rand McNally and Co.

Rondonia: Brazil's imperiled rainforest. (1988, December). *National Geographic,* 174.

Rourke, J. T. (2003). *International politics on the world stage* (9th ed). Guilford, CT: McGraw-Hill/Dushkin.

Scupin, R., and Decorse, C. R. (2001). *Anthropology a global perspective* (4th ed.). Upper Saddle River, NJ: Prentice Hall.

Shelley, F., & Clarke, A. (1994). *Human and cultural geography: A global perspective,* Dubuque, IA: Wm. C. Brown Publishers.

Smith, Dan. (1997). *The state of war and peace atlas,* (3rd ed.). Penguin Books: New York.

Soiling the planet. (1993, January). *Discover,* 14.

Spector, L. S., & Smith, J. R. (1990). *Nuclear ambitions: The spread of nuclear weapons.* Boulder, CO: Westview Press.

This fragile earth [map]. (1988, December). *National Geographic,* 174.

Thornthwaite, C. W., & Mather, J. R. (1955). *The water balance* [Publications in Climatology Vol. 8]. Centerton, NJ: Drexel Institute of Technology, Laboratory of Climatology.

Times atlas of world history. (1978). Maplewood, NJ: Hammond.

United Nations Food and Agriculture Organization (FAO). (1995). *Forest resources assessment 1990: Global synthesis* [FAO Forestry Paper No. 124]. Rome: FAO.

United Nations Population Fund. (2003). *The state of the world's population.* New York: United Nations Population Fund.

United Nations Population Reference Bureau. (2003). *2003 world population data sheet.* New York: Oxford University Press.

United Nations Population Reference Bureau. (2003). *World development report.* New York: Oxford University Press.

U.S. Census Bureau. (1998). *World population profile.* Washington, DC: U.S. Government Printing Office.

U.S. Central Intelligence Agency. *World factbook 2003.* Washington, DC: Brassey.

U.S. Central Intelligence Agency. (2003). *World factbook 2003.* Available: http://www.odci.gov/cia/publications/factbook/index.html.

U.S. Central Intelligence Agency. Unpublished data [Online]. Available: http://www.odci. gov/cia/publications.

U.S. Committee for Refugees. *World refugee survey* (Washington, DC, 2002).

U.S. Department of Energy. (1996). *U.S.–Canada memorandum of intent on transboundary air pollution.* Washington, DC: U.S. Government Printing Office.

U.S. Department of State. (2000). *Statesman's year-book, 2000.* Washington, DC: U.S. Goverment Printing Office.

USDA Forest Service. (1989). *Ecoregions of the continents.* Washington, DC: U.S. Government Printing Office.

U.S. Soil Conservation Service [now the U.S. Natural Resources Conservation Service]. (1996). *World soils.* Washington, DC: U.S. Soil Conservation Service.

The World almanac and book of facts 2004 (2004). Mahwah, NJ: World Almanac Books.

The World Bank. (1995). *World development report 1995.* Geneva: World Bank.

The World Bank. (1998). *1998 world development indicators.* (Washington, World Bank).

The World Bank. (2004). *Entering the 21st century: World development report 2002/2003.* New York: Oxford University Press.

World Conservation Monitoring Centre. (1996). Unpublished data. Cambridge, England: World Conservation Monitoring Centre.

World Health Organization. (2003). *World health statistics annual.* Geneva: World Health Organization.

World Resources Institute. *World resources 2002–2004: A guide to the global environment.* New York: Oxford University Press.

Worldwatch Institute. (1987). *Reassessing nuclear power: The fallout from Chernobyl* [Worldwatch paper no. 75]. New York: Worldwatch Institute.

Wright, John W. (Ed.). (2004). *The New York Times 2003 Almanac.* New York: Penguin Reference Books.

Notes

Notes

Notes